DR. ARNOLD'S WORKS.

I.

THE HISTORY OF ROME,

From the Earliest Period. Reprinted entire from the last English edition. One vol., 8vo. $3 00.

II.

HISTORY OF THE LATER ROMAN COMMON-WEALTH.

Two vols. of the English edition reprinted entire in 1 vol., 8vo. $2 50.

"The History of Rome will remain, to the latest age of the world, the most attractive, the most useful, and the most elevating subject of human contemplation. It must ever form the basis of a liberal and enlightened education, and present the most important subject to the contemplation of the statesman. It is remarkable, that until the appearance of Dr. Arnold's volumes, no history, (except Niebuhr's, whose style is often obscure) of this wonderful people existed, commensurate either to their dignity, their importance, or their intimate connection with modern institutions. In the preparation and composition of the history, Dr. Arnold expended many long years, and bent to it the whole force of his great energies. It is a work to which the whole culture of the man, from boyhood, contributed—most carefully and deeply meditated, pursued with all the ardor of a labor of love, and relinquished only with life. Of the conscientious accuracy, industry, and power of mind, which the work evinces—its clearness, dignity, and vigor of composition—it would be needless to speak. It is eminently calculated to delight and instruct both the student and the miscellaneous reader."—*Boston Courier.*

III.

LECTURES ON MODERN HISTORY.

Delivered in Lent Term, 1842, with the Inaugural Lecture delivered in 1841. Edited, with a Preface and Notes, by Henry Reed, M. A., Prof. of English Literature in the University of Pa. 12mo. $1 25.

"The Lectures are *eight* in number, and furnish the best possible introduction to a philosophical study of modern history. Prof. Reed has added greatly to the worth and interest of the volume, by appending to each lecture such extracts from Dr. Arnold's other writings as would more fully illustrate its prominent points. The notes and appendix which he has thus furnished are exceedingly valuable."—*Courier and Enquirer.*

IV.

RUGBY SCHOOL SERMONS.

Sermons preached in the Chapel of Rugby School, with an Address before Confirmation. One volume, 16mo. 50 cts.

"There are thirty Sermons in this neat little volume, which we cordially recommend to parents and others, for the use of the young, as a guide and incentive to deep earnestness in matters of religious belief and conduct; as a book which will interest all by its sincerity, and especially those who have become acquainted with Dr. A. through his Life and Letters, recently published by the Appletons."—*Evening Post.*

V.

MISCELLANEOUS WORKS.

With nine additional Essays, not included in the English collection. One volume, 8vo. $2 00.

"This volume includes disquisitions on the 'Church and State,' in its existing British combinations—on Scriptural and Secular History—and on Education, with various other subjects of Political Economy. It will be a suitable counterpart to the 'Life and Correspondence of Dr. Arnold,' and scholars who have been so deeply interested in that impressive biography will be gratified to ascertain the deliberate judgment of the Author, upon the numerous important themes which his 'Miscellaneous Works' so richly and clearly announce."

VI.

THE LIFE AND CORRESPONDENCE OF THOMAS ARNOLD, D. D.

By Arthur P. Stanley, A. M. 2d American from the fifth London edition One handsome 8vo. volume. $2 00.

'This work should be in the hands of every one who lives and thinks for his race and for his religion: not so much as a guide for action, as affording a stimulant to intellectual and moral reflection.' —*Prot. Churchman.*

LORD MAHON'S HISTORY OF ENGLAND.

D. Appleton & Company have just published,

HISTORY OF ENGLAND,

FROM

THE PEACE OF UTRECHT TO THE PEACE OF PARIS

BY LORD MAHON

EDITED BY

HENRY REED, LL.D.,

Prof of English Literature in the University of Pennsylvania

Two handsome 8vo. volumes. Price $5.

Mr. Macaulay's Opinion.

"Lord Mahon has undoubtedly some of the most valuable qualities of a historian—great diligence in examining authorities, great judgment in weighing testimony, and great impartiality in estimating characters."

Quarterly Review.

"Lord Mahon has shown throughout, excellent skill in combining, as well as contrasting, the various elements of interest which his materials afforded; he has continued to draw his historical portraits with the same firm and easy hand; and no one can lay down the book without feeling that he has been under the guidance of a singularly clear, high-principled, and humane mind; one uniting a very searching shrewdness with a pure and unaffected charity. He has shown equal courage, judgment, and taste, in availing himself of minute details, so as to give his narrative the pictu esqueness of a memoir, without sacrificing one jot of the real dignity of history .... His History is well calculated to temper the political judgment. It is one great lesson of modesty, forbearance, and charity."

Edinburgh Review.

"It was with no small satisfaction that we saw a history of this period announced from the pen of Lord Mahon, nor have we been disappointed in our expectations. His narrative is minute and circumstantial, without being tedious. His History of the Rebellion in particular is clear, distinct, and entertaining. In his judgment of persons he is on the whole fair, candid, and discriminating."

English Review.

"Lord Mahon's work will supply a desideratum which has long been f[illegible] a really good history of the last 150 years. It is written with an ease of style, a c[illegible]and of the subject, and a comprehensiveness of view, which evince the possession of high qualifications for the great task which the noble author has proposed to himself. Lord Mahon avails himself extensively of the correspondence and private diaries of the times, which gives unusual interest and life to the narrative........ The authorities quoted for Spanish or French details are always the original; and we can hardly remember a reference of his Lordship's on any subject which is not to the best testimony known or accessible."

Sismondi—Histoire des Français.

"Sur le Prince Charles Edouard, en 1745—nous renvoyons uniquement à l'admirable récit de cette expédition dans l'Histoire de Lord Mahon. Toutes les relations y sont comparées et jugées avec une saine critique, et le récit presente le vif interêt d'un roman.'

Professor Smyth—University of Cambridge.

"I may recommend to others, what I have just had so much pleasure in reading myself, the History lately published by Lord Mahon. All that need now be known of the era from the Peace of Utrecht to that of Aix-la-Chapelle, will be there found.'

COURSE OF THE HISTORY

OF

MODERN PHILOSOPHY.

BY M. VICTOR COUSIN.

TRANSLATED BY O. W. WIGHT.

IN TWO VOLUMES.

VOL. II.

NEW YORK:
D. APPLETON & COMPANY, 200 BROADWAY.
M DCCC LIII.

CONTENTS.

LECTURE IX.

SCHOLASTIC PHILOSOPHY.

LECTURE X.

PHILOSOPHY OF THE PERIOD OF THE REVIVAL.

LECTURE XI.

MODERN PHILOSOPHY. SEVENTEENTH CENTURY. SENSUALISM AND IDEALISM.

LECTURE XII.

MODERN PHILOSOPHY. SEVENTEENTH CENTURY. SKEPTICISM AND MYSTICISM.

SECOND SERIES—VOL. III.

LECTURE XIII.

CLASSIFICATION OF THE SCHOOLS OF THE EIGHTEENTH CENTURY.

LECTURE XIV.

SENSUALISTIC SCHOOL IN THE EIGHTEENTH CENTURY.

LECTURE XV.

LOCKE. HIS LIFE.

LECTURE XVI.

ESSAY ON THE HUMAN UNDERSTANDING. ITS SPIRIT. ITS METHOD.

LECTURE XVII.

ESSAY. FIRST BOOK, INNATE IDEAS. SECOND BOOK, OF SPACE.

LECTURE XVIII.

ESSAY. SECOND BOOK. TIME. INFINITY. IDENTITY. SUBSTANCE.

LECTURE XIX.

ESSAY, SECOND BOOK. OF THE IDEA OF CAUSE.

LECTURE XX.

ESSAY, SECOND BOOK. OF GOOD AND EVIL. THIRD BOOK, OF WORDS.

LECTURE XXI.

ESSAY, FOURTH BOOK. THEORY OF REPRESENTATIVE IDEAS.

LECTURE XXII.

ESSAY, FOURTH BOOK. REPRESENTATIVE IDEAS CONTINUED.

LECTURE XXIII.

ESSAY, THEORY OF JUDGMENT.

LECTURE XXIV.

ESSAY, FOURTH BOOK. CONTINUATION OF THE THEORY OF JUDGMENT.

LECTURE XXV.

ESSAY, LIBERTY. SOUL. GOD. CONCLUSION.

LECTURE IX.

SCHOLASTIC PHILOSOPHY.*

Scholastic Philosophy.—Its character and its origin.—Division of Scholasticism into three epochs.—First epoch.—Second epoch.—Third epoch. Birth of philosophical independence; quarrel of nominalism and realism, which represent idealism and sensualism in Scholasticism.—John Occam. His partisans and his adversaries.—Decrial of the two systems and of Scholasticism.—Mysticism.—Chancellor Gerson. His *Mystic Theology*. Extracts from this work.—Conclusion.

HITHERTO, both in India and in Greece, we have constantly seen philosophy spring from religion; and at the same time we have seen that it springs not from it at once, that a single day is not enough for it to raise itself from the humble submission by which it begins, to the absolute independence in which it terminates. Hitherto we have seen it passing through an epoch, somewhat preparatory, therein trying its forces in the service of a foreign principle, reduced to the modest employment of governing and regulating creeds which it did not establish, in expectation of the moment when it shall be able to search out truth itself at its own risk and peril. Modern philosophy presents the same phenomenon. It is also preceded by an epoch which serves it as an introduction, and, thus to speak, as a vestibule. This epoch is scholasticism. As the middle age is the cradle of modern society, so scholasticism is that of modern philosophy. What the middle age is to the new society, scholasticism is to

* These outlines of the entire system of Scholastic philosophy need to be strengthened and in some points rectified by study more limited but more solid than may be found in the *Introduction* of a work entitled: *Œuvres inédites d'Abélard*, Paris 1836, in-4. This *Introduction*, with some additions, forms the 3d volume of the *Fragments philosophiques*.

the philosophy of the new times. Now, the middle age is nothing else than the absolute reign of ecclesiastical authority, of which the political powers are only the more or less docile instruments. Scholasticism, or the philosophy of the middle age, could not then be any thing else than the labor of thought in the service of faith, and under the inspection of religious authority.

Such is scholastic philosophy. Its employment is limited, its bounds narrow, its existence precarious, inferior, subordinate. Well! here again philosophy is philosophy; and scarcely has it fortified itself by time, scarcely is the hand which was over it removed, or become less weighty, when philosophy resumes its natural course, and produces again the four different systems which it has already produced both in India and in Greece.

In the absence of chronology we cannot form a precise idea of the epoch corresponding to scholasticism in Indian philosophy. We distinguish the Mimansa school from the Sankhya school. But when did the Mimansa begin? When did the Sankhya begin? We are ignorant of this. Induction leads us to believe that the Mimansa must have preceded the Sankhya; nevertheless facts, in this India where every thing endures so long, where every thing exists in a state of confusion, facts show the Mimansa to be of a recent epoch. Thus Koumarila, the famous Mimansa doctor of whom I have spoken, was of the fourteenth century of our era. In Greece, we know at least when philosophy began; it began six centuries before our era with Thales and Pythagoras. But the epoch which precedes, that of the Mysteries, is covered with profound darkness. What took place between Orpheus and Pythagoras, between Musæus and Thales? How did the human mind go from the sanctuary of the temples to the schools of Ionia and of Greece at large? We know but ill, or rather we do not know at all.

In regard to the middle age we are much more fortunate. We know when scholasticism began, we know when it ceased, and we know its development between these two periods; we know its starting point, its progress, and its end.

When was scholasticism born? That is asking when the middle age was born; for scholasticism is the philosophic expression of the middle age. In order that scholasticism should have existed it was necessary that the middle age should exist, since scholasticism is only the middle age developed in the philosophy appropriate to it. The middle age, or the new society, was conceived, thus to speak, during the first century of the Christian era; but it appeared only with the triumph of its principle, that is, the Christian religion; and the Christian religion arrived at perfect dominion only after having been delivered from all the ruins of the ancient civilization, and after the soil of our Europe, at last secure against further invasions and barbarian devastations, had become more firm and capable of receiving the foundations of the new society which the Church bore in its bosom. Europe and the Church were firmly established only at the time of Charlemagne and by the aid of Charlemagne. Charlemagne is the genius of the middle age; he opens it and he constitutes it. He represents essentially the idea of order: his is above all the spirit of a founder and an organizer. He had more than one task to accomplish, and he was sufficient for all. 1st, It was necessary to establish material order, by putting an end to those invasions of every kind, which, continually agitating Europe, opposed every fixed establishment. So, with one hand Charlemagne arrested the Saracens in the South, and with the other the barbarians of the North, of whom he himself was a descendant, and thus he ceased to be a stranger in Europe; he became a European, a man of the new civilization. 2d, It was necessary to establish moral order. This could not be done except on the basis of the only moral authority of the times, religious authority; so this Charles, whose personality was so strong, did not hesitate to ask a new grant of the crown, which was already on his head, from the pontifical authority. 3d, It was necessary to establish scientific order. It was by the example of Charlemagne that his successors, or his rivals, Charles the Bald and Alfred the Great, everywhere sought the least sparks of ancient culture, in order to rekindle the flame of science. It was Charlemagne who first opened the schools, *scholæ*.* These schools were the abodes of science then: thus the science of that time was called *Scholasticism*. Behold the origin of the thing and of the word, and the character of scholasticism is already in its very origin. In fact, where did Charlemagne institute, and where could he institute schools? In places where most instruction still remained, where there was most leisure to acquire, where it was a duty to seek it and spread it abroad; that is, in the Episcopal sees, in the monasteries, in the cloisters, in the convents. Yes, the convents are the cradle of modern philosophy, as the Mysteries have been that of Greek philosophy; and scholasticism is stamped from its origin with an ecclesiastical character.

As you now know its origin, let us see what was its end. Scholasticism ended when the middle age ended; and the middle age ended when ecclesiastical authority ceased to be supreme, when other powers, and particularly political power, without neglecting the just deference and veneration always due to religious power, claimed and conquered its independence. It could not, then, be otherwise than that philosophy which always follows in the train of the great movements of society, should have claimed also its independence and conquered it little by little. I say little by little; for the revolution which caused philosophy to rise from the condition of a servant of theology to that of an independent power, was not accomplished in a day; it began in the fifteenth century but was completed at a later period, and modern philosophy did not really begin, as you know, until Bacon and Descartes.

The two extreme points are then settled; on the one hand the century of Charlemagne, on the other that of Bacon and Descartes, the eighth century and the seventeenth. It now remains to determine what occurred between these two extreme points;

---

* See the work of Launoy, *de celebrioribus Scholis a Carolo Magno et post ipsum instauratis*, Paris, 1672. Several times reprinted.

nothing is more simple. What is the commencement of scholasticism? the absolute submission of philosophy to theology. What is the end of scholasticism? the end of this submission and the claim of independence of thought. Then, the middle state of scholasticism must have been a condition between servitude and independence, an alliance wherein theology and philosophy lend to each other mutual support. Hence three distinct periods in scholasticism: 1st, absolute subordination of philosophy to theology; 2d, alliance of philosophy and theology; 3d, commencement of a separation, feeble at first, but which little by little increases, is extended and terminates in the birth of modern philosophy.

The first epoch of scholasticism is nothing else than the employment of philosophy as a simple form based on Christian theology. Theology comprised, with the holy Scriptures, tradition and the holy Fathers, especially the Latin Fathers, for the Greek Fathers were little known out of Constantinople; and among the Latin Fathers, he who represented all the others was Saint Augustine. All the resources of philosophy were reduced to a few ordinary writings, half-literary and half-philosophical, which contained the little knowledge that had escaped barbarism. These were the writings of Mamert,* of Capella,† of Boëthius,‡ of Cassiodorus,§ of Isadorus,‖ of the venerable Bede.¶ He, whom Charlemagne placed at the head of this regeneration of the human mind, Alcuinus,** had at his disposal few other aids than

* Of Vienna, in Dauphiny, died about 477 A. C. *De Statu Animæ.* Often reprinted.

† Marcien Capella, of Madaura, in Africa, flourished 474. *Satyricon de Nuptiis philologiæ et Mercurii, et de VII. Artibus liberalibus.* Often reprinted.

‡ Born in 470; senator of the Gothic king Theodoric, commented on Aristotle, wrote the treatise *de Consolationæ philosophiæ* in his prison of Pavia, which he left only to be beheaded. Opera, Basle, 1570, 1 vol. in-fol.

§ Born at Squillace about 480, died in 575. *De Septem Disciplinis.* Opp., 2 vol. in-fol. Rothomag., 1679.

‖ Bishop of Seville, died 636. *Originum seu Etymologiarum*, lib. xx. Opp., Romæ, 1796, 7 vol. in-4.

¶ Anglo-Saxon, born 673, died 735. Opp., Cologne, 1612, 8 vol. in-fol.

** Born at York, 726, died 804. Opp., Ratisbonne, 2 vol. in-fol., 1777. He

these, with the *Organum* of Aristotle.* That this first epoch may be well understood, it is necessary never to separate in the mind Saint Augustine and the *Organum ;* hence the grandeur of the theological basis and the poverty of the form. We encounter at this period an order of ideas and even of arguments much superior to these barbarous times; and if we are not aware of its source, we are tempted to admire too much these first essays of the philosophy of the middle age; it is to Christianity and to Saint Augustine that our admiration must be referred. As to the form, it is, as I have said, poor, feeble, uncertain; and this form was then the whole of philosophy.

The masters of scholasticism during this epoch do little else than comment on that beautiful expression of one of them :† "There

---

had as a pupil Rhabanus Maurus, died Archbishop of Mayence, 856. Opp., 6 vol. in-fol., Colog., 1626. See, on some unpublished writings on dialectics of Rhaban, the *Fragments de Philosophie scholastique*, pp. 104–110, and p. 311.

* Or rather some of its parts. For, strictly speaking, nothing was then known of the *Organum* except the *Introduction of Porphyry*, the *Categories*, and the *Interpretation.* See the *Fragments de Philosophie scholastique*, p. 70, sqq.

‡ John Scot, *de Prædestinatione* (Collection of Maugin, vol. 1, p. 103). "Non aliam esse philosophiam aliudve sapientiæ studium, aliamve religionem . . . Quid est de philosophia tractare nisi veræ religionis, qua summa et principalis omnium rerum causa. Deus, et humilitur colitur et rationabiliter investigatur, regulas exponere? Conficitur inde veram esse philosophiam veram religionem, conversimque veram religionem esse veram philosophiam." Alain de Lille, *Alanus de Insulis*, who closes this epoch of scholasticism, speaks like Scot, who begins it. Alain was a monk of Clairvaux, and a pupil of Saint Bernard; he died in 1203. Opp., Antwerpæ, 1 vol. in-fol., 1654. His principal work is entitled: *Ars fidei Catholicæ*, it is dedicated to Pope Clement III. (B. Pez. *Thesaurus anecdotorum novissimus*, Vol. 1, Col. 475.) Here is the introduction: "Cum nec miraculorum mihi gratia collata est, nec ad vincendas hæreses sufficiat auctoritates inducere, cum illas hæretici aut prorsus respuant aut pervertant, probabiles fidei nostræ rationes, quibus perspicax ingenium vix possit resistere, studiosius adornavi ut qui prophetiæ et Evangelio acquiescere contemnunt, humanis saltem rationibus inducantur, et nunc quasi per speculum contemplentur quod postea demum in perfecta scientia comprehendant. Itaque hoc opus in modum artis compositum, definitiones, distinctiones, propositiones ordinato successu propositas exhibet." It is divided in five books: 1st, *de uno eodemque trino Deo, qui est una omnium causa ;* 2d, de mundo, deque angelorum et hominum creatione et libero arbitrio· 3d de reparatione hominis lapsi· 4th *de Ecclesiæ Sacramen-*

are not two studies, one of philosophy and the other of religion; true philosophy is true religion, and true religion is true philosophy." I will dwell no longer on this point: it is more interesting to show you, in this unity, the progress which appears from age to age, from the eighth until the twelfth century; for it is in this progress that the different traits of these philosophers of the middle age are sketched. If they are alike in their complete submission to the Church, they differ as men, as thinkers, and as belonging to different times. Philosophy to them is only the form of theology, but this form is successively modified and perfected in their hands.

John Scot* is distinguished by an erudition which has deceived in regard to his originality. He understood the Greek, and translated Denis the Areopagite; and as Denis the Areopagite is a mystic writer who reflects more or less the Alexandrian mysticism, John Scot derived through study of his writings, a multitude of ideas which he scattered throughout his own two works, one on *Predestination and Grace,* the other on the *Division of Beings.* As these ideas did not belong to his own age, they astonished more than they instructed it, and in our times they have dazzled those who knew not their origin.

The true metaphysician of this epoch is Saint Anselm, born at Aosta in Piedmont, Prior and Abbé of Bec in Normandy, and at his death Archbishop of Canterbury.† To him was given the ap-

---

tis; 5th, *de resurrectione et vita futuri sæculi.* I place these divisions here because they are the ordinary divisions of the theological metaphysics of this epoch.

* Joannes Scotus Erigena, thus called because he was an Irishman, lived at the Court of Charles the Bald, who protected him; having fallen into disfavor, he returned to England at the invitation of Alfred the Great, and taught at Oxford, where he died in 886. He translated Denis the Areopagite into Latin. His other works are: 1st, *De divina Prædestinatione et Gratia,* in the collection of Maugin, vol. i. p. 103, sqq.; Paris, 1650. 2d, περὶ Φύσεως Μερισμοῦ, *de Divisione Naturæ,* lib. v., ed. Th. Gale, Oxford, 1681. Observe especially in this last work, a theory of the Creation (lib. iii. p. 106), by an explanation of a verse of Saint John. Every thing in it is referred to faith: Nesciendo scitur.—Lib. i. p. 25.

† Born 1034, died 1109. Opp., 1 vol. in-fol., 1675. The following works

pellation of the second Saint Augustine. Among his numerous works are two, the titles of which I will at least mention, for the titles indicate their spirit, and reveal, moreover, a remarkable progress. One is a monologue, wherein Saint Anselm supposes an ignorant man who is seeking truth by force of his reason only; a very bold fiction for the eleventh century, and the antecedent of the *Meditations:* it is entitled *Monologium, seu Exemplum Meditandi de ratione fidei,* Monologue, or Example of the manner in which one may account for his faith.* The second work is called *Proslogium, seu fides quærens intellectum,* Allocution, or the Faith which tries to demonstrate itself. In the first work, Saint Anselm does not suppose himself in possession of the truth, he is seeking it; in the second, he supposes himself in possession of the truth, and he tries to demonstrate it.† The name of Saint

---

should be designated: *De fide Trinitatis et de incarnatione Verbi.—De Veritate, dialogus.—De libero Arbitrio, dialogus.—Concordia præscientiæ Dei cum libero arbitrio.—Meditationes.*—Finally the *Monologium* and the *Proslogium.*

* *Monologium.*—"*Præfatio* . . . Quæcumque autem ibi dixi, sub persona secum sola cogitatione disputantis et investigantis ea quæ prius non animadvertisset, prolata sunt . . . Quæ de Deo necessario credimus, patet quia ea ipsa quislibet, si vel mediocris ingenii fuerit, sola ratione sibimetipsi magna ex parte persuadere possit. Hoc cum multis modis fieri possit, meum modum hic ponam, quem estimo cuique homini esse aptissimum." This mode, this plan, consists in drawing all theological truths from a single point, the essence of God; and the essence of God from the only ideal of beauty, of goodness, of grandeur which all men possess, and which is the common measure of all that is beautiful, etc. This ideal, this unity must exist, for it is the necessary form of all that exists. Unity is anterior to plurality, and it is its root. "Est ergo aliquid unum, quod, sive essentia sive natura sive substantia dicitur, optimum et maximum est, et summum omnium quæ sunt." This unity is God: Hence Saint Anselm draws, in seventy-nine chapters, the attributes of God, Trinity, Creation, relation of man, as intelligence, to God, in short, entire theology.

† *Proslogium:* "*Procemium.* Postquam opusculum quoddam velut exemplum meditandi de ratione fidei, cogentibus me precibus quorumdam fratrum, in persona alicujus tacite secum ratiocinando quæ nesciat investigantis, edidi, considerans illud esse multorum concatenatione contextum argumentorum, cœpi mecum quærere si forte posset inveniri unum argumentum quod nullo alio ad se probandum quam se solo indegiret. . . ." This argument is an abridgment of that of the Monologium. The maddest Atheist, *insipiens,* has in his thought an idea of a sovereign good, above which he can conceive no other.

Anselm is attached to the argument, which draws from the idea alone of an absolute *maximum* of greatness, of beauty, of goodness, the demonstration of the existence of its object, which can be only God. Without citing Saint Anselm, whom he did not probably know, Descartes has produced the same argument in the *Meditations*, when, on the simple idea of a perfect being, he establishes the necessity of the existence of that being, that is, God.* Leibnitz, in taking up the Cartesian argument,† refers it to Saint Anselm; but he was able to go farther back, he had found it in the genius of Christian idealism, and it was worthy of Saint Anselm, of Descartes, and of Leibnitz, to draw it from that source and diffuse it through modern philosophy.

In this rapid review I do not wish silently to pass by Abelard.‡ In this gross and pedantic age Abelard is a sort of beautiful classic spirit. He, too, was the first to apply philosophical criticism to theology, and he established a more liberal school of

---

This sovereign good cannot exist solely in the thought, for we might conceive a still greater. This we cannot do, therefore this sovereign good exists out of the thought, therefore God exists. The *Proslogium* is composed of twenty-six short chapters; its text is this passage: *Dixit insipiens in corde suo: Non est Deus.* A monk of Marmoutiers, Gaunillon, combated the argument of Saint Anselm in a small work under this title: *Liber pro Insipiente.* Anselm replied to it in his *Liber apologeticus contra Gaunillonem.* I have shown more at length the doctrine of Saint Anselm, especially in what regards nominalism and realism, *Fragments de Philosophie scholastique*, p. 140, etc.

* See, on the argument of Descartes, 1st Series, *passim*, and in this 2d Series, Lecture 11, of this volume.

† Throughout, and particularly correspondence of Korthold, vol. iv. p. 2.

‡ Born at Palais, near Nantes, in 1079, died in 1142. His works were collected by Amboise, Paris, 1616, in-4. This edition contains, among other works, the Letters of Abelard and Heloïse, and the Introduction to Theology. The *Ethica* was printed in the *Thesaurus anecdotorum novissimus* of B. Pez, vol. iv.; the *Theologia Christiana* and the *Hexameron* in the *Thesaurus anecdot.* of Martino, vol. v. We published in 1836, in-4, his unpublished treatises on dialectics, and the *Sic et non*, with an introduction and notices on different unpublished works of the ninth, tenth, eleventh, and twelfth centuries. We reproduced this introduction and these notices in the *Fragments de Philosophie scholastique*, adding to them a new unpublished treatise of Abelard, *de Intellectibus.*

theological interpretation. A disciple, by turns, of Roscellinus* and of Guillaume de Champeaux,† he vanquished them both, and introduced a new and afterwards celebrated system, Conceptualism.‡ As a professor his success was prodigious, and it contributed much to the establishment of the University of Paris.§

The school of Abelard was distinguished for refined taste and boldness. John of Salisbury was an enlightened and polished man, whom the grossness of the studies of his times and the jargon of scholasticism‖ deeply wounded. Peter the Lombard is commend-

---

* On Roscellinus, see *Fragments de Philosophie scholastique*, pp. 57, 119, etc.

† On Guillaume de Champeaux, ibid., pp. 152 and 232.

‡ Ibid., p. 224, etc.

§ Permit us to place here the portrait of Abelard, by which we commenced the special work consecrated to this man. *Fragments of Scholastic Philosophy*, p. 2: "Abelard of Palais, near Nantes, after having completed his first studies in his own country, and augmented his knowledge in the schools of different provinces, went to perfect himself at Paris, when from a pupil he soon became the rival of his renowned masters: he ruled, as it were, in dialectics. At a later period, when he mingled theology with philosophy, he attracted such multitudes from all parts of France, and even of Europe, that, as he himself said, the hotels were neither sufficient to contain them, nor the ground to nourish them. Wherever he went, the crowd and bustle followed him; the desert into which he retired became little by little an immense auditory. In philosophy he entered into the greatest quarrel of his times, that of realism and of nominalism, and he created an intermediary system. In theology, he placed himself on the side of the old school of Anselm, which exposed without explaining, and founded what is called rationalism. And he did not shine alone in the school; he moved the Church and the State, he occupied two great councils, he had as an adversary Saint Bernard, and one of his disdiples and friends was Arnold of Brescia. Finally, that nothing might be wanting to the singularity of his life and to the popularity of his name, this dialectician, who had eclipsed Roscellinus and Guillaume de Champeaux, this theologian against whom the Bossuet of the twelfth century arose, was handsome, was a poet, and a musician; in his native language he wrote songs which amused scholars and ladies; and as canon of the cathedral, professor of the cloister, he was loved even to the most absolute devotion by that noble creature who loved like Saint Theresa, wrote sometimes like Seneca, and whose grace must have been irresistible, since she charmed Saint Bernard himself. A hero of romance in the Church, a choice spirit in a barbarous period, the chief of a school and almost the martyr of an opinion, all concurred in making Abelard an extraordinary personage." See the work of M. de Remusat, at once so exact and so elegant, *Abelard*, 2 vol., 1845.

‖ As may be seen in the *Prolicraticus, seu de nugis curialium et vestigiis*

able for his skilful and regular exposition.* He compiled the Fathers of the Church, and attempted what would now be called a concordance of the arguments drawn from these different sources; he put them in such a methodical and convenient form for instruction, that he was the standard in the schools, where he remained during several centuries. It was impossible to go farther than the Lombard with the *Organum* alone. To advance required new aids for the human mind. He found them in the other works of Aristotle, which, until then, had remained unknown to Western Europe.

A great nation, the Arabs, after having subjugated a part of Africa and of Asia, had passed into Spain; they there had founded an empire, which little by little had become civilized; and little by little this civilization had borne its fruits, had had its philosophy. They had encountered everywhere on the eastern coasts of the Mediterranean the Alexandrians and Aristotle; and nothing was better adapted to their genius, which is made up of mystic exaltation and excessive subtilty. Hence the character of the Arabic philosophy, whose most celebrated representatives are Avicenna, a physician and philosopher;† Algazel, whose skepticism serves as a veil or instrument to religious faith;‡ and Averroes, the commentator, another Alexander of Aphrodisia.§ Christians, now and then, went to study in the schools

---

philosophorum, lib. viii. His most important philosophical work is the *Metalogicus*. Died in 1180. On John of Salisbury as pupil of Abelard, *Fragm. Philos.*, p. 304.

* Of Navarre, professor of theology at Paris, died in 1164. *Sententiarum libri* iv. Often reprinted; hence his surname of *Magister Sententiarum.*

† Born at Bochara, about 980, died in 1036. Opp., Venet., 1523, 5 vol. in-fol., Basil, 3 vol. in-fol. We have in French the *Logic of Avicenna*, Paris, 1658, in-12.

‡ Of Tus, died in 1127. *Logica et Philosophia.* Al-Gazelis Arabis, Venet., 1506.

§ Born at Cordova, died at Morocco in 1206. His Commentaries on Aristotle, translated into Latin, are in the two editions of Aristotle, Venet., 11 vol. in-fol., 1550–1552, and small in-4, 1560, with an index, 1562. Formerly his commentaries on the logic and rhetoric of Aristotle were published separately, Venet., 1 vol. in-fol., 1522–1523.

of Spain. Gerbert of Aurillac, afterwards Pope under the name of Sylvester II., studied at Cordova and at Seville; he brought thence, in the tenth century, the Arabic figures, and a very extensive knowledge of the philosophy of Aristotle, which he introduced into the monasteries instituted by him in Aurillac, his native country, at Rheims, at Chartres, and at Bobbio. But it was especially the Jews, who, admitted more easily than the Christians to the schools of the Arabs, obtained a knowledge of metaphysics, and of the natural and medical sciences, superior to the knowledge of the West; they translated into Hebrew the Arabic philosophers; these translations were soon reproduced in Latin, and spread throughout Europe. The Jews were at this epoch, if we may so express it, a species of philosophical courtiers between Spain and the West; they themselves produced some distinguished philosophers, and, among others, Moses Maimonides.* You may judge what a ferment was created in the monasteries of Europe, when instead of some parts of the *Organum*, or even instead of the entire *Organum*, all the works of Aristotle, metaphysical, physical, moral, and political, with Arabic commentaries, penetrated into them. It was thus that towards the first quarter of the thirteenth century, the second epoch of scholasticism was formed.

Three superior men represent this second epoch: Albert the Great, Saint Thomas Aquinas, Duns Scotus.

Albert of Bollstadt,† born at Lavingen in Suabia, was a Domin-

---

* Born at Cordova in 1139, died in 1207. *Rabi Mossei Ægyptii dux seu director dubitantium aut perplexorum*, Parisiis, 1520, in-fol. *Canones Ethici*, Amstelod. 1640, in-4.

† I should at least mention here, among other distinguished contemporaries of Albert, Alexander of Hales, of the County of Glocester, surnamed *Doctor irrefragabilis*, professor of theology in Paris, who died in 1245: *Summa universæ theologiæ*, Colog., 1622, 4 vols.; Guillaume d'Auvergne, Bishop of Paris, died in 1249; several works in theology, among which must be distinguished two treatises, *de Universo* and *de Anima*; Opp., Orleans, 1674, 2 vol. in-fol.; Vincent de Beauvais, a Dominican and preceptor of Saint Louis, who died in 1264; a compilation under the name of *Speculum doctrinale, naturale, historiale;* a division of sciences and their end: 1st, the theoretical part, comprising:

ican, and by turns professor of theology at Cologne and at Paris. In 1260 he was named Bishop of Ratisbon, but soon gave up his bishopric to devote himself exclusively to his studies at Cologne, in a convent of his order. He died in 1280. It is doubtful whether he knew the Arabic or even the Greek, but he studied deeply the new translations of Aristotle and his Arabic commentators, who were beginning to be introduced into Europe. Albert was occupied at the same time with theology, morals, politics, mathematics, and physics. He passed, during his times, about Cologne, for a magician. He was called the Great, by his contemporaries, and I am far from objecting to this title. Nevertheless, my superficial reading of some of his numerous writings* inclines me to believe that, error excepted, he is rather an indefatigable compiler, and thereby great for his age, than an original thinker. He produces upon me the impression of a German scholar of the thirteenth century.

Saint Thomas Aquinas was born rich and of an illustrious family,† who naturally wished to give him a good position in the world. He refused it, and entered quite early into the order of the Dominicans, in order that he might devote himself entirely to philosophy. He carried into his order the same disinterestedness; he constantly refused all dignities, and would consent to be only a professor; but he was an incomparable professor, and was called *Doctor angelicus*, the Angel of the school. He understood the importance of the Arabic and Greek philosophers; he greatly encouraged the translations of their works, and Europe is infinitely

---

theology, physics, mathematics; 2d, the practical part, comprising: monastics (individual morality), economics, politics; 3d, the mechanical arts; 4th, logic. There is a magnificent edition of Vincent de Beauvais in several vols. in-fol., Argentorati, 1473.

* Alberti Magni, Opp., ed. P. Jammy; Lyons, 21 vol. in-fol., 1651.

† At Aquino, near Naples, in 1225; studied under Albert at Cologne and at Paris; died in 1274, canonized in 1323. The first complete edition of his works was published at Rome, 1572, 18 vol. in-fol.; it was done by the orders of Sixtus V.; it contains the Commentaries of Cardinal Cajetan; is very correct and neat. Often reprinted at Paris, Lyons, and at Antwerp. The last edition at Venice, 28 vol. in-4, 1775.

indebted to him for all the translations he caused to be made. If Albert was more learned and, above all, better acquainted with the natural sciences, Saint Thomas was a better metaphysician, and, especially, a better moralist. He did not fall into asceticism as did his compatriot, John of Fidanza, otherwise called Saint Bonaventura, who nearly brought theology to mysticism, thereby obtaining the name of *Doctor seraphicus*, the Seraphic Doctor.* Saint Thomas Aquinas remained faithful to the philosophic spirit. If he submitted reason to the rule of faith, he never misconceived the extent and legitimate authority of our faculties.† The master work of Saint Thomas is the famous summation, *Summa Theologiæ*, which is one of the greatest monuments of the human mind in the middle age, and comprehends, with profound metaphysics, an entire system of morality, and even of politics; and that kind of politics too, which is not at all servile. Among other things, you find in it a defence of the Jews, who were then persecuted, and were so serviceable, not only to commerce, but to science. He could not dream of the civil equality of our days; but, as a Christian he recommended humanity in regard to them, even as a matter of policy. Saint Thomas is particularly a great moralist.‡

The English Duns Scotus§ possessed a mind of a healthy and

---

* Born in 1221, died in 1274. His most characteristic work is the *Itinerarium mentis ad Deum*, Opp., Rome, 1588–1596, 7 vol. in-fol.

† "Est in his quæ de Deo confitemur, duplex veritatus modus. Quædam namque vera sunt de Deo quæ omnem facultatem humanæ rationis excedunt, ut Deum esse trinum et unum; quædam vero sunt ad quæ etiam ratio naturalis pertingere potest, sicut est Deum esse, Deum esse unum et alia hujusmodi quæ etiam philosophi demonstrative de Deo probaverunt, docti naturalis lumine rationis."—*Summa Cathol. fidei contra Gentiles*, i. 3.

‡ We give some thoughts which betray the metaphysician and the superior moralist: *Summa theol.*, Quæst. 2, Art. 1. "Etiam qui negat veritatem esse, concedit veritatem esse; si enim veritas non est, non verum est non esse veritatem . . . Sed enim Deus est ipsa veritas; ergo veritatem esse verum est." Virtue is a means of faith and of science: Summa theol., Part i. Quæst. 82, Art. 4. "Qualis unusquisque, talis intelligit et talis finis videtur eidem."

§ Born at Dunston in Northumberland, according to others at Duns in Ireland, near 1275, died 1308. Opp., ed. Wadding, Lugd., 12 vol. in-fol., 1639.

powerful cast and uncommon solidity. He occupied himself with physics and mathematics. He wrote a small treatise on astronomy and optics. Less of a moralist than Saint Thomas, he was a greater dialectician. So also he was named by his contemporaries not the Seraphic Doctor, nor Angelic Doctor, but the Subtile Doctor, *Doctor subtilis.**

Saint Thomas and Duns Scotus founded two schools, between which the most animated discussions arose on different theological points, the same being also grave philosophical questions.† But

* I will cite some passages from his commentary on the *Master of Sentences.* He distinguishes two orders of ideas, that of sensational ideas and that of necessary and absolute ideas. The first order of verity may be certain and infallible, 1st, because the sensible world from which it is borrowed is itself changing; 2d, because the mind of man which forms them is also changing, etc.; therefore certain science can proceed from nothing perceived by the senses, although the mind of man may have referred it *quantum cumque per intellectum depuratum fuerit.* Every science exists in absolute ideas. God, *idea divina*, is not directly perceived by man, but indirectly, *non radio directo, sed reflexo.* This thought of Scot reminds us of the celebrated passage of Bacon, *De Aug. Scient.*: "Percutit natura intellectum nostrum radio directo, Deus autem, propter medium inæquale, radio tantum refracto; ipse vero homo sibimetipsi monstratur et exhibetur radio reflexo." In regard to necessary truths, sensation is the occasion and not the cause of them; they rest on the power of the mind which forms them. "Quantum est ad notitiam veritatum necessariarum, intellectus non habet sensus pro causa sed tantum pro occasione. Intellectus equidem non potest habere notitiam simplicem nisi acceptam a sensibus, ille tamen accepta potest simplicia componere virtute sua; et si ex ratione talium simplicium fit complexio evidenter vera, intellectus virtute propria assentiet illi complexioni ut veræ, non virtute sensuum a quibus accipit terminos tantummodo exterius, verbi gratia per visum aut auditum; non enim terminis assentitur ut visis et auditis externis, sed ob rationem eorum perspectam.—Statur in simplici experientia quod ita sit, qui quidem modus sciendi est ultimus, seu infimus gradus cognitionis scientificæ.—Cum sensus externi non cognoscant actus suos proprios, quippe cum nec visus nec auditus se ipsum percipiat, necesse erat ut præter sensus exteriores esset sensus quidam interior communis quo sentiamus nos videre, audire, etc.; hic sensus communis est unus." Very fine things in regard to free will. "Voluntati, in quantum est libera, essentiale est, 1, ut etiam quando producit velle, non repugnet eidem oppositum velle; 2, ut bonitas aliqua objecti cognita non causet necessario assensum voluntatis, cum voluntas libera assentit tam bono majori quam etiam minori; 3, ut voluntatis causa sit ipsa voluntas." The goodness of the human will is in its conformity to that of God.

† Saint Thomas, while he admits the liberty of God, is more struck with

let us bear in mind to what religious order Scotus and Saint Thomas belonged. The question of orders was an important question in the middle age, much more important than that of nationality; for where the unity of the Church prevails, national individualities, without being entirely effaced, are much enfeebled. The great matter then, was that of the orders: an order having once adopted a doctrine, or at least any tendency to it whatever, it preserved it a long time, and the history of the religious and learned orders of the middle age contains nothing less than the history of the human mind at this epoch. Saint Thomas belonged to the order of the Dominicans, Duns Scotus to that of the Franciscans. I do not mean to assert that the order of the Dominicans represents the theological idealism of the middle age, and the order of the Franciscans the little empiricism that then existed: the distinction would be much too absolute. But I observe that it was especially from the Scotists, and from the Franciscans, that successively proceeded, during nearly a century, those who were most distinguished by knowledge more or less extensive, in the physical sciences, and by the spirit of innovation. The fact is incontestable; and it is not a fact less incontestable, that the Thomists and especially the Dominicans produced the obstinate defenders of the scholastic theology. It must not be forgotten that at a later period the order of the Jesuits, which opposed the progress of the new spirit, was intimately connected with the Dominicans.

The summing up, and, as it were, the characteristic trait of this second epoch of scholasticism, was a project which, for a moment promising success, finally miscarried. Can you guess what

---

his intelligence, with his goodness, and the laws which result from his nature; it is on the nature of God, and not on his will, that he founds goodness, creation, etc. "Excluditur error quorumdam dicentium omnia procedere a Deo secundum simplicem voluntatem, ut de nullo oporteat rationem reddere, nisi quia Deus vult. Quod etiam divinæ Scripturæ contrariatur, quæ Deum perhibet secundum ordinem sapientiæ suæ omnia fecisse." *S. c. Gent.*, i. 86; ii. 24, 25, 29. On the contrary, Duns Scot deduces the moral law and the creation from the will alone of God; *Voluntas Dei absoluta summa est lex.*

it was? it was to canonize Aristotle as the philosopher *par excellence.** Thus we enter into the third and last epoch.

Two very different men, but both superior of their kind, mark its first moments. I mean Raymond Lully and Roger Bacon.

Raymond Lully† was a Majorcan, born at Palma, a small city of the island of Majorca, between Spain and Africa. His was a mind of Spanish, Arabic, African mould, exalted and mystical, *doctor illuminatus,* and at the same time very subtile, *magnus inventor artis.* Carried away by a lively imagination, he passed his life in running about the world; his youth had been spent in frivolity, his manhood was turbulent, and his end deplorable, but very honorable; he perished in Africa while occupied in the conversion of the infidels, which caused him to be regarded as a saint and a martyr, although his opinions had attracted canonical censures. His cabalistic mysticism was borrowed from the Arabs, but there was more originality in his dialectics. Raymond Lully invented, under the title of Universal Art, *Ars Universalis,* a species of dialectic machine in which all generic ideas were distributed and classified; so that one might procure at will, in such or such a case, in such or such a circle,‡ such or such a principle. Raymond Lully, in spite of these ridiculous things, caused a sensation during his times, and possessed considerable importance.

The Franciscan Roger Bacon was a man who stood alone in the thirteenth century on account of his taste and talent for physics, optics, and astronomy.§ He called his contemporaries

---

* See the work of Launoy: *de varia Aristotelis fortuna in Academia Parisiensi.* Often reprinted.

† Born in 1234, died in 1315. Opp., ed. Zalzinger, Mogunt., 1712–42, 10 vol. in-fol. We have never seen the last volumes, and we do not know that they have ever appeared.

‡ See the form of this *Ars Universalis* in Brucker, Vol. iv., p. 18–19.

§ Born at Ilchester in 1214, died in 1292.—*Opus Masus ad pap. Clement* IV., ed. Jebb., Lond., 1733, in-fol., reprinted in Venice in 1750.—*Specula Mathematica,* in-4, Francf., 1614.—*De secretis operibus artis et naturæ, et de nullitate magiæ diabolicæ, Epistol.;* ed. F. Rothscholz, Vol. iii., Theat. Chem. Norimberg, 1732.

to the study of the natural sciences, and the languages. You are acquainted with his life; you know that so long as Clement IV. lived he did himself honor by protecting a man of genius born three centuries too soon, but that as soon as this excellent pontiff died, ecclesiastical authority pursued Roger. He was imprisoned, it is said, as a sorcerer (*doctor mirabilis*) during many long years, by order of the Franciscan general. The Franciscans persecuted Roger Bacon, but, in fine, they had made him what he was.

These were but the beginnings of the third epoch of scholasticism. Everywhere a movement of independence was making itself manifest. This independence was also to be marked in philosophy, and it produced, little by little, the separation of philosophy from theology, by the enfeebling and destruction of scholasticism. How did this great event take place? How was war declared between the form and the foundation, between philosophy and theology, which until then had lived in such perfect agreement, and what was the battle-field? It was the old quarrel of the nominalists and the realists.

At the end of the eleventh century, in the times of Saint Anselm, on occasion of a passage of Porphyry's introduction to the *Organum* in regard to the different opinions of the Platonists and peripatetics relative to ideas of genus, a canon of Compiègne named Rousselin, or more elegantly, Roscelin, *Roscelinus*, pretended that genera are simple abstractions which the mind forms by the comparison of a certain number of individuals which it reduces to a common idea; he went even so far as to say that genera are mere words, *flatus vocis.* This opinion had its consequences. If every genus is a mere word, it follows that there is no reality except in individuals; then many unities may appear to be simple abstractions: among others, the unity that is above all unities, the unity that forms the basis of the Holy Trinity: there is nothing real in it except the three persons, and the Trinity itself is but a nominal unity, a simple sign representing the relation of the three. The poor canon was summoned before the

Council of Soissons in 1092; he retracted, *metu mortis*, says Saint Anselm, who wrote against him a treatise on the unity in the Trinity. Guillaume de Champeaux, going to the other extreme, maintained that genera, so far from being mere names, nominal entities, are the only entities that exist, and that the individuals, in which it has been attempted to resolve genera, have existence themselves only through relation to what is universal. For example, said he, that which exists is humanity, of which all men are but fragments. Abelard, without falling into the nominalism of Roscelin, and at the same time pretending that there is certainly reality in genera, does not agree with Guillaume de Champeaux that reality exists therein alone; he maintains that particulars constitute true essence, and that genera exist only in the mind, which is indeed a manner of existence quite real, but very different from that of individuals. He took, thus, a medium course; and, as always happens, he satisfied no one and displeased his master, the proud Guillaume de Champeaux. The quarrel stopped there. Realism triumphed; and this dispute slumbered during the second epoch of scholasticism.*

But at the commencement of the fourteenth century, a pupil of Duns Scotus, an Englishman and a Franciscan, took up, in an artful manner, the nominalistic opinion, and renewed the old warfare with vigor and perseverance. I must first tell who this Englishman was. He was an individual named John of Occam, in the county of Surrey, whence he was called John Occam, and sometimes simply Occam. He was a Scotist and a Franciscan, and taught with success, especially at Paris under Philip le Bel. This was the epoch when the political powers strove to emancipate themselves from the ecclesiastical power. You are ac-

* When, in 1829, we traced this rapid sketch of the first debates of realism and nominalism, like all historians of philosophy, we had at our disposal but two or three obscure texts, found here and there among writers of the eleventh and twelfth centuries. The subject has since been elucidated by the discovery of the *unpublished works of Abelard*. See the *Introduction* which accompanies these works and our *Fragments de Philos. scholast.*

quainted with the attempts and resistance of Philip le Bel. Occam, although a Franciscan, placed himself on the side of the political power; he wrote for Philip le Bel against the pretensions of the Holy See and of Pope Boniface VIII. He wrote also for the Emperor Louis of Bavaria, who took the same course as did the King of France, and resisted Pope John XXII. Occam said to Louis: *Tu me defendas gladio, ego te defendam calamo,* Defend me with the sword, and I will defend you with the pen. He was persecuted; and as Tennemann said, he died persecuted, but not conquered, at Munich,* at the court of Louis of Bavaria, with whom he had sought refuge. You may be well assured that a man so bold in politics could not have been timid in philosophy. His courage and his firmness procured for him the name of *Doctor invincibilis.* These are the principal features of his philosophy:

Genera can have existence only in things or in God. In things, there are no genera, for in them they would exist either wholly or partially; in God they are not as an independent essence, but as a simple object of knowledge;† in the mind they are nothing more. After having attacked universals, Occam found fault with another celebrated theory, connected with the first, the theory of sensible and intelligible forms. Until then all scholasticism had maintained that between the exterior bodies, placed before us, and the mind of man, there are images which belong to the exterior bodies, and make more or less a part of them, as the εἴδωλα of Democritus, of which I have already spoken to you, images or sensible forms which represent external objects by the conformity which they have with them. So the mind was supposed to be able to know spiritual beings

* In 1347. His works have not been collected. The principal are *Commentary on the Master of Sentences*, some *Quodlibetic Questions*, and a *Logic* which has been often reprinted.

† "Ideæ non sunt in Deo subjective et realiter, sed tantum sunt in ipso objective, tanquam quædam cognita ab ipso...." *In Magistrum Sententiarum*, i. dist. 35, q. 5.

only through the medium of intelligible species. Occam destroyed these chimeras, and maintained that there is nothing real but spiritual or material beings, and the mind of man, which directly conceives them. Gabriel Biel,* a pupil of Occam, exhibited with much sagacity and clearness, the theory of his master. You see that Occam renewed, without knowing it, the warfare of Arcesilaus against the Stoics; and he is in modern Europe the forerunner of Reid and of the Scotch school. The result of all this warfare was to call attention to words, which are the true medium between the mind and things, according to the nominalists, an opinion which was afterwards in high favor. Thence, finally this general rule, this axiom which does not perhaps belong to Occam, but which he has invoked more frequently than any other philosopher of the same epoch: Entities must not be unnecessarily multiplied, *Entia non sunt multiplicanda præter necessitatem. Frustra fit per plura quod fieri potest per pauciora.*

We have thus seen the good side of Occam; his other merits are far from being as pure. If he has done well to demonstrate that there is no immediate perception of God, that God is known only by his attributes—wisdom, goodness, power,† etc., he may be reproached with having obscured and enfeebled the proper notion of the essence of God. Because we arrive at substances only through their attributes, Occam concluded that we can have no idea of the nature of substances, and he drew from this principle its consequences. Even as God is known only through his attributes, so the soul is known only through its qualities.

* Born at Spire, died in 1495. *Epitome et Collectarium, Super* iv. *libr. Sententiarum*, Bas., 1508, in-fol., Lugd., 1514; *Supplementum*, Parisiis, 1521.

† "Essentia divina potest a nobis cognosci in aliquibus conceptibus qui de Deo verificantur, ut dum, exempli gratia, cognoscimus quid sit sapientia, justitia, charitas, etc.; licet enim hi conceptus dicant aliquid Dei, nullus tamen realiter dicit ipsum quod est Deus; sed dum caremus conceptu Dei proprio, quod ipsum intuitive non videmus, attribuimus ipsi quidquid Deo potest attribui, eosque conceptus prædicamus, non pro se, sed pro Deo," etc *Ibid.* i.. dist. 3, 7, 9.

We may observe these qualities, and account to ourselves for them; but in regard to the substance of the soul, as it is not directly perceived, it is not easy to say what it is; it is not easy, for example, to demonstrate that it is immortal, for it cannot even be demonstrated that it is immaterial. It cannot be demonstrated what is the *substratum*, the agent that resides under those qualities which we know; it is perhaps a natural and material agent. Here faith alone is allowable.* Is not this theory, borrowed from Duns Scotus, in the fourteenth and fifteenth centuries already the celebrated theory of Locke?† Nothing is more false than all this reasoning. In short, if there is no substance without attributes, then, an attribute of a certain character being given, a substance of a nature opposed to the character of this attribute is inevitably excluded; thought being given as a fundamental attribute, a material substance is thereby excluded from thought. I insist upon this, because it would not be impossible that, under a false appearance of method and circumspection, modern philosophy, which is not very far from nominalism, might pretend also that the question of substances, and consequently that of the material or immaterial principle of the phenomena of thought, is without importance, and that the observation of phenomena is that only which is important. Yes, doubtless the observation of intellectual phenomena is important; but it is that precisely, which giving us phenomena of a certain character, imposes upon us a substance of an analogous nature.‡ Another theory of Scot and of Occam, less seductive, and which

* Duns Scot, lib. ii., quæst. 1, num. 8. "Cæterum via naturali demonstrari nequit quod anima humana sit immortalis; quippe cum demonstrari nequit quod ipsa non subsit alicui agenti naturali, quantum adesse vel non esse."—Occam, *Quodlibeta*, i., q. 10. "Quod illa forma sit immaterialis, incorruptibilis ac indivisibilis non potest demonstrari, nec per experientiam sciri. Experimur enim quod intelligimus et volumus et nolumus, et similes actus in nobis habemus; sed quod illa sint e forma immateriali et incorruptibili non experimur, et omnis ratio ad hujus probationem assumpta assumit aliquod dubium."

† See the following volume, Lect. 25, and 1st Series, Vol. 3, Lect. 1, p. 66.

‡ 1st Series, Vol. 4, Lect. 12, p. 55–59; Lect. 20, p. 391; Lect. 21, p. 448.

nevertheless finds, at the present time, numerous partisans, and is attached to the general spirit of nominalism, is the theory which makes morality rest not on the nature of God, which would be very true, but on his will,* which, at the same time, destroys morality and God himself in his most holy attributes.

All that I have just told you shows plainly enough that there was more or less of sensualism in the school of Occam, and this is what I desired to accomplish. Certainly it is not that defined and consistent sensualism, such as we have seen in the independent schools of Greece; but it is, in fact, sensualism such as might have been expected at the close of scholasticism, under the reign of Christianity, under the influence of an authority already contested, but not yet shaken. Hence a school whose common character is disdain of the method and entities of scholasticism, and the taste for analysis and the physical sciences.

Do not believe that the old schools could have slept whilst the spirit of independence was everywhere aroused under the auspices of Occam. The Thomists and many of the Scotists, united, in so far as they were realists, against the new nominalism, made a long war upon it. In the school of realism, we must cite principally with Henry† de Gand, *doctor solemnis,* who also belongs to the thirteenth century, Walter Burleigh, *doctor planus et perspicuus,*‡ author of the first history of philosophy

---

* Occ., *Sentent.* "Ea est boni et mali moralis natura, ut, cum a liberrima Dei voluntate sancita sit et definita, ab eadem facile possit emoveri et refigi: adeo ut mutata ea voluntate, quod sanctum et justum est possit evadere injustum."

† Professor in Paris, died in 1293, author of a *Somme de Théologie* and *Questions Quodlibetiques.* He, with Saint Augustine, called ideas principal forms, *principales quædam formæ,* eternal reasons, *rationes æternæ,* contained in the divine intelligence and which are the model of the creature. Quodl., vii. q. 1. He pretended that man can discover truth only in the pure light of these ideas which is the divine essence, *in pura luce idærum quæ est divina essentia, Somm. theol.,* art. 1, q. 3.

‡ Flourished about 1337, professor in Paris and Oxford, author of Commentaries on Aristotle, Porphyry, etc. His historical compilation is entitled: *De vitis et moribus Philosophorum;* it begins with Thales and closes with Seneca. Nurnberg, 1477, in-fol. Often reprinted.

written in the middle age; Thomas of Bradwardin, a mathematician and at his death Archbishop of Canterbury;* Thomas of Strasburg, prior general of the order of the Hermits of Saint Augustine;† Marsile of Inghen, called *Ingenuus,* founder of the University of Heidelberg.‡ They attacked the doctrine of Occam as theologians and as philosophers. As theologians they accused Occam of Pelagianism. Among their philosophical arguments I will choose the three following: 1st, It is so true that there are genera, entirely distinct from the individuals, to which it is sought to reduce them, that nature, to which the nominalists incessantly appeal, sports with forms and preserves the genera. Every genus represents a real unity. And that again is the principle of a great school of naturalists of our age, which is founded on the unity of composition of each genus, and explains by circumstances the differences of individuals, instead of making genera of simple abstractions, all the reality of which is in the individuals, whether different or similar; 2d, human laws, like nature, neglect individuals and are occupied only with genera; human laws, then, recognize that there are not only resemblances in the human species, but an identical basis; 3d, we seek happiness in the different goods of this world; but all are relative, all variable, all insufficient; and we cannot do otherwise than elevate ourselves from these particular goods to a general good, which is not the union of all particular goods, but which is superior to them all, which is better than all, and which for us is the sovereign good, the unity itself of good. Our desires transcend the particular and the variable; then the absolute and the general exist.

All these arguments found answers more or less forcible in the school of nominalism.§ I content myself with remarking that this

* In 1439. His principal work is a treatise *de causa Dei Contra Pelagium, de virtute causarum et de virtute causæ causarum.* Lundini, 1618, in-fol.

† Died in 1357. Author of a Commentary on the *Master of Sentences.*

‡ Died in 1394.

§ The following are the names of the most celebrated nominalists:

Durand de Saint Pourçain, born in Auvergne, bishop of Meaux, died in 1333, *Doctor resolutissimus.*

controversy represents very well the struggle of empiricism and idealism. It was sustained on both sides with much talent and skill, and both parties enlisted very commendable names; it continued nearly a century. Nothing else than skepticism could have sprung from it. But what skepticism could there be in the middle age? The human mind had not yet arrived at that degree of independence which enabled it to question the basis itself, that is, theology; skepticism could then fall only on the form, that is, on scholastic philosophy, and it completely destroyed it. Hence the great decrial of scholasticism among all the good spirits of the fifteenth century, and hence still the formation of a new system, of that system which we have hitherto seen issuing, after skepticism, from the struggle between sensualism and idealism, I mean mysticism.

Doubtless in the middle age and under the reign of Christian theology, mysticism was very natural to the human mind. It had not ceased to exist from John Scot until the fourteenth century. Thus in the twelfth century Saint Bernard,* Hugues,† and Richard‡ de Saint Victor inclined to mysticism; in the thirteenth century Saint Bonaventura gave to it a character more systematic. But it was in the fourteenth and fifteenth centuries, after

---

Jean Buridan, de Bethune, professor in Paris; he perfected logic; a great partisan of the free will; died in 1358.

Robert Holcot, general of the order of the Augustins, died in 1349.

Gregory of Rimini, died in 1358.

Henry of Hesse, a mathematician and astronomer, died in 1397.

Matthew de Crochove, died in 1410.

Pierre d'Ailly, Chancellor of the University of Paris, a Cardinal, died in 1425.

Gabriel Biel, a pupil of Occam, a professor at Tubingen, died in 1495.

Raymond de Sébunde, professor at Toulouse, in 1436. In his opinion there are two books wherefrom man draws his knowledge, Nature and Revelation. See Montaigne, who translated the *Theologia Naturalis sive Liber creaturarum* of Raymond, and gives its apology in his *Essays*, Book ii. Chap. xii. The *Theologia Naturalis* was printed in 1502, at Nuremberg, in-fol., and very often reprinted.

* Opp., éd. Mabillon, 2 vol. in-fol. Paris, 1690.

† Opp., 3 vol. in-fol., Rothomagi, 1648.

‡ Opp., 1 vol. in-fol., Rothomagi, 165[illegible].

the warm debates of nominalism and of realism, that mysticism, separating itself from all other systems, acquired consciousness of itself, was called by its own name, and exposed its own theory. The most remarkable men of this epoch were almost all mystics, like the Dominican John Tauler, a preacher at Cologne and Strasburg,* and Petrarch, who, at the close of his life, abandoned profane studies in order to devote himself to contemplative philosophy. The last four works of Petrarch are: 1st, *de Contemptu Mundi,* the Contempt of the World; 2d, *Secretum, sive de Conflictu curarum,* the Secret, or the Combat carried on in the Soul by the cares engendered by human things; 3d, *de Remediis utriusque fortunæ,* Remedies against Good and Bad Fortune; 4th, finally, *de Vita Solitaria et de Otio religiosorum,* On Solitary Life and Religious Repose.† Then also appeared the celebrated book of the *Imitation of Jesus Christ;* whether it belongs to Thomas A-Kempis, or our own illustrious Gerson, it may be said to be the natural fruit and perfect image of those unhappy times when man, overwhelmed with the weight of present existence, anticipated the hour of deliverance by hoping in death and in God. This sad and sublime book then formed the constant reading of the religious, as may be seen by the great number of copies which are found in the convents of Germany, of Italy, and of France.

I have mentioned the name of Gerson;‡ he is the interpreter, the true representative of mysticism at this epoch. Gerson, *doctor Christianissimus,* was a pupil of the celebrated Pierre d'Ailly, an ardent nominalist; he succeeded him as Chancellor of the University of Paris. He had all the science of his times;

---

* Born at Strasburg in 1361. His works, in German, have been published at Francfort, by Spener, 1680–1692, and a Latin translation appeared at Colog., 1615. The *Divine Institutions* have been often reprinted at Paris.

† Born at Arezzo, in 1304, died at Padua in 1374. Opp., Basil., 1554, 2 vol. in–4.

‡ Born in the district of Rheims in 1363, died in 1429. Opp., Paris, 1706, 5 vol. in–fol., an edition due to the care of Ellies Dupin, who added to it dissertations on the life and works of Gerson.

and precisely because he had all the science of his times, it did not satisfy him; and at the close of his career he quitted his employment of Chancellor, whether voluntarily or involuntarily, and retired or was exiled to Lyons, and there became master of a school for little children, as may be seen in a very remarkable treatise, *de Parvulis ad Deum ducendis,* Of the Art of Leading Little Children to God. The most important work of Gerson is his treatise on Mystic Theology, *Theologia Mystica.* You will observe that he is not a recluse who falls naturally into mysticism, without knowing it; he is a philosopher, a man of business, of a practical mind, who voluntarily renounces the world and science, and who, in preferring mysticism, knows perfectly well what he does, what he takes and what he quits. The writings of the learned and virtuous Chancellor have this originality, that they are perhaps the first mystic writings in the world that have consented to be called by this name. The author of the Bhagavad-Gita, and afterwards Plotinus and Proclus, present themselves as ordinary philosophers; we have called them mystics. Here, on the contrary, it is mysticism which describes itself and analyzes itself. The *Theologie mystique* is little known; I think, then, it will be well to cite to you some characteristic morsels.

According to Gerson, ordinary philosophy proceeds by a train of arguments, and leads regularly but slowly to God, by setting out through a multitude of media either from nature or from man. The peculiar property of mysticism is that of being based upon immediate intuition.*—Mystic theology is not an abstract science, it is an experimental science; the experience which it invokes is neither the experience of the senses nor that of the reason, but the consciousness of a certain number of sentiments and phenomena which occur in the inmost recesses of the religious soul. This experience is real and leads also to a real system, but one which cannot be comprehended by those who have not proved

* Vol. iii. p. 366. "Quod si philosophia dicitur scientia procedens ex ex perientiis, mystica theologia vera erit philosophia."

facts of this order.*—True science is then that of the religious sentiment, or of the immediate intuition of God through the soul. Let a man possess this immediate intuition and he has true science; and were such a man otherwise ignorant either of physics, or metaphysics, or of all other worldly and profane sciences, were he of feeble mind or even an idiot, he would be a true philosopher.†—Immediate intuition is an operation of the soul, whose character is that of being accompanied with knowledge, and at the same time of not proceeding by successive argumentations, and of arriving directly at God, who, being once in contact with the soul, sends to it that light by means of which it discovers truth, the principles of all truth and all certitude; it is sufficient that the soul seize the terms in which these truths are expressed, in order to know these truths and believe in them immediately. Then reason is, as it were, on the verge of two worlds, on the verge of the corporeal world and of the intellectual world.‡—What immediate intuition is, in relation to knowledge, immediate desire of the highest good is in morals.§ In the order of knowledge, it is sufficient for the reason to conceive immediately the absolute good, to the end that, in the moral order, the mind may apply itself directly to this good, as soon as presented to it by the intelligence.

Mystic theology is, for many reasons, far superior to the speculative theology of the schools; here are four reasons:

* Vol. iii. p. 366. "Theologia mystica innititur ad sui doctrinam experientiis habitis intra in cordibus animarum devotarum. . . . illa autem experientia quæ extrinsecus habetur, nequit ad cognitionem immediatam vel intuitionem deduci illorum qui talium inexperti sunt."

† Ibid. "Eruditi in ea, quomodo libet aliunde idiotæ sint, philosophi recta ratione nominantur."

‡ Ibid., p. 370–371. "Intelligentia simplex est vis animæ cognoscitiva suscipiens immediate a Deo naturalem quamdam lucem in qua et per quam principia prima cognoscuntur esse vera et certissima, terminis apprehensis.—Ratio constituitur velut in horizonte duorum mundorum, spiritualis scilicet et corporalis."

§ Ibid. "Synteresis est vis animæ appetitiva suscipiens immediate naturalem quamdam inclinationem ad bonum, per quam trahitur insequi monitionem boni, ex apprehensione simplicis intelligentiæ præsentati."

1st, Mystic theology joins sentiment to intelligence; it elevates man above himself, warms him, gives him an experimental knowledge, and not an abstract knowledge, an experimental knowledge which is nothing less than God manifesting himself in man. 2d, In order to acquire it there is no necessity of being learned, it is sufficient to be a good man. 3d, It may arrive at the highest perfection without literature, whilst speculative theology cannot be perfect, if it does not attain step by step to the immediate intuition of God, to the apprehension of the sovereign good, that is, without a more or less intimate relation with mystic theology. Mystic theology, since it leads directly to God, can dispense with the science of the schools, and the science of the schools cannot dispense with mysticism if it would arrive at God. 4th, Mystic theology alone gives peace and happiness to the soul. Science is but a sterile exercise, in which man, believing that he is regularly approaching God, wanders from him, by wandering from himself; mystic theology is a salutary exercise, which sets out from the soul in order to arrive at God, and consequently never departs from reality.*

Finally, the end of mysticism is the exaltation, not of the imagination, not of the intelligence alone, but of the entire mind composed at once of imagination and intelligence, an exaltation which ends in unification with God.†

You see that this is nothing less than ecstasy,‡ the Alexandrian and Oriental ecstasy. Thus the mysticism of Gerson, the mysticism engendered by the debates of the two systems nominalism and realism, reproduced, little by little, the same mysticism which we have already encountered in Greece and India; and it reproduced it after a more or less considerable

---

* Ibid. Considerat. XXIX–XXXII., etc. † Ibid.

‡ Ibid. Consider. xxvi. p. 391: "Exstasim dicimus speciem quamdam raptus qui fit appropriatius in superiori portione animæ rationalis. . . . Est extasis raptus mentis, cum cessatione omnium operationum in inferioribus potentiis." See what follows on ecstatic love, and on its power of uniting the soul to God.

appearance of skepticism, after the more or less general decrial of idealism and of sensualism. The mysticism of Gerson stops at ecstasy, as the scholastic skepticism stops at the abandonment of the form of a false system of dialectics, as the sensualism of Occam stops at the contempt of the absurd entities of idealism, and as this idealism itself wanders not into all the follies into which, both in Greece and India, we have seen the Vedan idealism and the Neoplatonic idealism fall. Unfortunately it is not permitted us to bestow the honor of this sobriety upon the wisdom of the human mind; we are forced to refer it to its weakness and to the active and powerful surveillance of ecclesiastical authority. Under this severe control, philosophy, less independent, is constrained to be more prudent; meanwhile, it is still in these narrow limits more or less idealistic, sensualistic, skeptical, and mystical. In the next lecture we will examine what it was in its days of independence: we will enter into modern philosophy, properly so called.

LECTURE X.

PHILOSOPHY OF THE PERIOD OF THE REVIVAL.

Subject of this lecture: philosophy of the fifteenth and of the sixteenth century.—Its character and its origin.—Classification of all its systems into four schools. 1st, Platonic idealistic school: Marsilio Ficino, the Picos of Mirandola, Ramus, Patrizzi, Giordano Bruno.—2d, Peripatetic sensualistic school: Pomponatius, Achillini, Cesalpini, Vanini, Telesio, Campanella.—3d, Skeptic school: Sanchez, Montaigne, Charron.—4th, Mystic school: Marsilio Ficino, the Picos, Nicholaus Cusanus, Reuchlin, Agrippa, Paracelsus, Society of the Rosicrucians, Robert Fludd, Van Helmont, Böhme.—Comparison of the four schools.—Conclusion.

Scholasticism had its day. You have seen what, by turns, it necessarily became, at first the humble servant of theology, afterwards its respected ally, finally attempting liberty, and loosening gradually, without breaking, the bonds which it had borne during six centuries. We have distinguished these three momenta in the history of scholasticism; but it is not less true that its general character is the subordination of philosophy to theology, whilst that of modern philosophy is the complete secularization of philosophy. Scholasticism ceases then towards the commencement of the fifteenth century, and modern philosophy begins with the first days of the seventeenth. Between them there is a transition, an intermediate epoch, a precise idea of which it behooves us to obtain.

It is unnecessary to exhibit to you the great events which have distinguished the fifteenth and sixteenth centuries, in the social, scientific, and literary order; it is sufficient to remind you that what characterizes these two great centuries, is in general the spirit of adventure, a superabundant energy, which after being long nourished and fortified in silence under the severe discipline of the Church, is displayed in every sense and in every way when the passage is open to it. So it was with the philosophy of this age. Long captive in the circle of theology, it burst forth on every side, with wonderful ardor, but without any rule. Independence began,* but method had not yet commenced,† and philosophy precipitated itself at random into all the systems that were presented to it. What were these systems? This is what we must ascertain, for we are running over, we are studying every age in order to discover the innate tendencies of the human mind, and in some sort the organic elements of the history of philosophy. Now, the philosophy of the fifteenth and sixteenth centuries owed its character as well as its origin to an accident.

Among the great events which mark the fifteenth century, one of the most important is the taking of Constantinople. It was the taking of Constantinople that brought into Europe the arts, the literature, and the philosophy of ancient Greece, and which thereby completely changed the forms which art, literature, and philosophy till that time had possessed. The middle age, like every long and great epoch of humanity, had had its expression in art and literature. From the twelfth to the fifteenth century we see on all sides, proceeding from the social condition of Europe, and from Christianity, which is its basis, arts and a literature peculiar to Europe, the offspring of its creeds and its morals, and which represent them, that is, arts and a literature distinguished as romantic. True romanticism, in leaving arbitrary theories and insignificant imitations, in order to lay hold of history and original monuments, is nothing else than the spontaneous development of the middle age in art and literature. Call to mind Gothic architecture. Call to mind the admirable beginnings of Italian and Flemish painting; in regard to poetry think of the troubadours of Provence, of the masters of song in Germany, of the Spanish romancers; and remember that Dante in the thirteenth century, and Shakspeare even in the sixteenth, owed nothing to the new artificial culture brought into

---

* See Lecture 2.

† See Lecture 3.

Europe by the Greeks of Constantinople. It was not then, as has been declared, the importation of Greece into Europe during the fifteenth century that created our arts and our literature, for they were already in existence; but it was, in fact, from this source that flowed into European literature, the sentiment of beauty of form, peculiar to antiquity. Hence, between the romantic genius of Europe of the middle age, and the beauty of classic form, an alliance in which, as in all alliances, the terms have not been perfectly made and observed. However it may be, and in whatever manner we may be disposed to judge the memorable accident which so powerfully modified the form of art and literature in Europe during the fifteenth century, it cannot be denied that this same accident also had an immense influence on the destinies of philosophy.

When philosophic Greece appeared in the Europe of the fifteenth century, judge how its numerous systems, so free and clothed in such brilliant forms, must have impressed these philosophers of the middle age, still shut up in cloisters and convents, but sighing after independence! The result of this impression must have been a sort of enchantment and momentary fascination. Greece not only inspired Europe, it intoxicated it; and the character of the philosophy of this epoch is imitation of ancient philosophy without any criticism. The philosophical spirit was still incomparably below the systems which were presented to it; it was then inevitable that these systems should sweep it away and subdue it. Thus after having served the Church in the middle age, philosophy in the fifteenth and sixteenth centuries exchanged this dominion for that of ancient philosophy. Still it possessed, if you will, some authority; but what was the difference, I pray you? It was impossible to go immediately from scholasticism to modern philosophy, and make an end at once of all authority. It was, however, a benefit to fall under a new authority, entirely human, without any root in morals, without external power, divided against itself, and consequently very flexible and very durable; also, in my opinion, in the economy of the general history of the human mind, the philosophy of the period of the revival* was a transition without originality and without gran-

---

* I have several times expressed the same opinion in regard to the philosophy of the period of the revival, a great deal too much boasted of and little enough understood in Italy and even in Germany. *Introduction to the unpublished works of Abelard*, and *Philosophical Fragments*, SCHOLASTIC PHILOSOPHY, p. 81: "At the close of the fifteenth century, ancient philosophy appeared almost entire. The complete works of Aristotle are possessed, Plato is acquired; these two great minds are read in their own languages; all are enchanted, all are intoxicated by this wonderful antiquity; Platonism, peripateticism, Pythagoreanism, Epicureanism, Stoicism and the philosophy of the Academics, and of the Alexandrians, seize equally the mind; Christians are scarcely any longer found, and philosophers are rare enough. Learning consists in the possession, more or less, of imagination and enthusiasm; imitation is so successful as to deceive the most skilful; spirit abounds, genius is seldom found. The sixteenth century produced scarcely a single great man in philosophy, an original philosopher. The entire utility, the mission of this century was little else than to efface and destroy the middle age under the artificial imitation of antiquity, until, at length, in the seventeenth century, a man of genius, cultivated indeed, but without erudition, Descartes, gave birth to modern philosophy with its immense destinies." *Fragments of Cartesian Philosophy*, VANINI OR PHILOSOPHY BEFORE DESCARTES, p. 3. "Between scholastic philosophy and modern philosophy is that which may be properly called the philosophy of the period of the revival, because, if it is any thing, it is especially an imitation of antiquity. Its character is almost entirely negative: it rejects scholasticism, it aspires to something new, and makes something new of recovered antiquity. At Florence, Plato and the Alexandrians were translated, an academy was founded, full of enthusiasm, destitute of criticism, wherein were mingled, as formerly at Alexandria, Zoroaster, Orpheus, Plato, Plotinus and Proclus, idealism and mysticism, a little truth, much folly. Here the philosophy of Epicurus is adopted, that is, sensualism and materialism; there Stoicism, there again Pyrrhonism. If Aristotle is almost everywhere combated, it is the Aristotle of the middle age, it is the Aristotle of Albert the Great and of Saint Thomas, he who, well or badly understood, had served as a foundation and rule in Christian instruction; but still the veritable Aristotle is studied, is invoked, and at Bologna and at Padua for example, he is turned against Christianity. In fact, this short epoch does not reckon one man of genius who may be put in comparison with the great philosophers of antiquity, of the middle age, and of modern times, it produced no monument which has endured, and if we may judge it by its works, we may, with reason, be harsh towards it. But it is the spirit of the sixteenth century which must be considered in the midst of its greatest aberrations. The philosophy of the period of the revival prepared modern philosophy; it broke the ancient servitude, fruitful servitude, glorious even so long as it was unobserved, and so long as it was in some sort freely borne,

deur, but useful and even necessary, from the absolute slavery of the middle age to the absolute independence of modern philosophy.

The spectacle which the philosophy of the fifteenth and sixteenth centuries first presents is one of extreme confusion. Every thing is crowded and entangled in these centuries so completely crammed; systems no longer seem to succeed each other; they appear to exist all together. The first means of introducing some order and some light into this chaos, is, in setting out from the incontestable principle that the philosophy of this period is nothing else than a renewal of philosophical antiquity, to do for the copy what we have done for the original, and to divide the imitation of antiquity into as many great distinct parts as we have found in antiquity itself. Moreover it is not as true, as at first glance it appears, that the development of the philosophy of

---

but which, once felt, became an insupportable burden and an obstacle to all progress. In this point of view the philosophers of the sixteenth century have an importance very superior to that of their works. If they established nothing, they removed nothing; the greater part of them suffered, many died to give us the liberty which we enjoy. They have not only been the prophets, but they have been more than once the martyrs of the new spirit. Hence, on their account, two contrary judgments, equally true and equally false. When Descartes and Leibnitz, the two great philosophers of the seventeenth century, found under their pens the names of these bold thinkers of the sixteenth, partly in sincerity and partly through policy, they treated them with great disdain; they did not wish to be confounded with these turbulent spirits, and they forgot that without them, the liberty of thought which they enjoyed, might, perhaps, have never been obtained. There are still meddlers and utopians who, confounding a revolution to be maintained with a revolution to be made, take us back to the very cradle of modern times, and propose to us as models the disorderly enterprises in which the energy of the sixteenth century was consumed. We believe ourselves to be equitable in making little account of the philosophical labors of this age and in honoring their authors: it is not their writings that interest us, it is their destiny, their life, and especially their death. Heroism and martyrdom even are not proofs of truth: man is so great and so miserable that he may give his life for error and folly as well as for truth and justice; but devotion in itself is always sacred, and it is impossible for us to allow our thought to dwell upon the agitated life, the misfortunes, and the tragic end of many of the philosophers of the period of the revival without feeling for them a profound and painful sympathy.

the fifteenth and sixteenth centuries was simultaneous; it was really successive and progressive.

Although it should be proved that all the philosophical systems of antiquity, to some extent, burst forth together upon the West, and were known at the same time in Europe, it would not follow in the least that there would have resulted an adoption and a simultaneous imitation of all these systems; they might all, indeed, be offered to the human mind, and still the human mind might not with the same eagerness receive them all at once. It is more important here to take into consideration the disposition of those to whom the ancient systems were presented, than the nature of these systems in themselves. Thus, although the skeptical monuments of ancient philosophy might have been presented to the human mind simultaneously with the dogmatical monuments of peripateticism and of Platonism, it is impossible that the human mind, at the exit of the middle age, still thoroughly imbued with profoundly dogmatical habits, should have accepted skepticism with the same facility as dogmatism: it is also a very important and indisputable fact, that whilst Platonic and peripatetic dogmatism filled the entire fifteenth century, it was not until the sixteenth century that a ray of skepticism broke forth upon the philosophical horizon. Observe again that this skepticism, which appeared in the midst of the sixteenth century, proceeded not from Platonism, but from peripateticism, that is, from a school of empiricism and sensualism, according to the laws of the relative formation of systems which we have already noticed. Finally, if it is true that mysticism proceeded immediately from Platonic dogmatism, without waiting for the development of other systems, this phenomenon is explained by the character of Platonic dogmatism, such as it passed from Constantinople into Europe; it was Alexandrian Platonism, that is, a system of mysticism. This first mysticism, which you find at the commencement of the fifteenth century, is a small affair compared with that which existed at the end of this epoch. It must be acknowledged, in fact, that it was at the close of the sixteenth century, that is, after the greatest struggle between the two opposed systems of dogmatism, and after the appearance of skepticism, that a new mysticism arose, which was not only an artificial mysticism, a barren reproduction of Alexandrian mysticism, but an original and profound mysticism, which sprang from the natural development of the philosophical spirit of modern Europe. In this epoch of an imitation apparently so confused, we still find the regular laws of the development and of the progress of systems; those same laws which we have already deduced from the rapid but exact review of all the systems of scholasticism, of ancient philosophy, and of Oriental philosophy.

I am going to present to you the four great schools which, in the fifteenth and sixteenth centuries, still fill the history of philosophy, namely, Platonic idealistic dogmatism, peripatetic sensualistic dogmatism, skepticism, and mysticism. Doubtless in the confusion which reigned in the fifteenth and sixteenth centuries, more than one system combined, or rather mingled together, several of these elementary points of view; but in these powerless combinations, which the times so promptly swept away, a more severe analysis easily discerns the fundamental element which governs the entire combination, and reduces it to nothing more than a particular and exclusive system. All enter, then, into the four classes which I have just designated.

The systems which these four classes embrace are very numerous, and, at the same time, lack originality; for this, I repeat, is an epoch of fermentation and irregular imitation. It is impossible, and it would be useless for the end which we propose, to dwell upon each of these systems: the framework which embraces them being once completed, I shall be satisfied to fill it up with simple statistics.

If we had any clear light in regard to the state of philosophy in Constantinople, before the arrival of the Greeks into Italy, we should very probably behold peripateticism and Platonism, that is, sensualism and idealism, established at Constantinople, and there contending together. Scarcely, at least, had they crossed the sea and reached the soil of Italy, when they were announced by a quarrel. On one hand, Gemistus Pletho,* who came into Italy just at the commencement of the fifteenth century, to attend the Council of Florence, and his friend and disciple the Cardinal Bessarion,† made known in Europe the Platonic philosophy, such as it then was at Constantinople, that is, mingled with Neoplatonism. On the other hand, George Scholarius, called Gennadius, Theodore of Gaza, and especially George of Trebizond,‡ who had come into Europe at about the same time with the former, and, I believe, for the same object, all of these developed and defended the philosophy of Aristotle. Hence the most interesting discussions which occupied§ all Europe, discussions which were at first confined to the Greeks of Constantinople; little by little Europe takes part in them, and thence proceed two European schools, one Platonic and idealistic, of which Marsilio Ficino is the father, and the other peripatetic, and more or less sensualistic, of which Peter Pomponatius is the head. At these two schools we shall give a rapid glance.

I will mention the most distinguished men that mark the history and progress of idealistic and Platonic dogmatism, from the beginning of the fifteenth century until the seventeenth, from the end of scholasticism to the beginning of modern philosophy.

First we find Marsilio Ficino of Florence, who was born in 1433, and who died in 1489. Marsilio Ficino is rather a learned man than a philosopher, and as a philosopher he belongs rather to the Alexandrian than to the Platonic school. He has rendered immortal service to philosophy by translating into the Latin tongue the greatest monuments of idealism and of ancient mysticism, Plato, Plotinus, most of the works of Porphyry, of Jamblichus,

* Of Constantinople; he came from Florence in 1438. *De Platonicæ atque Aristotelicæ philosophiæ differentia.* Bas., 1574, in-4.

† Archbishop of Nice, afterwards Cardinal of the Roman Church, died in 1472. *In Calumniatorem Platonis*, lib. iv., Venetiis, Aldus, 1516, in-fol.

‡ Died about 1484. *Comparatio Aristotelis et Platonis.* Venet., 1523.

§ See on the debates, and on the works which they produced, Boivin, *Memoirs of the Academy of Inscriptions*, vol. ii. p. 776, and vol. iii. p. 308.

and of Proclus, independent of his own original writings, for example, *The Platonic Theology,* which embraces a complete treatise on the immortality of the soul.* What characterizes the erudition of Ficino is the absence of all criticism; what characterizes his philosophy is an enthusiasm, intemperate and without any method, for Alexandrian Platonism; and in this absence of method, the pretension of combining with the idealistic and mystic dogmatism which he received from the hands of antiquity, the creeds of Christianity; the very thing which gave the greatest success to Platonic philosophy. This success was so great, that Plato was on the point of obtaining the extravagant honor which had well nigh been decreed to Aristotle in the thirteenth century: a sort of legal consecration, as a philosopher, by the ecclesiastical authority. The Medici hastened to furnish Ficino with every facility for introducing and implanting Platonic idealism in Italy; and it was in 1460 that, under Cosmo de Medici, the celebrated academy was founded at Florence, from which went forth more than one learned man and distinguished philosopher.†

Marsilio Ficino numbered among his friends and pupils the two counts, John Pico‡ and Francis Pico§, of Mirandola: the former even abandoned the coronet of Mirandola in order to devote himself exclusively to the study of philosophy. He delivered himself up to it like a great lord: he contrived a sort of philosophical festival at Rome, where he intended to present nine hundred propositions, nine hundred theses, which he would sustain against any one, and in order to attract as many as possible, he declared that he would pay the travelling expenses of all the learned men

---

* *Theologia Platonica, sive de Immortalitate, animorum et æterna Felicitate,* lib. xviii. vol. i. of his works. Bas., 1576, in-fol.

† See the curious words of Bandini: *Specimen litteraturæ Florentinæ sæculi* xv. *in quo . . . acta Academiæ Platonicæ, amagno Cosmo excitatæ, cui idem præerat, recensentur et illustrantur,* 2 vol. in-8. Florence, 1748.

‡ Born in 1463, died in 1494. Among his works must be distinguished the *Heptaplus.*

§ Killed in 1533. The works of the two Picos were collected in two volumes in-fol. Basil., 1601.

who would accept his invitation. But as all this tended to nothing less than raising a sort of throne to Plato, even in the midst of Rome, the pope was made to understand the danger of such an assembly, more or less Christian, but especially philosophic. The assembly was forbidden, and from this time ecclesiastical authority commenced a strict watch over Platonism, which it had at first so favorably received.

Platonic idealism set out from the Florentine academy, from Ficino, and from the Picos of Mirandola, and marched regularly on to Giordano Bruno, who is the most eminent man, as well as the martyr of this school.

In this school we successively distinguish our own Ramus, the German Taurellus, the Dalmatian Patrizzi, and finally, the Neapolitan Bruno. I will give you only the most concise notices of these different philosophers.

Ramus (Pierre la Ramée) is the first celebrated antagonist of peripateticism in the University of Paris. Born in Picardy in 1515, of a very poor family, it is said that he commenced in the University by a service which could not apparently raise him to a very high philosophical rank. He arose gradually by dint of labor and of merit; but having expressed himself energetically against peripateticism, he made powerful enemies, and became the object of a violent persecution.* He could have found out of France honorable asylums; the most flattering invitations came to him from Italy and from Germany.† He preferred to

* "His books (*Institutiones dialecticæ—Animadversiones Aristotelæ:* Paris, 1543) were interdicted throughout the kingdom and burned before the Collège Royal. He was condemned to abandon the teaching of philosophy, and barely escaped being sent to the galleys. The sentence passed upon him was published in Latin and in French through all the streets of Paris . . . Pieces were performed in the theatre, in which he was introduced in a thousand ways, amidst the acclamations of the peripatetics." Teissier, *Eloge des hommes savants.*

† "After the death of Amaseo, the city of Bologna offered him a thousand ducats in order to engage him in his place. The King of Poland tried to draw him to Cracovia. John, King of Hungary, demanded him in order to give him the direction of the Academy of Weissemberg." *Ibid.*

suffer in his own country and for his own country. By turns deprived of his professorship, re-established in it, despoiled of it anew, forced to fly from France and continually returning to it again, the unfortunate man found himself at Paris, on the faith of treaties and solemn words, on the night of Saint Bartholomew: he was massacred. Doubtless he was suspected, and with reason, of protestantism; but if he was hunted as being secretly a Huguenot, he was not less hunted as being openly a Platonist. At this time the domination of nominalism was complete in the University of Paris, that same nominalism which had been for so long a time proscribed. Aristotle reigned without contradiction. The most fanatical peripatetic of that time was a professor named Charpentier, who, after having violently declared against Platonism, "bethought himself of means which had not yet been used," says Varillas, "by those excited against those doctrines: during the night of Saint Bartholomew he sent soldiers to the house of Pierre La Ramée, who, after having taken every thing from him under pretence of saving his life, assassinated him, and threw his body from the window of his room into the college-yard. The students, stirred up by their regents, tore out his bowels, and dragged him through the streets."* It must not be forgotten

* Varillas, *History of Charles IX.*, Book ix. De Thou said the same thing, ad ann. 1572, and Gouget, in his *Mémoires sur le Collège de France*, adopts the narration of De Thou. On Ramus, see our *Fragments of Cartesian philosophy*, p. 6: "What a life, what an end! Having sprung from the lowest ranks of the people, a domestic in the College of Navarre, admitted by charity to the lectures of the professors, afterwards a professor himself, by turns in favor and persecuted, driven from his chair, banished, recalled, always suspected, he was finally massacred on the night of Saint Bartholomew, as a Protestant, and at the same time as a Platonist. His adversary, the Catholic and peripatetic Charpentier, directed the blows. It would be difficult to believe this if it were not attested by a well-informed contemporary, De Thou. 'Charpentier, his rival,' says the faithful historian, 'excited a tumult, sent assassins who dragged him from the place where he was concealed, robbed him of his money, pierced him with their swords, and cast him from the window into the street; there some furious students, incited by their masters, tore out his bowels, submitted his body to every manner of outrage, and finally rent it in pieces.' Such was the fate of a man who, in the absence of great depth and originality, possessed an elevated mind adorned with every

that at about the same period, another peripatetic, the Spaniard Sepulveda,* the theologian and historiographer of Charles V., furnished the King of Spain with arguments in favor of enslaving the unfortunate Americans against the pious Barthelemy de Las Casas. Whenever, then, modern sensualism accuses idealism of having been behind in civilization, and boasts of having alone served the cause of liberty and humanity, think, I pray you, think of Charpentier and Sepulveda. Besides, God forbid that I should desire to brand sensualism, and render it injustice for injustice! Tyrannical and injurious at this period, you will see it hereafter, you have already seen it, useful and persecuted, as, for example, in the case of Occam. Systems have their good and their evil days, and their good days are not those of their prosperity and incontestable dominion. It does not belong to any system, whatever it may be, to serve civilization exclusively; and my sole wish is that you would draw from these words, and from all my instructions, a disdain and disgust for all fanaticism in philosophy as well as in other things, a habit of tolerance, and even of respect, for all systems, all the legitimate offspring of the human mind and of human liberty.

Pierre La Ramée, a martyr at the same time of protestantism and of idealism, had numerous partisans in France, in England, and in Germany, and in all protestant countries, where the spirit of reform extended itself to philosophy. In England, his treatise on anti-peripatetic logic had, at a later period, the honor of being reduced and arranged for classes by the author of *Paradise Lost*.†

---

kind of knowledge, who introduced among us Socratic wisdom, tempered and polished the rude science of his times by literary research, and first produced in the French language a treatise on dialectics. The most humble monument, however, has not been reared to his memory; he has never had the horor of a public eulogium, and his works even have not been collected."

* Born in 1490, died in 1573. *Joannis Genesii Sepulvedæ Cordubensis Opera.* Matriti, 1780, 4 vol. in-4.

† *Artis logicæ plenior institutio ad Petri Rami methodum concinnati*, p. 614,

For want of celebrated Platonists, Germany reckons a number of reasonable and moderate adversaries to Aristotle: at Altorf, Taurellus, who contended with Cesalpini, and appears to have possessed an excellent mind;* at Marburg, Goclenius,† remarkable especially as the author of a work, the title of which is: Ψυχολογία, *hoc est, de hominibus Perfectione Anima*, etc.‡ This is, I think, the first appearance of psychology under its own name, in modern philosophy. Goclenius had, as a pupil, Otto Casmann, who wrote a work similar to that of his master, entitled: *Psychologia anthropologica, sive animæ humanæ doctrina*;§ and these wise men founded at Marburg a true psychological school.

Francisco Patrizzi,‖ a Dalmatian, a professor at Ferrara and at Rome, attempted a conciliation between Aristotle and Plato in the Alexandrian manner, that is, in a manner whereby Aristotle is almost entirely sacrificed to Plato. He took the greatest pains to establish this combination, preparing himself for it by a long study of Aristotle, the fruits of which he deposited in his *Discussiones peripateticæ*.¶ He labored also on the Alexandrians, and even translated the *Theological Institutions* of Proclus.** At last he completed the work to which he hoped to fix his name, and which appeared to him the last word of philosophy, a work profoundly Christian, very orthodox, nowise peripatetic, and even of an extreme and intolerant Platonism. The following is the title of this work: *Nova de universis Philosophia, in qua Aristotelica*

---

vol. ii.; the Works of John Milton, historical, political, and miscellaneous, in-4, London, 1753.

* Born at Montheliard in 1547, died in 1606. His most celebrated writings are *Philosophiæ triumphus*, Basil., 1573, reprinted at Arnheim in 1617; *Alpes cæsæ*, 1597; *de rerum Æternitate*, Marburg, 1604; *Nicolai Taurelli in inclyta Noricorum Academia philosophiæ et medicinæ antecessoris celeberrimi, de Mundo et Cœlo, discussionum metaphysicarum et physicarum libr. IV. adversus Piccolominum aliosque peripateticos, editio nova.* Ambergæ, 1611.

† Born at Corbach in 1547, died at Marburg in 1628.

‡ Marburg, 1597.

§ Hanau, 1594.

‖ Born at Clisso, in Dalmatia, in 1529, died in 1597.

¶ Basil., 1581, 1 vol. in-fol.

** Ferrar., 1583, in-4.

*methodo, non per motum, sed per lucem et lumina, ad primam causam ascenditur; deinde nova quadam ac peculiari methodo tota in contemplationem venit divinitas; postremo methodo platonica rerum universitas a conditore Deo deducitur.** The book is dedicated to Pope Gregory XIV.

You can conceive that the destiny of the author would not have been very much troubled. Not so with that of Bruno. Giordano Bruno, born at Nola, about the middle of the sixteenth century, entered at an early age the order of the Dominicans. Religious and philosophical doubts soon made him quit his order, and he was also compelled to leave Italy. He went to Geneva, but could not agree with Theodore Beza, nor with Calvin. Thence he repaired to Paris, where he signalized himself as the adversary of Aristotle. He went also to England, and remained some time with Sir Philip Sidney, who was found wherever protection was needed for any attempt at philosophical, religious, or political independence. At a later period we find Bruno giving public and private lessons at Wittemburg, at Prague, at Helmstadt, and at Frankfort-on-the-Maine. The desire of revisiting Italy brought him again into that portion of the country then the most independent and the most liberal, the State of Venice; here during two years he led a tranquil life; then, from motives of which I am ignorant, the Venetians delivered him up or abandoned him in 1598 to the Inquisition. Transferred to Rome, he was tried, condemned as a violator of his vows and as a heretic, and burned the 17th of February, 1600.†

---

* Venetiis, 1593, in-fol.

† The following are the most remarkable works of G. Bruno: *Della causa, principio e uno;* Venet. (Paris), 1584.—*Dell' infinito universo e mondi;* Venet. (Paris), 1584.—*De monade, numero et figura,* etc.; Francf., 1591.—*Fragments of Cartesian Philosophy:* VANINI, OR THE PHILOSOPHY BEFORE DESCARTES, p. 8: "Bruno is delighted with Pythagoras and Plato, especially with the Pythagoras and Plato of the Alexandrians. Touched, and as it were intoxicated by the sentiment of universal harmony, he soars at once into the most sublime speculations, where analysis has not led him, where analysis cannot sustain him. Wandering upon precipices which he has imperfectly explored, without mistrust, and in default of criticism, he retreats from Plato to the

Giordano Bruno had less erudition than Marsilio, but was infinitely more original. He possessed an enlarged mind, a power-

Eleatics, anticipates Spinoza, and is lost in the abyss of an absolute unity, destitute of the intellectual and moral characters of divinity, and inferior to humanity itself. Spinoza is the geometrician of the system; Bruno is its poet. Let us render him justice in saying that, before Galileo, he renewed the astronomy of Copernicus. The unfortunate man, having early entered a convent of Saint Dominic, became one day inspired by a spirit opposed to that of his order, and left it. He sat down sometimes as a pupil, sometimes as a master, in the schools of Paris and of Wittemburg, spreading wherever he went a multitude of ingenious and chimerical works. The desire of revisiting Italy having taken him to Venice, he was delivered up to the Inquisition, led to Rome, judged, condemned, and burned. What was his crime? None of the proceedings in this questionable affair have been published; they have been destroyed, or they still remain in the archives of the holy office, or in a corner of the Vatican with those against Galileo. Was Bruno accused of having broken the ties which bound him to his order? But such a fault does not seem to justify such a punishment; and, besides, he should have been judged by the Dominicans. Or was he persecuted as a Protestant, and for having, in a small work under the title of the *Bestia trionfante*, seemed to attack papacy itself? Or was he merely accused of false opinions in general, of impiety, of atheism, the word pantheism not having yet been invented? This last conjecture is now shown to be the correct one. There was then at Rome a learned German, profoundly devoted to the Holy See, who was present at the trial and punishment of Bruno, and who relates what he saw to one of his Lutheran countrymen, in a Latin letter, found and published at a later period (*Acta litteraria* de Struve, fascic. v. p. 64). As it is little known, and has never been translated, we will here give a few extracts. It proves that Giordano Bruno was put to death not as a Protestant, but as an impious person, not for such or such an act of his life, his flight from his convent or his abjuration of the Catholic faith, but for the philosophical doctrine which he taught in his works and his discourses. Gaspard Schoppe to his friend Conrad Ritershausen . . . "This day furnishes me with a new motive for writing to you: Giordano Bruno, on account of heresy, has just been publicly burned alive in the Champ de Flore, before the theatre of Pompey . . . If you were now in Rome, the greater part of the Italians would tell you that they had burned a Lutheran, and that would doubtless confirm you in your idea of our cruelty. But you must know, my dear Ritershausen, our Italians have not learned to distinguish between heretics of every shade: every heretic is called a Lutheran, and I pray God to preserve them in this simplicity, that they may be always ignorant wherein one heresy differs from others. I myself would have perhaps believed, from the general report, that this Bruno was burned on account of Lutheranism, if I had not been present at the sitting of the Inquisition in which his sentence was pronounced, and if I had not thus learned of what sort of heresy he was guilty . . . (here follows an account of the life and journeys of Bruno, and the doctrines which

ful and brilliant imagination, an ardent soul, and a pen often lively and ingenious. He renewed the theory of numbers, and gave a detailed explanation of the decadal system. With him, God is the great unity which is developed in the world and in humanity, as unity is developed in the indefinite series of numbers. He also undertook the defence of the Copernican system. His errors belong to his qualities. The sentiment of universal unity takes from him that of human individuality and its distinctive characteristics. It cannot be denied that he has a sort of genius devoid of method. If he did not establish a durable system, he left, at least, in the history of philosophy, a luminous and bloody trace which was not lost to the seventeenth century.

---

he taught). It would be impossible to give a complete review of all the monstrosities which he advanced, either in his books or in his discourses. In a word, there is not an error of pagan philosophers, or of ancient and modern heretics, that he has not sustained . . . At Venice, he at last fell into the hands of the Inquisition; after remaining there some time he was sent to Rome, interrogated on several occasions by the holy office, and convicted by the first theologians. He was allowed forty days for reflection; he promised to abjure, then began to defend his follies, then asked a further delay of forty days; finally he made sport of the pope and of the Inquisition. Consequently, about two years after his arrest, on the 9th of February last, in the palace of the grand inquisitor, and in the presence of the illustrious cardinals, the consulting theologians, the secular magistrate, and the governor of the city, Bruno was introduced into the hall of the Inquisition, and there upon his knees heard the sentence pronounced against him. He was reminded of his course of life, his studies, his opinions, the zeal which the inquisitors had displayed to convert him, their fraternal warnings, and the obstinate impiety which he had shown. Afterwards he was degraded, excommunicated, and delivered to the secular magistrate, with the prayer that he would punish him with clemency and without the effusion of blood. To all this Bruno replied only in these words of menace: *The sentence which you pronounce troubles you, perhaps, more than me.* The guards of the governor then led him to prison; there they again tried to make him abjure his errors. It was in vain. To-day, therefore, he has been taken to the stake. The image of the crucified Saviour being presented to him, he rejected it with disdain. The unhappy man died in the midst of the flames, and I think has gone to relate in those other worlds which he imagined (an allusion to the innumerable worlds and to the infinite universe of Bruno) how the Romans are accustomed to treat impious men and blasphemers. This, my dear friend, is our mode of proceeding with monsters of this species. Rome, 17 February, 1600."

I pass to the peripatetic school. It is at bottom sensualistic, and conceals within it all the consequences belonging to sensualism; but these consequences are developed only successively.

In the peripatetic school of the fifteenth and sixteenth centuries, it is necessary to distinguish two points of view without which it is difficult or even impossible to trace the history of the peripateticism of this epoch.

As Marsilio Ficino and all the Platonic school of that period interpreted Platonism by Alexandrianism, so the peripatetic school interpreted Aristotle by Alexander of Aphrodisia, a celebrated ancient commentator of Aristotle, and Averroes, an Arabic commentator of the twelfth century. The difference between these commentators is, that Alexander of Aphrodisia is more methodical and more sensible and infinitely nearer the true meaning of Aristotle; whilst Averroes, as an Arabian, is at the same time subtile and enthusiastic; hence in Alexander of Aphrodisia, a peripateticism and logical sensualism, if I may so express myself, and in Averroes and his disciples a peripateticism and a sensualism which terminate in pantheism.

The father of the Alexandrian peripatetic school, as it was then called in opposition to the school of Averroes, was Peter Pomponatius, born at Mantua in 1462, professor at Padua and at Bologna, and died at Bologna in 1525. From him sprang the philosophical school of Bologna and of Padua, which has been almost constantly peripatetic and sensualistic, whilst those of Florence, of Rome, and of Naples, have been almost constantly Platonic and idealistic.

Peter Pomponatius wrote three works: the first, *de naturalium effectuum admirandis causis seu Incantationibus liber*, written at Bologna in 1520, printed at Bologna after the death of Pomponatius in 1556. Pomponatius is herein a peripatetic and a sensualist in that sense which repels the intervention of spirits: if he recognizes that of superior agents, according to him all these agents are physical.

His second work is entitled: *de Fato, libero Arbitrio et Providentia Dei,* in five books, published at Basle in 1525. To reconcile destiny, Providence and the liberty of man was a difficult question for any one, and especially for a peripatetic. There is something touching in the chapter* in which Pomponatius compares himself, with his zeal for knowledge and study, and with the enemies thereby made, to Prometheus fastened to Caucasus; he describes himself as devoured by the need of study as by a vulture, unable (I translate faithfully) either to eat, to drink, or to sleep; an object of derision for the foolish, of dread for the people, and of umbrage for the authorities. After many efforts, he arrives at no very precise solution. He gives the known solutions, drawn from the reigning scholasticism, confessing that they are rather illusions than veritable responses.†

The third work of Pomponatius is a treatise on a still more delicate subject, the immortality of the soul. It appeared at Bologna in 1516,‡ and has been very often reprinted, and the last time in Germany by Bardili:§ its conclusion is that of peripateticism, to wit, that the soul thinks by virtue of itself, but that it never thinks except on condition that there is also in the consciousness an external‖ image. Now if the soul thinks only on condition of an image, and if this image is attached to the sensibility, and this to the existence of the body, on the dissolution of the body the image perishes, and it seems that the thought must perish with it, and consequently it is not possible

---

* Lib. iii. c. vii. "Ista sunt quæ me premunt, quæ me angustiant, quæ me insomnem et insanum reddunt, ut vera sit interpretatio fabulæ Promethei. . . . Prometheus vero est philosophus qui, dum vult scire Dei arcana, perpetuis curis et cogitationibus roditur, non sitit, non famescit, non dormit, non comedit, non exspuit, ab omnibus irridetur, et tanquam stultus et sacrilegus habetur, et inquisitoribus prosequitur, fit spectaculum vulgi."

† "Videntur potius esse illusiones istæ quam responsiones."

‡ I have never seen more than one reprint in-12 without indication of place, dated 1534. *Petri Pomponatii Mantuani tractatus de Immortalitate animæ*, 1534.

§ Tubingæ, 1791, in-8.

‖ "Nequaquam anima sine fantasmate intelligit."

to give a demonstrative proof of the immortality of the soul.* He was accused of disturbing the public peace, by overturning the foundations of morality. He replied that men could be attached to their duties by the consideration that their happiness depends here below on the accomplishment of these duties. He added that the dignity of virtue had attractions great enough to seduce men in some manner, without the fear or the hope of the pains and of the recompenses of another life; a reply, it must be confessed, little enough in accordance with the principle of all sensualism. All this was unsatisfactory to the authorities. He was therefore placed in judgment, and escaped only by that distinction which the school of sensualism, since Peter Pomponatius, has always opposed to authority, the distinction between the truths of faith and the truths of philosophy; a convenient compromise which permits the denial on one side of what is apparently respected on the other, and characterizes wonderfully this epoch of transition and the passage from the complete servitude of reason to its complete independence. The Council of Lateran in 1512 cut short the question, and Pomponatius declared his submission to its decision.†

The school of Padua produced still other celebrated personages; among others are Zabarella‡ and Cremonini,§ eminent and bold peripatetics. Alexander Achillini began a new development of peripateticism, by taking as a guide Averroes, instead

* "Mihi itaque videtur nullus rationes adduci posse quæ cogant animam esse immortalem."

† P. Pomponatii philosophi et theologi doctrina et ingenio præstantissimi, Opera, Bas., 1567.

‡ Born at Padua in 1532, died in 1589. Jacobi Zabarellæ, Patavini, *de Rebus naturalibus*, libri xx., Colon., 1594. Opera philosophica, Francf., in-4, 1618.

§ Born at Centi, duchy of Modena, in 1552, died in 1630. Cæsaris Cremonini, Centensis, in schola Pativina philosophi primæ sedis disputatio de cœlo, etc., in-4, Venetiis, 1613.—Tractatus tres: primus, de sensibus externis; secundus, de sensibus internis; tertius, de facultate appetitiva. Opuscula hæc revidit Troylus Lancetta, auctoris discipulus. Venetiis, 1644, in-4.—De calido innato et semine pro Aristotele adversus Galenem, Lugd., Batav. Elzevir, 1634, small in-18.

of Alexander of Aphrodisia. He was called the second Aristotle; it was from his school that successively went forth the Neapolitan Zimara, who died in 1532; Cesalpini of Arezzo, born in 1509, and died 1603; finally, Julius Cæsar Vanini, born also in the State of Naples in 1585, and burned at Toulouse in 1619.

By this school God is considered not as the cause, but as the substance of the world. Consequently, the demonstration of God's existence is no longer made *per motum*, as among the Alexandrians, but by emanation, and especially by the emanation of light, *per lucem*. Such is the theory of Cesalpini of Arezzo. He was disturbed as well as Pomponatius, but he was physician to Clement VIII., and avoided difficulty by the distinction of the truths of faith from philosophical truths.*

Vanini was more courageous and more unfortunate. He wrote two works, the titles of which are as follows; first work: *Amphitheatrum æternum Providentiæ divino-magicum, christiano-physicum, nec non astronomico-catholicum, adversus veteres philosophos, atheos, epicureos, peripateticos et stoicos;* Lugduni, 1615. Second work: *De admirandis naturæ, reginæ dæeque mortalium arcanis, dialogorum inter Alexandrum et Julium Cesarem, lib. iv., cum approbatione Facultatis Sorbonicæ;* Lutet., 1616. Julius Cæsar Vanini was condemned at Toulouse as an atheist and burned as such. Was he an atheist or was he not? I should not decide in this matter, since I have not read the two works of Vanini, which are very rare.† I am, however, inclined to the negative from different passages cited by various authors. Vanini appears to have belonged to that particular sect of peripatetics who demonstrated God, not from the necessity of a first cause, but from the necessity of an Infinite Being, not as cause,

* Andreæ Cesalpini Questiones peripateticæ, Venet., 1571, in-fol.

† I have since wished to study Vanini myself, and have exhibited his two works and his true opinions in the article already several times referred to in the *Fragments of Cartesian philosophy*, VANINI, OR PHILOSOPHY BEFORE DESCARTES.

but as substance.* The philosophical difference is, certainly, very great, but hardly worthy of the stake. Strange enough! peripateticism reigned in Paris and in Spain; in the former it massacred Ramus, in the latter it persecuted the Americans, in both it supported the Inquisition, and on the other side of the Alps it was persecuted itself: one of the sects into which it was divided barely escaped the Council of Lateran; the other was in a manner burned at Toulouse in the person of Julius Cæsar Vanini.

But as yet it was only a sensualism without a well-defined character, and without any other greatness than an adventurous hardihood. Two men appeared at the end of the sixteenth century who renewed it with infinitely more wisdom and precision, and who were truly reformers in philosophy; I mean Telesio and Campanella.

Telesio and Campanella belong neither to the sect of Averroes nor to the Alexandrian sect of the peripatetics. They were independent philosophers, who even combated the authority of Aristotle; but who were still, in fact, unconsciously attached to the general spirit of peripateticism.

Bernardino Telesio was born at Cosenza, in the State of Naples, in 1508. He studied at Padua and was professor of natural philosophy at Naples. He revived the physics of Democritus, which, in antiquity, we have seen were always allied to sensualism. His great work is entitled, *De natura, juxta propria principia. Romæ,* 1565, in–4.† Doubtless, in the system of Tele-

---

* *Amphitheatrum,* exercit. i. "Omne ens aut finitum est aut infinitum, sed nullum ens finitum a se; quocirca satis patet non per motum (ad modum Aristotelis) sed per primas entium partitiones a nobis cognosci Deum esse, et quidem necessaria demonstratione. Nam alias non esset æturnum ens, et sic nihil omnino esset; alioqui nihil esse est impossibile, ergo et æternum ens non esse pariter est impossibile. Ens igitur æturnum esse adeoque Deum esse, necessarium est."

† Telesio published at Naples, in 1570, a new edition of this work. "Bernardini Telesii Cosentini de Rerum Natura, juxta propria principia, liber primus et secundus denuo editi. Neapoli, 1570, in-4." The base is the

sio, Parmenides is united with Democritus, but Democritus is most prominent. His general principle is, that it is necessary to set out from real entities and not from abstractions: *Realia entia, non abstracta;* he combats scholasticism, and recalls his age to the sentiment of reality, to the study of nature. He founded a free academy, which from his name, or from that of his country, is called *Academia Telesiana* or *Cosentina.* In the two books which compose the Roman edition, I can assure you, that everywhere, experience, and the experience of the senses, is his only rule. His preface, which I cannot read to you, is very remarkable: he therein declares that he will not reply to the objections which may be drawn from the logic of the schools, but that he will reply willingly to all the objections which shall be borrowed from sensible experience.* This is the character of his philos-

same, the form differs very much. Lib. i. c. i. "Mundi constructionem corporumque in eo contentorum naturam non ratione, quod antiquioribus factum est, inquirendam, sed sensu percipiendam, et ab ipsis habendam esse rebus." The last chapter of the second and last book is added: "Quæ Deum esse et rerum omnium conditorem nobis declarare possunt."—Telesio published at Naples, the same year, three small treatises: "Bernardini Telesii, Cosentini, De mari liber unicus.—De his quæ in aere fiunt et de terræ motibus liber unicus.—De colorum generatione, opusculum."—Antonio Persio, de Padoua, reprinted at Venice, in 1590, these three treatises and several others: "Bernardini Telesii, Consentini, varii de naturalibus rebus libelli, ab Antonio Persio editi, quorum alii nunquam antea excusi, alii meliores facti prodeunt."

* *Proœmium*, the last lines.—"Si qui nostra oppugnare voluerint, id illos insuper rogatos velim, ne mecum, ut cum aristotelico, verba faciant, sed ut cum Aristotelis adversario, neque igitur sese illius tueantur positionibus dictisque ullis, at sensu tantum et rationibus ab ipso habitis sensu, quibus solis in naturalibus habenda videtur fides; tum ne ut nobis notas illius afferant distinctiones terminosque, quas ingenue fateor percipere me nunquam satis potuisse; propterea reor, quod non sensui expositas, nec hujusmodi similes continent res, sed summe a sensu remotas et ab his etiam quæ percepit sensus, quales, tardiore qui sunt crassioreque ingenio, cujusmodi mihi ipsi, et nulla animi molestia, esse videor, percipere haud queant. Quæ igitur contra nos afferent, exponant oportet, et veluti in luce ponant, tarditatis meæ si libet commiserti, et rebus agant, non ignotis vocibus, quæ nisi res contineant, vanæ sunt inanesque. Illud pro certo habere omnes volumus, nequaquam pervivaci nos esse ingenio, aut non unius amatores veritatis, et libenter itaque errores nostros animadversuros, et summas illi gratias habituros, qui, quam solam quærimus colimusque patefecerit veritatem."

ophy. We should not stop at the few isolated thoughts, more or less idealistic, which the historians of philosophy have drawn from his work. We should adhere to the general spirit of the work, which almost makes Bernardino Telesio a forerunner of Bacon. He was also disturbed by the ecclesiastical authority; but foreseeing the result, left Naples and took refuge in his own country, where he died in 1588.

After Telesio comes another Calabrian, Thomas Campanella, a Dominican, born in 1568, who studied in Cosenza, the native city of Telesio, whose enterprise he continued and extended. Telesio had simply undertaken to reform the philosophy of nature; Thomas Campanella undertook to reform every part of philosophy. It seems that he did not limit himself to an attempt at philosophic reform, and that this energetic monk planned an insurrection in the convents of Calabria against Spanish domination; he was, at least, accused of it and cast into chains, where he remained during twenty-seven years. He endured this long captivity with admirable firmness of mind, and composed songs which here and there display an unusual vigor.* At the end of twenty-seven years he was set at liberty, left his native country, and sought an asylum in France under the protection of Cardinal Richelieu, the avowed enemy of the Austrian and Spanish power. He remained undisturbed at Paris in the convent of the Dominicans in the street St. Honore, where he died in 1639.

Doubtless the philosophical enterprise of Campanella was beyond his strength; he had more ardor than solidity, more stretch of mind than profundity. He recommended experience without practising it; he showed the necessity of a revolution, but did not consummate it. It would nevertheless be unjust to take no account of such noble efforts.† As an immediate pupil of Tele-

---

* *Scelta d'alcune poesie filosofiche*, di Settimontano Squilla, 1622. M. Orelli reprinted these poems at Lugano, in 1834. Read especially *Modo di filosofare, della Plebe, il Carcer, al Telesio, lamentevole Orazione dal profondo della fossa, etc.*

† Campanella, being in prison, confided his writings to Tobias Adamus,

sio and on account of many of his writings, it is necessary to refer Campanella to the empiric school; but he was, almost at all times, and particularly at the close of his life, far from sensualism. He was with Bruno the most powerful mind of the sixteenth century; their country, their misfortunes, their courage, associate them together, and they may both be considered, notwithstanding their differences, as the forerunners of Descartes.*

---

who published them successively at Francfort: 1st, *Prodromus philosophiæ instaurandæ*, Francf., 1617, in-4; 2d, *de Sensu rerum et magia*, Francf., 1620, in-4; 3d, *Apologia pro Galilæo*, Francf., 1622, in-4; 4th, *Philosophiæ realis epilogisticæ partes* iv., Francf., 1623, in-4. He himself published at Rome, *Atheismus triumphatus*, Romæ, 1630. In France he undertook a collection of his writings; he first put out, in 1636, a new edition of the *Atheismus triumphatus*, which he dedicated to King Louis XIII., with several other writings; then, in 1637 he reprinted the *de Sensu rerum*, which he dedicated to Cardinal Richelieu; then again in 1637 he dedicated to the Lord Chancellor Seguier his *Philosophiæ realis*, very much augmented; finally, in 1638, he dedicated to M. Bouillon, Controller of Finances, his Metaphysics, *Metaphysicarum rerum juxta propria dogmata partes tres*, in-fol. We give a few thoughts of Campanella: "Sentire est scire." Against scholasticism: "Cognitio divinorum non habetur per syllogismum, qui est quasi sagitta qua scopum attingimus a longo absque gestu, neque modo per auctoritatem quod est tangere quasi per manum alienam, sed per tactum intrinsecum..." As an apology for his conduct: "Non omnis novitas in republica et Ecclesia philosophis suspecta, sed ea tantum quæ principia æterna destruit.—Novator improbus non est qui scientias iterum format et reformat hominum culpa collapsas."

* *Fragments of Cartesian Philosophy*, p. 12. "Campanella, a Dominican, like Bruno, and an innovator, too, possessed a mind of another temper. He had more reason and more sagacity. Quite as ardent as Bruno against Aristotle, the reform which he undertook was at the same time more moderate and more vast. It deserves to be studied at the present time. Enthusiastic in the cause of right, he combated the moral and political doctrine of Machiavelli; from the recesses of his prison he defended the system of Copernicus, and composed an apology for Galileo during his trial before the Inquisition: an heroic victim writing in favor of another victim in the interval between two tortures! He wrote a very good work against atheism. His thoughts are those of a Christian, and far from attacking the Church, he glorifies it everywhere. But it seems that by reason of reading Saint Thomas, he acquired such a horror of tyranny, and such a passion for a government founded on reason and on virtue, that he thought of delivering his country from Spanish despotism, and contrived in the convents and castles of Spain a conspiracy of monks and gentlemen, which being unsuccessful, plunged him into an abyss of misfortunes. This affair is still enveloped in profound

The school of skepticism numbers few adepts in this age of enthusiasm; there are but three. The most decided skeptic of this age was Sanchez, a Portuguese physician and professor at Toulouse. The title of his work is: *de multum nobili et prima universali scientia* .... And what is this noble, first, and universal science? *Quod nihil scitur,* Tolosæ,* 1526. But he who

---

darkness. The last historian of Campanella, M. Baldachini, of Naples (*Vita e filosofia di Tommaso Campanella*, 2 vol. in-8, Napoli, 1840, 1842), has searched all the archives in vain for the trial of his celebrated compatriot; it has all disappeared, and we are reduced to the evidence of his enemies. All, at least, are unanimous in regard to his constancy and immovable courage. Having been confined in prison for a political crime, accusations in regard to his theology and philosophy were made against him, and he remained twenty-seven years in irons. A contemporaneous author, and one worthy of credit (J. N. Erythræus, *Pinacotheca Imaginum illustrium*, 1643–1648), relates that Campanella sustained, during thirty-five successive hours, a torture so cruel "that almost all the veins and arteries of his body being broken, the blood which flowed from the wounds could not be stopped, and that notwithstanding he supported this torture with so much firmness that he did not utter a single word unworthy of a philosopher." Campanella himself thus relates his sufferings in the preface of the *Atheism vanquished:* "I have been shut up in fifty prisons, and submitted seven times to the most severe torture. On the last occasion the torture continued forty hours. Bound with tight cords that broke my bones, suspended, my hands tied behind my back, above a sharp piece of wood which devoured the sixteenth part of my flesh and drew away ten pounds of blood, cured by a miracle after six months of sickness, I was thrown into a ditch. Fifteen times have I been placed in judgment. The first time, when it was asked: How then does he know what he has never learned? has he a demon at his command? I replied: In order to learn what I know, I have used more oil than you have drunk of wine. At another time I was accused of being the author of the book *of the three Impostors*, which was printed thirty years before my birth. I was again accused of entertaining the opinions of Democritus, I who have written books against Democritus. I was accused of fostering bad sentiments against the Church, I who have written a work on the Christian monarchy, wherein I have shown that no philosopher could have imagined a republic equal to that which was established at Rome under the Apostles. I have been accused of being a heretic, I who have composed a work against the heretics of our times.... Finally, I have been accused of rebellion and heresy for having said that there are spots upon the sun, the moon, and the stars, contrary to Aristotle, who makes the world eternal and incorruptible... It was for that that they cast me, like Jeremiah, into the dungeon, where there was neither air nor light."

* Often reprinted, Lugduni, 1581; Francf., 1618; Rotterdam, 1649. Ex-

spread and popularized skepticism in France was Montaigne, born at Bordeaux in 1533, died in 1592. He had as a friend La Boëtie, who died in 1563, and who himself possessed a cultivated and independent mind. As sensualism and idealism were then little else than peripateticism and Platonism, that is, borrowed systems, so the skepticism of Montaigne is also only a skepticism revived from antiquity. It must, nevertheless, be confessed that there was something essentially skeptical in the spirit of the Gascon noble, and that doubt was the most agreeable pillow to his well-shaped head. The *Essays*, which appeared in 1580 and were completed in 1588,* soon became, as it is said, the breviary of free-thinkers. The friend and pupil of Montaigne, Pierre Charron, born in Paris in 1521, died in 1603, is more

---

tract from the preface of Sanchez.... "A prima vita naturæ contemplationi addictus minutim omnia inquirebam; et quamvis initio avidus animus sciendi quocumque oblato cibo contentus esset, utcumque, post modicum tamen tempus, indigestione prehensus revomere cœpit omnia. Quærebam jam tunc quid illi darem quod et perfecte amplecteretur et frueretur absolute; nec erat qui desiderium expleret meum. Evolvebam præteritorum dicta, tentabam præsentium corda; idem respondebant; quod tamen mihi satisfaceret omnino nihil.... Ad me proinde memetipsum retuli, omniaque in dubium revocans, ac si a quopiam nihil unquam dictum, res ipsas examinare cœpi.... Quo magis cogito, magis dubito. Despero. Persisto tamen. Accedo ad doctores, avide ab iis veritatem exspectaturus. Quisque sibi scientiam construit ex imaginationibus tum alterius tum propriis; ex his alia inferunt.... quousque labyrinthum verborum absque aliquo fundamento veritatis produxere.... Decipiantur qui decipi volunt. Non his scribo, nec proinde scripta legant mea.... Cum iis mihi res sit qui nullius addicti jurare in verba magistri proprio marte res expendunt, sensu rationeque ducti. Tu igitur quisquis es ejusdem mecum conditionis temperamentique, quique de rerum naturis sæpissime tecum dubitasti, dubita modo mecum, ingenia nostra simul exerciamus." The conclusion of this preface, and, as it were, the symbol of the skepticism of Sanchez, is the celebrated formula, *Quid?* Is this the source of the *What do I know?* of Montaigne? It is difficult to suppose that the work of the professor of Toulouse had not come to the knowledge of the translator of Raymond de Sebunde.

* First edition at Bordeaux by Millanges, 1580, two books in two volumes in-12; the second includes the three books, in-4, by the same Millanges, 1588. Montaigne prepared a new edition, which Mademoiselle de Gournay, his adopted daughter, published in 1595, in-fol.

methodical and less ingenious. It was* from Charron that Lamothe Le Vayer, and the skeptics of the seventeenth century sprang.

Mysticism embraces a more numerous family: it has two characters and a single source. This single source is the neoplatonic, idealistic, and mystic school of Florence. Now, the Alexandrian mysticism was allied on the one hand to the positive religion of the times by allegorization, and on the other to theurgical operations. Hence two tendencies of the Florentine mysticism of Marsilio Ficino, the one allegorical in religion, the other theurgical and alchemistic. Sometimes these two tendencies are divided, sometimes they are united. I shall give a list of the principal mystics of the fifteenth and sixteenth centuries.

The most sensible and most discreet mystic was unquestionably the Cardinal Nicolas, improperly called de Cusa, which leads to the belief that he was an Italian, while in fact he was a German, of Cuss, a small place near Treves. He reproduced the Pythagorean part of Neoplatonism, with this reservation, that the Neoplatonists had admitted that, although with the theory of number, we may account for the phenomena of the exterior world, and ascend to their principle in the primitive unity, we do not know this unity in itself. He goes farther: he pretends that the direct knowledge of truth has not been given to man. He wrote an apology for learned ignorance, *de docta Ignorantia*, in which there is a very judicious mixture of Platonism, skepticism, and mysticism: this work does the highest honor to this man of the fifteenth century, for Cardinal Cuss was anterior to Reuchlin and to Agrippa, and contemporary with Ficino. He died in 1464.†

John Reuchlin, of Pforzheim, born in 1455, died in 1522, made personal acquaintance with Ficino and the Picos of Miran-

---

* *La Sagesse* is of 1601, also at Bordeaux, by Millanges, in-12; the second at Paris, 1604; and the third, 1607.

† Nicholai Cusani, Opp., 3 vol. in one, in-fol., Basil., 1565.

dola during a journey in Italy, and brought into Germany a decided taste for mysticism. He was less an alchemist than an allegorist, and wrote a treatise on the cabalistic art, *De Arte Cabalistica*, and another, *De Verbo Mirifico*.* He studied the Oriental languages, in particular the Hebrew and the Talmud, and defended the persecuted Jews. Agrippa of Nettesheim, who was born at Cologne in 1486, and who died at Grenoble in 1535, was a friend of Reuchlin, whose work, *De Verbo Mirifico*, he commented upon and expounded even at the University of Dole, at that time a flourishing institution. He had composed a work, *De Philosophia Occulta*; but as it was necessary to draw attention to mysticism by decrying every species of philosophy, he wrote another, *De Vanitate Scientiarum*.† Agrippa of Nettesheim, like Reuchlin, was an allegorist; but he applied himself to alchemy and theurgy. Paracelsus, who was born at Einsielden, in Switzerland, in 1493, and who died at Saltzburg in 1541, was a chemist and an ingenious physician.‡ He travelled a great deal in Italy and in Germany; he occupied the first public chair of chemistry at Basle. Bacon remarked that the greatest fault of Paracelsus was that he concealed his real experience under a mysterious appearance. The doctrine of Paracelsus consists in three principles, the union of which forms the *Archæum Magnum* with which he explains all nature. Valentine Weigel, a Lutheran minister, who was born in Misnia in 1533, and who died in 1588, followed the theurgical tendency of Paracelsus, in uniting to it

* Reprinted in the collection of Pistorius, Bas., 1587, in-fol.

† H. C. Agrippæ Opp., 2 vol. in-8, Lugduni, per Beringos fratres, without date. The following are thoughts of Agrippa drawn from his letters:

"Supremus et unicus rationis actus religio est."

"Omnium rerum cognoscere opificem, atque in illum tota similitudinis imagine, cam essentiali contactu sine vinculo, transire quo ipse transformeris efficiareque Deus, ea demum vera solidaque philosophia est.

"Sed quomodo qui in cinere et mortali pulvere se ipsum amisit Deum inveniet? Mori nimirum oportet mundo et carni et sensibus omnibus, si quis velit ad hæc secretorum penetralia ingredi. . . "

‡ Phil. Theophrasti Paracelsi volumen medicinæ paramirum, Argentorati, 1575, in-fol.

the moral and religious mysticism of Reuchlin, of Tauler, and of Gerson.* Leibnitz said that he was "a man of spirit,† even of too much spirit." At the commencement of the seventeenth century the doctrines of this school, allegorical as well as theurgical, passed into a secret society, the society of the Rosicrusians,‡ where they were preserved as in deposit. We may also place among the mystics of this epoch Jerome Cardan of Pavia, who was born in 1501, and who died in 1576, a physician and a celebrated naturalist, of extensive knowledge, and who, in the midst of great extravagances, often presented the most elevated views.§ After Paracelsus I ought to speak of Von Helmont, who sprang from him: he was a mystical alchemist, and was born at Brussels in 1577, and died in Vienna in 1644. His son Mercurius Von Helmont, who published his works,‖ belongs to the seventeenth century. Robert Fludd, an English physician, of the

---

* "Libellus de vita beata, non in particularibus ab extra quærenda, sed in summo bono intra nos ipsos possidendo; item exercitatio mentis de luce et caligine divina; collectus et conscriptus a M. Valentino Weigelio, Halæ Saxonum, 1609."

† Theodicea, discourse on the conformity of reason with faith, ix. p. 11 of Vol. i. of the Edit. of Amsterdam, 1747.

‡ Formed at the commencement of the seventeenth century, on the occasion of a poem by the theologian Andreæ: *Mariage chimique de Christian Rosencreutz*, 1603.—*Réformation universelle au moyen de la* fama fraternitatis *des rose-croix*. Ratisb., 1614.

§ The following are some specimens of his great work: *De subtilitate et varietate rerum*.—"Est aliquid in nobis præter nos. . . Incitari autem nemo ad virtutem poterit aut verum experiri, qui id quod in se est præter se obruit atque sepelit. XVIII.—Quod si quis vel exiguo tempore ex se ipso exire possit unirique Deo, hunc momento fieri beatissimum necesse est. . . Atque hæc illa exstasis solis probis sapientibusque concessa, et infinite melior omni humana felicitate. XXI.—Animæ immortalitatem non nunc primum, sed semper agnovi; sentio enim aliquando intellectum sic Deum esse adeptum, ut nos prorsus unum cum eo esse intueamur." *De utilitate ex advers. capiend.*, II. 6. His works have been collected in ten volumes in-fol., Lugd., 1663.

‖ Among others Ortus medicinæ, id est initia physicæ inaudita, progressus medicinæ novus, in morborum ultionem, ad vitam longam, autnore J. B. Van Helmont, &c., edente authoris filio; edit. nova, Amstelodami, 1651, in-4, Elzevir.

county of Kent, who was born in 1574, and who died in 1627, tried to combine Paracelsus with the assiduous study of *Genesis*, allegorically interpreted.* But the most profound and at the same time the most unaffected of all the mystics of the sixteenth century was Jacob Böhme, who was born in 1575, and who died in 1624. He was a poor shoemaker of Görlitz, without any literary attainments, for which reason he remained for a long time in obscurity, occupied solely with two studies, which every Christian and every man may always pursue, the study of nature ever spread out before his eyes, and that of the sacred Scriptures. He is called the Teutonic philosopher. He wrote a multitude of works which afterwards became the gospel of mysticism. They have often been reprinted† and translated into different languages. One of the most celebrated, published in 1612, is called *Aurora*.‡ The fundamental points of the doctrine of Böhme are: 1st, the impossibility of arriving at truth by any other process than illumination; 2d, a theory of the creation; 3d, the relations of man to God; 4th, the essential identity of the soul and of God, and the determination of their difference as to form; 5th, the origin of evil; 6th, the reintegration of the soul; 7th, a symbolical exposition of Christianity.

Such, briefly, are the four great schools with which history fills the fifteenth and sixteenth centuries. The rough statistics which I have just given you are sufficient to demonstrate that, even in this epoch of artificial culture and imitation, the human mind remained faithful to itself, and to the laws which we have already observed, to the four tendencies which impel it, everywhere and always, to seek truth either in the senses and empirical observation, or in consciousness and rational abstraction, or in the negation of all certitude, or finally in enthusiasm and the

---

* Philosophia Mosaica, Gudæ, 1638, in-fol.—Historia macro et microcosmi metaphysica, physica et technica, Oppenheim, 1617, in-fol.

† The preferable edition is that of 1730, 7 vol. in-12.

‡ It has been translated into French by Saint-Martin. See the following volume, Lecture 13.

immediate contemplation of God. This is the classification under which all the systems of the fifteenth and sixteenth centuries are arranged. It remains to be known which of the four schools has reckoned the most partisans, and which consequently reflects best the general spirit of the two centuries. Assuredly it is not skepticism, for it is reduced, as you have just seen, to three men of mind. Nor is it the sensualistic peripatetic school, nor the idealistic Platonic school, both almost equally fertile in distinguished men and celebrated systems: it is the mystic school in its double allegoric and alchemic development. Examine and you will see, in fact, that the number and importance of systems is on the side of mysticism. Mysticism is even found in the empiric school; and this inconsistency proceeds from the domination of mysticism. Whenever one point of view predominates it attracts to it all the others, even those which are foreign to it, even those which are hostile to it.

Let us take another view of these four schools; let us consider their division among the different countries of Europe. In the middle age there was scarcely any other distinction than that of religious orders; but towards the fifteenth century national individualities appear; and it is curious to see how, in the nascent independence of Europe, the different nations have, thus to speak, shared the philosophic points of view. We find, 1st, that there was no skepticism except in France; the three men who then represented skepticism being two Frenchmen and one Portuguese naturalized in France; 2d, that Italy was the classic ground of the double peripatetic and Platonic dogmatism, and that it was from Italy that it passed into all the other countries of Europe; 3d, that mysticism, although it came from an Italian source, spread chiefly throughout Germany; so that in considering only the general results we should say that dogmatism belongs to Italy, skepticism to France, and mysticism to Germany. England plays but a feeble part in the philosophy of the fifteenth and sixteenth centuries.

There is still another view to be taken of these four schools.

What have been their means of expression? What languages have they used? This is important, for the introduction of the vulgar tongues into philosophy, therein exhibits more or less the independence and originality of thought. I do not find that any peripatetic then wrote in a vulgar tongue. In the Platonic school, near the close, and even towards the middle of the sixteenth century, the employment of a national language began; we find the *Dialectics* of Ramus* in pretty good French; and Giordano Bruno wrote several works in Italian.† As to skepticism, Sanchez excepted, it always made use of a vulgar tongue, the French. I conclude then that sensualism and idealism were, especially during the fifteenth century, borrowed systems, and that there was more originality in skepticism. I say as much of mysticism. If in its first developments, in the Florentine school, it speaks the appropriate language of this school, the Latin, it ended by speaking in Böhme a vulgar tongue. It must be observed that Jacob Böhme wrote all his works in the only language that he knew, and that was known around him, the German; a circumstance which makes of the mysticism of Böhme a system more natural and serious than that of Ficino and of the Picos of Mirandola.

Finally, if I seek out the good and the evil part in the philosophy of these two centuries, it seems to me that the good is especially found in the immense career which the free imitation of antiquity has opened to the human mind, and in the fruitful fermentation which systems so numerous and so diverse must have excited in European philosophy. This is a benefit which must balance all inconveniences, for from that must have proceeded whatever was good in the future. When we read the

---

* *Dialectique de Pierre de La Ramée, à Charles de Lorraine cardinal, son Mécène*, Paris, in-4, 1555.

† *Della causa, principio et uno.—Degli eroici furori.—La Bestia trionfante.—Dell' infinito, universo e mondi;* finally the *Candelaio, come diadel Bruno Nolano, achademico di nulla achademia, detto il fastidito.* "*In tristitia hilaris, in hilaritate tristis*," Pariggi, 1582.

life, the adventures, and the enterprises of Ramus, of Giordano Bruno, of Telesio, and of Campanella, we feel that Bacon and Descartes are not far off. The evil is in the predominance of the spirit of imitation which engenders immense confusion and is betrayed by the absence of method. Absence of method, such is the capital fault of the philosophy of the fifteenth and sixteenth centuries. It is marked in two ways: 1st, This philosophy scarcely establishes the relation of the different parts of which it is composed; metaphysics, morals, politics, physics are not therein united among themselves by those intimate ties which attest the presence of a single and profound thought. 2d, It cannot discern, and does not seek out among the different parts which it embraces that which must be the fundamental part and the basis of the whole edifice. We thus begin in every thing, to go, we know not to what; there is no order of research which may be accepted as the fixed and necessary point from which philosophy must set out in order to reach its ultimate aim. Or if we wished to find a point of departure common to all systems, we might say that this point of departure is taken in ontology, that is, outside of human nature. We begin in general by God or by external nature, and we arrive as well as we can at man, and that too, without any very well-defined rule, without establishing this manner of proceeding as a principle and as a method. Hence the necessity of a revolution whose character must have been the opposite of that of the philosophy of the fifteenth and sixteenth centuries, to wit, the introduction of a method, and of a method which must have been the opposite of the confused practice of the preceding epoch, the opposite of ontology, that is, psychology. It is this fruitful revolution, with the great systems which it has produced, that I propose to make known to you in my next lecture.

LECTURE XI.

MODERN PHILOSOPHY. SEVENTEENTH CENTURY. SENSUALISM AND IDEALISM.

Modern philosophy.—Its general character.—Two ages in modern philosophy: the first age is that of the philosophy of the seventeenth century, properly so called.—Schools of the seventeenth century. Sensualistic school: Bacon, Hobbes, Gassendi, Locke.—Idealistic school: Descartes, Spinoza, Malebranche.

THE philosophy of the fifteenth and sixteenth centuries released the human mind from scholasticism, from slavery to a foreign principle—authority; at the same time it prepared it for modern philosophy, for absolute independence; and conducted it from scholasticism to modern philosophy by the intermediation of an epoch wherein authority still reigned, but an authority much more flexible than that of the middle age, the authority of philosophic antiquity. The philosophy of the fifteenth and sixteenth centuries is, as it were, the education of modern thought by ancient thought. Its character is an ardent and often blind imitation; its necessary result was a universal fermentation, and the want of a definitive revolution. This revolution was consummated in the seventeenth century; it is modern philosophy properly so called.

The most general feature which distinguishes it is an entire independence; it is independent both of the authority which reigned in scholasticism, the ecclesiastical authority, and of the authority which reigned in the fifteenth and sixteenth centuries, the admiration of ancient genius. It breaks with every thing past, thinks only of the future, and feels capable of drawing the future from itself. On one hand it might be said that from fear of being charmed by the genius of Plato and of Aristotle, it turns away from them designedly, and even ignorance and disdain of them seem the ransom of independence. Bacon and Leibnitz excepted, all the great philosophers of the new era, Descartes, Spinoza, Malebranche, Hobbes, Locke, and their disciples, have no knowledge of, and no respect for antiquity; they scarcely read any thing else than what is found in nature and in consciousness. On the other hand, the progressive secularization of philosophy is evident on all sides: inquire, for example, who are the two great men that founded modern philosophy? Do they belong to the ecclesiastical body, that body which, in the middle age, furnished scholasticism with such great interpreters? No, the two fathers of modern philosophy are two laymen; and, with a few exceptions, it may be said that from the seventeenth century up to our own times, the most illustrious philosophers have not come from the ranks of the Church. Philosophical instruction was, in the middle age, confined to cloisters and convents. Universities were soon after established; this was a considerable step, for in the universities, even of the middle age, were found professors taken from among the laity. The seventeenth century witnessed the establishment of a new institution, which is to universities what universities were to convents; I mean academies. They began in Italy towards the close of the sixteenth century, but it was especially in the seventeenth century that they spread throughout Europe. There are three which from their first institution acquired the greatest glory, and were extremely useful to the free culture of thought. These are, 1st, The Royal Society of London, established on the plan of Bacon;* 2d, the Academy of Sciences at Paris, a useful creation of the genius of Colbert, as the French Academy had been the brilliant creation of the genius of Richelieu; 3d, the Academy of Berlin, not only founded† on the plan of Leibnitz, but by Leibnitz himself, who was its first president, and who edited the first volume of its transactions.

---

* First at Oxford in 1645, then permanently with privilege, at London in 1663. Newton, Locke, &c., were members.

† In 1700.

The second characteristic of modern philosophy is, as I have already told you, the determination of a fixed point of departure, the adoption of a method; and this point of departure, this method, is the study of human nature, the foundation and necessary instrument of all science and of all philosophy, that is, psychology.

In entering into modern philosophy, to study more particularly its systems, after having recognized its general characteristics, the first reflection presented to us is, that modern philosophy is of very recent date. Without speaking of the East and of India, where dates are so uncertain, in Greece the movement of independent philosophy continued twelve centuries, from Thales and Pythagoras to the end of the school of Athens; whilst the corresponding movement of philosophy in which we all participate, and of which we are the agents and products, this philosophical movement reckons scarcely two centuries. Judge of the vast future that is before modern philosophy, and let this consideration embolden and encourage those who find it so ill assured in its proceedings, so undecided in its results. Although still young it is already great, and in two centuries it has produced so many systems, that in this movement, which is, as it were, of yesterday, one may distinguish two ages: the first, which commences with the seventeenth century and extends towards the middle of the eighteenth; the second, which embraces all the last half of the eighteenth century with the commencement of our own.* These two ages have this much in common, that they both participate in the general spirit of modern philosophy; and each of them has this in particular, that it participates more or less in it, and in a different degree: there is harmony between them, but at the same time there is progress from one to the other. I must to-day speak of the first, the philosophy of the seventeenth century.

* This distinction of two epochs in modern philosophy, according to the progress of method itself, is already indicated in the first Series, for example Vol. 2, *Discours d'Ouverture*, p. 6.

Two men open and constitute it, Bacon and Descartes. We must know how to recognize in these two men their unity; for they must have a unity, since they are the founders of a philosophy which is one in its spirit; at the same time we must recognize their difference, since they have placed modern philosophy on two entirely different routes. Both had, what is very rare in men who achieve a revolution, a design to achieve it, and a consciousness of having achieved it. Bacon and Descartes knew that a reform was necessary, that already it had been attempted and that it had been frustrated; and it was voluntarily and knowingly that they renewed this great enterprise and executed it. In all their works breathes the sentiment of the spirit of their times, of which they recognize and conduct themselves as the interpreters. Add to this that they were both what they should have been in order to accomplish the revolution which they undertook. Both were laymen, one a soldier and the other a lawyer. Both were natural philosophers and geometricians, and the nature of their studies removed them from false scholasticism. Both were experienced in the world and in business, and had that sentiment of reality so necessary to be introduced into philosophy. In fine, both were skilled in literature, and were in their respective languages great, or at least excellent writers, and hence they were able to spread and render popular the taste for philosophy. Behold the unity of Bacon and Descartes, it was the unity of modern philosophy itself. But under this unity were manifest differences. Bacon was particularly occupied with physical sciences; Descartes, although a great natural philosopher, was a still greater geometrician. Both started by analysis; but one first rested analysis on the exterior observation of the phenomena of nature, the other on the interior observation of thought; one trusted more to the evidence of the senses, the other to that of consciousness. Hence inevitably two opposite tendencies, and on the same basis two entirely distinct schools, one sensualistic, the other idealistic.

I have often told you, and I shall have frequent occasions to repeat to you, that every thing always begins well. The chief of a school does not at first perceive all the consequences of his principles; he exhausts his boldness in the invention of principles, and thus overlooks, in a great part, the extravagance of the consequences. Thus Bacon* put the modern sensualistic school in the world; but in vain would you seek in Bacon the sad theories at which this school finally arrived. Bacon created no system, he simply established a method; and this method was far from being as exclusive with the master as with his disciples. It is singularly curious to meet in Bacon a eulogy on the rational method; he even goes so far as to excuse mysticism. In reading Bacon attentively I have found in his works a number of passages which are sufficient to defend his memory from the charge of an exclusive sensualistic tendency.

"I believe" says he,† "that I have, forever and legitimately, united the empiric method and the rational method, the divorce of which is fatal to science and humanity."

---

* Francis Bacon, Lord of Verulam, Viscount of Saint-Alban, and Chancellor of England, was born in London in 1561, and died in 1626. A deplorable stain rests upon his memory, one that can be explained only by this passage from the *De augm.*, viii. 3: "Ad litteras potius quam ad quidquam natus, et ad res gerendas nescio quo fato contra genium suum abreptus." Of the great work which he undertook, *instauratio magna*, we have only two fragments; one of them is entitled: *Of the proficience and advancement of learning*, London, 1605, small in-4; and this work, translated into Latin by skilful hands, reviewed by Bacon himself, and very much augmented, has become the *De dignitate et augmentis scientiarum;* the second fragment is the *Novum organum*, which, it is said, appeared first in English, though the Latin edition was first known to us; in-fol., Londini, 1620, with the celebrated epigraph: *Multi pertransibunt et augebitur scientia.* Among his other works we must notice *The Essays or Counsels, civil and moral*, of which he published a newly enlarged edition one year before his death, London, 1625, small in-4. In the Latin translation the *Essays* are called *Sermones fideles sive interiora rerum.* Complete works of Bacon, by Mallet, London, 1740, 4 vol. in-fol.; and 1765, 5 vol. in-4. All new editions are reproductions of the latter.

† "Inter empiricam et rationalem facultatem (quarum morosa et inauspicata divortia et repudia omnia in humana familia turbavere), conjugium verum et legitimum in perpetuum nos firmasse existimamus." *Instaur. mag.* præfat., p. 10, ed. 1620.

Here are farther passages from Bacon on mysticism, on divination, and even on magnetism. I do not invent them, I do not justify them; I merely cite them.

"Prophetic inspiration, the divining faculty,* has as a foundation the hidden virtue of the soul, which when it retires within itself, can foresee the future in dreams, in ecstasy, and at the approach of death; this phenomenon is more rare in the wakeful state and in health."

"It is possible for one person to act upon another, by the force of the imagination of one of these two persons; for, as the body receives the action of a body, the mind is apt to receive the action of another mind."†

Bacon was unwilling that magic should be entirely abandoned; he thought that on this road‡ it was not impossible to find facts that might not be found elsewhere; facts obscure, but real, into which it behooves science to bear the lamp of analysis, instead of abandoning them to the extravagant who exaggerate and falsify them.

These are rules truly remarkable for their independence, their moderation, and their extent. But I need not add that they disappear, before the great number of those that are stamped with quite another character, with the exclusive character of sensualism. Here citations are useless. Bear in mind only that the same man who wrote the preceding lines said also that it is solely

---

* "Divinatio naturalis, ex vi scilicet interna animi ortum habens....hoc nititur suppositionis fundamento, quod anima in se reducta atque collecta nec in corporis organa diffusa, habeat ex vi propria essentiæ suæ aliquam prænotionem rerum futurarum; illa vero optime cernitur in somniis, exstasibus atque in confiniis mortis, rarius inter vigilandum aut cum corpus sanum est et validum." *De augm.*, lib. iv. c. 3.

† "Fascinatio est vis et actus imaginationis intensivus in corpus alterius... ut multo magis a spiritu in spiritum, quum spiritus præ rebus omnibus sit et ad agendum strenuus et ad patiendum tener et mollis." *Ibid.*, iv. 3.

‡ "Nos magiam naturalem illo in sensu intelligimus, ut sit scientia formarum abditarum quæ cognitionem ad opera ad miranda deducat, atque, quod dici solet, activa cum passivis conjungendo, magnalia naturæ manifestat." *Ibid.*, iii. 5.

in the interpretation of external nature that the human mind shows its strength, and that when it returns upon itself and seeks to comprehend itself, it is like the spider, that can merely draw from itself fine and delicate threads, but without solidity and of no use.* It is established and acknowledged that it is the sensualistic tendency that governs in Bacon. According to our habit, let us consult history and the times.

To the school of Bacon immediately attach themselves three men who are his official successors, Hobbes, Gassendi, Locke. It may be said that these three men have transported the spirit of Bacon into all parts of philosophy, and that they divided, as it were, among them, the different points of view of their common school. Hobbes is its moralist and politician, Gassendi its scholar, Locke its metaphysician.

Hobbes† was a friend and an avowed disciple of Bacon. He joined, it is said,‡ with Rawley and several other persons, in translating the beautiful English of Bacon into a Latin which also has its beauty. And what is the philosophy of this disciple, of this translator of Bacon? I will tell you in a few words.§

There is no other certain evidence than that of the senses. The evidence of the senses attests only the existence of bodies; then there is no existence save that of bodies, and philosophy is only the science of bodies.

There are two sorts of bodies: 1st, Natural bodies, which are the theatre of a multitude of regular phenomena, because they

---

* See Lecture 3.

† Born at Malmsbury in 1588, died in 1679, Opp., 1668. Amstelod., 2 vol. in-4. These are only his Latin works; Hobbes also wrote much in English. A new edition, large in-8, due to the care of Molesworth, London, 1839–1845, devotes five volumes to the Latin works and eleven to the English works.

‡ *Vitæ Hobbianæ Auctarium.* "Illis temporibus, in amicitiam receptus est Francisci Baconi, etc., qui illius consuetudine magnopere delectatus est, et ab ipso in nonnullis scriptis suis latine vertendis adjutus, qui neminem cogitata sua tanta facilitate concipere atque T. Hobbium passim prædicare solitus est."

§ We have related in detail the philosophy of Hobbes, and particularly his moral and political philosophy, 1st Series, Vol. 3, Lectures 7, 8, 9, and 10.

take place by virtue of fixed laws, as the bodies with which physics are occupied, and those which are called spirits, souls with which metaphysics are occupied; 2d, Moral and political bodies, societies which continually change and are subject to variable laws.

Hobbes' system of physics is that system of which Bacon has spoken* with so much eulogium, that of Democritus, the atomistic and corpuscular philosophy of the Ionic school. His metaphysics are its corollary: all the phenomena which pass in the consciousness, have their source in the organization, of which the consciousness is itself simply a result. All the ideas come from the senses. To think, is to calculate; and intelligence is nothing else than an arithmetic. As we do not calculate without signs, we do not think without words; the truth of the thoughts is in the perception of the relation of the words among themselves, and metaphysics are reduced to a well-made language: Hobbes is completely a nominalist. With Hobbes there are no other than contingent ideas; the finite alone can be conceived; the infinite is only a negation of the finite; beyond that, it is a mere word invented to honor a being whom faith alone can reach. The idea of good and of evil has no other foundation than agreeable or disagreeable sensation; to agreeable or disagreeable sensation it is impossible to apply any other law than escape from the one and search after the other; hence the morality of Hobbes, which is the foundation of his politics. Man is capable of enjoying and of suffering; his only law is to suffer as little as possible and to enjoy as much as possible. Since such is his only law, he has all the rights that this law confers upon him; he may do any thing for his preservation and his happiness; he has the right to sacrifice every thing to himself. Behold, then, men upon this earth, where the objects of desire are not superabundant, all possessing equal rights to whatever may be agreeable or useful to them, by virtue of the same capacity for enjoyment and suffering. This is

* De Augm., iii. 4.

a state of nature, which is nothing less than a state of war, the anarchy of the passions, a combat in which every man is arrayed against his neighbor. But this state being opposed to the happiness of the majority of individuals who share it, utility, the offspring of egotism itself, demands its exchange for another, to wit, the social state. The social state is the institution of a public power, stronger than all individuals, capable of making peace succeed war, and imposing on all the accomplishment of whatever it shall have judged to be useful, that is, just. But as the restrained passions are naturally and necessarily in revolt against the new authority, this authority cannot be too strong; and Hobbes places the human species between the alternative of anarchy, or of a despotism which will be so much the more conformed to its end as it shall be the more absolute. Hence absolute monarchy as the ideal of true government.

Such are the politics of Hobbes, politics very consistent with his morality, which is deduced from his general philosophy, whose root is in the sensualistic tendency of Bacon. That which characterizes Hobbes, and gives him a superior rank in the history of philosophy, is consistency. He carried it from theory into practice, he was a man of his doctrines. In 1628, foreseeing the troubles that threatened his country, he made a translation of Thucydides in order to disgust his fellow-citizens with a liberty which leads to anarchy. At a later period he left England with the family of the Stuarts, faithful to this family through fidelity to his own principles. When Cromwell established a power agreeable to his idea of monarchy, Hobbes asked nothing better than to yield his submission, not to the republican Cromwell, but to the dictator Cromwell; consistent, too, in this, whatever may be said of it.* And as then the ecclesiastical power was at vari-

---

* Lord Clarendon relates in his Memoirs the following anecdote: "In returning from Spain I passed through Paris; Hobbes frequently came to see me. He told me that he was then printing in England his book which he intended to entitle *Leviathan*, that every week he received and corrected a proof-sheet, and that he thought it would be completed in one month at most. He added that he was well aware that I would not approve of his book, when I should read it; and thereupon enumerated some ideas con-

ance with the civil power, Hobbes did not hesitate to abase the ecclesiastical power before the State, the whole strength of which resides in unity, and he made war upon the Church as well as upon democracy.

Gassendi was a Frenchman, a native of Provence, an ecclesiastic.* As his first writings are posterior to those of Bacon, and as he often cites the English philosopher, it must be admitted that Bacon has, at least, seconded the natural direction of his mind and of his studies. Although he belongs to the seventeenth century and to modern philosophy, it may be said that he is a wreck of the sixteenth; for it is antiquity rather than his own century that inspires and guides him. Tennemann said with reason that he was the most learned among philosophers, and the most philosophic among the learned. Thus he wrote only in Latin, and scarcely ever in French. His life was devoted to the renewal of the philosophy of Epicurus; he took great care, however, even in the title† of his book, to declare that he rejected from it every thing that was contrary to Christianity. But how could he succeed in this? Principles, processes, results, every thing in Epicurus is sensualism, materialism, atheism. Was this inconsistency? Was it ecclesiastical prudence? It is of little consequence: the thought of Gassendi must not be sought for in these reserves. It is found in the ardor with which he combated the nascent idealism of Descartes. He could not prevent himself, whatever may have been his moderation, from exclaiming against Descartes in very lively expressions, half serious, half sportive; he frequently addresses him: *O mens! O spirit!* To which Descar-

---

tained in it; whereupon I asked him why he published such doctrines. After a half-pleasant and half-serious conversation, he replied: 'The fact is, I wish to return to England.'"

* Born in 1592, in Provence, professor in the College of France in Paris, died in 1655. *Petri Gassendi Opera*, Lugd., 1658, 6 vol. in-fol.

† *Syntagma philosophiæ Epicuri, cum refutationibus dogmatum quæ contra fidem christianam ab eo asserta sunt; præfigitur Sorberii dissert, de vita et moribus P. Gassendi.* Hag. Com., 1655–1659; several times reprinted. He had before published, Lugduni, 1649, *Epicuri philosophia*, *Animadversiones in decimum librum Diogenis Laertii*, 3 vol. in-fol.

tes responds: *O matter! O Caro!* He was so zealous a partisan of the philosophy of Hobbes, that his friend and his pupil, Sorbière, informs us that some months before his death, having received the work of Hobbes, *De corpore politico*, he kissed it with respect, and exclaimed that it was a very small work, but that it was full of precious sweets, *medulla scatet.** He also greatly prized the *De Cive.*†

To Gassendi, that is, to the scholar of the sensualistic school, must be added several philosophers of the same kind who are not his pupils, but who, like him, explored antiquity to the profit of sensualism. I will name two Frenchmen, the one Guillemert de Berigard or Beauregard, a professor in Italy, who was born at Moulins in 1578, and who died at Padua in 1667: he renewed the physics of the Ionians;‡ the other Jean Chrysostome Magnen, born at Luxeuil, a professor in Pavia, and a great partisan of the doctrine of Democritus.§

I ought also to call your attention to the success of the philosophy of Gassendi in France. Doubtless the high clergy, Port-Royal, the Oratoire, the *élite* of literature, the great minds of the century of Louis XIV.‖ were, for the most part, Cartesians; but Gassendi spread his ideas throughout a small circle of pupils and zealous partisans, among whom, with his biographer Sorbière, we may distinguish the traveller Bernier, Chapelle, Cyrano, and our great Molière.¶ This was the foundation of that society of free-thinkers of the Temple from which Voltaire drew his first inspira-

* Preface of Sorbière.

† See, on the head of the *De Cive*, the letter of Gassendi to Sorbière.

‡ *Circuli pisani*, Undine, 1643–1647, reprinted at Padua in 1661.

§ *Democritus reviviscens*, Ticini, 1646; often reprinted.

‖ *Fragments of Cartesian Philosophy*, passim.

¶ Grimarest testifies that Molière observed for some time during his youth the teachings of Gassendi, and that he translated, partly into verse and partly into prose, the epicurean poem of Lucretius. He places in the mouth of Eliante, in the *Misanthrope*, a charming imitation of several verses of Lucretius, on the illusion of lovers who see nothing but beauty in the beloved object. Grimarest informs us that in time Molière left Descartes and continued faithful to Gassendi.

tions, before he had found in the conversation of Bolingbroke, and in his Voyage to England, Epicurean philosophy under a regular and scientific form. Locke was the true master of Voltaire.* He was the metaphysician of the sensualistic school; he was its most elevated and purest expression in the seventeenth century.

In order to obtain a just idea of the philosophy of Locke,† it is necessary to read in the first pages of his work the passage where he refers to the occasion upon which it was written. Locke relates that in a conversation in which he took part, a question, foreign to philosophy, produced a discussion wherein the most opposite opinions were advanced, without resolving the difficulty. On reflection he suspected that its cause was especially in the use of notions whose nature, reach, and limits had not been recognized; and generalizing this observation, he concluded that, since after all we think and philosophize only with the human mind, it is this human mind that it behooves us first to know. Hence the *Essay on the Human Understanding,* wherein Locke determines its nature and its powers, the exact extent and limits of our cognitions. This great and simple thought is the whole philosophy of Locke; herein is the originality of this philosophy; hereby it has rendered an immortal service to the human mind. But it is enough to render a single and memorable service to the human mind; the greatest man may therein exhaust himself, and Locke, after having opened the road of true philosophy, tottered himself upon it, and wandered insensibly into a narrow and exclusive path.

Locke assigns two sources of human knowledge, sensation and reflection. Reflection is applied to the operations of the understanding, and is limited to making them known to us such as they are. These operations are comparison, reasoning, abstraction,

---

* See, on the philosophy of Voltaire, Vol. 3 of this 2d Series, Lecture 13, and especially 1st Series, Vol. 3, Lecture 1, p. 38; 2d Lecture, p. 80; 4th and 5th Lectures, p. 201.

† On Locke, his life, writings, philosophy, and influence, see 1st Series, Vol. 3, Lecture 1, and Vol. 3, almost entire, of this Series.

composition, association, all the faculties which separate or combine the elements which are derived from sensation, but add nothing to it; there is not one that has the power of conveying to the understanding any contingent whatever of notions proper to it. All our knowledge, then, has its first and last root in sensation. Such is the theory of Locke brought back to its principle. The principle once laid down, you easily guess the consequences. The natural sagacity of Locke has in vain attempted to retain them; they escape him on all sides and connect him with that chain of sensualistic philosophers, the first link of which is Hobbes. Locke is Hobbes with all necessary differences. He does not often quote him, he often reproduces him. His chapter on the influence of language, in all respects, resembles an analogous chapter of Hobbes. Hobbes and the whole sensualistic school assimilate more or less the soul to the body; this you know. Locke did not go so far; but with Occam and Scot* he pretends that it is very difficult to prove, except by revelation, that the subject of the operations of the understanding is spirit and not matter; and he supposes that God could have endowed matter with the faculty of thinking. Locke was religious, it is true; but Leibnitz showed that the Christianity of Locke inclined to Socinianism,† a doctrine that has always been poor enough in regard to God and the soul. Finally, if Locke possesses the liberality so deficient in Hobbes, it remains to be known which of the two is wanting in consistency.

Such is the sensualistic school of the seventeenth century in its historical development. It terminated in Locke, who closes the seventeenth century and opens the eighteenth. His sensualism shall hereafter be the subject of our inquiry. Now let us examine the parallel development of the idealism of the seventeenth century.

---

* See Lecture 9.

† "Inclinasse eum ad socinianos quorum paupertina semper fuit de Deo et mente philosophia." *Epist. ad Bierling.*, Correspondence of Korthold, Vol. iv. p. 15.

The founder of the modern idealistic school is Descartes.* But Descartes, as well as Bacon, does not begin by an exclusive doctrine; he falls into it unconsciously, or rather he conducts to it. Like Bacon, he begins with the sagest principles, which belong to no school, and which are the soul of entire modern philosophy. He is far from having neglected studies, whose object is exterior nature. Remember that Descartes was one of the greatest natural philosophers of his age, that he spent his life in making experiments; but he was above all a great geometrician and an observer of human nature.

Descartes seeks the fixed and certain point of departure, whereupon philosophy may rest. He finds that thought may question every thing, every thing save itself. In short, although we should doubt all things,† we could not doubt that we doubt: now, to doubt is to think; whence it follows that we doubt not that we think, and that thought cannot deny itself, for it could do it only by itself. We have here a circle, out of which it is impossible for skepticism to go. This is, then, the firm and certain point of departure sought by Descartes; and as thought is attested to us through consciousness, behold consciousness taken as the point of departure and the foundation of all philosophical research.

Follow out the consequences of this principle. I think, and since I cannot doubt that I think, I cannot doubt that I exist in so far as I think. Thus I think, therefore I exist,‡ and existence

---

* Born in 1596, died in 1650. The only complete edition of his works is that published in Paris, 1824–1826, eleven vols. in-8. The first work of Descartes is the *Discours de la méthode pour bien conduire sa raison et chercher la vérité dans les sciences; plus la dioptrique, les météores et la géométrie, qui sont des essais de cette méthode*, in-4, 1637.—*Meditationes de prima philosophia*, 1641, in-4.—*Principia philosophiæ*, 1644, in-4. The French translation is preceded by a French preface by Descartes.—*Traité des passions*, in-12, 1650.

† On the nature of Cartesian doubt, see our writings *passim*, and especially the *Defence of the University and of Philosophy*, p. 221.

‡ Of the true sense of the Cartesian enthymeme, 1st Series, Vol. 1, p. 27, Vol. 4, p. 67 and p. 512, Vol. 5, p. 213.

is given me in thought. This is the first consequence; behold the second:

What is the character of thought? it is that of being invisible, intangible, imponderable, without dimensions, simple. Now, if the conclusion from the attribute to the subject is good, thought being admitted as the fundamental attribute of the subject that I am, the simplicity of the one implies the simplicity of the other, that is, of the *me* or of the soul; and from the second step, Cartesian philosophy naturally and invincibly arrives at the spirituality of the soul,* which all other philosophers attained only after many circuits and much uncertainty.

But does this thought, which is to me existence since it is that in which I can alone perceive it, does this thought always and infallibly attain to truth? Doubtless I have no other means of knowing truth than my thought; but I must admit that, in more than one case, this thought is at fault, that it does not always go as far as I could wish, and that imperfection is one of its manifest characteristics. Now this notion of the imperfect, of the limited, of the finite, of the contingent, elevates me directly to that of the perfect, of the absolute, of the illimited, of the infinite, of the necessary; it is a fact that I have not and cannot have one without the other. I have, then, this idea of the perfect and of the infinite, but who am I, I who have such an idea? A being whose attribute is finite, limited, imperfect thought. On the one hand, I have the idea of the infinite and of the perfect, and on the other I am imperfect and finite. Hence the demonstration of the existence of a perfect being; for if the idea of the perfect and of the infinite did not suppose the real and substantial existence of a perfect and infinite being, it is only because it was I who had formed this idea. But if I had formed it, I could destroy it, I could at least modify it. Now, I can neither destroy it nor modify it; I have not then formed it; it is then in me without belonging to me: it is related to a model

* Ibid.

foreign to myself and which is peculiar to it, namely, God; so that from the fact alone that I have the idea of God, it follows that God exists.*

Behold then the existence of the soul and the existence of God proved by the authority of thought alone. Behold the existence of the soul and the existence of God established, and yet there has been no question concerning the existence of the exterior world. Descartes concludes that we have a more direct certainty of the existence of the soul and of the existence of God than of the existence of bodies.

In the mean time, this great natural philosopher, far from denying the existence of bodies, seeks its demonstration; but seeking it only in thought, he cannot easily find it. In the complex phenomenon of thought, Descartes encounters sensation; he does not deny it; nor does he deny that this phenomenon, foreign to the will, must have a cause, and a foreign, exterior cause. Thus far Cartesian philosophy reaches; but if there is incontestably a cause of our sensations, what is this cause? Is it spiritual or material, deceitful or true? The senses say nothing about it. Descartes would hesitate then, if the senses alone could decide; and he asks if by chance he could not make the supposition of an evil genius, who behind all these appearances might be the true author of this phantasmagoria. But Descartes is in possession of the existence of God; God is with him perfection itself: now, perfection comprehends, among other attributes, both wisdom and veracity. If then God is true, it cannot be that he who is in the last analysis the author of these appearances which seduce us to believe in the real existence of the exterior world, has shown us these appearances only as a snare and as a deception. It is not then a snare, a deception; that which appears to exist does then exist, and God is our warrant for the legitimacy of our natural persuasion.

---

* On the demonstration of the existence of God by the idea of him, see 1st Series, Vol. 4, Lect. 12, pp. 63–68, and Vol. 5, Lect. 6, p. 213.

Without examining whether there is or whether there is not a paralogism in the process which makes the certainty of the existence of the world rest upon the divine veracity,* let us limit ourselves to observing, that if Descartes has given proof of good sense and depth by not placing the existence of the soul and the existence of God at the mercy of an argumentation, and by drawing these two convictions from the primitive decisions of thought, he has committed a grave fault, an evident anachronism in the history of consciousness, by not placing upon the same line, the conviction of the existence of the exterior world. According to Descartes, man could believe in the existence of the world only after a complicated train of reasoning, the basis of which should be the veracity of God. In fact, it is not so, and the belief in the existence of the world is infinitely nearer the point of departure of the thought; it is more immediate and more profound. Now, the existence of the exterior world once placed after the existence of the soul and the existence of God, the door is open to idealism. Follow Descartes in his two immediate disciples, Spinoza and Malebranche, and you will recognize the fruits oi the master's principles.† With them, God is every thing; the world and man nothing, or scarcely any thing. I say man as well as the world, and for this reason: struck particularly, in consciousness, with the phenomenon of thought, Descartes neglected that of free and voluntary agency. He does not, doubtless, deny liberty, he often speaks of it,‡ but he does not apply himself to giving an exact and profound analysis of it; he often confounds the will and desire,§ phenomena entirely distinct, for desire is passive and impersonal, the will is the type itself of ac-

---

* See the reply to this accusation, 1st Series, Vol. 4, Lect. 22, p. 514.

† The resemblances which attach Spinoza and Malebranche to Descartes are here shown; but it was also necessary to take account of their differen ces and essential differences. This is what was done in the *Mémoire sur les* RAPPORTS DU CARTESIANISME ET DU SPINOZISME, *Fragments de philosophie Cartesienne*, 429–470.

‡ *Fragments de la philosophie Cartesienne*, p. 466.

§ Ibid., p. 465.

tivity and of personality, the most eminent characteristic of man. The confounding of desire and the will debased, therefore, and enfeebled the notion of human personality in Cartesianism, while at the same time a manifest anachronism compromised that of the world. The notion alone of God, of a perfect, necessary and absolute being, was always in it, inviolable and sacred. It was quite natural that, in the progress of the school, this sublime notion remaining always the same during the continual dissipation of the notion of the exterior world and of the notion of the will and of human personality, it is quite natural, I say, that the first should absorb the other two:* this is the common vice of the philosophy of Spinoza and of Malebranche.

Instead of accusing Spinoza† of atheism, the opposite reproach might be cast upon him. Spinoza sets out with the perfect and infinite being of Descartes; he shows that before the infinite being every thing else has but a phenomenal existence; that a substance being that which possesses existence of itself,‡ and the finite being that which shares existence without possessing it of itself, a finite substance implies two contradictory notions. Thus, in the philosophy of Spinoza, man and nature are mere phenomena, simple attributes of sole and absolute substance, but attributes that are coeternal with their substance; for, as there are no phenomena without a subject, no imperfect without perfect, no finite without infinite, and as man and nature suppose God, so there is no substance without phenomena, no perfect without imperfect, no infinite without finite; and God implies also humanity and nature. The evil here is in the preponderance of the relation

---

* On this predominance of the idea of God in the Cartesian philosophy and on the general spirit of the seventeenth century, see *The Thoughts of Pascal*, preface, p. 46, the last pages of *Jaqueline Pascal*, and the *Fragments of Cartesian Philosophy*, p. 469.

† Born at Amsterdam in 1632, died at Haye in 1677. Opp. ed. Paulus, Jen., 1802-1803, 2 vol. in-8.

‡ This false definition of the substance is the source, too little known, of Spinozism. Now, Descartes did not definitely admit it. *Fragments of Cartesian Philosophy*, p. 467.

of the phenomenon to the being, of the attribute to the substance, over the relation of the effect to the cause. When man has not been conceived as a free and voluntary cause, but as a desire often impotent, and as a thought always imperfect and finite, God, or the supreme model of humanity, can be but a substance and not a cause, the immutable substance of the universe, and not its productive and creative cause. In Cartesianism, the notion of substance played a greater part than that of cause; this notion of substance grown entirely predominant constitutes Spinozism.*

* *Philosophical Fragments*, the article entitled: Spinoza, and the Synagogue of the Portuguese Jews at Amsterdam. "In confounding desire with will, Spinoza has destroyed the true character of human personality, and, in general, too much obscured personality in existence. With him, God, being in itself, the eternal, the infinite, overwhelms too much the finite, the relative, and that humanity without which the most profound and most holy attributes of God are unintelligible and inaccessible. Far from being an atheist, of which he is accused, Spinoza possesses so strongly the sentiment of God, that he loses the sentiment of man. This temporary and limited existence, every thing that is finite seems to him unworthy of the name of existence, and for him there is no true being but the eternal being. This book, bristling as it is, in the manner of the times, with geometrical formula, so dry and so repulsive in its style, is at foundation a mystic hymn, a transport, a yearning of the soul towards him who alone can legitimately say: I am that I am. Spinoza calumniated, excommunicated, and persecuted by the Jews as having abandoned their faith, is essentially a Jew, much more so than he believed himself to be. The God of the Jews is a terrible God. No living creature has value in his eyes, and the soul of man is to him as the grass of the fields and the blood of the beasts of burden. (Ecclesiastes.) It belonged to another epoch of the world, to lights different from those of Judaism, to establish the boundary between the finite and the infinite, to separate the soul from all other objects, to tear it from nature to which it was, as it were, enslaved, and by a mediation and a sublime redemption, to place it in just relation with God. Spinoza was ignorant of this mediation. For him the finite remained on one side and the infinite on the other; the infinite producing the finite only to destroy it, without reason and without aim. Yes, Spinoza was a Jew, and when he prayed to Jehovah, he prayed sincerely in the spirit of the Jewish religion. His life was the symbol of his system. Adoring the eternal, ever in the presence of the infinite, he disdained this passing world; he knew neither pleasure, nor action, nor glory, for he did not suspect his own. Young, he desired to know love; but he knew it not, because he did not inspire it. Poor and suffering, his life was spent in waiting for and meditating upon death. He lived in a suburb of this city, where gaining, as a polisher of glass, the little bread and milk necessary for his subsistence, hated, repu-

The point of departure of Malebranche* is the Cartesian theory that human thought cannot recognize itself as imperfect, and as relative, without conceiving God, perfect and absolute being; now as there is not a single thought which is not accompanied by the feeling of imperfection in itself, it follows that there is not a thought which is not accompanied by the conception of God, which communicates to it a force and superior authority. Thus the idea of God is contemporaneous with all our ideas, and the basis of their legitimacy; and, for example, the idea which we form of exterior bodies and of the world, would be vain, if this idea was not given in that of God. Hence the famous principle of Malebranche, that we see every thing, and the material world itself, in God; which means that our vision and conception of the world is accompanied by a conception of God, of infinite and perfect being, that adds its authority to the uncertain evidence of our senses and our thought. On the other hand, Malebranche does not destroy the notion of cause as Spinoza has done; he maintains it in God, but he degrades it in man; he makes the liberty of man very feeble and the action of God infinite. Hence the theory of God as the author and principle of our desires, of our acts, and of our thoughts; hence the theory of occasional

---

diated by the men of his communion; suspected by all others, detested by all the clergy of Europe whom he wished to subject to the State, escaping persecutions and outrages only by concealment, humble and silent, of a gentleness and patience that were proof to every thing, passing along in this world without wishing to stop in it, never dreaming of producing any effect upon it, or of leaving any trace upon it. Spinoza was an Indian mouni, a Persian soufi, an enthusiastic monk; and the author whom this pretended atheist most resembles, is the unknown author of the *Imitation of Jesus Christ.*"

* Born at Paris in 1638, died in 1715. His principal works are: *Examination of Truth*, Paris, 1674, a single volume in-12; there were six editions of it published in France during the life of Malebranche; the last is of 1712, 2 vol. in-4, and 4 vol. in-12; *Christian Conversations*, 1677; *Of Nature and of Grace*, 1681; *Christian Meditations*, 1683; *Discourses on Metaphysics and Religion*, 1688; *Conversation between a Christian philosopher and a Chinese philosopher*, 1708; *Reflections on Physical Predetermination*, 1715.

causes,* found almost at the same time by Geulinx.† The last term of this system is the absorption of man in God.

Such is the state in which sensualism and idealism, the school of Bacon and that of Descartes, were found at the close of the seventeenth century. It remains for me to speak of their struggle and of its results.

---

* On Malebranche, see the *Introduction* to the works of P. André, the *Preface to the Thoughts of Pascal*, p. xxxii., and in the *Fragments of Cartesian Philosophy*, the correspondence of Malebranche and Leibnitz, as well as that of Malebranche and of Mairan on the system of Spinoza.

† Of Antwerp, born in 1625, died in 1669. Among other works: *Logica fundamentis suis, a quibus hactenus collapsa fuerat, restituta*, Lugd. Bat., 1662. Γνῶθι σεαυτόν, *sive Ethica*, Amstelod., 1665. *Metaphysica vera*, etc., Amstelod. 1691.

LECTURE XII.

MODERN PHILOSOPHY. SEVENTEENTH CENTURY. SKEPTICISM AND MYSTICISM.

Struggle between sensualism and idealism. Leibnitz: an attempt at a conciliation which is resolved into idealism.—Skepticism: Huet, Hirnhaim, Glanville, Pascal, Lamothe Le Vayer, Bayle.—Mysticism: Mercurius Van Helmont, More, Pordage, Poiret, Swedenborg.—Conclusion. Entrance into the second age of modern philosophy, or philosophy of the eighteenth century properly so called.

In the last lecture we saw modern philosophy divided from its birth into two opposite schools, equally exclusive, equally defective, which are represented and summed up at the beginning of the eighteenth century, on one side by Locke, and on the other by Malebranche. The struggle between these two great schools fills the first quarter, and almost the half of the eighteenth century; this struggle began at their very origin. You have seen Gassendi attack the idealism of Descartes, and Descartes the empiricism of Gassendi. At a later period, Locke, taking up the quarrel, submitted to a severe analysis the pretended innate ideas of Descartes,* and the vision in God of Malebranche;† and even in the country of Locke, the friend and pupil of Locke, Shaftesbury,‡ combated the principles and consequences of the *Essay on the Human Understanding*: in the midst of all this Leibnitz arrived.§

That which most especially characterized Leibnitz, among many

* Book 1st of the *Essay on the Human Understanding*.

† *Examination of the Opinion of Father Malebranche*.

‡ Letter to a gentleman who is studying at the University, 1716.

§ Born at Leipsic in 1646; Journey in France in 1672, in England in 1763, in Germany and in Italy in 1687–1689; President of the Academy of Berlin in 1699, died in Hanover in 1716. *Complete Works*, ed. Dutens, 6 vol. in-4, Geneva, 1768.

other eminent qualities, was breadth of mind. He then conceived the idea of closing the struggle which divided philosophy, by combating equally the two extreme parts, and by uniting them in the centre of a vaster theory, which should comprehend while it modified them.

Leibnitz wrote against Locke a work on the same plan and under the same title as that of his adversary, divided into as many books, and into as many chapters, in which he follows him gradually, from principle to principle, from consequences to consequences.* He guards against denying the intervention of sensibility; he does not destroy the axiom: there is nothing in the intelligence which is not received through the senses; but he makes this reservation: yes, but the intelligence excepted. The reservation is immense: in fact, if intelligence does not come from the senses, it is, then, an original faculty; this original faculty has, then, a development which is peculiar to it, and engenders notions which belong to it, and which, added to those that spring from the simultaneous exercise of the sensibility, complete and constitute the entire domain of human knowledge. The exclusive theory of empiricism is destroyed by the following objection: The senses attest what is, they do not say what should be, they do not give the reason of phenomena; they may tell us that this or that is so, of such or such a manner; they cannot teach what exists necessarily. It must be proved that no necessary idea is in the intelligence, or this order of ideas must be accounted for by sensation: now this order of ideas cannot be denied, nor can it be accounted for by sensation; then, the senses and empiricism, which explain a certain number of notions, cannot explain them all, and those which they do not explain are precisely the most important.

So much for the school of Locke. Leibnitz did not attack the Cartesian school less vigorously; he is the first who seized the

* *New Essays on the Human Understanding*, published by Raspe; 1 vol. in-4, 1765.

feeble side of Cartesianism, the predominance of the idea of substance over the idea of cause. Call to mind how Descartes arrives at God. He arrives at him through the impossibility which exists, the idea of the imperfect and the finite being given, of not conceiving the idea of the perfect and the infinite, and, consequently, an infinite and perfect being, a real and substantial type of this idea. God is given to him as being and substance, and not as cause. I do not say that Descartes has denied the idea of cause, but he has neglected it too much. Spinoza converted this negligence of Descartes into a system. Spinoza placed and wished to place simply a principle and a substance, where a cause also should have been seen, and the result is, that the world and humanity, all visible phenomena, those of the mind and those of matter, are no longer effects, but modes, and modes coeternal with their substance. Both the creative virtue of God and the peculiar activity of man perish in this coeternity. Malebranche is a Christian Spinoza, somewhat more orthodox, and much less consistent. If with Malebranche, restrained by the Christian faith, God is still the creator of the world and of man, Malebranche, like Spinoza, despoils the human race of all voluntary and free agency; for, like Spinoza, he identifies the will with the desire, the will which attests a personal agency, with the desire which is passive and related to God, if you please, in the last analysis, but at first to the first object which fills the soul with involuntary desires.* The philosophy of Malebranche, and that of Spinoza, is nothing less than the suicide of liberty and of humanity to the profit of eternal substance. Leibnitz discovered and exposed the hidden vice of the whole Cartesian school, and established the new principle, that all substance is essentially cause. In fact, either substance is as if it were not, or it manifests and develops itself in modalities and in attributes: now it cannot do this, if it has not in itself the power of manifesting and

* On the essential difference between desire and will, 1st Series, Vol. 2, Lecture 18, pp. 231–236; Vol. 3, Lecture 3, p. 116; Vol. 4, Lecture 23, p. 566, etc.

developing itself, that is, if besides being a substance it is not also a cause. Take away from it this causative power, it is no longer any thing more than an abstract substance, a scholastic entity. Thus, according to Leibnitz, every real and not verbal substance is endowed with energy, it is a force ;* hence God, according to Leibnitz, is essentially creator; hence, at the same time, a creation not accidental and arbitrary, but which proceeds necessarily from the nature of God, which develops it and manifests it, and which, consequently, is perfectly regulated; hence a world composed of beings which are forces; hence, in short, a human soul like that which we have, and in which we all believe, a soul which is not only subject to the action of the world and of God, but which has also in itself a power of action which belongs to it, and proceeds only from itself.

Thus far every thing works very well; the vice of the empiric school and that of the Cartesian school could not be better seized. The first discussion is known; the second is not so well known, nevertheless it is the best title which Leibnitz has to glory. This title, obscured and almost lost, has been restored to him during these latter times; it has been placed in highest honor by one of our own countrymen, one worthy to be the interpreter of Leibnitz, M. de Biran, whose name I cannot here pronounce without painful emotion, when I think that he was so suddenly taken away from French philosophy, already so much his debtor !†

Behold Leibnitz, then, separating himself equally from the sensualism of Locke and from the idealism of Descartes, and absolutely rejecting neither the one nor the other: this in my opinion is the fundamental idea of Leibnitz, and you perceive that I applaud it with all my heart. Why should I not say so? Since precedents are sought to these feeble lectures, I willingly acknowl-

* On the relation between cause and substance, see 1st Series, Vol. 2, Lecture 6, p. 76.

† Works of M. de Biran, *Examination of the Lectures of M. Laromeguière*, and the article *Leibnitz* in the 1st Vol., with the editor's preface.

edge that they are found in Leibnitz; for Leibnitz is not only a system, but a method, and a method at the same time theoretical and historical, whose eminent characteristic is to reject nothing, and to comprehend every thing, in order to use every thing. Such is the direction which we strive to follow, and which we shall not cease to recommend as the only, as the true star on the obscure road of the history of philosophy. But it is necessary to distinguish this general direction of the spirit of Leibnitz from his system; for he also finished by a system, and by a system which unfortunately resembles an hypothesis. Of this system we have nothing more than morsels, *disjecta membra poetæ;* for Leibnitz has left no true systematic monument. Distracted by his employments and by that unbounded curiosity which led him to pursue every branch of human knowledge and to maintain a vast correspondence with all scientific Europe,* Leibnitz was unable to write out the whole of his philosophy: it must be sought here and there in the fragments which have escaped, at different periods, from his pen. The basis of all his thoughts is monadology and pre-established harmony. Monadology rests upon this axiom: Every substance is at the same time a cause, and every substance being a cause, has therefore in itself the principle of its own development: such is the monad; it is a simple force. Each monad has relation to all others; it corresponds with the plan of the universe; it is the universe abridged; it is, as Leibnitz says, a living mirror which reflects the entire universe under its own point of view. But every monad being simple, there is no immediate action of one monad upon another; there is, however, a natural relation of their respective development, which makes their apparent communication: this natural relation, this harmony which has its reason in the wisdom of the supreme director, is pre-established harmony.

---

* On Leibnitz, on his character and whole career, see in the *Fragments of Cartesian Philosophy* the article entitled: UNPUBLISHED CORRESPONDENCE BETWEEN MALEBRANCHE AND LEIBNITZ.

It would hence follow, that each monad, for example the human soul, draws every thing from itself, and in nowise receives the influence of this aggregation of monads called the body, and that the body in nowise submits to the influence of the soul. There would not be between the body and the soul reciprocity of action, there would be simple correspondence: they would be like two watches wound up at the same hour, which correspond exactly, but whose interior movements are perfectly distinct. But to deny the action of the body over the soul and that of the soul over the body, is, at the outset, to deny an evident fact which we may every moment prove both in the phenomenon of sensation and in the phenomenon of effort; then if it is not openly denying the existence of exterior objects, it is condemning the soul to ignorance of them, for it is condemning it not to go forth from itself, and reducing it to mere consciousness; it is then engaging philosophy in the way of idealism. Thus, after having some time suspended the struggle of systems, Leibnitz has therein fallen himself; after having tried to arrest the progress of exclusive schools, he has facilitated and hastened it: for it is Leibnitzism which has sown everywhere throughout Germany those seeds of idealism which at a later period bore their fruits.

You conceive that empiricism is not destroyed by the hypothesis of pre-established harmony: it is a general rule that one exaggeration is never corrected by another; the greatest strength of our enemies lies in our own faults, and that which injures all schools is their exaggerated pretensions. You conceive, then, that the partisans of Locke, far from being arrested by the idealistic hypotheses of Malebranche and of Leibnitz, are, on the contrary, authorized by the manifest vices, and, we may say, by the ridiculousness of these hypotheses, to plunge farther and farther into sensualism, and to push their principles even to the most deplorable consequences. In England, the friend and pupil of Locke, Collins,* denies positively the liberty of man. Locke

* Born in 1676, died in 1729.

had insinuated that it was not impossible that matter might think; Dodwell* changes this doubt into certitude, and undertakes to demonstrate the materiality of the soul, which greatly reduces the chances of immortality. In fine, Mandeville,† finding in Locke the theory of the useful as the only basis of virtue, concludes that there is no essential difference between virtue and vice, and thinks that too much evil has been said of vice, that after all, vice is not so much to be despised in the social state, that it is the source of a great number of precious advantages, of professions, of arts, of talents, of virtues which, without it, would be impossible.‡ Behold the extravagances of the empiric school; and what has it thereby accomplished? It has raised against itself new adversaries. Newton§ and his disciple, Samuel Clark,‖ contended against the irreligious consequences of the empiric school; Shaftesbury¶ combated its moral and political tendency. Finally, Arthur Collier** and G. Berkeley,†† in order to put an end to materialism, denied the existence of matter. Berkeley, setting out with this scholastic theory preserved by Locke, that we conceive exterior objects only by the intervention and the image of sensible ideas, destroys the hypothesis of ideas, which should

* Born at Dublin in 1642, died in 1711.

† A Hollander of French origin, a physician at London; born at Dordrecht in 1670, died in 1735.

‡ *Fable of the Bees*, London, 1706, 1714, 1728, translated into French, 4 vol. in-12, 1750. Helvetius has drawn much from it.

§ See his quarrel with Locke in the following volume, Lecture 15.

‖ Born in 1675, died in 1729. See his controversy with Collins and Dodwell, his sermons on the existence of God and his attributes, and his correspondence with Leibnitz. *Complete Works*, London, 4 vol., 1738–1742.

¶ On Shaftesbury and his opinion of Locke, 1st Series, Vol. 4, Lecture 11, p. 4–7.

** London, in-8. *Clavis Universalis*, 1713. We are acquainted only with the recent reprint made by Doctor Parr: *Metaphysical Tracts by English Philosophers of the Eighteenth Century*, London, 1837.

†† An Irishman, born in 1684, bishop of Cloyne in 1734, died in 1755. *Complete Works*, 2 vol. in-4, 1784, and in-8, 3 vol., 1820. His two most celebrated works are the *Alcyphron* and the *Dialogue between Hylas and Philonoüs*, both translated in French. On Berkeley, see 1st Series, Vol. 1st, Lectures 8 and 9.

represent bodies, and hence, thinks that he has taken away the foundation of the belief in the material world, which he regards as an illusion of philosophy to which the human race has never given any credit.

From England, turn your eyes to France, you there find the same struggle between the school of Descartes and that of Gassendi. In Germany, if Wolf,* the professor *par excellence*,† spreads Leibnitzism everywhere, do not forget the resistance, the persecutions even which he encountered; do not forget that there was more than one pupil of Locke among his adversaries. The struggle was more unequal in Italy. Fardella, at Padua,‡ was an Augustinian and an idealist like Malebranche; at Naples, Vico,§ while violently combating the very unjust contempt which Descartes had shown for the authority of history and languages, does not the less adopt his general philosophy, and he belongs to that noble idealistic school which has never been destroyed in the country of Saint Thomas and of Bruno. Nevertheless, Genovesi arose.‖

Such, in 1750, was the state of empiric dogmatism and of idealistic dogmatism in Europe. You have seen that neither of these two systems escaped the consequences resulting from their principles; a struggle of an entire century presented conspicuously

---

* Born at Breslau in 1679, *privat Docent* at Jena from 1703 to 1707, professor at Halle until 1723, driven away, afterwards reinstated, and died at Halle in 1754. His Latin and German works compose a whole library.

† Vol. 1st, Lecture 12.

‡ Professor at Padua, died in 1718. His greatest work is entitled: "*Animæ humanæ natura ab Augustino detecta* . . . exponente Michaele Angelo Fardella, Drapanensi, sacræ theologiæ doctore, et in Patavino lycæo astronomiæ et meteorum professore. . . Opus potissimum elaboratum ad incorpoream et immortalem animæ humanæ indolem, adversus, Epicureos et Lucretii sectatores, ratione prælucente, demonstrandam." Venetiis, 1698, in-fol.

§ Born at Naples in 1668, died in 1744. On Vico, see the preceding volume, Lecture 11. The great work of Vico is: *Principi di Scienza Nuova d'intorno alle Commune Natura delle Nazioni*, Naples, 1725. The last edition which he himself published is the 3d, in-8, 1744.

‖ In 1712, died in 1788.

all the vices attached to both. Hence should have arisen, and in fact soon enough did arise, a skepticism in proportion to the dogmatism which engendered it. As far, generally, as the extravagances of dogmatism are pushed, so far the boldness of skepticism will go; always, however, on two conditions: 1st, it is necessary that we should be in a century of liberty and independence, where alone, the extravagances of dogmatism bear their best fruits; we dare neither to doubt nor to appear to doubt, and terror stifles skepticism in thought itself or therein retains it; 2d, it is not enough to be independent, it is necessary moreover to be accustomed to recur to self, to examine different principles, the different processes of systems, and to gather together their consequences and their principles; it is necessary, in fine, that the spirit of criticism should have acquired some strength. Now, call to mind that we are in the century of Bacon and of Descartes, in the century which established philosophy on the double basis of independence and of method. Skepticism, too, was not wanting in the seventeenth century; it was, as it must have been, in proportion to the vast and rich dogmatism, whose distinct momenta and principal representatives I have pointed out to you.

In casting my eyes over the long list of skeptic philosophers which have appeared in the first age of modern philosophy, I cannot forbear dividing them at first into two classes, the true and the false. And here is presented a phenomenon of which I have already spoken to you,* and which we shall hereafter see reproduced, but which must be pointed out at its origin.

Call to mind the necessary order of the development of the human mind, such as we have seen it by the rapid history which I have presented to you: we have everywhere seen philosophy spring from the midst of theology. Having sprung from it, it was at first divided into two dogmatisms, which have often resulted in the maddest consequences. It was impossible that the-

---

* See Lecture 4.

ology should patiently behold an independent philosophy rise up beside it; and theology must have been so much the more afflicted to see the human mind escape it, as it saw it make a feeble trial of its strength. So, with very good intention, theology undertook (and this was its right and its duty) to recall the human mind to the sentiment of its weakness. It was thereby of great service; for it is of the utmost importance to remind dogmatism continually, that its basis is human reason, and that human reason has its limits. But if theology is still serviceable to the human spirit by reminding it of its weakness, this service is not entirely disinterested, and the secret or avowed, but very natural aim of theology, is to bring back the human spirit through the sentiment of its weakness, by exaggerating this sentiment somewhat, to the ancient faith, to the ancient authority from which philosophy set out.

In fact, scarcely had independent philosophy, in the seventeenth century, produced a few attempts at idealistic and empiric dogmatism, when theology, gaining credit by the errors into which philosophy had fallen, hastened to place before it the picture of its faults in order to disgust it with its independence, and bring it back to faith. This artifice must have been often practised in Europe, for its secret was soon known. In 1692 this disguised skepticism was unmasked and combated, in a book whose title is very remarkable, *Pyrrhonismus pontificus.**

Nothing is more clear than the aim of Huet: he is dogmatical and theological. Bishop of Avranches, employed in the education of the youth of France, celebrated besides as a learned man, Huet, the warm adversary of Descartes and the friend of the Jesuits, after having written his famous *Censure of the Cartesian Philosophy*, left a *Treatise on the Weakness of the Human Mind*, the last conclusion of which is, that it is necessary to return to faith and adhere to it. This pretended skeptic is the author of the *Evangelical Demonstration.* But to whom is this demon-

* By Fr. Turretini, of Geneva; printed at Leyden.

stration addressed? to the human mind apparently, to that same human mind which Huet has just convicted of inability to attain to truth, and which, consequently, must be incapable of seizing the truth of the evangelical demonstration.*

Jerome Hirnhaim was a Premonstrante, and a doctor of theology in Prague.† His work is a declamation unworthy of the attention of the historians of philosophy. Its spirit is sufficiently indicated by its title, which is as follows: *De typho generis humani, sive de scientiarum humanarum inani ac ventoso tumore, difficultate, labilitate, falsitate, jactancia, præsumptione, incommodis et periculis, tractatus brevis in quo etiam vera sapientia a falsa discernitur, simplicitas mundo contempta extollitur, idiotis in solatium, doctis in cautelam conscriptus.* Prag., in-4, 1676.

The Englishman, Joseph Glanville, is a skeptic of more mind, but strangely inconsistent. He is, at the same time, avowedly antidogmatic and superstitious to the utmost degree. A member of the Royal Society of London, he defended that illustrious association against the accusation of irreligion which had been made against it, and which has been since made against similar institutions. At the same time, chaplain ordinary of the king, he wrote more than once in favor of apparitions and spirits, striving to prove their possibility and their reality.‡ This is a very singular sort of skepticism: it is somewhat analogous to that of the mystic Agrippa.§ His most celebrated work is entitled: *Scientific*

---

* Born at Caen in 1630, died in 1721. *Censura philosophiæ Cartesianæ*, in-12, 1689. See, on this book, the beautiful letter of Arnauld, cited in the Preface of our *Thoughts of Pascal*, PREFACE, p. xxii. The *Philosophical Treatise on the Weakness of the Human Understanding* is a posthumous work, which appeared at Amsterdam, in-12, 1721. See our opinion of it in the book just cited, Preface, pp. xvi.-xix. See also on Huet, the *Philosophical Fragments, Correspondence of Leibnitz and the abbé Nicaise.*

† Died in 1679.

‡ *Saducismus triumphatus, or Full and plain evidence concerning witches and apparitions, in two parts, the first treating of their possibility, the second of their real existence*, 1666. There is a 3d edit., 1689, in-8.

§ See Lecture 10.

*skepticism,** or *Confest ignorance the way to science, in an essay oj the vanity of dogmatizing and confident opinion.* It is a regular attack upon the most accredited dogmatism of that period, idealistic dogmatism. Without dwelling upon this work, I will cite an important passage from Chapter XXV., in which Glanville examines and refutes dogmatism in relation to the idea of cause. In his opinion we cannot know any thing, if we do not know it in its cause. Causes are the alphabet of science, without which we cannot read in the book of nature.† Now we know effects alone, and by means of our senses too.‡ Our senses do not reach beyond phenomena, and when we wish to relate phenomena to causes invisible and above our senses, we can resort only to hypotheses. Descartes himself, that great secretary of nature,§ although he may have surpassed all the philosophers who preceded him in the explanation of the system of the world, has, nevertheless, given this explanation only as an hypothesis. In short, if we knew causes we should know every thing, so that the pretension of dogmatism in regard to causes implies that of omniscience. Doubtless there is not much to be boasted of in this work, which does not contain more than two or three pages, and which, too, is superficial enough, but it must be observed that Glanville is an Englishman, who enjoyed much celebrity in his own times, that Hume in his youth must have found his reputation great enough to warrant him in reading his works, and that this attack upon the knowledge of causes must be considered as the antecedent in England of that of Hume.

Pascal‖ is much above all these skeptics, but he is one of them.

---

* *Scepsis scientifica, or Confest ignorance the way to science, in an essay of the vanity of dogmatizing and confident opinion*, 1665. He has left also *Essays on several important subjects in philosophy and religion*, in-4, 1676. Among the essays the first two are: *Against confidence in philosophy; Of skepticism and certainty.*

† P. 154. "These are the alphabet of science, and nature cannot be read without them."

‡ "We know nothing but effects, and those by our sense."

§ "The great secretary of nature, the miraculous Descartes."

‖ Born in 1623, died in 1662. In my work *Des pensées de Pascal*, in estab-

Pascal is incontestably skeptical in many of his *Thoughts;* and the avowed design of his book the apology of the Christian religion. Neither his skepticism nor his theology contains any thing very remarkable. His skepticism is that of Montaigne and Charron, which he often reproduces in the same terms; in it you find no new view nor any new argument. It is nearly the same with his theology. What, then, places Pascal so high, and makes his originality? It is that, whilst with other skeptics skepticism is nothing more than a play of wit, a combination coolly invented to frighten the human mind with itself and bring it back to faith, that of Pascal is profoundly sincere and serious. The uncertainty of all opinions is not a bugbear in his hands; it is a phantom imprudently evoked which troubles and pursues him. In his *Thoughts* there is one which, though rarely expressed, rules and makes itself felt everywhere, the idea of death. Pascal, one day, saw death unexpectedly near at hand, and was terrified. He fears death, he does not wish to die; and having, as it were, taken in some sort this resolution, he endeavors as much as possible to secure to himself the immortality of the soul. It is for the immortality of the soul, and for that alone, that he seeks God; and from the first glance which this young geometrician, till then almost a stranger to philosophy, casts over the works of philosophers, he does not find a dogmatism which satisfies his geometrical habits and his wants, he throws himself into the arms of faith, of the most orthodox faith; for this teaches and promises with authority what Pascal would hope for without fear. He is not ignorant that this faith has difficulties; it is for this reason, perhaps, that he clings to it still more, as to the only treasure that remains to him, and devotes himself to strengthen every kind

lishing, for the first time, the true text of several thoughts, and in drawing new and unexpected thoughts from the original manuscripts, hitherto neglected, I believe that I have established the skepticism of Pascal as a philosopher. See *Journal des Savants*, April to November, 1842. *On the Necessity of a new Edition of the Thoughts of Pascal; Thoughts of Pascal*, in-8, 1842; 2d edition, much augmented, 1844, and 3d edition, with a new preface, 1847; see also *Jacqueline Pascal*, in-12, 1845.

of argument, good and bad; here solid reasons, there resemblances, there even chimeras. Given up to itself, the reason of Pascal would incline to skepticism; but skepticism is nothingness; and this horrible idea rejects it even in the most imperious dogmatism. Thus, on one hand, a skeptical reason; on the other, an invincible necessity of believing: hence, an uneasy skepticism, and a dogmatism which also has its inquietudes; hence, too, even in the expression of thought, that melancholy and pathetic character which, joined to the severe habits of a geometrical mind, displays in Pascal's writings a style unique and of superior beauty.

The skeptical school of Gassendi is of a very different character. In it, in my opinion, faith is but a reserve or a habit. The point of departure of this school is empiricism; its instrument and its form is erudition, which, among other advantages, had that of presenting skepticism under the respected cloak of antiquity. Lamothe le Vayer follows, at the same time, Charron and Gassendi; he is a sincere skeptic, except the restraint imposed upon him as preceptor of the youth of France.* The abbé Foucher† was surnamed the restorer of the new academy, and he wrote a book against the dogmatism of Descartes and of Malebranche.

Bayle is the ideal of this school of learned skeptics. He was made for skepticism by his good faith and his mobility: his life was the image of his character.‡ Born in the Protestant faith, he became a Catholic; no sooner was he a Catholic than he returned to Protestantism; after many adventures he retired to Holland;

* Born at Paris in 1586, died in 1672. His *Five Dialogues in imitation of the ancients by Horatius Tuberon* are still read. His complete works have been published by his son, 15 vol. in-12, 1671.

† Born in 1644, died in 1696. *Criticism on the Examination of Truth*, in-12, 1675. *Reply to the Criticism*, in-12, 1676. *Dissertation on the Examination of Truth, containing the history and the principles of the philosophy of the Academics*, in-12, 1693. On Foucher, see the *Philosophical Fragments, Correspondence of Leibnitz and the abbé Nicaise*, pp. 280, 284, 289–291; and *Fragments of Cartesian Philosophy*, p. 396.

‡ Born at Carlat, County of Foix, in 1648; died in Holland in 1706.

at last, it is said, he concluded to return to France and to Catholicism; for the one was then the only door to the other.* Bayle is, above all, a friend of paradox. He places himself almost always behind some name, or behind some decried opinion which he takes up in an underhand manner, without adopting it clearly and frankly, and which he excels in elucidating, in fortifying, and in putting into circulation. Nevertheless, to be just towards him, it must be confessed that he has given to the world, as his own, a number of paradoxes which belong to him. For example, in the *Thoughts on the Comet* was, for the first time, found the famous principle, since much in vogue, and which is not far from the truth: That an idea false or unworthy of God is worse than indifference or atheism. Again, Bayle advances that one may be an honest man and an atheist; that a people without religion is still capable of social order, and that every society is not essentially religious. But if these paradoxes, and many others,† betray in Bayle a skeptical spirit, they do not constitute a regular whole, a system of skepticism. Bayle is much more the father of Voltaire than of Hume.

It remains to me to speak of the mystic school. Thus far we have constantly seen the follies of idealism and of sensualism producing skepticism, and skepticism, unable to destroy the necessity of belief inherent in the human mind, constraining dogmatism to

---

* *Of Public Instruction in Holland*, ROTTERDAM, p. 184. "At Rotterdam, near the Great Market, opposite to the statue of Erasmus, is the house where Bayle lived and died, in disgrace with the Protestant party. Singular was the destiny of this man of the South of France, who, to escape the superstitions of his own country, fell into the hands of the Synod of Dordrecht, and passing from one extreme to the other, ended in skepticism. Bayle is not a systematic skeptic like Sextus and Hume, avowing his principles, and pushing them intrepidly to their last consequences. His skepticism is, as it were, the fruit of weariness, and the work of a curious and mobile mind, which floats at random in a sea of erudition."

† See the *Pensées sur la Comète*, 4 vol. in-12, 1681, and the articles *Manichéens*, *Pauliciens*, in the *Dictionnaire historique et critique.* Edit. de Desmaiseaux, 4 vol. in-fol., 1540. His works, with the exception of his *Dictionnaire*, have been collected in 4 vol. in-fol., Haye, 1737.

clothe the form of mysticism. Besides, as skepticism is always, in an epoch of liberty and of criticism, in direct proportion with dogmatism, so mysticism is almost always in direct proportion with both skepticism and dogmatism: so, in the first age of modern philosophy, there were as many important mystics as there were great skeptics and celebrated dogmatists.

Mysticism despairs of the regular processes of science: it believes that we may attain directly, without the aid of the senses, and without the aid of reason, by an immediate intuition, the real and absolute principle of all truth, God.* It finds God either in nature, and hence a physical and naturalistic mysticism, if I may so express it, or in the soul, and hence a moral and metaphysical mysticism. In short, it has also its historical views; and you conceive that in history it considers especially that which represents mysticism in full and under its most regular form, that is, religions; and you conceive again that it is not to the letter of religions, but to their spirit, that it clings; hence an allegorical and symbolical mysticism. These three points of view may be distinguished in the development of mysticism, and I pray you not to forget them; but it is sufficient that I have pointed them out to you. Without following them farther, I shall be satisfied with giving you the names of the principal mystics of each nation of Europe in the seventeenth century.

Germany, which has always been the classic ground of mysticism, first offers us the son of the celebrated Van Helmont, Mercurius Van Helmont, born in 1618, died in 1699, who spent his life in travelling in England and in Germany, and left several works, among others, *Opuscula philosophica*, in-12, Amsterdam 1690, and *Seder Olam, sive ordo sæculorum, hoc est historica enarratio doctrinæ philosophicæ per unum in quo sunt omnia*, in-12, 1693. Among the German mystics, must be named John Amos, born in 1592 at Comna in Moravia, and therefore called Comenius; his death occurred in 1671. He

* For mysticism, we have already referred, and we refer again, to the 2d Vol. of the 1st Series, Lectures 9 and 10, *Mysticism*.

tried to reform physics by mysticism: *Synopsis physices ad lumen divinum reformatæ*, 1633.* Amos supposes two substances, matter and spirit, and light as intermediary.

In England it is not just to place Cudworth† among the mystics; he is a Platonist of a firm and profound mind, who bends somewhat under the weight of his erudition, and with whom method is wanting; but H. More is decidedly mystic. He was at first a Cartesian, and Descartes addressed several letters to him; then he passed from Cartesianism to mysticism, which is natural enough; for, in general, remember that as we have seen, thus far, that skepticism proceeds from empiricism, so we have seen, and still see, that mysticism proceeds from idealism.‡ We must not forget among the English mystics of this period, John Pordage, a preacher and physician, who introduced into England the ideas of the German Böhme, and presented them under a regular and systematic form.§

In France, mysticism had not less success. Like some historians of philosophy, I do not count Pascal among the mystics; for if Pascal abandoned reason for faith, it was for orthodox

---

* See also *Joannis Amos Comenii* V. Cl. *pansophiæ prodromus*, Lugd. Batav., 1644, in-8.

† Died in 1688, author of *The True Intellectual System of the Universe*, London, in-fol., 1678; new edit., 4 vol. in-8, Lond., 1820; translated into Latin by Mosheim, Jena, in-fol., 1735, and 2 vol. in-4., Lugd. Bat., 1773. See also an excellent posthumous work entitled: *Treatise concerning eternal and immutable Morality*, in-8, Lond., 1731.

‡ More was a colleague of Cudworth at Cambridge; he was born in 1614 and died in 1687. He published a multitude of writings, and among others: *Immortality of the Soul, by Henry More, Fellow of Christ's College in Cambridge*, in-8., Lond., 1659. *Enchiridion Ethicum*, Lond., in-8, 1660; there is a 4th edit. in-8, Lond., 1711. Several of his English philosophical writings have been collected under this title: *A Collection of several Philosophical Writings*, one vol. in-fol., 2d edit., Lond., 1662, in-fol.; 4th edit., 1712.—*H. Mori Catabrigiensis opera omnia, tum quæ Latinæ scripta sunt, nunc vero Latinitate donata*, 2 *vol. in-fol. Lond.*, 1679, 1 *vol.*—*H. Mori, Cant. opera theologica, anglice quidem scripta nunc vero per auctorem Latinæ reddita*, in-fol., 1700, Lond.

§ Born in 1625, died in 1698. *Metaphysica vera et divina*, 3 vols., 1725, Francfort and Leipzic. *Sophia, sive detectio cœlestis sapientiæ de mundo interno et externo*, Amstelod., 1699. *Theologia Mystica*, Amst., 1698.

faith; whilst mysticism always inclines to heterodoxy. Nor will I place Malebranche in this class; for at first Malebranche does not subject reason to faith, but he establishes the conformity of the one to the other; then, too, the faith of Malebranche is orthodox, like that of Pascal. I should be more tempted to place Fenelon among them; for the author of the *Maxims of the Saints* prefers contemplation to thought and pure love to action and it may now be said that his faith is not very orthodox. Fenelon is therefore a mystic; but whether from weakness, or humility, or good sense, he does not go beyond that degree of moral mysticism which is called quietism.* The most decided French mystic of this epoch is Pierre Poiret, a Protestant minister who was born at Metz in 1646, and who died in Holland in 1719. A Cartesian like More, he, like More, abandoned Cartesianism, or rather he overstrained all its consequences, which led him to mysticism. He was the editor of the works of Antoinette Bourignon, 19 volumes in-8, 1679–86; and he himself wrote a great number of works. The most celebrated is written in French: *Economy of Divine Providence*, 1687, 7 vols. in-8, translated into Latin in 2 vols. in-4, Amstelod., 1705, reprinted in 1728. We must notice also the *Cogitationes rationales de Deo, anima et malo*, in-4, 1677, and with great augmentations, Amstelod., 1685; a third edition in-4, 1715. Herein is found a free Cartesianism, with a well-defined mysticism and a solid refutation of Spinoza. *Theology of the Heart*, 2 vols. in-12, 1690; *Theology of Love*, 1691; *De eruditione solida, superficiaria et falsa*, 1692, 2d edition, 2 vols. in-4, 1707; *Fides et ratio collatæ ac suo utraque loco redditæ adversus principia J. Lockii*, Amstelod., 1707; *Vera et cognita omnium prima, sive de natura idæarum*, 1715; a new edition of several writings of

* *Explication des Maximes des Saints*, in-12, 1697. The refutation of Bossuet is also of 1697, *Instruction sur les Etats d'oraison*, in-4. See on Quietism, 1st Series, Vol. 2, Lectures 9 and 10, p. 106, etc., and the opinion of Leibnitz on this great controversy, *Fragments philosophiques*, *Correspondence de Leibnitz et de Nicaise*, p. 314.

Madame Guyon and some of the spiritual works of Fenelon. After his death was published: *Petri Poireti Posthuma*, in-4, 1721, with a notice of his life and his works. The only one of which I shall here speak, is a very curious letter in which he gives a pretty clear idea of mysticism, enumerates its most essential points of view, and concludes by a history, or at least by an extended nomenclature of mystic authors.* This short letter is a mystic monument which may take the place of many others. According to Poiret, the foundation of mysticism is partly in the impotence of the reason and partly in the corruption of the will; hence the necessity of receiving every thing from God, truth by faith and revelation, virtue by grace. Practical perfection consists in being a mere instrument of divine action, *pati Deum Deique actus*. The mysticism of Poiret is especially moral and practical, whilst Pordage, Amos, and Van Helmont are rather naturalistic mystics. Towards the middle of the eighteenth century a vaster mysticism arises, which includes the three essential points of view of mysticism, sentimental and moral mysticism, naturalistic mysticism, and allegoric mysticism. You see that I allude to the doctrine of the famous Swedenborg.† Swedenborg closes all the mysticism of the seventeenth century, as Bayle closes the skepticism of the same age, and as Leibnitz and Locke represent and sum up its empiricism and its idealism.

I have shown to you the opposition and the struggle of these

---

* *Bibliotheca mysticorum*. Amstelod., 1708. In the middle of the book is the letter in question: *Epistola de principiis et characteribus quibus præcipui ultimorum sæculorum auctores mystici et spirituales fuere instructi*. At the end, some *Annotationes et additiones*, with a *catalogus auctorum mysticorum*.

† His works are innumerable. The principal are as follows: *Emmanuelis Swedenborgii Opera philosophica et mineralia*, 3 v. in-fol., Dresdæ et Lipsiæ, 1734.—*Prodromus philosophiæ ratiocinantis de infinito et causa finali creationis, deque mecanismo operationis animæ et corporis*, Dresdæ et Lipsiæ, 1734, in-12. *Doctrina novæ Hierosolymæ*, in-4. Amstelod., 1763.—*De cœlo et ejus mirabilibus, et de inferno ex ejus auditis et visis*, in-4. Lond., 1758.—*Delitiæ sapientiæ de amore conjugali; post quas sequuntur voluptates insaniæ de amore scortatorio*, in-4. Amstelod., 1768.—*Vera Christiana religio continens universam theologiam novæ ecclesiæ*, in-4. Amstelod., 1771.

four schools, but we must not forget their unity; it is in that of the common spirit of the seventeenth century, it is in that of the great movement which all these schools have in their way served. They are united to one another, they act upon one another. The honor of our Descartes is in having inspired or aided them all. Hobbes and Gassendi follow Descartes even in their writings against him; Locke proceeds directly from him, although he separates from him; Berkeley continues Malebranche; Leibnitz is a Cartesian; Wolf, who is a Leibnitzian, is consequently a Cartesian. On the other hand, Pascal and Huet have their eyes upon Descartes. Finally, More and Poiret come from Descartes, whom they refute and whom they abandon; and Swedenborg has before him, as a bugbear, the mathematical abstractions of Wolf. They suppose and produce one another, and compose by their strife an indivisible group: the same period, the same spirit, with the diversities necessary to place this unity in relief; the same point of departure, if not the same aim; finally, the same language and common terminology. We feel that they spring from the same trunk, although they form different branches and belong to the same family whose father is Descartes, or rather the spirit of the seventeenth century.

If this spirit has sent its roots into the eighteenth century, as for instance in Berkeley and Wolf, these roots have not the less sent their roots into the seventeenth century, and there indeed is their native soil. Berkeley is the offspring of Malebranche; and Wolf is Leibnitz himself with less genius. The spirit of a century neither dies nor is born upon a certain day; the spirit of the seventeenth century no more ceased to exist in 1700 than that of the eighteenth in 1799. The spirit of a period may change several times in a single century, or embrace several. In general the first years of a century do not belong to it; they are the prolongation and the echo of that which preceded and which in a manner died during the uncertain period when the following century was born. So to the spirit of the seventeenth century we must refer the first third of the eighteenth. Then, and then only, the first age of modern philosophy closed and an entirely new development began for it: a new dogmatism, a new empiricism, and a new idealism appear, which will produce a new skepticism, which will engender a new mysticism; then, in short, begins the second age of modern philosophy, which is the philosophy of the eighteenth century properly so called. Before entering upon it, let us cast a last look upon the age which I have traced, and which we will abandon to-day.

Observe that this great period of the history of philosophy, viewed in all its phenomena, has resolved itself into the same classification in which the systems of India, of Greece, of scholasticism, and of the Revival have arranged themselves. Here we have not only the same classification of systems, but moreover the same formation. Idealism and empiricism first present themselves; they rapidly produce skepticism, and it is only when skepticism has decried idealistic and empiric dogmatism that mysticism begins to appear, or at least to take a high importance. Thus behold modern philosophy, at its commencement, provided with the four elementary systems of all philosophy. Behold it constituted. In fact, a philosophy is not constituted so long as it has not all its organic elements, and it has all its organic elements only when it is in possession of the four systems which I have designated to you. Modern philosophy has taken a century and a half to form itself and to acquire the elements which are necessary to it; its first age extends from the first years of the seventeenth century to the middle of the eighteenth. Then only it was constituted; but it was constituted, and its future is secure; and unless some great catastrophe should suddenly take place, the principles which it contains must receive their development.

So much for its interior constitution; its exterior constitution is equally good. In the fifteenth and sixteenth centuries, modern philosophy had but one home, or at least it had a principal home, Italy. It was in Italy that the philosophy of the fifteenth and sixteenth centuries shone forth in splendor; other countries did little else than reflect it. But in the seventeenth century all

Europe became the theatre of philosophy; philosophy was everywhere acclimated; it thrust its roots into the very heart of Europe, in France, in England, in Germany; these were the equal and different homes of modern civilization. If philosophy had remained in Italy, where would it now be? But, thank God, it descended to the seventeenth century, from that ingenious and unfortunate Italy, into those strong and fruitful lands which belong ever to the new spirit, France, England, Germany; and there it has materially secured, thus to speak, the immense future which its interior constitution promised to it.

Add that in the fifteenth and sixteenth centuries, philosophy had scarcely any means of expression save a single language, and that too a dead language, the Latin; there were doubtless some exceptions, but in the seventeenth century the Latin language became the exception; then philosophy everywhere began to make use of national languages, which it enriched and regulated. There are very few great philosophical works in the seventeenth century which are not written in French* or in English;† the Latin language was still sustained in the North and in Germany,‡ yet somewhat barbarous and destitute of language and of literature. Leibnitz, however, was beginning to write § in German on philosophical matters, inviting his compatriots to imitate his example, and Wolf sometimes followed it.

Behold modern philosophy then, at the end of the seventeenth century, constituted, I repeat it, interiorly and exteriorly; it possessed its four necessary elements; it was naturalized in the three great nations which represented civilization; it had at its service living languages, full of the future, and which placed it in direct communication with the masses. Thus it marched for-

---

* Descartes, Malebranche, Arnauld, Fenelon, Bossuet, often Leibnitz, Bayle, Poiret in part.

† Several parts of Bacon and of Hobbes, Locke, Glanville, Cudworth, Berkeley.

‡ The Hollander Spinoza, Leibnitz, and Wolf in part, Swedenborg.

§ See *Leibnitz's Deutsche Schrifften*, of M. Guhrauer, 2 vol. in-18, 1838-1840.

ward, to become one day an independent, universal, and almost popular power.

In closing, I should make some apologies to you for reaching so slowly the very heart of my subject, the history of philosophy in Europe during the eighteenth century. I fear lest you may have found these prolegomena both too short and too long. But one may abridge and not be superficial, and I flatter myself that in this rapid sketch not one celebrated school, not one important name, and consequently not a single important element of the history of philosophy, has been omitted. As to length, I shall be pardoned if you form a clear idea of my true aim. This aim is to draw philosophical conclusions from the study which we must pursue together of the philosophy of the eighteenth century: my road is historical, it is true, but my aim is dogmatical; I tend to a theory, and this theory I demand from history. But every theory founded upon history is related to it, and is measured by the extent of the historical space run over. Suppose that I operate upon a single century, the eighteenth for example: I believe that in examining closely this single century we shall find in it idealism, empiricism, skepticism, and mysticism, and thence we shall be able to draw a certain theory of the human mind and of its laws; but this theory will necessarily be as limited in its legitimate results as the single experience that serves it as a basis; for do you know whether all centuries resemble the eighteenth? Do you know whether all the systems of every century enter into the plan of the classification of the systems of the eighteenth century? This page of the human mind, thus opened before you, is certainly more or less important; but thereby we can conclude nothing in regard to the human mind itself, for there are many other pages; its history fills many other centuries; and a legitimate theory of its nature and its laws must rest on a vast number of experiments. Now this theory is our avowed aim. In order to arrive at it, it was necessary then, in taking a single century, in order to study it thoroughly, it was necessary, I say, to rest this century on all anterior centuries, so that it might be its crown and pinnacle, and identify so well the essential elements of which it is composed, with those which the entire history of philosophy comprehend, that this single century might be legitimately taken for the faithful representative of universal history. Then the eighteenth century is no longer an accident, an isolated arbitrary experience; it is not by chance that the eighteenth century is divided into idealism, into empiricism, into skepticism, into mysticism; it was thus developed, because it could not be otherwise than thus developed, because in all the great epochs of philosophy we have found always and everywhere these four great systems which we may consider as the necessary, simple, and indecomposable elements of the history of philosophy.

At the commencement of the fourth lecture proposing this question: What is the philosophy of the eighteenth century? in what does it resemble the philosophy of anterior ages, in what does it differ from it? I answered that the philosophy of the eighteenth century resembles that of anterior ages in that it continues it, and that it differs from that philosophy in that it continues it in greater proportions and on a greater scale. What I then advanced I now repeat with more authority; for I now speak from the summit of the entire history of philosophy, and in the name of the laws of the human mind which three thousand years of experience have made known to us.

Let that be my excuse and my apology for these long prolegomena. You have thus far aided me by the promptness of your intelligence, while we have been travelling together through the centuries on the perilous heights of science and of history. I need the assistance of all your patience, now that I must lead you through the vast details of the philosophy of the eighteenth century.

COURSE OF THE HISTORY

OF

MODERN PHILOSOPHY,

SECOND SERIES.

VOL. III.

HISTORY OF PHILOSOPHY

IN THE EIGHTEENTH CENTURY.

YEAR 1829—SECOND HALF-YEAR.

SENSUALISTIC SCHOOL. SYSTEM OF LOCKE.

LECTURE XIII.

CLASSIFICATION OF THE SCHOOLS OF THE EIGHTEENTH CENTURY.

Of the method of observation and of induction in history.—That induction, resting upon the observation of all the anterior facts in the philosophy of history, divides at first the philosophy of the eighteenth century into four systems.—Confirmation of induction by facts.—Division of the European schools of the eighteenth century into four schools: sensualistic, idealistic, skeptical, mystical. Division of this course into four corresponding parts.—Order of the development of these four schools, and consequently the order to follow in their exposition.—Spirit of this course.—Its last aim.

The analysis of the human mind has demonstrated to us that in its natural development it ends at four fundamental points of view, which measure it and wholly represent it. These four points of view, in their scientific expression, give four elementary systems: sensualism, idealism, skepticism, and mysticism. And, as the history of philosophy is the manifestation of the human mind in time and space, there must be in history all that there is in the human mind: so, we have not feared to affirm, in advance, that the history of philosophy would constantly reproduce these four systems.

This is not a hypothetical method, it is a rational method, as

Bacon says;* it consists in going from the human mind, which is the material of history, to history, which is the manifestation of the human mind, and in confirming one by the other. And we have not confined ourselves to the rational method, we have joined to it the experimental method; we have interrogated history as we have interrogated the human mind. I have exhibited to you all the great epochs of the history of philosophy; I have shown you successively the East, Greece, scholasticism, the philosophy of the fifteenth and sixteenth centuries, finally all the first period of modern philosophy, from the first years of the seventeenth century up to 1750. Not only have I run over with you all these epochs, but I am not conscious of having omitted in each one of these any important school, and in each of these schools any celebrated system; and entire history at each one of these epochs has adjusted itself to the frame itself which the analysis of the human mind had furnished us. The last result of the experiences of history has been the constant recurrence, in each epoch, of the four systems which are intimately connected without being confounded, which are developed unequally, but harmoniously, and always with a marked progress. Why, then, have we not the right to convert the constant recurrence of this phenomenon into a law of history?

Call to mind by what processes and upon what conditions we obtain a law in the physical order. When a phenomenon presents itself with such a character in such a circumstance, and when, the circumstance changing, the character of the phenomenon changes also, it follows that this character is not a law of the phenomenon; for this phenomenon can still appear, even when this character no longer exists. But if this phenomenon appears with the same character in a succession of numerous and diverse cases, and even in all the cases that fall under the observation,

---

* Preceding Vol., Lecture 9.—On the necessity of uniting the rational method and the experimental method, see Vol. 1 of this Series, Lecture 4, and first Series, Vol. 2, *Discours d'Ouverture*, and Lecture 1.

we hence conclude that this character does not pertain to such or such a circumstance, but to the existence itself of the phenomenon. Such is the process which gives to the physical philosopher and to the naturalist what is called a law. When a law has been thus obtained by observation, that is, by the comparison of a great number of particular cases, the mind in possession of this law transfers it from the past to the future, and predicts that, in all the analogous circumstances that can take place, the same phenomenon will be produced with the same character. This prediction is induction: induction has for a necessary condition a supposition, that of the constancy of nature; for leave out this supposition, admit that nature does not resemble herself, and the night does not guarantee the coming day, the future eludes foresight, and there no longer exists any thing but arbitrary chance: all induction is impossible.* The supposition of the constancy of nature is the necessary condition of induction; but this condition being granted, induction, resting upon sufficient observation, has all its force. In the moral order, the same processes severely employed conduct to the same results, to laws which give to the moralist and the historian, quite as well as to the physical philosopher and the naturalist, the right to foresee and to predict the future. All the epochs of the history of philosophy being given, that is, all the experiments upon which observation of this kind can bear, when all these experiments, very different by reason of external circumstances, have always offered us the same phenomenon with the same character, that is, the constant recurrence of these four elementary systems, distinct from each other and developed by each other, I ask, what is wanting to give us the right to consider this result as the law itself of the history of philosophy? Will it be said that observation bears upon too small a number of cases? But we have commenced with the East, and we have been as far as to 1750:

---

* See on the stability of the laws of nature as the condition of all induction, 1st Series, Vol. 4, Lecture 20, p. 382; and Lecture 22, p. 485.

we have five great experiments, one of which embraces twelve hundred years. Observation bears therefore upon a sufficiently great number of particular cases; it bears at least upon all existing cases; we have omitted none: each great philosophical experiment has presented the same character, the division into four elementary systems. There remains only one condition to be fulfilled, to wit, the supposition of the constancy of the human mind, a supposition as necessary here as that of the constancy of nature in the physical order. But what right has the physical philosopher to suppose that nature is rather constant to herself, than the moralist to suppose that the human mind is constant to itself? All human life is founded upon the supposition of the constancy of human nature.* You suppose that humanity will do to-morrow what it has done to-day, the circumstances being analogous, as you suppose that nature will not fail to reproduce what has already been produced. Induction, therefore, has the same value in one case as in the other. So, when, after having met, in all the great epochs of the history of philosophy from the East up to 1750, the same phenomenon with the same character, I come to the philosophy of the eighteenth century, induction founded upon the experience of three thousand years authorizes me to predict that if this new experiment is extended, developed, completed (for an incomplete experiment proves nothing), the human mind, constant to itself in the eighteenth century, will reproduce the same philosophical phenomena which it has thus far produced, with the same characters, and that the philosophy of the eighteenth century will also be resolved into sensualism, into idealism, into skepticism, and into mysticism. Historical induction incontestably bears us thus far; it only remains to submit this legitimate conjecture to a last and decisive proof, that of facts.

The philosophy of the eighteenth century forms a great experiment. Never, at any epoch of history, has there appeared in less time a greater number of systems; never have more

---

* First Series, Vol. 4, Lecture 22, p. 484.

schools disputed with more ardor the empire of philosophy. The experiment is very rich, and at the same time it is perfectly clear; for, with a little instruction, one may easily possess himself of all the systems of which the European philosophy of the eighteenth century is composed. Now, an attentive study of all these systems gives precisely the same result which induction, drawn from the laws of history and from the laws of the human mind, would in advance suggest; and I undertake to demonstrate that in fact, in the eighteenth century, as in the seventeenth, as in the period of the Revival, as in the middle age, as in Greece, as in the East, there were only four fundamental systems, the four which you have already seen. Everywhere, it is true, reigns a contrary prejudice. The eighteenth century is a century so great, so glorious for the human mind, that it is very natural that all the schools should contend for it among themselves. Here, it is almost a dogma that sensualism constitutes the whole philosophy of the eighteenth century, and sums up civilization. There, sensualism is regarded as a sort of anomaly, as an insignificant phenomenon the whole office of which, in a picture of modern philosophy, is to cast a shadow upon the fundamental system, idealism. On another side, there are not wanting people who honor the eighteenth century for quite another reason, as having expanded and firmly established in the world, contempt of all systems, skepticism. Hear also the disciple of Swedenborg; he will say to you that the eighteenth century is the definite advent of divine philosophy. Whence come these contrary prejudices? From a very simple cause: each one, instead of elevating himself to a European point of view, usually stops at the point of view of his own country. But a country, whatever it may be, in Europe, is only a fragment of Europe, and represents there only one side of the human mind and of things. It is therefore natural that in each country of Europe a particular system should reign, and that all those who are within the horizon of this system should not see beyond it, and should make Europe in the image of their native land. But just because in each country of Europe a particular system has reigned, as there is more than one country in Europe, I conclude that for this very reason, no particular system has reigned exclusively in Europe, and that European philosophy in the eighteenth century is the triumph of a single thing, of a thing much greater than all systems, philosophy itself.

Yes, philosophical Europe in the eighteenth century belongs only to philosophy; it contains all systems, it is ruled by no one of them; I go farther, and I say that if the general philosophy of Europe, which it is always necessary to have in view, comprises in itself the different systems which rule in the different countries of Europe, each one of these countries, in order to be a part of the great European unity, taken in itself is also a unity more or less considerable; and that this particular unity, if it is somewhat rich, and if the philosophical spirit takes in it a development of some extent, still presents, under the domination of such or such a particular system, all the other systems, obscure, it is true, but not entirely smothered by the vanquishing system; so that the philosophy of each great country of Europe is a complete philosophy, which has four distinct elements, among which there is one which it elevates above all the rest.

It is certain that in France the philosophical system which reigned in the eighteenth century was that which derived every thing from sensible data;* but it must not be supposed that other systems were entirely wanting to France. Without speaking of the ancient spiritualism of Descartes and Malebranche, which was not extinguished among us with the seventeenth century, and which had as a representative in the eighteenth the Abbé de Lignac, the author of some excellent works, among others the *Témoignage du Sens intime*,† can one say that spiritualism was destitute of splendor in the country where Rousseau wrote? Is Rousseau any thing else than energetic opposition to

---

* First Series, Vol. 3, Condillac, Helvetius, Saint-Lambert, etc.

† First Series, Vol. 1, Lecture 18, p. 150.

the spirit of the philosophy of his times? Neglect the earliest works produced when Rousseau was ignorant of himself and was searching for himself, consider only the great monuments of the maturity of his talent, and in them you will everywhere find, under forms more or less severe, an avowed system of spiritualism; everywhere Rousseau defends conscience, disinterested virtue, human liberty, the immateriality and the immortality of the soul, and divine providence. It is sufficient to mention the first part of the *Profession de Foi du Vicaire Savoyard.* We know that Rousseau had written a refutation of the book of Helvetius; but the parliament having condemned Helvetius and burned his book, Rousseau suppressed his refutation.* Turgot, a man very inferior to the author of *Emile* as a writer, but who was much superior as a philosopher, also declared himself an adversary of Helvetius in a confidential letter to Condorcet, which Dupont de Nemours has published. His *Discourses on Universal History,* and the article entitled *Existence* in the *Encyclopédie,* bear a somewhat undecided but real impress of spiritualism.† As to skepticism, in order not to perceive it in France in the eighteenth century, it would be necessary to forget Voltaire. What, in fact, is Voltaire?‡ good sense somewhat superficial; and, in this degree, common sense always leads to skepticism. Voltaire doubtless attached himself to the sensualistic school, as skepticism usually does; but he constantly rejected its most bitter consequences, when he seriously explained himself. If he supported with all his talent the philosophy of Locke, which he regarded as the philosophy of the new times, against the philosophy of Descartes exaggerated and compromised by Malebranche, he took good care not to adopt the extravagances of Helvetius and d'Holbach;

---

* First Series, Vol. 3, Lectures 4 and 5, p. 203.

† On Turgot, in this Series, Vol. 1, Lecture 9, and First Series, Vol. 1, Lecture 17, p. 147; Vol. 3, Lectures on Helvetius, p. 208; Vol. 4, Lecture 16, p. 201.

‡ On Voltaire, in this Series, Vol. 2, Lecture 1, and First Series, Vol. 3, Lecture 1, p. 38; Lecture 2, p. 80; Lectures 4 and 5, p. 201.

his philosophy consisted in adopting no system, and in ridiculing all systems; he is skepticism in its most brilliant and lightest dress. It is also just to recognize that mysticism has never had in France an interpreter more profound, more eloquent, and who has exercised more influence, than Saint-Martin. The works of Saint-Martin, celebrated in all Europe, have made a school among us.*

If in England you only look at London in the eighteenth century, you will doubtless there see little else than sensualism. But even at London you would find, by the side of Priestley, Price, that ardent friend of liberty, that ingenious and profound economist, who renewed and brilliantly sustained the Platonic idealism of Cudworth.† I know that Price is an isolated phenomenon at London; but the whole Scotch school is more or less spiritualistic. Not without glory are the names of those professors who have succeeded each other in Scotland in the chairs of Aberdeen, of Glasgow, of Edinburgh, from the first quarter of the eighteenth century up to our day—Hutcheson, Smith, Reid, Ferguson, Beattie, and Dugald Stewart.‡ In regard to skepticism, it will be sufficient for me to name Hume, who by himself alone is an entire school.§ Mysticism is found in every part of

---

* He has by turns published translations or imitations of Böhme and original writings. They are as follows, in chronological order: *Of Errors and Truth*, Lyons, 1775, 1 vol. in-8; *Natural Picture of the Relations which exist between God, Man, and the Universe*, Edinburgh, 1782, 2 vol.; *The Man of Appetite*, Lyons, 1790, 1 vol.; *Ecce Homo*, 1 vol., Paris, 1792; *The New Man*, Paris, in-8, 1 vol., the fourth year of liberty; *Concerning the Spirit of Things*, 1800, 2 vol.; the *Dayspring*, 1800, 2 vol.; *The Three Principles of the Divine Essence*, 1802, 2 vol.; *The Ministry of the Human Spirit*, Paris, 1802, 1 vol.; *Four Questions in regard to the Soul*, 1807, 1 vol; *Concerning the Triple Life of Man*, 1809, 1 vol.; *Posthumous Works*, Tours, 2 vol., 1807.

† Richard Price, born in 1723, died in 1791. List of his philosophical writings: *Review of the Principal Questions in Morals*, London, 1758, 3d edition, London, 1787; *Four Dissertations on Providence, on Prayer, etc.*, 2d edition, 1768; *A Free Discussion of the Doctrine of Materialism and Philosophical Necessity, in a Correspondence between Dr. Price and Dr. Priestley*, by Dr. Priestley, London, 1778.

‡ First Series, Vol. 4, *Scotch School.*

§ First Series, Vol. 1, Lecture 10; and Vol. 4, *passim.*

England. Recollect that Swedenborg, during his sojourn at London, founded there a mystical school which numbers many partisans, has its periodical organs, journals, and, it is said, even several chapels.

Doubtless that which rules beyond the Rhine is idealism. Such is the general character of the great philosophy which sprang up at Kœnigsburg in 1781, with the *Critique of pure Reason,** and has been maintained with a continually increasing progress up to our times, by an uninterrupted course of superior men whose names begin to pass beyond the limits of their own country. Idealism is enthroned in Germany, but it must not be supposed that it has there entirely effaced the other systems, not even sensualism. Kant found a very strong opposition in Feder and Weisshaupt,† in Tiedemann,‡ especially in Herder, who wrote several works against the doctrine of Kant, and whose philosophy of history was composed in the sense of the philosophy of Locke.§ Skepticism had as a representative in Germany M. Schulze, the spirited author of *Ænesidemus.*‖ Quite as ingenious and profound as Schulze, Frederic Jacobi¶ equally combated empiricism and idealism, and renewed the skepticism of Hume by changing its character in favor of sentiment and enthusiasm; an original thinker, a writer of the first order, whose renown has increased since his death, and equals that of his illustrious rival, Schelling. As to mysticism, we are very sure of finding it in abundance in the country of Böhme and Swedenborg.

This very incomplete review is sufficient to demonstrate what it was necessary to establish, that, if in each country of Europe there reigned perhaps a particular system, this particular system nowhere abolished the other systems. Now take from all these different countries the analogous systems, and place them by the side of each other; put together all the sensualistic systems of

---

* First Series, Vol. 5.

† See the following Lecture.

‡ Ibid., and Vol. 1, Lecture 12.

§ Ibid., and Vol. 1, Lecture 11.

‖ Ibid.

¶ On Jacobi, see farther on in this Lecture.

France, of Germany, and of England, then all the idealistic systems, then the skeptical systems, then the mystical systems, and you will have upon the stage of European philosophy four great schools, all of which are recommended by considerable services, and present to impartial posterity names almost equally celebrated. If, moreover, we search for the part of each country in the general work, we shall find that France and England especially represent sensualism and skepticism; Scotland and Germany, in different degrees, spiritualism; in regard to mysticism, there is a little of it everywhere, and particularly in Germany.

Such is the result which observation gives us: observation, then, confirms the theory. Induction, resting upon the entire history of the past, divided in advance the philosophy of the eighteenth century into four great schools; and we have found that in fact this epoch of the history of philosophy is thus divided. This division, which in itself would be only a real but arbitrary fact, becomes a necessary fact by its relation to the entire history which it continues; it expresses a law of this history. Let us carefully follow it. As philosophical Europe in the eighteenth century is divided into four great schools, so this course will be divided into four parts.

I shall exhibit in turn to you the sensualistic school, the idealistic school, the skeptical school, the mystical school. But by which of these shall I commence? In what order should I present them to you?

Analysis of the human mind has given us not only four different points of view; it has given us those four points of view in an intimate correlation which it is important to observe. The human mind does not start by negation; for, in order to deny, it is necessary to have something to deny, it is necessary to have affirmed, and affirmation is the first act of thought. Man, therefore, commences by believing perhaps in this; perhaps in that, and the first system is necessarily dogmatical. This dogmatism is sensualistic or idealistic, according as man puts more confidence in thought or sensibility, but it is impossible that we should begin by skepticism. On the other hand, if skepticism presupposes dogmatism, mysticism in its turn presupposes skepticism. For what is mysticism? it is, once more, an act of despair on the part of human reason, which, after having naturally believed in itself, and having started by dogmatism, frightened and discouraged by skepticism, takes refuge in sentiment, in pure contemplation and immediate intuition. Behold the necessary movement of systems in the human mind.* In drawing conclusions from the human mind in regard to its history, we have not feared to affirm that here too history would reproduce what the analysis of the human mind had given us; and the experimental method, always agreeing with the rational method, has everywhere shown us, in each of the great epochs of the history of philosophy, sensualism and idealism, skepticism and mysticism, reciprocally developed by each other in an invariable progress and order. Everywhere, in the first part of each epoch, we have encountered two dogmatisms which soon, engaging in contest with each other, wound each other, and end by producing skepticism; this, in its turn, reacts upon them and modifies them, while they also exercise a powerful influence upon its course and its character; and then appears mysticism, which, produced, as it were, out of fear of skepticism and distrust of all dogmatism, equally shuns both, and attaches itself to them again through the warfare itself which it raises against them. This constant order of the development of systems, we can establish as a law, which shall have the same validity as that of the division of systems into four classes; and consequently we can, with the same certainty, predict that in the eighteenth century not only will the same systems be reproduced, but that they will be reproduced in the same order. In fact, if you attentively examine the four great schools which contend for philosophical domination, without ever obtaining it exclusively, in the eighteenth century,

---

* See on different systems, Lecture 4 of Vol. 2.

you will see that they all exist with the same mutual relation which I have just determined.

There is not in the eighteenth century a single philosophical school which acts upon all other schools and resists their influence; it is this relative development of schools, this reciprocity of action, this perpetual action and reaction which constitutes the philosophic life of Europe in the eighteenth century.

Get an exact idea of the real situation of philosophy at this epoch. The seventeenth century had everywhere terminated, except in England, with the domination of idealism; idealism had not extinguished, but it had conquered sensualism; and it had ruined itself by its own faults, by the ingenious but chimerical hypotheses which mark the triumph and bring the ruin of Cartesianism. It was then that the philosophical minority of the seventeenth century, strengthened by the extravagances of the majority, became the majority in its turn; sensualism, which received a certain number of partisans in the seventeenth century, obtained in the eighteenth century the domination, first in England, then in France: towards 1750, Locke was the philosopher of enlightened Europe. The idealism of the seventeenth century doubtless resisted, but it was beaten down at every point. Later appeared a new idealism, that of the eighteenth century, that of Rousseau and Turgot, that of the Scotch school and the German school. But Rousseau is evidently an opposer, a man of the minority, who contends against the sensualistic majority, represented by the encyclopedists. So Reid is an antagonist of Locke; the Scotch school, as I have already said, is a protestation of the permanent good sense of humanity against the extravagances of the new majority; for we are never the majority with impunity. Kant is Reid enlarged, that is, an antagonist of Locke. Thus, whilst the sensualism of the eighteenth century is a reaction against the idealism of the seventeenth, the idealism of the end of the eighteenth century is a reaction against the sensualism which precedes it. As to skepticism, try, I pray you, to comprehend Hume without Locke and Berkeley. What is Hume?

The last term* of the sensualistic system of Locke and the idealistic system of Berkeley. In Germany, Schulze-Ænesidemus† and Hume-Jacobi‡ are incomprehensible without a sensualistic school and an idealistic school, without Condillac and without Kant, for their skepticism, above all that of Jacobi, falls at once upon both. And by way of parenthesis, remark how history is formed, how the spirit which presides in it forms every thing in its time with weight and measure, and produces systems when it is good that they should come: after Locke and Berkeley, after Condillac and Kant, skepticism was necessary, and it was then that it came. In regard to mysticism, who could comprehend Saint-Martin without Voltaire and Condillac? Was not Saint-Martin driven to his mysticism through fright of skepticism, which he wished to escape, and the sad dogmatism of his times? It is the same with Frederic Schlegel, with Baader, and with other German mystics of our age.§ They are, in my opinion, the offspring of a period worn out with speculation, the last products of a discouraged philosophy which abjures itself. All, or nearly all, have been ardent dogmatists, whom the strife and the movement of mutually destructive systems have precipitated towards skepticism, and of whom some have found refuge in the orthodox mysticism of the ancient faith and the Church, but the most part in a heterodox mysticism, at once arbitrary and chimerical. But finally, all this mysticism is the result of the despair of speculative reason, and we arrive at despair only after having passed through illusion. I regard it, therefore, as an incontestable point, that there are not only four great schools in

---

* First Series, Vol. 4, Lectures on Reid, *passim.*

† Schulze wrote a work entitled: *Ænesidemus, or the Foundations given to German Philosophy by Professor Reinhold, with a defence of Skepticism against the pretensions of the Critique of Reason.* See *Manuel of Tennemann*, French translation, 2d edition, vol. ii., p. 327.

‡ Jacobi is the author of the treatise: *David Hume and concerning Faith, or Idealism and Realism*, *Manuel of Tennemann*, vol. ii., p. 321.

§ See on Fr. Schlegel and Franz Baader the *Manuel of Tennemann*, vol. ii., pp. 301, 302.

the eighteenth century, but that these four great schools are regularly developed: first sensualism, then idealism, then skepticism, then mysticism.

I shall do as the human mind and history do. The human mind and history give four points of view, four schools, always and everywhere, and so in the eighteenth century; I shall therefore divide the history of the philosophy of the eighteenth century into four parts. Moreover, the human mind and history make these four points of view appear, these four great schools, in their determined order; I shall present them to you in the same order: I shall begin with sensualism; I shall go from that to idealism, then to skepticism, and shall end with mysticism. But I shall take great care, in presenting to you successively and isolatedly each one of these four schools, to show you always their intimate relation and their reciprocal action in all the degrees of their development. Such will be the order of this course.

Now, what shall be its spirit? On which side shall I rank myself, in this great battle of European philosophy in the eighteenth century? Shall I be a sensualist, an idealist, a skeptic, or a mystic? Once more, I shall do like the human mind and history. The human mind and history produce four systems; therefore these four systems are true, at least in part; for nothing exists, nothing can exist, which has no relation to truth. Pure error, I have already said, would be impossible, and it would be unintelligible: as error penetrates the mind of a man only by the truth which is in it, so it is admitted by other minds, is sustained in the world only by that, and the success of every system supposes that there is some common sense in it. The eighteenth century could produce these four systems, and they had in it great success; therefore these four systems have their truth. On the other hand, these four systems contended together, and strongly contradicted each other. The day when absolute truth shall appear in the world, there will be no more contradiction and strife, all combat will cease; for truth has the power to rally to itself all minds. But, in the eighteenth century, as in all the great epochs of the history of philosophy, I behold strifes, a lively antagonism between these four systems; I conclude thence, that these four systems, in order to have existed, had a cause for existing, their part of truth; they also had, and necessarily, their part of error, in order to have been contradicted, in order thus to have fallen into strife and antagonism; they exist, therefore they are more or less true; they are four in number; therefore they are more or less false: this is for me mathematically exact. What, then, is the duty of the historian? Here as elsewhere, as always, his duty is to do as the human mind and history have done: he must not reject these four systems, for they have existed; and at the same time he must not be the dupe of any of these, for they have fallen into contention, for they have existed, not one, but four; they have been only particular systems, consequently exclusive systems, consequently more or less erroneous and vicious. I shall therefore do two things: I shall defend the foundation and the general principles of the four schools which the philosophy of the eighteenth century presents; I shall defend each one of these schools against the three others, in the name of the human mind and history, which, having admitted them in spite of the other three, have had on account of that, I think, excellent reasons which I shall give; and in defending the foundation of each one of these schools against the other three, I shall overwhelm by the weight of the other three, as the human mind and history have done, the exaggerated and exclusive pretensions of each of them. History has produced all four of them, therefore I will accept them all; history has contradicted them by each other, therefore I shall contradict them by each other, and shall embrace none of them. Thus, in the examination which I shall make of each one of the great schools of the eighteenth century, there will always be two parts: 1st, an apologetical part, which will represent, thus to speak, the reasons of the existence of each school in history; 2d, a critical part, which will represent the strife and the defeats to which each has been subjected.

Such is the plan, such are the divisions, the order, and the spirit of the history of the four great schools of the eighteenth century which I propose to present to you. But shall I limit myself to this part of the historian? Is this impartiality, which appears like indifference, and which rests, on the contrary, upon a profound sympathy for humanity and for every thing which comes from it, the only task which I propose? No; I must propose to myself still another; and I tell you beforehand that all this tends to, and will end at, dogmatical conclusions.

There is, incontestably, a foundation of truth under the contrary errors of the four fundamental systems of philosophy, without which these very errors would be impossible. But it is the error which is diverse; the truth is one. These four systems, although different in their errors, can and must agree in the truths which they contain. The errors of the systems which destroy each other, cover truths which do not pass away, and the history of philosophy contains a true philosophy, and, as Leibnitz said, *perennis philosophia*, an immortal philosophy, concealed and not ruined in the eccentric developments of systems. This is the common foundation upon which we all live, people and philosophers: we live in truth and by truth, thus to speak; and it is sufficient to disengage this immortal foundation from the defective and variable forms which at once obscure it and manifest it in history, in order to attain to true philosophy. I have long since* said, if philosophy does not already exist, you will search for it in vain; you will not find it. Would it not be absurd, in fact, if here, in 1829, I should pretend to show the truth, finally discovered, in this point of time and space, which had escaped three thousand years of fruitless researches, and so many generations of men of genius? The pretension is insane, and every philosophy which is thus presented is a philosophy which it is easy

---

* 1st Series, *passim.*

to confound, even before having heard the revelations which it promises. If, on the contrary, under all errors, there is in the history of philosophy as well as in the human mind, a philosophy always subsisting, always ancient and always new, it is only necessary to re-collect it. It is necessary to elevate the true side of all the systems which the history of philosophy contains, to put it in harmony with the true side of all the points of view of the human mind, to collect and offer to men that which they know already but confusedly, that which is in philosophers but in fragments, and, as it were, in shreds, that which has belonged to all time, that which will always be, but everywhere and always more or less mixed, altered, corrupted by the movement of time and human things, by the feebleness of reflection, and the systematic illusions of genius.

Such, you know, is the end of all my labors; this history of the philosophy of the eighteenth century will therefore be, properly speaking, a course of philosophy under the form of the history of philosophy, in the limits of a single epoch, an epoch which is greatest and most recent. I shall end, and wish to end, at theoretical conclusions; but these conclusions will be nothing else than the elevation and reunion of all the truths which have been put into the world, and expanded in the world by the four great schools of the eighteenth century. Every great epoch of the history of philosophy has, thus to speak, a clear result, which is composed of all the errors and all the truths which are due to this epoch: such is the legacy which it bequeathes to the epoch which follows it. The eighteenth century, also, has its clear result; it has a legacy to bequeath to the nineteenth century. I accept this legacy with gratitude, but without binding myself to discharge its obligations; I wish to clear it from dross, and present it thus to the rising generation, as its patrimony, and the foundation upon which it should work.

You comprehend the reach of the philosophical and historical enterprise which I propose to execute with you and before you. The end is good, I believe, but the route will be long; neither in a few months, nor in a year, shall we be able to arrive at its termination. It is important, therefore, that we should take the first steps as soon as possible, and I shall take up, in the coming lecture, the first great school which offers itself to us in the eighteenth century, to wit, the sensualistic school.

LECTURE XIV.

SENSUALISTIC SCHOOL IN THE EIGHTEENTH CENTURY.

Subject of this Lecture: Review of the different systems of the sensualistic school in Europe during the eighteenth century, in England, France, and Germany.—That, even for the sake of fidelity, the historian should attach himself to the most celebrated systems.—In what order must they be studied? Ethnographical method. Three objections: 1st, arbitrary; 2d, shows not the concatenation, the reciprocal action of systems; 3d, unfavorable to scientific instruction.—Of the true method of its characters: To follow at once the dates of systems, their reciprocal dependence, and the analogy of subjects.—To commence with the metaphysicians and Locke.

The last lecture gave you the general classification of the systems which fill up the philosophy of the eighteenth century. We reduced these systems so diverse and so numerous to four schools; we determined the order in which these four schools have appeared, and consequently the order in which it is necessary to reproduce them. It is the sensualistic school which precedes the others: we will therefore examine it first.

But this school is vast; it embraces several nations and many systems! Where shall we commence? Observe that it is not I that detains you some time yet upon this preliminary question; it is method itself, method, which checks the natural impetuosity of thought, and condemns it to undertake nothing of which it has not rendered to itself a strict account. It is the peculiarity of nascent philosophy to let itself be carried away by its object, to precipitate itself at first into every route that is offered to it; but it is the character of a more advanced philosophy to borrow from reflection the motives of all its proceedings, and to set out upon no route without having wholly measured it, without having recognized its point of departure and its issue. Thus, as we have not approached the eighteenth century at hazard, and as we have commenced by searching out the order in which we should study the different schools of which it is composed, so we cannot approach at venture the sensualistic school; before engaging in it, it is necessary to search out also the order in which we should study the different systems which this school contains.

But we cannot classify systems of which we have not the least idea; it is, therefore, necessary to commence by a kind of recognition, by a rapid review, of all the monuments of the sensualistic school of the eighteenth century. Surely I ought not, neither do I wish to, enter into any detail, for I should anticipate the extended lectures which are to follow; I only wish to cite for you some proper names, some titles of works, and some dates; but, finally, these proper names, these titles, these dates are absolutely necessary in order that we may be able to find our way in the world where we are now taking the first steps. I am about to designate to you nearly all the phenomena which it is necessary to classify and to distribute into a convenient order.

Locke is the father of the sensualistic school of the eighteenth century; placed between the seventeenth and eighteenth centuries, he forms the transition from one to the other; he is the last term of the sensualistic school of the seventeenth century, and the first term of the sensualistic school of the eighteenth. In fact, run over all the sensualistic philosophers of the eighteenth century, there is not one who does not invoke the authority of Locke; and I do not speak merely of metaphysicians, but of moralists, publicists, and critics. Locke is the chief, the avowed master of the sensualistic school of the last century. Behold now the disciples and the representatives of this school.

In England, without speaking of Collins, Dodwell, and Mandeville,* whom you know, we find, somewhat later, David Hartley, with his *Observations on Man*.† It is the first attempt to join

---

* See, in the preceding volume, the 12th Lecture, and in Vol. 3 of the 1st Series, Lecture 2, p. 79.

† David Hartley, a physician, born in 1704, died in 1757. He published:

the study of intellectual man to that of physical man. The author of *Zoonomy** follows the work of Hartley. Contemporaneous with Darwin, Priestley, so well known as a physical philosopher, travelled in the same route and left a great number of works, the most celebrated of which is the treatise on *Matter and Spirit*,† in which he identifies spirit and matter. He combats the Scotch school; he is also a theologian, a heterodox theologian, as you would suppose; finally, he is a hardy publicist. He died in 1804. Horne Tooke, so famous for his political adventures, applied to grammar‡ the general principles of the English sensualistic school. He died in 1812. There come in course two publicists, who are still living, Godwin, the author of *Political Justice*;§ and Bentham, who is now the great representative of the sensualistic political school of all Europe: his age, his renown, his foreign character, give us, I think, the right to occupy ourselves with a philosopher who belongs to history.‖

Observations on Man, his Frame, his Duty, and his Expectations, London, 1749, in-8. The best edition, with the notes and additions of Pistorious, translated into English, is that of London, 1791, 3 vol. This edition has been several times reprinted. There is a French translation, by the Abbé Jurain, 2 vol., Rheims, 1755. Priestley gave a posthumous work of Hartley, entitled: *Theory of Human Mind*, London, 1775, not translated.

* It has been translated into French, Gand, 4 vol. in-8, 1810–1812.

† Principal works of Dr. Priestley: *An Examination of Dr. Reid's Inquiry into the Human Mind, Dr. Beattie's Essay on the Nature and Immutability of Truth, and Dr. Oswald's Appeal to Common Sense*, London, 1774.—*Letters on Materialism and Hartley's Theory of the Human Mind*, London, 1776.—*Disquisitions relating to Matter and Spirit*, London, 1777.—*The Doctrine of Philosophical Necessity Illustrated*, etc., London, 1777.—*Three Dissertations on the Doctrine of Materialism and Philosophical Necessity*, London, 1778.—*Letters to a Philosophical Unbeliever containing an examination of the principal objections to the doctrines of Natural Religion, and especially those contained in the writings of Mr. Hume*, Bath, 1780.—*Additional Letters*, 1781–1787.—*A continuation of the Letters*, 1794.—His discourses on History and Politics have been translated into French, Paris, 4th year of the republic, 2 vol. in-8.

‡ In his work entitled: Ἔπεα πτερόεντα, or *Diversions on Purley*, 1786, Vol. 1st; the second appeared in 1805.

§ *Inquiry concerning Political Justice*, 2d edition, London, 1796, 2 vol. Godwin is celebrated for his romance of *Caleb Williams*.

‖ We did not dare to take this liberty in 1819, 1st Series, Vol. 3, p. 7.

If we pass into France, we there find at the head of the movement which is made on every hand towards the middle of the eighteenth century, Condillac, whose numerous works are known to you.* He applied his principles to all parts of philosophy; but he excels as a metaphysician. He died in 1780. We cannot speak of the eighteenth century in France without mentioning Diderot and the *Encyclopédie;* for the *Encyclopédie* is the monument which best represents the eighteenth century among us, with all its grandeur and its hardihood, and with all its irregularities. Diderot is especially remarkable for his ideas on the theory of the fine arts; he is a paradoxical and enthusiastic critic.† Helvetius‡ died, it is true, in 1771, that is, before Condillac; but the work *de l'Esprit* is several years posterior to the first writings of Condillac. The book *de l'Esprit* appeared in 1758, whilst the *Essai sur l'Origine des Connaissances Humaines* belongs to 1746, the *Traité des Systèmes* to 1749, and the *Traité des Sensations* to 1754; so that it is impossible not to place Helvetius after Condillac, although he died before him; for it is less the date of their death than that of their works which constitutes the age of philosophers. After Helvetius comes Saint-Lambert,§ whose *Catechism of Universal Morality* obtained the honor in the competition for prizes at the commencement of this century. Saint-Lambert died in 1803. You can place at nearly the same epoch, Condorcet, Dupuis, and Cabanis. Condorcet belongs to the history of philosophy on account of his *Sketch of the Progress of the Human Mind.*‖ He died prematurely, in 1794. Dupuis, whose work on the *Origin of Worships* is so widely circulated, died in 1809. Cabanis, who played in France, with his *Relations between the Physical Con-*

---

* First Series, Vol. 3, Lectures 2 and 3.

† First Series, Vol. 2, Lectures 15 and 16, p. 204; Vol. 3, *Discours d'Ouverture*, p. 6.

‡ First Series, Vol. 3, Lectures 4 and 5.

§ First Series, Vol. 3, Lecture 6.

‖ See Vol. 1 of this Series, Lecture 11.

stitution and Morality, nearly the same part which Hartley and Darwin played in England, died in 1808. Volney, author of the *Ruins*, died a few years since; Gall, quite recently. To this list I might, I should perhaps, but I shall not dare to do it, add a man who, by his age, belongs to this generation of celebrated men, rather than to the century and the movement in which we are; the respectable old man who, by the elevation and goodness of his character, by the vigor of his thought and the lucidness of his style, is now among us the most faithful and complete representative of the sensualistic school of the eighteenth century: you are all thinking of our compatriot so justly and so generally esteemed, M. Destutt de Tracy.

In Germany, without speaking of some fine minds, whether French* or German, belonging to the court of Frederic, the sensualistic school gives us Feder, a distinguished professor of the University of Gottingen, who preceded the revolution of Kant and survived† it; Tittel, his disciple,‡ Weisshaupt,§ and several other metaphysicians or logicians who belong to the school of Locke, and of whom the best known are Herder and Tiedemann. Herder has written much against Kant; but the work to which his name is attached is the *Philosophy of the History of Humanity.*‖ Tiedemann has served the sensualistic school by a multitude of theoretical and historical writings, especially by his *Spirit of Speculative Philosophy.*¶

If you will consider the other parts of Europe, you will find for the school which occupies us, scarcely more than two names

---

* For example, La Methrie, born in 1709, died in 1751. His principal works are: *l'Homme Machine*, 1748, and *l'Homme Plante*, 1748. His works have been collected in 2 vol. in-8. Amsterdam, 1753–1764.

† Born in 1740, died in 1821. *Institutiones Logicæ et Metaphysicæ*, 1777.—*On Time and Space as serving for the examination of the Philosophy of Kant* (German), 1787, etc.

‡ *Of the Forms of Thought, or Categories of Kant* (German), 1788, etc.

§ *Doubts in regard to the doctrine of Kant, on the subject of Space and Time* (German), 1788, etc.

‖ See Vol. 1 of this Series, Lecture 11.

¶ Ibid., Lecture 12.

worthy the attention of history. There is, first, in Italy, Genovesi, of Naples;* his writings retain something of the philosophy of the seventeenth century and of Leibnitz; but Locke predominates in them, and in the end appears there alone. In Switzerland, you have Bonnet, who seems formed in the school of Hartley, a sincerely religious and openly materialistic naturalist and metaphysician, who belongs to the history of philosophy by reason of his *Analytical Essay on the Faculties of the Soul.*†

Such is the list of the names and the systems which fill up the sensualistic school of the eighteenth century: it is upon this list that it is necessary to work. I believe it to be nearly complete, or at least there are wanting to it only names and works of little renown. To each must be accorded the place in history which really belongs to him, that is, we must occupy ourselves only with the men who have advanced science, and have left upon it their trace. Let it, then, be a principle with us that we will give our attention only to the great representatives of the sensualistic school, and that we will leave in obscurity, doubtless mentioning them, but without according to them a lengthy analysis, all those who have done nothing else than to follow beaten paths, and to group themselves around illustrious men, who alone should interest us. This first consideration already reduces our task; it remains to know in what order we should accomplish it; it is necessary to fix this order, under penalty of marching blindly on the route before us.

It seems that we might adopt the order which we have just been following. What have we done? We have run over Europe from nation to nation; we have considered England, then France, then Germany, then Italy and Switzerland: this is what is called the ethnographical order. But to this order we may make three fundamental objections.

---

* Born in 1712, died in 1769.

† Born in 1720, died in 1793. His complete works appeared in 9 vol. in-4, from 1779 to 1783.

At first, it has pleased us to begin with England; but why have we commenced with England, and not with France or Germany? What reason is there for commencing with one nation rather than with another? It will be replied that the choice is not arbitrary, because it is an Englishman, Locke, who is the founder of the whole modern sensualistic school; hence it is necessary to commence with Locke. That is true in regard to Locke; but towards 1750, the principles of Locke are spread through all Europe; they are developed everywhere else as well as in England. For example, after Locke and Hartley, according to the ethnographical order, you should take Darwin and Priestley; but they are no more the disciples of Locke than were Voltaire, Helvetius, and Saint-Lambert, and especially Condillac, who kept himself so near to Locke, and propagated his metaphysics. Moreover, when you shall have exhausted England, with what nation will you continue? Will you go from England to France, or to Germany, or to Switzerland, or to Italy? Will you commence with Condillac, or with Herder, or with Bonnet, or with Genovesi? There is no particular reason for choosing France rather than any other country. Thus, whatever step you take, you cannot escape what is arbitrary.

Behold another impropriety of the ethnographical method. When you start with such or such a country, with England, for example, should you pursue there the entire development of the sensualistic school, and successively run over Locke, Hartley, Darwin, Priestley, Horn Tooke, Godwin, Bentham, before having made known Condillac, Helvetius, Saint-Lambert, etc., you would do nothing less than destroy the real relations of the European systems to each other, and the reciprocal action of these systems upon each other. When Priestley wrote, Condillac had created a lively sensation in Europe; consequently, the mind of Condillac must have had some influence on that of Priestley: if you neglect this relation, you do not make the character, the merit, and true place of Priestley understood. But this remark is much more applicable to Godwin and Bentham, who are disciples of the sensualistic school of France quite as much as of this same school in England. I might multiply examples, but one is sufficient to show that the ethnographical method has the great inconvenience of destroying the natural relations of systems, their order of dependence, and thereby the most general character of European philosophy in the eighteenth century, that is, its unity. In fact, Europe is one in the eighteenth century. That which commences in England is developed in France, reacts upon England, repasses into France, returns again into England, and it is from this action and reaction, and by these perpetual counterstrokes, that the European philosophy is formed. This concatenation is the very life of history, and, at the same time, it is the light of history, for it alone teaches causes from effects and effects from causes; where this relation of cause to effect, this progressive order, this logic of events does not exist, there are many materials for history, but there is no real history.

The ethnological order does more, it objects that from history there should spring any scientific result. You commence with England, and you meet at first the father of the English school, Locke. Locke is a metaphysician. You will, in course, meet Hartley, Darwin, Priestley, who are, properly speaking, physiologists; you, therefore, lose sight of metaphysics, in order to plunge into physiology. Then you pass to Horn Tooke, who is a grammarian, and you leave physiology as you have just left metaphysics. Finally, you arrive at Bentham, who is a publicist, and you are separated at once from metaphysics, and physiology, and grammar. In going from England into France, you find Condillac, with whom you resume your metaphysical studies, soon to abandon them, and to take up your studies of politics and morals with Helvetius and Saint-Lambert. You therefore traverse the same interruptions which had at each step broken the chain of your studies in England. They await you in Germany. You continually abandon one subject for another, then this second in order to return to the first. Now, I ask, what do metaphysics gain, what do morals, æsthetics, all the parts of philosophic science gain, by studies which are begun only to be suspended, and resumed only to be abandoned again? It is impossible thus to acquire any thing else than a superficial and incomplete instruction, and the history of philosophy thus studied, entirely fails of its highest aim, which is the advancement and the formation of science.

Such are the three objections which, in my opinion, do not permit us to think of adopting the ethnographical method. We must, therefore, find a method which may be free from these objections: 1st, a method which may not be arbitrary; 2d, which shows the connection of systems; 3d, which sheds a true light upon each one of the sciences of which history is composed.

Against the peril of what is arbitrary we shall employ chronology. There is nothing less arbitrary than figures and dates. By taking successively all systems in chronological order throughout Europe, you take an order which is that of reality itself; you do not put yourselves in the place of history, you take history such as it has been made. Under this relation, the chronological method is that which we should adopt; but this alone would not suffice, and it is necessary to fertilize and elucidate the chronological order by joining to it that of the reciprocal independence of systems. As soon as a system is given with its date (and we here suppose a system capable of exercising some influence in Europe, for otherwise it would not belong to history), we ought to search out what are the effects of this system, that is, what are the systems which it directly or indirectly engenders, and which are joined to it, whether as reproducing it, or as combating it. We must not here confine ourselves to such or such a country; all Europe must be given as a theatre. Wherever the effect of a cause may appear, it must there be pursued, and this effect must be related to its cause; if the cause is in England and the effect in Germany, we must go from England to Germany in order to proceed in course, if it is necessary, from Germany to Italy, or to return to England. We have no jurisdiction over reality; and if being produced by each other from end to end of Europe is a real character of philosophic systems in the eighteenth century, it is the duty of history to retrace this movement and this connection. In the drama of the European philosophy of the eighteenth century, unity of place is of no consequence; we must attach ourselves to the unity of action. By uniting the order of the reciprocal dependence of the systems and their chronological order, you will preserve yourselves from what is arbitrary, and thereby from what is incoherent. This is not all; it is still necessary to consider the systems by the analogy of subjects of which they treat. It would be absurd to mix metaphysicians with publicists, moralists with naturalists, historians with critics and grammarians; metaphysicians must be put with metaphysicians, moralists with moralists, grammarians with grammarians, etc.; so that the relation and the combination of all the analogous developments of a science, of metaphysics, for example, in each of the countries of Europe, may give the whole metaphysics of the sensualistic school in Europe in the eighteenth century. I might say as much for morals, for politics, for æsthetics, for grammar. It is in this manner, and in this manner alone, that history can take a scientific character, and that the history of philosophy will become what I wish it to become, a lesson of philosophy.

These three conditions are indeed excellent, provided they are possible, you will say; but can we establish and prefix the dates of these systems, their reciprocal dependence, the analogy of subjects, the chronological order, the historical order, and the scientific order?

I believe so, and an attentive examination demonstrates, in my opinion, that these three orders are intimately connected. At first, you cannot deny that one system, in order to produce another, must have preceded it. This is not all: not only every system precedes that which it produces, but it produces that which it precedes, to speak with some latitude. If we were at an epoch wherein the different nations of Europe might be isolated from each other, it would certainly be possible for a system to appear at London without having any influence upon that which might afterwards appear at Paris. But, once more, Europe was one in the eighteenth century. Rapid and continual communications of every kind, printing and the periodical press, unite England, France, and Germany; and as soon as a system appears in such or such a point of civilized Europe, it is spread and is almost immediately known at the most distant point from that where it first saw the light. There may be thinkers so solitary, or so thoughtful of their originality, that they are ignorant of or undertake to ignore what is going on around them; they are exceptions more or less fortunate; but in general nothing is isolated in Europe in the eighteenth century, and the same year produces a discovery and spreads it from one end of the world to the other. Thus, we say that when a system appears, supposing—and remember this is always hypothesis—that this first system attracts sufficient attention, the systems which shall come afterwards must inevitably attach themselves more or less to it, and sustain with it a relation either of resemblance or opposition. The chronological order is then the condition and the principle of the historical order.

It is the same with the order of subjects. But I shall be asked whether there is an order of subjects. I answer that the different parts of philosophy, metaphysics, morals, æsthetics, grammar, history of philosophy, certainly follow an order in their development. It is impossible to suppose applications before principles. Now in philosophy metaphysics are the principle; all the rest is consequence and application. Metaphysics are evidently the foundation of morals, of æsthetics, of history, of politics. There is even in the different applications of metaphysical principles a certain order the rigor of which must not be exaggerated, but which, nevertheless, is not without reality. For example, in a school, whatever it may be, the history of philosophy can appear only so far as the metaphysics of this school and all the great moral, æsthetical, and political applications shall have been developed. Without this the school in question will not have a measure which can be applied to all systems, and do not expect that it will produce a historian.*

This is what reason says; facts are in accordance with it.

Consult facts and you will see that this necessary order has been everywhere followed. In England, the chronological order gives Locke and metaphysics, then the applications of metaphysics, Hartley, Priestley, Bentham. Try to disarrange the terms of this series; try to put Hartley, Priestley, and Bentham before Locke; you cannot do it; therefore the order of subjects, as I have deduced it from the nature of things, is here realized in the history of English philosophy; it is equally realized in the history of philosophy in France. Do you think of Condorcet, Saint-Lambert, and Helvetius before Condillac? Facts declare, as well as reason, that Condillac came and flourished before them all. It is the same in Germany. Feder died after Herder and after Tiedemann; but Feder, who lived to the most advanced old age, taught the philosophy of Locke at Gottingen, and had formed around him an empirical school with Lossius, Tittel, etc., before Tiedemann and Herder had arrived at the complete development of their historical views. The different parts of philosophy follow in time the same order as in thought; time everywhere only manifests the nature of things: the nature of things and time, theory and history equally give us this same result, that metaphysics precede, that the moral, æsthetical, and political applications follow, and that that which terminates is the regard, the judgment which a completely established school bestows upon the past, that is, history, and particularly the history of philosophy. Therefore the chronological order and the order of subjects are the same. Now, we have seen that the chronological order contains the reciprocal dependence of systems, the historical order; therefore the chronological order, well understood, comprises the other two; thus the harmony of the three

* See the First Vol. of this Series, *Introduction to the History of Philosophy*, Lecture 12.

orders which the true historian should follow, is found to be demonstrated by facts, as well as by the nature of things.

If the historian of the philosophy of the eighteenth century wishes to embrace all the phases of the numerous phenomena which come under his observation, he must consider them at first in their chronological succession; he must then consider them in their reciprocal dependence; finally, he must consider them in their relation with such or such a given subject. And these three points of view, equally necessary, are only three distinct parts of one and the same order, which is the true order, the philosophical spirit applied to history.

This chronological order is, without contradiction, the foundation of history; but employed alone or badly understood, it is not a torch, it gives only insignificant dates, various and more or less interesting expositions, but expositions without unity and without light, in a word, mere chronicles. Chronicles are excellent when they are true, in the infancy of the civilization of nations, when man, without comprehending, and without endeavoring to comprehend what takes place under his eyes, reproduces it with unsophisticated fidelity, and transmits it to future generations. But, at this time, the chronicle, as such, is a real anachronism. History can no longer be a simple literary amusement, addressed to the imagination alone; it should speak to the reason of man. It is not sufficient that it should be a picture; it must be a lesson, and it can be such only so far as it relates effects to causes, and presents facts not only in their chronological succession, but in that concatenation which explains them by each other in deducing them from each other. It is only by this that it can make certain facts, certain systems, comprehensible. Such or such a metaphysical system considered alone, resists the most penetrating attention, and remains obscure. But put this system in relation with those which follow it, and which it has produced, and the scene changes; this obscure mass is elucidated, and is converted into a luminous and fecund principle which reveals to you its nature by its effects, by the systems which are its consequences;

these consequences produce others which develop the first, until, from consequences to consequences and from systems to systems, the power of the principle or the primitive system is exhausted. If, perchance, this system is false, judge of what importance it is to follow it in all its consequences, whose extravagance exposes the view of their principle, which, taken alone, might have escaped your attention. The order of dependence can alone give you this high instruction; and the order of dependence is, doubtless, contained in the chronological order, but it is not the imagination, it is profound reason which can discover it there. Finally, it is not sufficient to show the concatenation of systems among themselves; the history of philosophy would not be true to itself, unless it were a philosophical education. What is the life of an individual, if not his continual education? What is political history, if not a social education? What can be the history of philosophy, if not the education of philosophy? But philosophical education is not accomplished by hastily running over subjects without any connection between them, and over topics that change, and are continually metamorphosed under the eye which considers them. It is necessary to dwell upon a large collection of analogous subjects, in order to draw real instruction from them. The analogous order of subjects among themselves should be joined to the order of dependence of systems, which is derived from their succession, from the chronological order, the necessary base and efficacious principle of the other two.

These three points of view will guide us in the history of the sensualistic school of the eighteenth century. I shall scrupulously follow the chronological order; but I shall interpret it by the historical order, by investigation of the filiation and genealogy of systems; and I shall take good care not to separate what the nature of things, what history and dates have brought together; I shall put all the systems of metaphysics with each other, then I shall examine all the important applications of metaphysics to morals, to æsthetics, to society, and I shall terminate as every school terminates, whatever may be its character, by their applications to general history, and to the history of philosophy, which is the crown of all.

In order to be faithful to the order which I have just designated to you, I should commence with the first series of the sensualistic school, that is, with the series of metaphysicians. Locke is at the head of the sensualistic metaphysicians of the eighteenth century: he it was who produced all the others, and who furnished for his successors the very subjects with which they were occupied. With Locke, then, it is necessary to commence. His merited glory, his genius, his immense influence of every kind, command us to study him seriously, and to make him the subject of a profound examination.

LECTURE XV.

LOCKE. HIS LIFE.

Locke: his biography.—Sprang from a liberal family.—His first studies.—Descartes disgusts him with scholasticism.—He pays particular attention to medicine.—He enters into the political world; his friendship with Shaftesbury.—His varied fortunes.—Driven from the University of Oxford.—His refuge in Holland.—Revolution of 1688.—Favor of Locke until his death.—His character: disinterestedness, prudence, firmness, tolerance.—Review of his works.—The *Essay on the Human Understanding.*

Locke is the father of the whole sensualistic school of the eighteenth century. He is, incontestably, in time as well as in genius, the first metaphysician of this school. And, as we have said, morals, æsthetics, politics, are merely applications of metaphysics, applications which are themselves the bases of the history of philosophy. Moreover, Locke was not simply a metaphysician; he himself carried his metaphysics into the science of government, into religion, into political economy: his works of this class have served as a foundation to analogous works of the sensualistic school. In order to understand this school, it is then necessary to have a thorough understanding of the metaphysics of Locke; for this reason I propose to examine him with the most scrupulous care, and at sufficient length.

But before exposing to you the philosophy of Locke, it is important that you should know what was the life and character of this man, who has exercised such a powerful influence over the moral and intellectual destiny of so great a number of his fellow-beings.

John Locke* was born at Wrington, a few leagues distant from

* We have made use of the Life of Locke, written in French, by his intimate friend Leclerc, and inserted in the 4th vol. of the *Bibliothèque Choisie*, 1705; of the Eulogy of Locke by Coste, contained in a letter to the author of

Bristol, in the county of the same name, on the 29th of August, 1632. Very little is known of his family, except that his father was the clerk of a justice of the peace, that he took part in the political troubles of 1640, and even served as a captain in the parliamentary army under Colonel Alexander Popham. Young Locke pursued his first studies in Westminster College, London. Here he remained until the age of nineteen or twenty years, until 1651 or 1652, when he went to the University of Oxford, to the identical Christ's College where, at a later period, he was examiner.

The University of Oxford was then, as it appears to be now, much attached to the cause of the past: and the cause of the past, in philosophy, was then peripatetic scholasticism. A single man turned it aside from this sterile study, and this man was our Descartes, the common master of all the great minds of his times, even the most opposite. Locke, in reading the works of Descartes, admired the perfect clearness of his exposition, without adopting his system; and he became disgusted with the barbarous philosophy that was taught at Oxford; so that Descartes has the honor and the merit of having contributed to the formation of his most redoubtable adversary.* Locke received the degree of Bachelor of Arts in 1655, and that of Master of Arts in 1658. The study to which he applied himself particularly was medicine. He did not take the degree of doctor; nor did he practise, on account of the extreme feebleness of his health; neither had he any professorship; but procured at Christ's College a simple benefice, that is, a title, that of fellow, a prebend without functions. But although he had never practised nor professed medicine, Locke acquired considerable reputation at

---

the *Nouvelles de la Republique des Lettres*, and published in these *Nouvelles*, February, 1705; of the life of Locke in the classical edition of his works; finally, of the excellent chapter of Dugald Stewart on Locke, in his preliminary discourse in the ENCYCLOPÆDIA BRITANNICA, *On the progress of metaphysical and moral sciences in Europe after the revival of letters.*

* This curious fact is attested to by Leclerc, who declares that he received it himself from Locke. Dugald Stewart has repeated it.

Oxford, if we may judge by the testimony of one of the most skilful practitioners of that period, Sydenham, who in the dedication of his *Observations* on Acute Diseases,* congratulates himself on the approbation of Locke. Such were his occupations until the year 1664. Observe the nature of these occupations and their influence on the direction of the mind. The study of medicine supposes that of the physical and natural sciences; it develops the taste and the talent for observation, and, in this respect, it may be said that the study of medicine is an excellent preparation for metaphysics; but, it must be added, for a well-formed mind,† for when we are continually surveying phenomena of organic life, it is easy, it is natural to be surprised and carried away by the appearance, and to confound with these phenomena other phenomena which are very different; and I pray you not to forget that, in fact, in the review which I have presented to you of all the philosophical schools, we have seen sensualism and empiricism, as well as skepticism, often proceed from schools of natural philosophers and physicians: call to mind, in antiquity, Sextus Ænesidemus, and more than one successor of Aristotle.

In 1664, Locke accompanied William Swan, as secretary, to the Court of Berlin. At the end of one year he returned to Oxford, and it was there, in 1666, at the age of thirty-four years, that he made an acquaintance which decided his destiny. Ashley Cooper, afterwards Earl of Shaftesbury, having come to Oxford for his health, was introduced to Locke; and after having consulted him as a physician, he became attached to him as a friend, and never did they separate. Locke shared the prosperity of his friend, but he also shared his adversity; he joined him in his exile, he closed his eyes in a foreign land, and he undertook, at a later period, to write his life and vindicate his memory.

Who was Shaftesbury? History seems to point him out as a man of strong mind, without settled convictions, as an ambitious

---

* Published in 1676.

† In regard to this, see Dugald Stewart, discourse already cited.

politician, who more than once changed his position, but an ambitious person of great talent, and even of great character. A strange friend for a philosopher! I give you this opinion as that of historians, and not as my own; I have not sufficiently studied the affairs of this period to pass a safe opinion on the men who took part in it. I know that in these revolutionary times the same end was often pursued by the most different ways; I find no essential contradiction in all the changes with which Shaftesbury is reproached; it is possible that, under the appearance of intrigue, and with intrigue itself, there was in him a sincere patriotism, and I confess that the friendship and high esteem of a man as sensible and as virtuous as Locke, protect, in my opinion, the doubtful memory of this ardent and uneasy statesman, at one time engaged with Lord Falkland in the party of the court, then united with that of the parliament, afterwards lending a hand in the re-establishment of Charles II., and minister of this prince; finally, conspiring perhaps against him, and leaving his country to die in Holland.

Ashley drew the young physician from the peaceful solitude of Oxford, and placed him in the brilliant circles of London. Locke there became connected with the most important personages, Lord Halifax, the Duke of Buckingham, and the Earl of Northumberland, whom he accompanied to France in 1668. A few years after, in 1674, having gone to Montpelier for his health, which had always been very delicate, he made the acquaintance of Lord Herbert, Earl of Pembroke, to whom he afterwards dedicated his great work on the *Human Understanding.*

On returning from Montpelier, he passed through Paris and formed connections with some of the learned men, and, among others, with the traveller Bernier, the Calvinist Justel, who afterwards, being obliged to quit France, became a bookseller to the King of England, and with the antiquary Toinard, with whom he held a regular* correspondence during all his life.

* A great part of this unpublished correspondence is in the hands of M. Brunet, the learned author of the *Manuel du Libraire.*

Ashley was one of the eight lords to whom Charles II. conceded the territory of Carolina. These eight proprietors applied to Locke for a constitution, and it appears that this constitution, which I have not read, was much more favorable to the rights of the proprietors than to those of the inhabitants, since in 1719 the inhabitants demanded the repeal of this constitution which had been given to them by the liberal Ashley and the philosopher Locke, and besought the crown to take them again under its immediate authority. In 1668 Locke was named member of the Royal Society of Sciences. In 1672, Ashley having been made Earl of Shaftesbury, and having been elevated to the dignity of Lord Chancellor of England, gave to Locke an important office, that of secretary of presentations. A ministerial revolution in 1673 deprived the minister of his office, and the philosopher of his situation. In 1679 Shaftesbury was again restored to favor, and his renewed favor was shared by the philosopher; finally, renewed disgrace fell upon them both, more severely, too, than before, and much more prolonged. The Earl of Shaftesbury, thrown into the ranks of the opposition, was accused of having carried opposition even to faction, was imprisoned, placed in the Tower of London, compelled afterwards to leave England and take refuge in Holland, where he died in 1683. Locke followed him thither and inherited all the hostility of the opposite party. The Court of Charles II. determined that the University of Oxford should dispossess him of his employment in Christ's College; and as Dean Fell made some resistance to this, on the twelfth of November, 1684, a warrant signed *Charles II.* struck Locke from the list of the members of the University of Oxford, without judgment or previous inquest. The hatred of his enemies went still farther. It was the time when the Earl of Monmouth was engaged in foreign conspiracies against the throne of the Stuarts. Locke was implicated in these conspiracies; his extradition* was demanded, and if he had been delivered up, he would

* See Leclerc for the details of this affair.

doubtless have ascended the scaffold and closed his life like Sydney. Fortunately, he had found friends in Holland: he concealed himself, and suffered the storm to pass. Some time after, with some theologians and physicians of Holland, he formed a small philosophical society, which bore its fruit. Among these men were Leclerc, the author of the *Bibliothèque Universelle,* and Limborch, a Protestant minister, a remonstrant and Arminian, men penetrated, like Locke, with the liberal spirit which prevailed in religion and politics. The first efforts of Locke as a writer were there made, his *Methodus Adversariorum,* inserted in the journal of Leclerc, and his letter to Limborch on Toleration,* a veritable manifesto of the persecuted minority. There, too, he completed the great philosophical work which he had undertaken many years before, the work entitled the *Essay on the Human Understanding;* but at first he published a mere abridgment, a sort of prospectus, in the *Bibliothèque Universelle,* of January, 1688.

In the mean time the revolution of 1688 took place. You can easily conceive that Locke, who in his exile had been, as it were, the intellectual chief of the whole persecuted party, received at London in 1689 the most honorable reception. King William accorded to him his entire confidence; and, if his health, and perhaps the modesty of his tastes, had not been opposed to it, Locke would have acquired the highest political fortune. He was offered the appointment of minister to the Court of Vienna or to that of Berlin, or to any other court that he might choose.† He contented himself with a more humble employment, but still one of some importance, first with that of member of the Board of Commissioners of Appeals; afterwards with that of member of the Board of Commissioners of Trade. Besides his great work

---

* The following is the title: *Epistola ad clarissimum virum* T. A. R. P. T. O. L. A., scripta a P. A. P. O. J. L. A.; that is, *Theologiæ apud remonstrantes professorum, tyrannidis osorem, Limburgum, Amstelodunensem, scripta a pacis amico, persecutionis osore, Johanne Lockio, Anglo.*

† See Leclerc.

on the *Human Understanding*, he published several writings which aided powerfully in strengthening and popularizing in England the constitutional government of 1688, that government which conciliates, at the same time, the tutelar power of the crown and the rights of the people; that government which, in the eighteenth century, inspired Montesquieu, and at a later period served as a model for that which sprang from the French Revolution. Locke is therefore in this respect one of the benefactors of humanity. About the year 1700 the condition of his health compelled him to renounce a political career; he retired to Oates, in the county of Essex, to the family of Lady Masham, daughter of the celebrated Doctor Cudworth, an accomplished person and much distinguished for nobility of character and rare qualities of mind. The last years of his life, completely occupied in preparation for death, were passed between the reading of the Holy Scriptures and the services of friendship. Thus he died at the age of seventy-three years, on the 28th of October, 1704.

Such was the life of Locke: let us now examine his character. All his contemporaries, and, what is better, all the known actions of his life testify, that no one was more sincerely and constantly attached to truth, virtue, and the cause of human liberty. He loved and served this noble cause; he even had the honor of suffering for it, but without ever departing from the most perfect moderation. Locke was, in some sort, born a sage. Moderation and cautiousness were, as it were, in his temperament. It may be said that he had something of Socrates, or at least of Franklin, in him. I shall not blame him for having loved his country so much as to be associated with its destinies; but those who would blame a philosopher for having left his solitude, and having mingled in public affairs, cannot deny at least that he therein showed the greatest disinterestedness. In 1700, when on account of his health he resigned his place as one of the Commissioners of Trade, the king wished to continue his salary, which was very considerable,* and at the same time dispense with his

* Coste and Leclerc.

services. Locke refused to receive a salary for a situation which he could not fill.

He was extremely prudent, reserved, and discreet. During the exile of Shaftesbury, and during the violent persecution of the whole liberal party, the enemies of Locke sought diligently for an opportunity to deprive him of his place in Christ's College. The minister, Lord Sunderland, wrote to Dean Fell to obtain information concerning him ; Fell replied :* I have for several years past had my eyes upon him ; but he is so cautious, that I cannot say that there is a person in the college who has heard him utter a single word on politics. . . . Having spoken before him both in public and private against the honor of Lord Shaftesbury, against his party and his designs, he has never, either by word or gesture, manifested the least interest in what was said. There is no man who is so perfectly the master of his passions and of his tongue.

You must not fancy that this prudence arose from pusillanimity. At the death of Charles II., when James II. ascended the throne, William Penn, who, as a philanthropist perhaps, had everywhere secured acquaintances and even favor at the court, offered his quondam fellow-student Locke, to procure for him a pardon. Locke replied, although he was then an exile and in distress, that there was no reason for pardon where there was neither crime nor fault.

But that which I admire most in Locke, that which renders him most particularly dear to me, if I may dare to make use of such an expression, is a quality which, in my opinion, is still better than prudence and firmness, I mean indulgence and tolerance. A learned ecclesiastic of the times, Doctor Lowde, having publicly accused him of enfeebling by his system the distinction between good and evil, Locke, instead of being displeased, exclaimed :† The brave man is right ; it is consistent with his profession

---

* Leclerc.

† *Essay on the Human Understanding*, preface to the second edition.

to take umbrage at such a point, and to be alarmed at expressions which, if considered alone, would be offensive and productive of just suspicions. He showed his philosophical toleration on a more important occasion, and of which I will speak.

Newton, although a good natural philosopher, was not at all materialistic; perceiving at once the consequences of the system of Locke, he became alarmed. He took him for a partisan of Hobbes, which was doing him a very great injustice. He even conceived suspicions of the honesty of Locke; and, in a moment of singular humor, learning that Locke was sick and even unlikely to live, he went so far as to say that it would be well if he were already dead. This speech is relieved of its cruelty by the perfect candor with which Newton himself confessed it to Locke, asking at the same time his pardon. "Pardon me, I pray you," said he, "for this want of charity." The letter is signed "*Your very humble and very unfortunate servant, Isaac Newton. September*, 1693." I cannot forego the pleasure of reading to you the reply of Locke; it was published for the first time by Dugald Stewart.* It breathes, as Dugald Stewart well observes, a true philosophical magnanimity, and a genuine kindness.

OATES, Oct. 5th, '93.

SIR:—I have been ever since I first knew you, so entirely and sincerely your friend, and thought you so much mine, that I could not have believed what you tell me of yourself, had I had it from anybody else. And though I cannot but be mightily troubled that you should have had so many wrong and unjust thoughts of me, yet next to the return of good offices, such as from a sincere good-will I have ever done you, I receive your acknowledgment of the contrary as the kindest thing you could have done me, since it gives me hopes that I have not lost a friend I so much valued. After what your letter expresses, I shall not need to say any thing to justify myself to you. I shall

* *Discourse*, etc., Vol. 2, p. 75.

always think your own reflection on my carriage, both to you and to all mankind, will sufficiently do that. Instead of that, give me leave to assure you, that I am more ready to forgive you than you can be to desire it; and I do it so freely and fully, that I wish for nothing more than the opportunity to convince you that I truly love and esteem you; and that I have still the same good-will for you as if nothing of this had happened. To confirm this to you more fully, I should be glad to meet you anywhere, and the rather, because the conclusion of your letter makes me apprehend it would not be wholly useless to you. But whether you think it fit or not, I leave wholly to you. I shall always be ready to serve you to my utmost, in any way you shall like, and shall only need your commands or permission to do it.

"My book is going to the press for a second edition; and though I can answer for the design with which I writ it, yet since you have so opportunely given me notice of what you have said of it, I shall take it as a favor, if you would point out to me the places that gave occasion to that censure, that by explaining myself better, I may avoid being mistaken by others, or unawares doing the least prejudice to truth or virtue. I am sure you are so much a friend to them both that were you none to me, I could expect this from you. But I cannot doubt that you would do a great deal more than this for my sake, who after all have all the concern of a friend for you, wish you extremely well, and am, without compliment, etc."

It remains to me to speak of the works of Locke. But I will simply mention the titles of these works, that I may speedily arrive at that which must be for us a subject of long examination. The first work of Locke is a small Latin essay, entitled *Methodus Adversariorum*, that is, a model of the manner to be employed in preparation of collections and arrangements of extracts obtained in reading, translated into French and published for the first time in the *Bibliothèque Universelle*, July, 1686, Vol. ii., p. 315;

the second is the famous letter to Limborch on Toleration, of which we have already spoken, and which was also translated into French and inserted into the *Bibliothèque* in 1688. It was in 1690 that the *Essay on the Human Understanding* appeared in London. The same year Locke published the *Essay on Civil Government.* The aim of this *Essay* was to reply to the partisans of the Stuarts, who accused the new dynasty of usurpation. Locke endeavors to show that the legitimacy of a government rests on the sanction of the people; whence it follows that the people sanctioning the new dynasty, this dynasty is legitimate. In this work the republican spirit prevails with some monarchical traits. The sovereignty of the people, which was the reigning dogma among the Puritans and Independents of England, among whom Locke had received his first impressions, is the philosophical principle of this treatise, which served as a model to the *Social Contract.* His letters *on Education* (1693) also inspired the *Emile. Reasonable Christianity,* which appeared in 1693, had, like the *Essay on Civil Government,* a particular aim. In order to introduce some toleration and union among all the sects which divided England, it was necessary to seize upon and settle the point which was common to all; and it was precisely this point that Locke tried to establish as the basis itself of Christianity. In short, the book *On Commerce* is, I believe, the starting point of all the analogous works which appeared in the eighteenth century. I do not know a book anterior to that on political economy which produced any sensation in the world. But Locke's true title to glory is his *Essay on the Human Understanding.* It is with this work that I wish to occupy you, contenting myself at present with the consideration of its exterior, before entering into the spirit itself of the work, and submitting it to a close examination.

The *Essay on the Human Understanding* appeared for the first time in London in 1690, in folio form. It had immense success. Many were the causes of it, and above all the celebrity of the author as the friend of religious and political liberty. It was at the period of the revocation of the edict of Nantes; and all those who, throughout Europe, adhered to the proscribed cause, expected and received with the utmost eagerness and with the greatest favor, all the publications of Locke, who, after the appearance of his letter *on Toleration,* was regarded as their representative. Everywhere the liberal minority which was already formed, and which was the basis of the present majority, had their eyes on the writings of Locke. Hence the prodigious success of the *Essay on the Human Understanding;* editions and translations multiplied rapidly. During the life of Locke, four editions were published in England, in 1690, 1694, 1697, and 1700; and in all these editions Locke made considerable alterations: the best chapters, for example that on the *Association of Ideas,* appeared only in the fourth edition. He was preparing a fifth when he died; it appeared in 1705; a tenth edition was published in 1731. Dugald Stewart informs us that he possesses a copy of the thirteenth edition, of 1748. What contributed especially to spread the *Essay on the Human Understanding,* was the French translation of Coste. The French was becoming the universal language of Europe. This translation, made in 1700, during the life of Locke, passed through five editions, between the years 1700 and 1750. Wynne, bishop of Saint Asaph, published an English extract from the original work, which was translated into French by Bosset, in 1720.* There are three Latin translations: one which appeared in London in 1701,† reprinted at Leipsic in 1709, and again reprinted at Amsterdam in 1729; the best is that of Thiele, Leipsic, 1731. There are many Dutch and German translations.‡ Finally, a version in modern Greek was published in Venice in 1796.

Nothing was opposed to the success of Locke except the anger of the enemies of all political and religious liberty. The Univer-

---

* Reprinted at Geneva in 1738.

† In fol., with a portrait of Locke.

‡ Three German translations, that of Poleyen, 1727, of Tittel, in 1791, and of Tennemann in 1797

sity of Oxford proscribed his work, as it had proscribed his person. It was agreed in an assembly that if a public manifesto was not made against the *Essay on the Human Understanding*, all the professors would unite in closing their doors upon him.

What, then, is this work which from its origin attracted the admiration of some and the criticism of others? As I have before said, I mean to consider it here simply in its exterior. The general composition partakes of the agitated life of its author. It is needless to look in it for the rigorous connection and unity of the *Meditations* of Descartes. The *Essay on the Human Understanding* has two grave defects: first, it contains innumerable repetitions; then it has considerable variations and contradictions; it is therefore necessary to adhere to the general spirit of the book, and with this spirit to interpret the contradictory passages, to neglect the inconsistencies of detail, and to consider especially the basis and scope of the work, for herein is the system of the author.

In regard to style, it is generally agreed that the prose of Locke is the best of his times; and it requires no great knowledge of the English to perceive in it the manners of a man who has lived in the best society, and who expresses his thoughts without pedantry, in the most clear, most simple, and most familiar terms. There is a certain mundane spirit spread throughout the book which has contributed not a little to its success. Dugald Stewart remarks,* that if the style of the *Essay* has grown somewhat antique, it still preserves a certain ease and elegance which gives us an idea of the fine conversations in which the friend of Ashley must have taken part. I need not tell you that the eminent characteristic of this style is clearness. In order to obtain it Locke prolongs his developments beyond measure; he presents the same thought under an infinite variety

---

* *Discourse*, Vol. ii., p. 19. See also the opinion of Shaftesbury, *First Letter to a Young Gentleman who is Studying at the University*. Mackintosh cites several pieces from Book ii., chap. x., as remarkable for the beauty of its developments.

of forms, as if he wished that this thought might, by some means, be introduced into every mind. Precision is doubtless true clearness, but it is the clearness of the strong; a little diffuseness is necessary for the weak, who, saving error, are destined yet to make a large majority, even among philosophers.

At our next meeting, I shall enter into a philosophical examination of the *Essay on the Human Understanding.*

ADDITION

TO THE LECTURE ON THE LIFE OF LOCKE.

Almost at the same time that this Lecture was published, Lord King published a *Life of John Locke, with Extracts from his Correspondence, Journals, and Common-place Books,* two volumes in-8, London, 1829; second edition, London, 1830. After the death of Locke all his papers fell into the hands of Sir Peter King, his nearest relation and his executor. These consisted of the originals of several of his works already printed, some unpublished manuscripts, an extensive correspondence with several friends in England and abroad, the Journal of Locke's travels in France and in Holland, finally some small books in which he deposited his notes and recollections. These papers were religiously preserved in the family of King, and from them the inheritor and last head of this family, Lord King, has drawn a new life of Locke founded on authentic documents; this life confirms and develops that written by Leclerc. We will extract a few passages for the purpose of elucidating and enriching our lecture.

William Swan is the name applied by Leclerc and other biographers, to the envoy of the King of England at the German Court, whom Locke accompanied as secretary in 1664. Lord King calls him Vane, an illustrious name in the constitutional history of England. When Locke returned to England, it seems certain, according to several letters cited by Lord King, that he was invited to proceed to Spain, as an attaché to the English legation. He refused the mission thus offered to him.

It was at Oxford, in 1670, that he undertook the *Essay on the Human Understanding*. It appears that he finished it in 1671, for Lord King declares that he has in his possession a copy dated 1671, by Locke's own hand; and the first sketch of this work may be found in his Common-place Book, with this commencement: "Sic cogitavit de intellectu humano Johannes Locke, ann. 1671." Locke did not publish it until eighteen years after, in 1690, and during this long interval, he made considerable corrections and alterations in it.

We cannot read, without interest, the Journal of his travels in France, and his opinions upon various things. It is France of the seventeenth century seen by the eyes of a liberal of our own times. Lord King merely gives fragments of this Journal; I could wish that he had published it entire. The travels of Locke on the Continent continued four years, from December, 1675, to the month of May, 1679.

Lord King throws light especially upon the persecutions which Locke endured during the years which preceded the Revolution of 1688. All the trickery which was used in 1684 on account of his benefice at Christ's College, Oxford, are exposed in the greatest detail. Lord King cites a very fine passage from the history of Fox in regard to this affair. He cites also a work of Lord Grenville, entitled *Oxford and Locke*. The following is the entire correspondence between the minister and chief of the college to which Locke was attached, Dean Fell, bishop of Oxford:

To the Lord Bishop of Oxford.

"WHITEHALL, Nov. 6, 1684.

"MY LORD—The King being given to understand that one Mr. Locke, who belonged to the late Earl of Shaftesbury, and has upon several occasions behaved himself very factiously and undutifully to the Government, is a student of Christ's College; his Majesty commands me to signify to your Lordship, that he would have him removed from being a student, and that, in order thereunto, your Lordship would let me know the method of doing it.

"I am, my Lord, &c.,

"SUNDERLAND."

To the Right Hon. the Earl of Sunderland, Principal Secretary of State.

"Nov. 8, 1684.

"RIGHT HON.—I have received the honor of your Lordship's letter, wherein you are pleased to inquire concerning Mr. Locke's being a student of this house, of which I have this account to render: that he being, as your Lordship is truly informed, a person who was much trusted by the late Earl of Shaftesbury, and who is suspected to be ill affected to the Government, I have for divers years had an eye upon him, but so close has his guard been on himself, that after several strict inquiries, I may confidently affirm there is not any one in the college, however familiar with him, who has heard him speak a word either against, or so much as concerning the Government; and although very frequently, both in public and in private, discourses have been purposely introduced, to the disparagement of his master, the Earl of Shaftesbury, his party, and designs, he could never be provoked to take any notice, or discover in word or look the least concern; so that I believe there is not in the world such a master of taciturnity and passion. He has here a physician's place, which frees him from the exercise of the college, and the obligation which others have to residence in it, and he is now abroad upon want of health; but notwithstanding that, I have summoned him to return home, which is done with this prospect, that if he comes not back, he will be liable to expulsion for contumacy; if he does, he will be answerable to your Lordship for what he shall be found to have done amiss; it being probable that though he may have been thus cautious here, where he knew himself to be suspected, he has laid himself more open in London, where a general liberty of speaking was used, and where the execrable designs against his Majesty, and his Government, were managed and pursued. If he does not return by the first day of January next, which is the time limited to him, I shall be enabled of course to proceed against him to expulsion. But if this method seem not effectual or speedy enough, and his Majesty, our founder and visitor, shall please to command his immediate remove, upon the receipt thereof, directed to the dean and chapter, it shall accordingly be executed by,

"My Lord, your Lordship's

"Most humble and obedient servant,

"J. OXON."

To the Bishop of Oxford.

"WHITEHALL, Nov. 10, 1684.

"MY LORD—Having communicated your Lordship's of the 8th to his Majesty, he has thought fit to direct me to send you the inclosed, concerning his commands for the immediate expulsion of Mr. Locke.

"SUNDERLAND."

To the Right Reverend Father in God, John, Lord Bishop of Oxon, Dean of Christ Church, and our trusty and well-beloved the Chapter there.

"Right Reverend Father in God, and trusty and well-beloved, we greet you well. Whereas we have received information of the factious and disloyal behavior of Locke, one of the students of that our college; we have thought fit hereby to signify our will and pleasure to you, that you forthwith remove him from his student's place, and deprive him of all the rights and advantages thereunto belonging, for which this shall be your warrant; and so we bid you heartily farewell. Given at our court at Whitehall, 11th day of November, 1684.

"By his Majesty's command,

"SUNDERLAND."

To the Right Hon. the Earl of Sunderland, Principal Secretary of State.

"November 16, 1684.

"RIGHT HON.—I hold myself bound in duty to signify to your Lordship, that his Majesty's command for the expulsion of Mr. Locke from the college is fully executed.

"J. OXON."

To the Bishop of Oxon.

"MY LORD—I have received your Lordship's of the 16th, and have acquainted his Majesty therewith, who is well satisfied with the college's ready obedience to his commands for the expulsion of Mr. Locke.

"SUNDERLAND."

Lord King shows still more the extreme weakness, not to say the baseness of Fell, in publishing from time to time several letters in which he calls Locke his *esteemed friend*, his *affectionate friend*. It is lamentable to be obliged to confess that Fell was a learned man, author of an excellent edition of Cyprian.

Lord King published, for the first time, the memoir presented by the English minister at Haye to the States-General, in the name of his government, to obtain the extradition of several persons, among whom was Locke, under the title of Secretary to the last Earl of Shaftesbury.

Leclerc has related the offer which William Penn made to Locke to procure his pardon from the king. The Earl of Pembroke, whom he knew at Montpellier, was equally interested in his behalf, and did not cease to give him marks of his high esteem and affection. It was in remembrance of this conduct that Locke dedicated to Lord Pembroke his *Essay on the Human Understanding.*

In Vol. i. p. 357, is a letter of Mr. Tyrrell to Locke, wherein he informs him of the following facts: all the heads of the University of Oxford had united and proposed to enjoin upon all the tutors not to read to their pupils the *Essay on the Human Understanding*, and the philosophy of Leclerc. This resolution was like, at first, to have passed, but Dr. Dunstan remarked that in proscribing these books they would but excite the curiosity of the pupils. At another meeting they resolved that instead of proscribing these books, that all the heads of the houses should give the tutors private instructions not to read those books to their pupils, and to prevent their doing it by themselves, as much as lay in their power.

In reading this letter, Locke might have been reminded that in the journal of his travels in France, he wrote these words under date of March 22, 1676: "The new philosophy of Descartes prohibited to be taught in the universities, schools, and academies."

Pages 388–434, may be found different letters of Newton, among which is the extraordinary letter to which Locke made such an admirable reply. This letter of Newton must be attributed to the disordered state of mind in which this great man had fallen. It is of the 16th September, 1693. It must be observed especially with what candor Newton confesses and asks pardon for his evil thoughts. This candor is his own; the rest is his disorder. So when he received Locke's letter, he could not even remember what had occasioned it. He answers from Cambridge, the 5th of October: "Sir, the last winter, by sleeping too often by my fire, I got an ill habit of sleeping; and a distemper, which this summer has been epidemical, put me farther out of order,*

* In regard to the undeniable derangement of Newton, see in the *Universal Biography*, the article of M. Biot, and the articles of the same ingenious and skilful writer, *Journal des Savants*, June, 1832, and May, 1834.

so that when I wrote to you, I had not slept an hour a night for a fortnight together, and for five nights together not a wink. I remember I wrote to you, but what I said of your book I remember not. If you please to send me a transcript of that passage, I will give you an account of it if I can. I am your most humble servant, Is. Newton." Locke did not preserve any remembrance of this affair, and throughout all his correspondence was ready to yield homage to the genius of Newton. On page 39 of the second volume, in a letter to his cousin, Peter King, afterwards Lord Chancellor, and which is dated the 30th of April, 1703, may be found the following lines, which prove what reputation Newton enjoyed as a theologian: "Mr. Newton is really a very valuable man, not only for his wonderful skill in mathematics, but in divinity too, and his great knowledge in the Scriptures, wherein I know few his equals."

Among the philosophical pieces published for the first time by Lord King, there are some truly precious. We will mention particularly, 1st vol. p. 134, a few pages dated in the year 1696, and which are an examination of the Cartesian proof of the existence of God, deduced from the idea of a necessary being. Locke rejects this proof, which, for our part, we regard as excellent, though very incomplete. We think that this fragment should be translated and referred to that part of the *Essay on the Human Understanding*, where Locke himself produces his proof of the existence of God. This fragment is posterior and very superior to the passage of the *Essay*.

We will close these extracts by expressing our regrets at not having found in these two volumes more details in regard to the intimate friendship between Locke and Lady Masham, the daughter of Cudworth, with whom he passed the last years of his life. It appears that she was a person as remarkable for her mind as she was for the charms of her manners. Several writings attributed to Locke are really by this lady, among others a treatise on divine love, translated into French by Coste, and printed at Amsterdam in 1705. Lord King reproduces the passage from the biography of Leclerc, in which are related the last moments of Locke, and his pious and calm death, as it were in the arms of Lady Masham.

"In October, 1704, his disorder greatly increased: on the 27th of that month, Lady Masham, not finding him in his study as usual, went to his bedside, when he told her that the fatigue of getting up the day before had been too much for his strength, and that he never expected to rise again from his bed. He said that he had now finished his career in this world, and that in all probability he should not outlive the night, certainly not be able to survive beyond the next day or two. After taking some refreshment, he said to those present that he wished them all happiness after he was gone. To Lady Masham, who remained with him, he said that he thanked God he had passed a happy life, but that now he found that all was vanity, and exhorted her to consider this world only as a preparation for a better state hereafter. He would not suffer her to sit up with him, saying, that perhaps he might be able to sleep, but if any change should happen, he would send for her. Having no sleep in the night, he was taken out of bed and carried into his study, where he slept for some time in his chair: after waking, he desired to be dressed, and then heard Lady Masham read the Psalms apparently with great attention, until perceiving his end to draw near, he stopped her, and expired a very few minutes afterwards, about three o'clock in the afternoon of the 28th October, in his seventy-third year."

Locke was buried in a small church in the village of High-Laver. On his modest tomb, now in ruins, was placed this epitaph, which he himself had composed:

Hic juxta situs est
JOANNES LOCKIUS.
Si qualis fuerit rogas,
Mediocritate sua contentum
Se vixisse respondet.
Litteris innutritus eousque

Tantum profecit
Ut veritati unice litaret.
Hoc ex scriptis ejus disce,
Quæ quod de eo reliquum est
Majori fide tibe exhibebunt,
Quam epitaphii suspecta elogia.
Virtutes si quas habuit,
Minores sane quam sibi laudi
Duceret,
Tibi in exemplum proponeret:
Vitia una sepeliantur.
Morum exemplum si quæras,
Tu Evangelia habes,
Vitiorum utinam nusquam!
Mortalitatis certe (quod prosit)
Hic et ubique.
Natum anno Domini MDCXXXII,
Mortuum XXVIII Octobris MDCCIV.
Memorat hæc tabella
Brevi et ipsa interitura.

LECTURE XVI.*

ESSAY ON THE HUMAN UNDERSTANDING. ITS SPIRIT, ITS METHOD.

General spirit of the *Essay on the Human Understanding*.—Its method: study of the human understanding as the necessary foundation of all true philosophy.—Study of the human understanding in its phenomena or ideas.—Division of inquiries with respect to ideas, and determination of the order in which these inquiries should be made. To postpone the logical and on tological question of the truth or falsity of ideas, of the legitimacy or illegitimacy of their application to such or such objects, to adhere to the study of ideas in themselves, and in that to commence by establishing the actual characters of ideas, and then to proceed to the investigation of their origin. —Examination of the method of Locke. Its merit: he postpones and places last the question of the truth or falsity of ideas; its fault: he entirely neglects the question of the actual characters of ideas, and he starts by that of their origin. First error of the method; chances of errors which it involves; general tendency of the school of Locke.

The first question which we shall put in regard to the *Essay on the Human Understanding* is: Upon what authority does it rest in the last analysis? Does the author search for truth at his own risk and peril by the single force of reason, such as it has been given to man, or does he recognize a foreign and superior authority to which he submits, and from which he borrows the motives of his judgments? In fact, this is, you know, the question upon which it is necessary to interrogate at first every philosophical work, in order to determine its most general character, and its place in the history of philosophy, and even in that of civilization. Now, a single glance at the *Essay on the Human Understanding,* is sufficient to show that Locke is a free seeker of truth. Everywhere he addresses himself to reason; he

* The third volume of the 1st Series contains a lecture devoted to the examination of the philosophy of Locke, p. 35–76.

starts from this authority, and from this alone; and if he subsequently admits another, it is because he arrives at it by reason: so that it is always reason which governs him, and holds in some sort the reins of his thought. Locke belongs, therefore, to the great family of independent philosophers. The *Essay on the Human Understanding* is a fruit of the movement of independence in the seventeenth century, and it has fortified that movement. This character passed from the master into his whole school, and was thereby recommended to all the friends of human liberty. I should add, that in Locke independence is always united to a sincere and profound respect for every thing which should be respected. Locke is a philosopher, and, at the same time, a Christian. Such is the chief. As to the school, you know what it has been. Its independence passed rapidly to indifference, and from indifference to hostility. I mention all this, because it is important that you should continually have in hand the thread of the movement of the sensualistic school.

I pass to the question which comes immediately after that of the general spirit of the whole philosophical work, to wit, the question of method. You know the importance of this question; it should now be evident to you that, as the method of a philosopher is, so will his system be, and that the adoption of a method decides the destinies of a philosophy. Hence our strict obligation to insist on the method of Locke, with all the care of which we are capable. What, then, is this method which, in its germ, contains the entire system of Locke, the system which produced the great sensualistic school of the eighteenth century? We will let Locke speak for himself; in his preface he expresses himself thus:

"Were it fit to trouble thee with the history of this Essay, I should tell thee, that five or six friends, meeting in my chamber, and discoursing on a subject very remote from this, found themselves quickly at a stand by the difficulties that arose on every side. After we had awhile puzzled ourselves without coming any nearer a resolution of those doubts which perplexed us, it came into my thoughts that we took a wrong course; and that before we set ourselves upon inquiries of that nature, it was necessary to examine our own abilities, and see what objects our understandings were or were not fitted to deal with. This I proposed to the company, who all readily assented; and thereupon it was agreed that this should be our first inquiry. Some hasty and undigested thoughts on a subject I had never before considered, which I set down against our next meeting, gave the first entrance into this discourse; which having been thus begun by chance, was continued by entreaty; written by incoherent parcels; and after long intervals of neglect, resumed again, as my humor or occasions permitted; and at last, in a retirement, where an attendance on my health gave me leisure, it was brought into that order thou now seest it."

He returns to the same thought in the introduction which follows the preface:

Chap. II. "I shall not at present meddle with the physical consideration of the mind, or trouble myself to examine wherein its essence consists, or by what motions of our spirits, or alterations of our bodies, we come to have any sensations by our organs, or any ideas in our understandings; and whether those ideas do, in their formation, any or all of them, depend on matter or no: these are speculations which, however curious and entertaining, I shall decline, as lying out of my way, in the design I am now upon. It shall suffice to my present purpose, to consider the discerning faculties of a man, as they are employed about the objects which they have to do with."

Locke is persuaded that this is the only means of repressing the rashness of philosophy, and, at the same time, of encouraging useful investigations.

Chap. IV. "If, by this inquiry into the nature of the understanding, I can discover the powers thereof, how far they reach, to what things they are in any degree proportionate, and where they fail us; I suppose it may be of use to prevail with the busy mind of man to be more cautious in meddling with things exceeding its comprehension; to stop when it is at the utmost extent of its tether; and to sit down in a quiet ignorance of those things, which, upon examination, are found to be beyond the reach of our capacities. We should not then, perhaps, be so forward, out of an affectation of a universal knowledge, to raise questions, and perplex ourselves and others with disputes about things to which our understandings are not suited, and of which we cannot frame in our minds any clear or distinct perceptions, or whereof (as it has, perhaps, too often happened) we have not any notions at all. If we can find out how far the understanding can extend its views, how far it has faculties to attain certainty, and in what cases it can only judge and guess, we may learn to content ourselves with what is attainable by us in this state."

Chap. VI. "When we know our own strength, we shall the better know what to undertake with hopes of success; and when we have well surveyed the powers of our own minds, and made some estimate what we may expect from them, we shall not be inclined either to sit still, and not set our thoughts on work at all, in despair of knowing any thing; or, on the other side, question every thing, and disclaim all knowledge, because some things are not to be understood."

And again, in the same section:

"It is of great use to the sailor to know the length of his line, though he cannot with it fathom all the depths of the ocean. It is well he knows that it is long enough to reach the bottom, at such places as are necessary to direct his voyage, and caution him against running upon shoals that may ruin him."

I shall make but one more and a decisive citation:

"This was that which gave the first rise to this essay concerning the understanding. For I thought that the first step towards satisfying several inquiries the mind of man was very apt to run into, was to take a survey of our own understanding, examine our own powers, and see to what things they were adapted. Till that was done, I suspected we began at the wrong end. . . . ."

I have purposely brought together these citations, in order to convince you that they contain, not merely a fugitive view, but a fixed rule, a method. This method is, in my opinion, the true method, that which is at the present time the strength and the hope of science. Let me present it to you in language somewhat more modern.

Whatever may be the objects you know or seek to know, God or the world, entities the most remote or the nearest, you know them, and can know them, only on this condition, that you are capable of knowing in general; and you know, and can know them, only in proportion to your general faculty of knowing. All the knowledge you can acquire, the highest as well as the lowest, rests in the last result upon the reach and value of this faculty. You may call it what you choose, spirit, reason, mind, intelligence, understanding. Locke calls it understanding. A wise philosophy, instead of blindly using the understanding and applying it at venture, should first examine it, and search out what it is and what it can accomplish; otherwise it is exposed to misconceptions without number. The study of the human understanding is, then, above all things else, the study of philosophy. There is no part of philosophy which does not presuppose this and from it borrow its light. What, for example, can logic be, that is, the knowledge of the rules which should govern the human mind, without the knowledge of that which we are seeking to govern, to wit, the human mind itself? What can morals be, the knowledge of the rules of our actions, without the knowledge of the subject itself of all morals, of the moral agent, of man himself? Politics, the science or the art of the government of social man, rests equally upon the knowledge of man whom it develops, but whom it does not constitute. Æsthetics, the science of the beautiful and the theory of arts, have their roots in the nature of the being capable of knowing the beautiful and of reproducing it, capable of feeling the particular emotions which attest its presence, capable of awakening these emotions in the souls of others. If man were not a religious being, if none of his faculties reached beyond the bounded and finite sphere of this world, God would not exist for man; and God indeed exists for him only according to the measure of his faculties; the examination of his faculties and of their reach is, therefore, the condition of every good theodicea. In a word, man is implied in all the sciences, which are in appearance the most foreign to him. The study of man is, then, the necessary introduction to every science that claims a separate existence; and, whatever name we give to it, psychology, or something else, it is necessary to conceive that this study, though certainly not the whole of philosophy, is its foundation and its point of departure.

But is psychology, the knowledge of human nature, possible? No doubt it is; for consciousness is a witness which makes known to us every thing that takes place within the soul. It is not the principle of any of our faculties, but it is the light of all. It is not because we have a consciousness of what takes place within, that it does take place; but that which takes place within us would be as though it had not taken place, if it were not attested by consciousness: it is not by it that we feel, that we will, that we think; but it is by it that we know that we do all this. The authority of consciousness is the last authority into which that of all the other faculties resolves itself, inasmuch as, if the authority of consciousness were overthrown, since by it the action of all our other faculties comes to our knowledge, their authority, without being destroyed in itself, would be nothing for us. So there is no one who does not put full confidence in his own consciousness. At this point skepticism expires; for, as Descartes has said, let one doubt of every thing else, yet he could not doubt that he doubts.* Consciousness has, then, an incontestable authority; its testimony is infallible, and it is wanting to no one. In fact, consciousness is more or less distinct, more or less vivid, but it is in all men. No one is unknown to himself, although very few know themselves perfectly, because all, or nearly all, make use of consciousness without applying

* Throughout the first Series and in this.

themselves to perfect it, to elucidate, and to understand it, by will and attention. In all men, consciousness is simply a natural process; some elevate this natural process to the height of an art, of a method, by reflection, which is in some sort a second consciousness, a free reproduction of the first; and as consciousness gives to all men a knowledge of what passes within them, so reflection can give to the philosopher a certain knowledge of every thing that falls under the eye of consciousness. And observe that the question is not here concerning hypotheses and conjectures, for the question is not even concerning the processes of reasoning; the question is only concerning facts, and concerning facts which can be observed quite as well as those which take place on the scene of the world. The only difference is, that on the one hand they are exterior, on the other interior, and that the natural action of our faculties carrying us outward, it is easier for us to observe the former than the latter. With a little attention, resolution, and practice, we may succeed in interior observation as well as in exterior observation. Finally, psychology, even were it more difficult than physics, is by its nature, like physics, a science of observation, and consequently it has the same title and the same right to the rank of a positive science.

But it is indeed necessary to recognize its true objects. The objects of psychology are those of reflection, which again are those of consciousness: now, it is evident that the objects of consciousness are neither the exterior world nor God, nor the soul itself in so far as substance, for if we had a consciousness of the substance of the soul, we should dispute no longer in regard to its nature, whether it is material or spiritual. Being in itself, whatever it may be, that of bodies, that of God, that of the soul itself, does not fall under consciousness. True philosophy does not exclude ontology, but adjourns it: psychology does not dethrone metaphysics, but precedes and elucidates them; it makes no romance on the nature of the soul; it studies the soul in the action of its faculties, in the phenomena which consciousness and reflection can attain, and directly do attain.

This can bring clearly to view the true character of the *Essay on the Human Understanding.* It is a work of psychology, and not of ontology. Locke does not investigate the nature and the principle of the understanding, but the action itself of this faculty, the phenomena by which it is developed and manifested. Now, Locke calls the phenomena of the understanding *ideas.* This is the technical term which he everywhere employs to designate that by which the understanding manifests itself, and that to which it immediately applies itself.

Introduction, § 8. "I have used it," he says, "to express whatever is meant by phantasm, notion, species, or whatever it is which the mind can be employed about in thinking..... I presume it will be easily granted me that there are such ideas in men's minds; every one is conscious of them in himself, and men's words and actions will satisfy him that they are in others."

It is very evident that ideas are here the phenomena of the understanding, of the mind, which the consciousness of each one can perceive in himself when he thinks, and which are equally in the consciousness of other men, to judge of them by their words and actions. Ideas are to the understanding what effects are to causes. Hereafter we shall examine the advantages and the disadvantages of this term, and the theory which it involves. For the present, it is sufficient to state it, and to designate it as the very watchword of the philosophy of Locke. For Locke and his whole school, the study of the understanding is the study of ideas: hence the recent and celebrated expression ideology, to designate the science of the human understanding. The source of this expression is in the *Essay on the Human Understanding,* and the ideological school is the natural offspring of Locke.

Here then you see the study of the human understanding reduced to the study of ideas; this study contains several orders of researches which it is important to determine well.* According-

* All the distinctions which follow are in the opening discourse of the year 1817, *Classification des questions et des écoles philosophiques*, Vol. 1st, p. 221 of the First Series.

ing to what has been previously said, we may consider ideas under two points of view: we may investigate whether in their relations to their objects, whatever the objects may be, they are true or false; or, omitting the question of their truth or falsity, of their legitimate or illegitimate application, we may investigate solely what they are in themselves and as consciousness manifests them to us. These are the two most general questions which we can propose in regard to ideas, and the order in which it is proper to treat of them cannot be doubtful. It is sufficiently evident that to commence by considering ideas in their relation to their objects, without having ascertained what they are in themselves, is to commence at the end, is to commence by investigating the legitimacy or illegitimacy of the consequences, while ignorant of the principles. It is then necessary to commence by the investigation of ideas, not as true or false, as legitimately or illegitimately applicable to such or such an object, and consequently as being or not being sufficient foundations for such an opinion, for such a belief, but as simple phenomena of the understanding, marked by such or such characters. It is incontestably thus that a true method of observation should proceed.

This is not all, and within these limits there is still matter for two distinct orders of researches.

We can at first study the ideas which are in the human understanding, developed as it now is in the present state of things. The question would then be that of collecting the phenomena of the understanding as the consciousness gives them, and of carefully stating their differences and their resemblances, so as to arrive from step to step to a good classification of all these phenomena. Here is then the first rule of the method of observation: to omit none of the phenomena which consciousness shall attest. In fact, you have over them no right; they exist, and for this sole reason then must they be recognized; they are in reality, in the consciousness, therefore they should be found in the framework of your science, or your science is only an illusion. The second rule is: to imagine none. As you are not to deny what is, so you are not to assume what is not; you should neither invent nor retrench any thing. To omit nothing, to suppose nothing, such are the two rules of observation, the two essential laws of the experimental method applied to the phenomena of the understanding, as to every other order of phenomena. And what I say of the phenomena of the understanding, I say of their characters; none must be omitted, none supposed: and thus having omitted none and having supposed none, having embraced all the real phenomena, and only the real phenomena, with all their characters, you will have the greatest number of chances for arriving at a legitimate classification which shall comprehend the whole reality, and nothing but the reality, at the exact and complete statistics of the phenomena of the understanding, that is, of ideas.

These statistics being collected, you know the understanding as it now is; but has it always been what it now is? Since the time when its action commenced, has it not undergone many changes? Have these phenomena, whose characters you have with so much penetration and fidelity analyzed and reproduced, always been what they are and what they appear to you? May they not have had at their birth certain characters which have disappeared, or have wanted at first characters which they have since acquired? Hence the important question of the origin of ideas, or the primitive characters of the phenomena of the understanding. When this second question shall be resolved, when you shall know what have been in their birth-place these phenomena which you have studied and know in their actual form, when you shall know what they were and what they have become, it will be easy for you to find the routes by which they have arrived from their first state to their present state; you will easily seize their generation, after having recognized their actual state, and after having penetrated their origin; and it is only then that you will perfectly understand what you are, for you will know both what you were and what you now are, and how you have come from what you were to be what you are. Thus will be completely known to you, both in its actual state and in its primitive state, and also in its metamorphoses, this faculty of knowing, this intelligence, this reason, this spirit, this mind, this understanding, which is for you the foundation of all knowledge.

The question of the present state of our ideas and that of their origin are therefore two distinct questions, and both are necessary to constitute a complete psychology. So far as psychology has not surveyed and exhausted these two orders of researches, it is ignorant of the phenomena of the understanding, for it does not know them under all their phases; it does not possess their secret. But where should we commence? Is it necessary to commence by recognizing the actual character of our ideas, or by searching out their origin?

Shall we commence with the question of the origin of our ideas? It is doubtless a very curious, very important point. Man aspires to the origin of all things, and especially to that of the phenomena which take place within him; he can be satisfied only after having penetrated thus far. The question of the origin of ideas is certainly in the human mind, it has then its right in science, it must come in its time; but must it come first? At first, it is full of obscurity. Thought is a river which we cannot easily ascend; its source, like that of the Nile, is a mystery. How, in fact, shall we find the fugitive phenomena by which nascent thought is marked? Is it by the memory? But you have forgotten what then passed within you, for you were not aware of its existence. At that time we live and think without paying attention to the manner in which we live and think, and memory does not render up a deposit that we never intrusted to it. Will you consult others? They are in the same perplexity as you. Will you study infants? but who will unfold what passes under the veil of an infant's thought? The deciphering of these hieroglyphics easily conducts to conjectures, to hypotheses. Would you thus commence an experimental science? It is evident that if you start with the question of the origin of ideas, you start with precisely the most difficult question. Now, if a wise method should go from the best known to the least known, from the most easy to the least easy, I ask whether it should commence with the origin of ideas. This is the first objection; and behold another. You commence by seeking the origin of ideas; therefore you commence by seeking the origin of that of which you are ignorant, of phenomena which you have not studied, and in regard to which you cannot say what they are and what they are not. What origin of them, then, could you find except a hypothetical origin? And this hypothesis will be either true or false. Is it true? Very well; you guessed rightly: but as guessing, even that of genius, is not a scientific process, truth, thus discovered, does not take rank in science, and is still nothing but hypothesis. Is it false? Instead of truth under the vicious form of hypothesis, have you only an hypothesis without truth? Then behold what will be its result. As this hypothesis, that is, this error, will have taken a place in your mind, when you shall come to explain with it the phenomena of intelligence as it now exists, if they are not what they should be to justify your hypothesis, you will not for all that renounce it, and for it you will sacrifice reality. You will do one of two things: either you will deny all ideas which shall not be explicable by your hypothetical origin, or you will arrange them by caprice and for the support of your hypothesis. It was not necessary to choose with so much show the experimental method, in order to wholly falsify it afterwards by putting it upon a route so perilous. Wisdom, good sense, logic, demand therefore that, provisionally neglecting the question of the origin of ideas, we should content ourselves at first with observing ideas as they now exist, and the characters which the phenomena of intelligence actually present in the consciousness.

This done, in order to complete our researches, in order to go to the extent of our powers, to the extent of the wants of the human mind and the demands of experimental questions, we shall ask ourselves, What, in their origin, have been these ideas which we now possess? Either we shall discover the true origin of our ideas, and experimental science will be achieved; or we shall not discover it, and then nothing will be either lost or compromised. We shall not have attained all truth; but we shall have attained a great part of truth. We shall know what is, if we do not know what was, and we shall always be ready to resume the delicate question of the origin of ideas; whereas, once having wandered into this premature research, a primary error vitiates all subsequent researches, and in advance perverts observation. So the regular order of psychological questions may be fixed in the following manner:

1st, To search out, without any systematic prejudice, by observation alone, with simplicity and good faith, the phenomena of the understanding in their actual state, and as consciousness now presents them to us, by dividing and classifying them according to the known laws of scientific divisions and classifications;

2d, To search out the origin of these same phenomena or ideas by all the means which are in our power, but with the firm resolution not to let what observation shall have given us be wrested from us by any hypothesis, and with our eyes always fixed upon present reality and its incontestable characters. To this question of the origin of ideas is joined that of their formation and generation, which evidently depends upon it, and is, as it were, enveloped in it.

Such are, in their methodical order, the different problems which philosophy embraces. The slightest inversion of this order is full of perils, and may lead to the gravest mistakes. You indeed conceive that if you treat the question of the legitimacy of the application of our ideas to their objects, before understanding well what is the nature of these ideas, what are their actual and their primitive characters, what they are and whence they come, you wander at venture and without a torch into the unknown land of ontology. You again conceive that if, within the very limits of psychology and ideology, you commence by wishing to carry by main force the question of the origin of ideas before you know what they are, and before you have recognized them by observation, you seek for light in the darkness, which will not yield it to you.

Now, how has Locke proceeded, and in what order has he treated these philosophical questions?

Introduction, § 3. "I shall pursue," he says, "this following method:

"First, I shall inquire into the original of those ideas, notions, or whatever else you please to call them, which a man observes, and is conscious to himself he has in his mind; and the ways whereby the understanding comes to be furnished with them.

"Secondly, I shall endeavor to show what knowledge the understanding hath by those ideas; and the certainty, evidence, and extent of it.

"Thirdly, I shall make some inquiry into the nature and grounds of faith or opinion; whereby I mean that assent which we give to any proposition as true, of whose truth yet we have no certain knowledge: and here we shall have occasion to examine the reasons and degrees of assent."

It is evident that the last two points here indicated are related to one and the same question, the general question of the legitimacy or illegitimacy of the application of our ideas to their objects; and this question is here given as the last question of philosophy. It is nothing less than the adjournment of the whole logical and ontological inquiry until after psychology. This is the fundamental character of the method of Locke and the originality of his *Essay.* We entirely agree with Locke in this respect, under this special reservation, that the adjournment of ontology shall not be its suppression.

The first point remains, which is wholly psychological, and occupies the greatest part of the work of Locke. He therein declares that his first inquiry will be that of the origin of ideas. But in that there are two radical errors in regard to method: 1st, Locke treats of the origin of ideas before having sufficiently studied these ideas; 2d, he does more; he not only puts the question of the origin of ideas before that of the inventory of ideas, but he entirely neglects this last question. It was already venturing much to put one question before the other; for it was seeking at the outset an hypothesis, with the exception of afterwards confronting the hypothesis with reality; but what will this amount to when even this chance of return to truth is interdicted, when the fundamental question of the inventory of our ideas and of their actual characters is wholly omitted?

This is the first error of Locke. He recognizes and proclaims the experimental method; he proposes to apply it to the phenomena of the understanding, to ideas; but not having sufficiently fathomed this method which was then in its infancy, he has not discerned all the questions to which it gives rise; he has not arranged these questions in due order; he has misconceived and omitted the most important experimental question, the observation of the actual characters of our ideas; at the very outset he has fallen into a question which should have been adjourned, the obscure and difficult question of the origin of our ideas. What, therefore, will be the result? Either Locke will hit upon the true origin of our ideas by a sort of good fortune and divination, at which I should rejoice; but however true it may be in itself, this origin will be demonstrated to be true, will be legitimately established only on this condition, that Locke should subsequently demonstrate that the characters of our ideas are all, and in their whole extent, explicable and explained by the origin supposed. Or indeed Locke will be deceived: but, if he is deceived, an error of this kind will not be a particular error concentrated upon a single point and without influence upon the rest; it will be a general error, an immense error, which will corrupt, even at its source, the whole of psychology, and thereby the whole of metaphysics. In order to be faithful to his hypothesis, to the origin which he shall have assigned to all ideas without understanding them fully, he will be obliged to sacrifice all ideas which shall refuse to be referred to this false origin. The falsity of the origin will be extended even to the actual state of the intelligence, and will conceal from the eyes of consciousness itself the real characters of our ideas; hence, from applications to applications, that is, from aberrations to aberrations, the human understanding and human nature will be more and more misconceived, reality will be destroyed, and science perverted.

Such is the rock; it was necessary to point it out. We know not whether Locke has been wrecked upon it; for we know not yet what he has done, whether he has had the good fortune to divine correctly, or whether he has had the fate of most diviners and of those who start at venture upon a route which they have not measured. We suppose ourselves now to be ignorant of it, we shall subsequently examine it; but we are already able to remark, that it is in great part from Locke that, in the eighteenth century, in his whole school, comes the systematic habit of placing the question of the origin and the generation of ideas at the head of all philosophical researches. In metaphysics, this school is preoccupied with inquiring what are the first ideas which enter into the mind of man; in morals, the actual state of man's moral nature being neglected, what are the first ideas of good and evil, which arise in man considered in the savage state or in infancy, two states in which observation is not very sure and may easily be arbitrary; in politics, what is the origin of societies, of governments, of laws. In general, it searches for right in fact, and philosophy is reduced for it to history, and to history the most obscure, that of the first age of humanity. Hence the political theories of this school, often opposite in their results, yet identical in the method which presides in them. Some, plunging into ante-historical or anti-historical conjectures, find at the origin of society the empire of force and conquerors: the first government which history presents to them is despotic; therefore the idea of government is the very idea of despotism. Others, on the contrary, in the convenient obscurity of the primitive state, think they perceive a contract, reciprocal stipulations, and titles of liberty which despotism subsequently caused to disappear, and which the present time should re-establish. In either case, the legitimate state of society is deduced from its first form, from that form which it is almost impossible to find, and the rights of humanity are at the mercy of a venturous erudition, at the mercy of an hypothesis. Finally, from origin to origin, the true nature of man has even been sought for in the most absurd geological hypotheses: the last term of this deplorable tendency is the celebrated work of Maillet, *Telliamed.**

To recapitulate, the most general character of the philosophy of Locke is independence; and here, with all the necessary reservations, I openly rank myself under his banner, if not side by side with the chief, at least side by side with his followers. As to method, that of Locke is the psychological or ideological method, for the name is of little consequence; and here again I declare myself of his school. But, as he did not sufficiently fathom the psychological method, I accuse Locke of having commenced by an order of researches which necessarily puts psychology on the road of hypothesis, and deprives it more or less of its experimental character, and here I differ from him.

Let us understand at what point we are in this examination. We have seen Locke upon a perilous route; but has he had the good fortune, in spite of this bad choice, to arrive at the truth, that is, at the veritable explanation of the origin of our ideas? What, according to him, is this origin? This is the foundation of the *Essay on the Human Understanding*, the system to which Locke has attached his name. This will be the subject of our future lectures.

---

* On the dangers into which, in all these orders of researches, the question of origins, prematurely undertaken, throws us, see especially Vol. 3 of the first Series, Lecture 7, p. 260, etc.

LECTURE XVII.

ESSAY. FIRST BOOK, INNATE IDEAS. SECOND BOOK, OF SPACE.

First Book of the *Essay on the Human Uunderstanding*. Of innate ideas.—Second Book. Experience, the source of all ideas. Sensation and reflection.—Of the operations of the mind. According to Locke, they are exercised only upon sensible data. Basis of sensualism.—Examination of the doctrine of Locke concerning the idea of space.—That the idea of space, in the system of Locke, should be reduced and is reduced to that of body.—This confusion is contradicted by facts and by Locke himself. Distinction of the actual characters of the ideas of body and of space.—Examination of the question of the origin of the idea of space. Distinction between the logical order and the chronological order of our ideas.—The idea of space is the logical condition of the idea of body; the idea of body is the chronological condition of the idea of space.—Of reason and experience, considered in turn as the reciprocal condition of their mutual development.—Merit of Locke's system.—Its vices: 1st, it confounds the measure of space with space; 2d, the condition of the idea of space with this idea itself.

Locke, doubtless, is not the first who instituted the question concerning the origin of ideas; but it is Locke who first made it a great philosophical question, and since Locke, it has preserved this rank in his school. Besides, if this question is not that which a severe method should first agitate, it is certain that in its place, it is of the highest importance: let us see how Locke has resolved it.

In entering upon the investigation of the origin of ideas, Locke encounters an opinion which, if it were well founded, would cut short the question; I mean the doctrine of innate ideas. In fact, if ideas are innate, that is, if, as the word seems to indicate, ideas are already in the mind at the moment when it begins to enter into exercise, it does not acquire them, it possesses them from the first day, precisely as they will be at the last; and, properly speaking, they have no progress, no generation, and no origin. This doctrine, which Locke imputes to his adversaries, is opposed to his design of beginning with the question of the origin of ideas; it is moreover opposed to the solution which he wished to give of this question, and to the system which preoccupied him. First of all, he should have removed this obstacle, refuted the doctrine of innate ideas. Hence the polemic discussion which fills the first book of the *Essay on the Understanding.* I must give you an account of this discussion.

According to Locke there are philosophers who consider certain principles, certain maxims, and certain propositions in metaphysics and in morals as innate. Now by what reason may propositions be called innate? Two reasons may be and have been given: 1st, that these propositions are universally admitted; 2d, that they are primitively admitted, that they are known as soon as reason is exercised.

Locke examines successively these two reasons.

In metaphysics, he takes the two following propositions: What is, is; it is impossible for the same thing to be, and not to be; and he examines whether in fact all men admit these two propositions. Leaving civilized men who have read the philosophers, he addresses savages, and he asks whether a savage knows that what is, is, that it is impossible for the same thing to be and not to be. He answers for the savage, that the savage knows nothing about it and cares little for it. He interrogates the child, and finds that the child is in the same case as the savage. Finally, supposing that savages and children, like civilized people, admit that what is, is, that it is impossible for the same thing to be and not to be, Locke has in reserve an objection which he imagines to be unanswerable: the idiot does not admit these propositions; and this single exception would suffice, according to Locke, to demonstrate that they are not universally admitted, and consequently that they are not innate; for the soul of an idiot is also a human soul. Examining afterwards whether these propositions are primitive, whether they are the first that are acquired as soon as we begin to make use of reason,

Locke, taking again a little child for the subject of his experiment, maintains that in the child a multitude of ideas precede them: the idea of colors, the idea of bodies, the idea of existence; and that thus the propositions in question are not the first which preside at the development of intelligence.

So much for speculation: it is the same with practice. Locke submits moral propositions or maxims to the same tests to which he has submitted metaphysical propositions. Then, more than ever, he rests upon the manners of savages, the narrations of travellers, and the observation of children. His conclusion is that there is no moral maxim universally and primitively admitted, and consequently, innate.

Such are the first two chapters of the first book of the *Essay on the Human Understanding*. The last goes farther still. If the propositions and maxims, metaphysical as well as moral, previously examined, are neither universally nor primitively admitted, what must be thought of the ideas which are contained in these propositions and which are their elements? Locke chooses two, upon which he establishes a long discussion, the idea of God and the idea of substance. He has recourse to his ordinary arguments to prove that the idea of God and the idea of substance are neither universal nor primitive; in evidence of this he appeals to savages who, according to him, have not the idea of God; he addresses himself to children in order to know whether they have the idea of substance, and concludes that these ideas are not innate, and that no particular idea, nor any general speculation or moral idea, is anterior to experience.

As from the time of Locke, the question of the origin of ideas has become the fundamental question in the sensualistic school, so you will observe that from Locke polemical discussion upon innate ideas is, as it were, the obligatory introduction of this school. And not only the subject, but the manner of treating it comes from Locke. From him arose the habit of appealing to savages and to children, in regard to whom observation is so difficult; for, in regard to the former, it is necessary to refer to travellers who are often prejudiced, and who do not understand the languages of the people that they visit; and as to the latter, we are compelled to make use of very equivocal signs. The polemics of Locke, in substance and in form, have become the basis of all the polemics of his school against innate ideas.

And what is the real value of these polemics? Permit me to postpone this question;* for if its discussion should be too general, we should learn nothing, and if too profound, we should anticipate particular discussions which the examination of the *Essay on the Understanding* will successively introduce. Thus in making my reservations on the conclusions of this first book, I enter immediately upon the second, which contains the special theory of Locke on the origin of ideas.

"Let us then suppose, says Locke (B. II. Chap. I. § 2), the mind to be, as we say, white paper, void of all characters, without any ideas; how comes it to be furnished? Whence comes it by that vast store which the busy and boundless fancy of man has painted on it, with an almost endless variety? Whence has it all the materials of reason and knowledge? To this I answer, in one word, from experience; in that all our knowledge is founded, and from that it ultimately derives itself."

Let us see what Locke understands by experience. Let him speak for himself:

B. II. Chap. I. § 2. "Our observation, employed either about external sensible objects, or about the internal operations of our minds, perceived and reflected on by ourselves, is that which supplies our understandings with all the materials of thinking. These two are the fountains of knowledge from whence all the ideas we have, or can naturally have, do spring."

§ 3. "*The objects of sensation one source of ideas.*—First, Our senses, conversant about particular sensible objects, do convey into the mind several distinct perceptions of things, according to those various ways wherein those objects do affect them: and

---

* See the close of Lecture 22.

thus we come by those ideas we have of *yellow, white, heat, cold, soft, hard, bitter, sweet,* and all those things which we call *sensible qualities;* which, when I say the senses convey into the mind, I mean, they from external objects convey into the mind what produces there those *perceptions*. This great source of most of the ideas we have, depending wholly upon our senses, and derived by them to the understanding, I call *sensation.*"

§ 4. "*The operations of our minds the other source of ideas.*— Secondly, The other fountain from which experience furnisheth the understanding with ideas is the perception of the operations of our own mind within us, as it is employed about the ideas it has got, which operations, when the soul comes to reflect on and consider, do furnish the understanding with another set of ideas, which could not be had from things without; and such are *perception, thinking, doubting, believing, reasoning, knowing, willing,* and all the different actings of our own minds; which we, being conscious of, and observing in ourselves, do from these receive into our understandings as distinct ideas, as we do from bodies affecting our senses. This source of ideas every man has wholly in himself; and though it be not sense, as having nothing to do with external objects, yet it is very like it, and might properly enough be called *internal sense.* But as I call the other *sensation,* so I call this *reflection,* the ideas it affords being such only as the mind gets by reflecting on its own operations within itself. By *reflection,* then, in the following part of this discourse, I would be understood to mean, that notice which the mind takes of its own operations, and the manner of them; by reason whereof there come to be ideas of these operations in the understanding. These two, I say, viz., external material things, as the objects of *sensation,* and the operations of our minds within, as the objects of *reflection,* are to me the only originals from whence all our ideas take their beginnings. The term *operations* here I use in a large sense, as comprehending not barely the actions of the mind about its ideas, but some sort of passions arising sometimes from them, such as is the satisfaction or uneasiness arising from any thought."

§ 5. "*All our ideas are of the one or the other of these.*—The understanding seems to me not to have the least glimmering of any ideas, which it doth not receive from one of these two. *External objects furnish the mind with the ideas of sensible qualities,* which are all those different perceptions they produce in us: *and the mind furnishes the understanding with ideas of its own operations.* These, when we have taken a full survey of them and their several modes, combinations, and relations, we shall find to contain all our whole stock of ideas; and that we have nothing in our minds which did not come in one of these two ways."

Locke here evidently confounds reflection with consciousness. Reflection, strictly speaking, is a faculty analogous without doubt to consciousness,* but distinct from it, and belongs more particularly to the philosopher; while consciousness belongs to every man as an intellectual being. Moreover, he reduces very much the reach of reflection or of consciousness, by limiting it to the operations of the soul: it is manifest that the consciousness or reflection has for its objects all the phenomena which pass within us, sensations or operations. Consciousness or reflection is a witness and not an actor in the intellectual life. The true powers, the special sources of ideas, are sensations on the one hand, and on the other the operations of the soul, under this general condition, that we have a consciousness of the one as well as of the other, and that we may fall back upon ourselves and reflect upon them, and upon their products. These, then, are the two sources of ideas to which, strictly, the theory of Locke is reduced.

Now, is it the sensibility, is it the operations of our soul that enter first into exercise? Locke does not hesitate to say that our first ideas are furnished to us by the sensibility, and that those which we owe to reflection come later. He declares it, Book II. Chap. I. § 8; he declares it still more expressly, *ibid.*, § 20. "I

* See the preceding lecture; and 1st Series, Vol. 4, Lecture 26, p. 411.

see no reason to believe that the soul thinks before the senses have furnished it with ideas to think on." And again, § 23: "If it shall be demanded, then, when a man begins to have any ideas, I think the true answer is, when he first has any sensation . . . ."

Thus Locke places the acquisitions of the senses before those of thought. We might stop him here: we might ask him if this order is real; if it is possible to conceive, not a sensation perhaps, but an idea of sensation, without the intervention and concurrence of some of the operations of the soul. But without entering into this objection, let it suffice us to state that Locke does not admit the operations of the soul until after the sensations. It remains to know what these operations are, and what are their peculiar functions, on what and in what circle they act, and whether, in supposing that they do not enter into exercise until after the sensibility, they are or are not condemned to work solely on the primitive data which are furnished to them by the senses. For this, it is necessary to examine with care the nature and the object of the operations of the soul, according to Locke.

Locke is the first who has given an analysis, or rather an attempt at an analysis of the sensibility, and of the different senses of which it is composed, of the ideas which we owe to each of them, and to the simultaneous action of several (Book II. Chap. II. § 2; Chaps. III. IV. and V.); he, too, first gave the example of what, at a later period, in the hands of his successors, became a theory of the faculties of the soul. That of Locke, curious, precious even for the times, is in itself extremely feeble, vague, and confused. Nevertheless, faithful to the general spirit of his philosophy, Locke tries to present the faculties in the order of their probable development.

The first of which he treats is *perception* (Book II. Chap. IX. § 2.): "What perception is, every one will know better by reflecting on what he does himself, what he sees, hears, feels, etc., or thinks, than by any discourse of mine. Whoever reflects on what passes in his own mind, cannot miss it: and if he does not reflect, all the words in the world cannot make him have any notion of it." § 3: "This is certain, that whatever alterations are made in the body, if they reach not the mind; whatever impressions are made on the outward parts, if they are not taken notice of within; there is no perception." § 4: "Wherever there is sense, or perception, there is some idea actually produced, and present to the understanding." And, § 15: "Perception is the first degree towards knowledge." The perception of Locke is what is now called consciousness, the faculty of perceiving what is actually taking place within us.

After perception comes *retention* (Chap. X. § 1), or the power of retaining actual perceptions, ideas, of *contemplating* them when they are present, or of *recalling* them when they have disappeared. In this last case, retention is *memory*, the aids of which are *attention* and *repetition.*

After this comes the faculty of *distinguishing ideas* (Chap. XI.), and that of *comparing* them: whence arise all the ideas of relation, without forgetting the faculty of *composition*, whence arise complex ideas, which come from the combination of several simple ideas. At a later period, finally, the faculty of *abstraction* and *generalization* is developed. Locke does not reckon any other faculties. Thus, in the last analysis, perception, retention, or contemplation and memory, discernment and comparison, composition, abstraction, such are the faculties of the human understanding, for the will, with pleasure, and pain, and the passions, which Locke gives as operations of the mind, form another order of phenomena.

Now, what is the character and what is the employment of these operations? On what is perception exercised? to what is it applied? to sensation. And what does it do? It simply perceives the sensation, simply has a consciousness of it. Add, according to Locke, that the perception is passive (Chap. IX. § 1), forced, inevitable; it is, then, little else than an effect of sensation. The first faculty of the soul adds nothing then to sensation; it simply takes cognizance of it. In retention, contemplation prolongs this perception; having vanished, the memory recalls it. Discernment separates, composition reunites the perceptions; abstraction seizes their most general characters; but finally the materials are always, in the last analysis, ideas of sensation due to perception. Our faculties add to the knowledge which they draw from them nothing but that of their own existence and of their action.

Thus, on one hand, sensation precedes; on the other, the understanding is, for Locke, only an instrument whose whole power is spent upon sensation. Locke, doubtless, has not confounded sensation and the faculties of the soul; he very explicitly distinguishes them: but he makes our faculties play a secondary part in concentrating their action upon sensible data: hence confounding them with sensibility itself was but a step, and in philosophy was already deposited the still feeble germ of the future theory of sensation transformed, of sensation as the sole principle of all the operations of the soul. It was Locke who, without knowing it, and without wishing it, opened the road to that exclusive doctrine, by adding to sensation only faculties whose whole office is to act upon it, without any original power. The sensualistic school will be constituted only when it shall have arrived at this point. In waiting for the future to push thus far the system of Locke, let us take this system for what it is, or rather for what it claims to be: its pretension is to explain all ideas which are, and which may be in the human understanding, by sensation and by reflection, that is, by the sentiment of our own operations.

"If we trace the progress of our minds," says Locke (Chap. XII.), "and with attention observe how it repeats, adds together, and unites its simple ideas received from sensation or reflection, it will lead us farther than at first perhaps we should have imagined. And I believe we shall find, if we warily observe the originals of our notions, that even the most abstruse ideas, how remote soever they may seem from sense, or from any operations of our own minds, are yet only such as the understanding frames to itself, by repeating and joining together ideas, that it had either from objects of sense, or from its own operations about them: so that even those large and abstract ideas are derived from sensation or reflection, being no other than what the mind, by the ordinary use of its own faculties, employed about ideas received from objects of sense, or from the operations it observes in itself about them, may and does attain unto. This I shall endeavor to show in the ideas we have of space, time, and infinity, and some few others, that seem the most remote from those originals."

All this is well enough. It has somewhat the appearance of a challenge; let us accept it, and see how Locke will draw, for example, the idea of space from sensation and from reflection.

I am somewhat embarrassed in trying to explain to you Locke's opinion in regard to space, and must call to your remembrance an observation which I have already made. Locke is the chief of a school; you must not expect, then, that Locke has drawn from his principles all the consequences which they contain; you must not expect the inventor of a principle to establish it with clearness and precision. This remark, which is applicable to the whole *Essay on the Human Understanding*, is particularly true of the chapters wherein Locke treats of the idea of space. Herein we find, under a clearness sometimes real and sometimes apparent and superficial, an extreme confusion, and contradictions are not only met from chapter to chapter, but from paragraph to paragraph in the same chapter. It is, without doubt, the duty of the historian to exhibit these contradictions, in order to characterize both the epoch and the man; but history is not simply a monograph, it is not interested solely in an individual, however great he may be; it is the germ of the future which it seeks in the past. I shall endeavor, then, after having designated to you, once for all, the innumerable inconsistencies of Locke, to disengage from the midst of these sterile inconsistencies whatever has been fruitful, whatever has borne its fruits, what constitutes a system, the veritable system of Locke. This system consists, you know, in drawing all ideas from two sources, sensation and reflection. The idea of space must then be derived from one or the other of these two sources. Assuredly the idea of space is not acquired by reflection, by the consciousness of the operations of the understanding. It comes, then, from sensation. Behold the systematic principle. We will let Locke set out from this principle, and arrive at the idea of space. But Locke does not wish to reform the human understanding, he only wishes to explain it; he wishes to show the origin of what is, not of what could or should be. Then the trial for him, as for every other philosopher, is this: the principle of his system being admitted, to draw from it what at present exists, to wit, the idea of space, such as it is in the minds of all men. So we will let him proceed according to his system; we will then take from the very hands of this system the idea of space, such as it gives it to us, and we will confront it with the idea of space such as we have it, such as all men have it independently of any system whatever.

According to Locke,* the idea of space comes from sensation. But from what sense does it come? It is not from the smell, it is not from the taste, it is not from the hearing; it is then from the sight and from the touch. This is, too, what Locke says, Book II. Chap. XIII. § 2: "We get the idea of space both by our sight and touch, which I think is so evident, that...." If the idea of space is an acquisition of the sight and of the touch, in order to know what it should be on this condition, let us recur to the preceding chapters wherein Locke treats of the ideas which we receive by sight, and especially by touch. Let us see what touch can give according to Locke and according to every one.

The touch, aided or not aided by sight, suggests to us the idea of something that resists; and to resist is to be solid. "The idea of solidity," says Locke (Chap. IV. § 1), "we receive by our touch, and it arises from the resistance which we find..." And

* On the idea of space in Locke, 1st Series, Vol. 3, Lect. 1, p. 53–57, and in general on the idea of space, 1st Series, Vol. 3, opinion of Condillac, p. 133; Vol. 4, opinion of Reid, Lect. 21, p. 436, and Vol. 5, opinion of Kant, Lect. 4, transcendental æsthetics, p. 81, etc.

what are the qualities of a solid, of this something which resists? more or less solidity, resistance. More solidity is hardness, less, is softness; hence, perhaps, also figure with its dimensions. Charge with different qualities this solid, this something which resists, and you have all that touch can give, whether aided or not aided by sight. This something which resists, which is solid, which is more or less so, which has such or such a figure, in a single word, is body.

Is it true that the touch, with the sight, suffices to give that which resists, the solid with its qualities, body? I do not wish to examine it too far. Analysis would perhaps force me to admit the necessary intervention of something besides the sense of touch.* I prefer, however, to suppose that in fact touch, sensation, gives the idea of body. I grant that sensation may go thus far; but that it goes farther, Locke does not pretend. In the chapter where, almost without any of the spirit of system, Locke examines what may be derived from sight and from touch, he deduces from them nothing more than the solid, that is, body. If, then, at a later period, and in a systematic manner, he pretends, as we have seen, that the idea of space comes from sensation, to wit, from sight and from touch, it follows that he reduces the idea of space to the idea of body, and that for him space is nothing more than body itself, body enlarged, multiplied in an indefinite manner, the world, the universe. In fact, § 10, Chap. XIII.: "The idea of place we have by the same means that we get the idea of space (whereof this is but a particular and limited consideration), viz., by our sight and touch...." Same chapter, same paragraph: "To say that the world is somewhere, means no more than that it does exist...." This is clear: the space of the universe is equivalent to neither more nor less than to the universe itself; and as the idea of the universe is, after all, only the idea of body, it is to this that the idea of space is reduced.

* First Series, Vol. 1st: Course of 1817, Lect. 11, p. 296; and Vol. 4, Lect. 21, p. 426.

Such is the necessary origin of the idea of space in the system of Locke.

That there are throughout these different chapters contradictory paragraphs, and that the contradiction is often gross, is true; but it is not less true that the system of Locke being given, that is, sensation as the only principle of the idea of space, the necessary result is the idea of space such as Locke has just determined it. But is this systematic result the reality? The idea of space derived from sensation, from touch and from sight, is this the idea of space such as it is in your mind and in the minds of all men? Let us see now, such as we are, whether we confound the idea of body and the idea of space, whether for us they are but one and the same idea.

In making any such experiment upon ourselves, let us guard against two things which corrupt every experiment: let us guard against having in view such or such a systematic conclusion; let us guard against thinking of any origin whatever, for the preoccupation of the mind by such or such an origin would, unconsciously even, lead us to attribute to ideas, such as they are at present in our consciousness, such or such a character more in relation with the origin which we inwardly prefer. We shall see hereafter the conclusions which may be drawn from the experiment which we wish to institute; hereafter we will ascend even to the origin of the idea which it concerns us and suffices us first to state without any prejudice, without any foreign view.

Is the idea of space reduced in the understanding to the idea of body? Such is the question; it is a question of fact. Let us take any body that you please; let us take this book which is under our eyes, under our hands; it resists, it is solid, it is more or less hard, it has figure, etc. Do you think of nothing more in regard to it? Do you not think, for example, that this body is somewhere, in a certain place? Do not be astonished at the simplicity of my questions; we must not be afraid of bringing philosophers to the most simple questions; for it is précisely because they are the most simple that they are often neglected, and that, for want of interrogating and collecting evident facts, philosophers are precipitated into absurd systems.

Is this body somewhere? is it in a place? Yes, doubtless, all men will answer. Well! let us take a more considerable body, let us take the world. Is the world also somewhere? is it in a place? No one doubts it. Let us take thousands of worlds, myriads of worlds; can we not in regard to these thousands of worlds, ask the same questions which I have just asked concerning this book? Are they somewhere? are they in a place, that is, are they in space? We may ask the question in regard to one world or thousands of worlds as in regard to this book, and to all these questions you will equally reply: This book, this world, these thousands of worlds are somewhere, are in a place, are in space. There is not a human creature, except perhaps a philosopher preoccupied by a system, who can doubt what I have just said to you. Take the savage to whom Locke so often appeals, take the child, take the idiot, unless he be completely one; and if any of these human creatures has the idea of any body whatever, book or world, or thousands of worlds, he will naturally believe that this book, this world, these thousands of worlds are somewhere, in a place, in space. What does this amount to? It is to recognize that the idea of a book, of a world, of thousands of worlds, solid, resisting, situated in space, is one thing, and that the idea of space wherein this book, this world, or these thousands of worlds are situated and contained, is another thing.

This is so evident that Locke himself, when he is not under the yoke of his system, distinguishes perfectly the idea of body, of solid from that of space, and establishes the difference between them. Book II. Chap. XIII. § 11: "For I appeal to every man's own thoughts, whether the idea of space be not as distinct from that of solidity as it is from the idea of scarlet color? It is true, solidity cannot exist without extension, neither can scarlet color exist without extension; but this hinders not but that they are distinct ideas. Many ideas require others as necessary to their existence or conception, which yet are very distinct ideas. Motion can neither be, nor be conceived, without space; and yet motion is not space, nor space motion: space can exist without it, and they are very distinct ideas; and so, I think, are those of space and solidity." Several considerations follow on the difference which separates body and space, considerations which fill more than ten paragraphs, to which I refer you in order not to multiply quotations. I cannot, however, forbear giving you here a very decisive and curious passage: Chap. IV. § 5: "Of pure space then, and solidity, there are several (among which I confess myself one), who persuade themselves they have clear and distinct ideas; and that they can think on space without any thing in it that resists or is protruded by body. This is the idea of pure space, which they think they have as clear as any idea they can have of the extension of body; the idea of the distance between the opposite parts of a concave superficies being equally as clear without as with the idea of any solid parts between: and on the other side they persuade themselves that they have, distinct from that of pure space, the idea of something that fills space, that can be protruded by the impulse of other bodies, or resist their motion. If there be others that have not these two ideas distinct, but confound them, and make but one of them, I know not how men, who have the same idea under different names, or different ideas under the same name, can in that case talk with one another, any more than a man who, not being blind or deaf, has distinct ideas of the color of scarlet and the sound of a trumpet, could discourse concerning scarlet color with the blind man I mentioned in another place, who fancied that the idea of scarlet was like the sound of a trumpet."

Thus, according to Locke himself, the idea of space and the idea of body are totally distinct. In order to place this distinction in a clear light, let us observe the difference of characters which these two ideas present.

You have the idea of a body, you believe that it exists; but can you suppose it not to exist? I ask you, can you not suppose this book to be destroyed? Without doubt you can. And can you not also suppose the whole world to be destroyed, and no body whatever to be in existence? You can. For you, constituted as you are, the supposition of the non-existence of bodies implies no contradiction. And what do we call the idea of a thing which we can conceive as not existing? We call it a contingent and relative idea. But if you can suppose this book to be destroyed, the world destroyed, all matter destroyed; can you suppose space to be destroyed? Can you suppose that when all bodies should cease to exist, there would no longer remain any space for bodies which might come into existence? You cannot; if it is in the power of man's thought to suppose the non-existence of bodies, it is not in his power to suppose the non-existence of space; the idea of space is then a necessary and absolute idea. Here then are two characters entirely different which separate the two ideas of body and of space.

Moreover, every body is evidently limited; you seize its limits in every part. Enlarge, extend, multiply this body by thousands of analogous bodies; you will have simply removed the limits of this body, you will not have destroyed them, you will conceive them still. But with space it is not so. The idea of space is given to you as that of a continuation, in which you can, indeed, make divisions useful and convenient, but artificial, under which the idea of a space without any limit still subsists. For beyond any determinate portion of space, there is space still; and beyond this space, there is space always and forever. Body has in all its dimensions, something else which limits it, to wit, space which contains it; but space has no limits.

The idea of body is not complete without that of form and figure, and you can always represent it under a determinate form; it is always an image. Far from that, space is a conception and not an image; and as soon as you conceive space imaginatively, as soon as you represent it under any determinate form whatever, it is no longer the space which you conceive, but something else, a body in space. The idea of space is a conception of reason, distinct from every sensible representation.

I could prolong this opposition of the characters of the idea of body and of the idea of space. It is sufficient to have established these three fundamental characters: 1st, the idea of body is a contingent and relative idea, whilst the idea of space is a necessary and absolute idea; 2d, the idea of body implies the idea of limit, and the idea of space implies the absence of all limit; 3d, finally, the idea of body is a sensible representation, and the idea of space is a pure, and entirely rational conception.

If these characters are truly those of the idea of space and of the idea of body, these two ideas are profoundly different, and every philosophy which shall pretend to rest on observation should never confound them. Nevertheless, their confusion is necessarily derived from the system of Locke. Condemned to proceed from sensation, and being able to proceed neither from smell, nor from hearing, nor from taste, the idea of space must necessarily proceed from sight and from touch; and, proceeding from sight and from touch, it could not be any thing else than the idea of body more or less generalized. Now, it has been demonstrated that the idea of space is not that of body; it does not then come from sight and from touch, it does not then come from sensation; and as it does not come from reflection, from the sentiment of our operations, and as it still exists, it follows that all ideas are not derived from sensation and reflection only, and that the system of Locke, on the origin of ideas, is incomplete and vicious, at least as regards the idea of space.

That we may better penetrate this system, it is necessary that we ourselves should take the same ground that Locke occupies and examine the question which, with him, is especially the philosophical question. After having determined the characters which the idea of space and the idea of body have already in the intelligence of all men, and after having shown that these characters make a profound difference between these two ideas, it is necessary to seek out their origin, the origin of the idea of space relatively to the idea of body. Thus far, I hope, every thing has been simple and clear; for we have not gone out of the human intelligence, such as we now find it. Let us proceed, and let us not extinguish the lights which we owe to an impartial observation, in the darkness of any hypothesis.

There are two sorts of origin; in human cognitions there are two orders of relations which it is necessary to distinguish.

Of two ideas, we may inquire, whether one does not suppose the other, whether one being admitted, it is not necessary to admit the other in order to escape the reproach of inconsistency? This is the logical order of ideas.

If the origin of the ideas of body and of space is met under this point of view, behold what is the result.

The idea of body and the idea of space being given, which supposes the other? Which is the logical condition of the admission of the other? Evidently it is the idea of space which is the logical condition of the admission of the idea of body. In fact, take any body that you please, you can admit the idea of this body only on condition that you admit, at the same time, the idea of space; if you do not, you would admit a body which would be nowhere, which would have no place, and such a body is inconceivable. Take an aggregate of bodies, or take a single body, since every body is an aggregate of parts, these parts are more or less distant from each other, and at the same time they coexist; these are the conditions of all bodies, even the least. Do you not see what is the condition of coexistence and of distance? Space still. For how could there be distance between bodies, or between the parts of a body, without space? and what coexistence is possible without some continuity? It is the same with contiguity. Destroy by thought the continuity of space, no distance is appreciable, no coexistence, no contiguity is possible. Besides, continuity is extension. It must not be believed, and Locke has well established it (Book II. Chap. XIII., § 11), that the idea of extension is adequate to the idea of body. The fundamental attribute of body is resistance; hence solidity;

but solidity does not imply in itself that this solidity is extension.* Extension exists only on condition of a continuity, that is, of space. The extension of body, therefore, supposes space; space is not body or resistance, but that which resists, resists only on some real point; now, every real point whatever is extended, is in space; then take away the idea of space and of extension, and no real body is supposable. Then as a last conclusion, in the logical order of human cognitions, it is not the idea of body which is the logical condition of the admission of the idea of space; it is, on the contrary, the idea of space, the idea of a continuity, the idea of extension, which is the logical condition of the admission of the least idea of body.

This is beyond doubt; and when, under the logical point of view, we meet the question of the origin of ideas, this solution, which is incontestable, overwhelms the system of Locke. Now it is here that the idealistic school has taken, in general, the question of the origin of ideas. By the origin of ideas, it usually understands the logical filiation of ideas among themselves. For this reason it could say, with its last and most illustrious interpreter, that so far is the idea of body from being the foundation of the idea of space, that it is the idea of space which is the foundation of the idea of body.† The idea of body is given to us by touch and by sight, that is, by experience, and by the experience of the senses. On the contrary, the idea of space is given to us on occasion of the idea of body, by the thought, the understanding, the mind, the reason, in short, by a power different from sensation. Hence this Kantian formula: the pure and rational idea of space comes so little from experience, that it is the condition of all experience; and this bold formula is perfectly correct, taken in a certain respect, that is, in respect to the logical order of human cognitions.

But this is not the only order of knowledge; and the logical

* 1st Series, Vol. 1, Lecture 11, p. 297, etc. See also in the Essays of D. Stuart, *Essay on the Idealism of Berkeley.*

† 1st Series, Vol. 5, Lecture 4, p. 83.

relation does not exhaust all the relations which ideas sustain among themselves. There is still another, that of anteriority or of posteriority, the order of the relative development of ideas in time, their chronological order; under this point of view we may meet the question of the origin of ideas. Now, is the idea of space, which, as we have just seen, is the logical condition of all sensible experience, also the chronological condition of all experience and of the idea of body? I do not believe that it is. No, taking ideas in the order in which they are produced in the intelligence, seeking only their history and their successive appearance, it is not true that the idea of space is antecedent to the idea of body. It is so little true that the idea of space supposes, chronologically, the idea of body, that if you had not the idea of body, you would never have the idea of space. Take away all sensation, take away sight and touch, and you have no longer any idea of body, neither have you any idea of space. Space is the place of bodies: whoever has no idea of a body will never have an idea of the space which contains it. Rationally, logically, if you have not the idea of space, you cannot have the idea of a body; but the reciprocal is chronologically true, and in fact the idea of space comes only with the idea of body; and as you have not the idea of body without at once having the idea of space, it follows that these two ideas are contemporaneous. I will go farther. Not only may we say that the idea of body is contemporaneous with the idea of space, but we may say, but we must say, that it is anterior to it. In fact, the idea of space is contemporaneous with the idea of body, in this sense, that as soon as the idea of body is given to you, you cannot help having the idea of space; but finally, it was necessary for you first to have the idea of body, in order that that of the space which contains it should appear to you. It is then by the idea of body that you arrive at the idea of space; one may then be called the historical and chronological condition of the other.

Undoubtedly (I cannot repeat it too often, for it is the very knot of the difficulty, the secret of the problem), undoubtedly as soon as the idea of body is given, at that very moment the idea of space arrives; but if this condition were not fulfilled, the idea of space would never enter the understanding. When it is there, it is established there and remains there, independent of the idea of body which introduced it there: for we may suppose space without body, whilst we cannot suppose body without space. The idea of body was the chronological condition of the idea of space, as the latter is the logical condition of the former.* The two orders are inverse, and, in a certain sense, we may say, every one is right and every one is wrong. Logically, idealism and Kant are right in maintaining that the pure idea of space is the condition of the idea of body and of experience; and chronologically, empiricism and Locke in their turn are right, in pretending that experience, to wit, here sensation, the sensation of sight and of touch, is the condition of the idea of space and of every exercise of the understanding.

In general, idealism neglects more or less the question of the origin of ideas, and seldom regards ideas except in their actual characters. Placing itself at first on the understanding such as it now is, it does not investigate its successive acquisitions; it does not trouble itself in regard to the chronological order of ideas, it stops at their logical connection; it sets out from reason, not from experience. Locke, on the contrary, preoccupied with the question of the origin of ideas, neglects their actual characters, confounds their chronological condition with their logical basis, and the power of reason with that of experience which precedes it and guides it, but does not constitute it. Experience, put in its right place, is the condition, not the principle of knowledge. Does it go farther, and does it pretend to constitute all knowledge? It is then nothing else than a system, and an incomplete, exclusive, vicious system; it is empiricism, or the opposite of idealism, which, in its turn, is the exaggeration of the

* On the distinction between the logical order and the historical, or chronological order of human cognitions, see 1st Series throughout.

proper power of reason, the usurpation of reason over experience, the destruction or forgetfulness of the chronological and experimental condition of knowledge, in the excessive preoccupation of its logical and rational principles.

Locke introduced and accredited empiricism in the philosophy of the eighteenth century. He plainly saw that we could have no idea of space, if we had not some idea of body. Body is not space, but it is body which fills or which measures space; if then space is not body, we can know nothing of space except what body gives us. Locke saw this; and this is his merit. His fault is: 1st, in having confounded what fills and measures space and reveals it to us, with the idea itself of space; 2d, and this second fault is much more general and more comprehensive than the first, in having confounded the chronological condition of ideas with their logical condition, experimental data, external or internal, on condition of which the understanding conceives certain ideas, with these ideas themselves.

This is the most general critical point of view which rules all the metaphysics of Locke. I deduce it from the examination to which I have just submitted his theory of the idea of space; I may apply it and I shall apply it in the next lectures to his theory of the idea of the infinite, of time, and of other ideas which Locke has boasted, as you know, of easily deducing from experience, from sensation, or from reflection.

LECTURE XVIII.

ESSAY. SECOND BOOK. TIME. INFINITY. IDENTITY. SUBSTANCE.

Continuation of the examination of the Second Book of the *Essay on the Human Understanding*. Of the idea of time.—Of the idea of the infinite.—Of the idea of personal identity.—Of the idea of substance.

I SHALL commence by exhibiting to you the results which the last lecture has given us; the question was concerning space.

A sound philosophy should not, without doubt, retrench or destroy the ontological questions concerning the nature of space in itself, whether it is material or spiritual, whether it is a substance or an attribute, whether it is independent of God or is related to God; for all these questions are in the human mind; but it should adjourn them until psychological observations, correctly made and skilfully combined, shall permit us to resolve them; it will then first of all occupy itself with the psychological question of the idea of space.

It is sufficient to interrogate the human understanding as it now exists in all men, in order to recognize in it the idea of space with these three distinguishing characters: 1st, space is given us as necessary, whilst body is given us as being able to exist or not to exist; 2d, space is given us as without limits, body is given us as limited on all sides; 3d, the idea of space is entirely rational, that of body is accompanied by a sensible representation.

The preliminary question concerning the actual characters of the idea of space being thus resolved, we can, without danger, approach the quite as difficult and obscure question of the origin of the idea of space. Here, we have carefully distinguished two points of view intimately connected together, but which analysis ought to separate, the logical order of ideas and their chronological order. To the eyes of reason and logic, body presupposes space; for what is body? The juxtaposition, the coexistence of resisting points, that is, solids: but where could the juxtaposition and the coexistence be produced, if not in a continuity, in space? On the other hand, if in the order of reason and nature body presupposes space, it is necessary to recognize that in the chronological order there is a contemporaneousness between the idea of body and the idea of space, since we cannot have the idea of body without that of space, nor that of space without that of body. And if, in this contemporaneousness, we can distinguish an antecedent, it is not the idea of space which is anterior to that of body, it is that of body which is anterior to that of space: it is not by the idea of space that we start; and if sensibility, if touch did not take the lead and suggest to us the idea of resistance, of solid, of body, we should never have the idea of space. Doubtless the idea of solid and body cannot be formed in the mind, unless we already have the idea of space; but it is not produced first in the mind; it precedes, in some degree, the idea of space, which follows it immediately.

Here then are two orders perfectly distinct from each other. In the order of nature and reason, body presupposes space. In the order of the acquisition of knowledge, it is, on the contrary, the idea of solid and body which is the condition of the idea of space. Now, the idea of body is acquired by the perception of touch, aided by sight; it is therefore an acquisition of experience; hence it is correct to say that, in the chronological order, experience and a certain development of the senses are the condition of the acquisition of the idea of space; and at the same time, as body presupposes space, and as the idea of space is given us by reason, and not by the senses and experience, it is logically correct to say that the idea of space and a certain exercise of the reason render all experience possible.

From this point of view we discover the real character, the merit and the defects of Locke's theory. What has Locke done? I believe that he has destroyed the ontological questions of the nature of space, instead of contenting himself with adjourning them: but in fine he has had the wisdom to put the psychological question of the idea of space in the first rank. He should have dwelt longer on the actual characters of this idea, and it was in him a grave fault to throw himself first into the question of its origin. His general system on the origin of ideas being that all our ideas are derived from two sources, reflection or consciousness and sensation; as the idea of space cannot come from consciousness, it was necessary that it should come from sensation; and to draw the idea of space from sensation, it was necessary to reduce it to the idea of body. This is what Locke has done in the systematic parts of his work, though contradicting himself more than once, for often he speaks of space as wholly distinct from solidity. But when his system comes up, when the necessity of drawing the idea of space from sensation comes up, then he affirms that the idea of space is acquired by sight and touch; and as touch, aided by sight, gives us only body and not space, for this reason alone Locke reduces space to body; he does this explicitly when he says that to ask whether this universe exists somewhere, is to ask whether the universe exists. The confusion of the existence of space and the existence of the universe is the confusion of the idea of space and the idea of body; and this confusion was necessary that the system might be, at least in appearance, rigorous. But the universal belief of the human race declares that body is one thing, and the space which contains it is another thing; that the world, and all possible worlds are one thing, and the infinite and unlimited space which embraces them, is another thing. Bodies measure space, and do not constitute it. The idea of body is indeed antecedent to that of space, but it is not this idea itself.

Behold where we now are: let us advance; let us successively interrogate the second book of the *Essay on the Human Understanding*, on the origin of the most important ideas, and we shall see that Locke continually confounds the order of the acquisition of our knowledge with its logical order, and the necessary antecedent of an idea with this idea. I propose to examine at the present in the system of Locke the idea of time, the idea of the infinite, the idea of personal identity, the idea of substance. I commence, like Locke, with the idea of time.*

Here, the first rule, you know, is to neglect the question of the nature of time, and to seek solely what is the idea of time in the human understanding, whether it is there, and with what characters is it there. It is unquestionably there. There is no one, as soon as he has before his eyes, or presents to himself in imagination any event whatever, who does not conceive that this event has passed, or is passing in a certain time. I ask you whether you can suppose an event of which you are not forced to conceive that it has taken place at such an hour, such a day, such a week, such a year, such a century? You can suppose even the abolition of every event, but you cannot suppose the abolition of time. Before a horologe we can, indeed, make the supposition that from hour to hour no event has happened; notwithstanding you are none the less convinced that time has passed away, even when no event has marked its course. The idea of time is, therefore, a necessary idea, like the idea of space. I add that, like space, time is unlimited. The divisions of time, like those of space, are purely artificial, and suppose a unity, an absolute continuity of time. Take millions of events, do with these millions of events what you did with bodies, multiply them indefinitely, and they will not equal the time which precedes them and which follows them. Before all finite periods, and beyond all finite periods, there is still time unlimited, infinite, inexhaustible. Finally, like the idea of unlimited and necessary space, the idea of necessary and unlimited time is a pure idea of reason, which escapes all representation, and all the efforts of the imagination and the sensibility.

* On the idea of time, see 1st Series, Vol. 1, Lectures 25 and 26; Vol. 3, 1st Lecture, opinion of Locke, p. 56, 3d Lecture, opinion of Condillac, p. 131; Vol. 4, opinion of Reid, Lecture 21, p. 443; and Vol. 5, opinion of Kant, Lecture 4, p. 88.

It is with the origin of the idea of time as with the origin of the idea of space. You are still to distinguish between the order of the acquisition of our ideas and their logical order. In the logical order of ideas, the idea of any succession of events presupposes that of time; there can be succession only on condition of a continuous duration, to the different points of which the different members of the succession may be attached. Take away the continuity of time, and you take away the possibility of the succession of events; as, the continuity of space being taken away, the possibility of the juxtaposition and the coexistence of bodies is destroyed. But, in the chronological order, it is, on the contrary, the idea of the succession of events which precedes the idea of the time which includes them. I do not mean, in regard to time as well in regard to space, that we have a clear and complete idea of a succession, and that, in course, there arrives in the understanding the idea of a time which includes this succession: I only say that we must first have the perception of some events, in order to conceive that these events are in time. Time is the place of events, as space is that of bodies: whoever has not the idea of an event, cannot have the idea of time. If, therefore, the logical condition of the idea of succession is in the idea of time, the chronological condition of the idea of time is in the idea of succession.

You see we have been conducted to the result, that the idea of succession is the occasion, the chronological antecedent of the necessary succession of time. But every idea of succession is an acquisition of experience; it remains to see of what experience. Is it the experience of the senses or that of the operations of the mind? Is the first succession given us in the spectacle of exterior events, or in the consciousness of events that pass within us?

Take a succession of exterior events: in order that these events may succeed each other, there must be a first, a second, a third event, etc. But if, when you see the second event, you do not remember the first, there would be no second, there would be no succession for you; you would always be fixed at a first, which would not have the character of first, since there would be no second. The intervention of memory is therefore necessary, in order to conceive of any succession whatever. Now, the memory has for its direct object nothing external; it is not immediately related to things, but to us. When we say, we remember a person, we remember a place, this means nothing else than that we remember to have been seeing such a place, seeing or hearing such a person. We have memory only of ourselves, for there is memory only on condition that there has been consciousness. If, then, consciousness is the condition of memory, as memory is the condition of the idea of succession, it follows that the first succession is given us in ourselves, in consciousness, in the proper objects and phenomena of consciousness, in our thoughts, in our ideas. But if the first succession which is given us is that of our ideas, as to all succession is necessarily attached the conception of time, it follows again that the first idea which we have of time is that of the time in which we are; and as the first succession is for us the succession of our ideas, so the first duration for us is our own duration; the succession of exterior events, and the duration in which these events are accomplished, are only known to us afterwards. I do not say that the succession of exterior events is only an induction from the succession of our ideas, neither do I say that exterior duration is only an induction from our personal duration; but I say that we can have an idea either of exterior succession or of exterior duration, only after having had the consciousness and the memory of some interior phenomena, and, consequently, the conception of our own duration. Thus, summarily, the first duration which is given us is our own, because the first succession which is given us is the succession of our own ideas.

A profound analysis can go farther still; there is a crowd of ideas, of phenomena, under the eye of consciousness: to seek what is the first succession which is given us, is to seek what are our first ideas, the first phenomena which fall under consciousness, and form the first succession. But it is evident, in regard to our sensations, that they are phenomena of consciousness only on condition that we pay attention to them. Thousands and thousands of impressions may assail my sensibility; if I do not give them my attention, I have no consciousness of them. It is the same in regard to many of my thoughts which, if my attention is directed elsewhere, do not come to my consciousness, and vanish in reveries. The essential condition of consciousness is attention; the phenomenon most intimately connected with consciousness is, therefore, attention, and the series of the acts of attention is necessarily the first succession which is given us. But what is attention?* It is nothing less than the will itself; for no one is attentive who does not wish to be so. The first succession is, therefore, that of our voluntary acts. Now, succession measures time, as body measures space; whence it follows that, the first succession being that of voluntary acts, the will is the primitive measure of time; and this measure has the excellence of being equal to itself; for every thing differs in the consciousness, sensations, and thoughts, whilst the acts of the attention, being eminently simple, are essentially similar.

Such is the theory of the primitive and equal measure of time, which we owe to M. de Biran; and you may see it expressed with a perfect originality of analysis and style in the lectures of M. Royer-Collard.† M. de Biran continually repeats that the element of duration is the will; and in order to pass from our duration to exterior duration, from the succession of our acts to the succession of events, from the primitive and equal measure of time for us, to the ulterior and more or less uniform measure of time without us, M. de Biran relied upon a double phenomenon of the will, which regards both the interior world and the exterior world. According to M. de Biran, the type of the sentiment of

* 1st Series, *passim*, and particularly Vol. 3, Lecture 3, p. 115, and Vol. 4, Lecture 23, p. 569.

† Works of Reid, Vol. iv. pp. 394–411; and 1st Series, Vol. 1, p. 210.

the will is in the sentiment of effort.* I make an effort to move my arm, and I move it; I make an effort to walk, and I walk. The effort is a relation to two terms. One is internal, to wit, the will, the act of will; the other external, to wit, the movement of the arm, or the step which I have made, which has its cause and its measure in the internal movement of the will. The determination is nothing else than the most simple act of the will. It is, at first, entirely interior; then it passes without, in the movement produced by the *nisus* or the effort, a movement which reflects that of the will, and becomes the measure of all subsequent exterior movements, as the will is the primitive and indecomposable measure of the first movement which it produces.

Without taking upon myself either the honor or the responsibility of all the parts of this theory, I hasten to arrive at that of Locke. The merit of Locke is to have established that the idea of time, of duration, of eternity, is suggested to us by the idea of some succession of events, and that this succession is not taken in the exterior world, but in the world of consciousness. See Book II. Chapters XIV. XV. XVI. For example, Chap. XIV. § 4: "Men derive their ideas of duration from their reflection on the trains of the ideas they observe to succeed one another in their own understandings." *Ibid.*, § 6: "The idea of succession is not from motion." And § 12: "The constant and regular succession of ideas is the measure and standard of all other successions." The analysis of Locke does not go far enough; it does not determine in what particular succession of ideas the first succession, the first duration, is given us. When it is said that Locke, in deriving the idea of duration from reflection, derives it consequently from the sentiment of the operations of the soul, as, according to Locke, the operations of the soul are not all active and voluntary, his theory is still very far from that which we have exhibited. Herein is the merit of Locke's theory; its vice is

* Works of M. de Biran, Vol. i., Introduction of the Editor; for the appreciation of the theory of M. de Biran, see Lecture 25 of this volume.

more considerable; but it is closely connected with the merit. Locke saw that the idea of time is given us in succession, and that the first succession for us is necessarily the succession of our ideas. Thus far Locke merits only praise, for he gives the succession of our ideas only as the condition of the acquisition of the idea of time; but the condition of a thing is easily taken for the thing itself, and Locke, after having taken the idea of body, the mere condition of the idea of space, for the idea of space, takes also the condition of the idea of time for the idea itself; he confounds succession with time; he no longer simply says: The succession of our ideas is the condition of the conception of time; but he says: Time is nothing else than the succession of our ideas. Book II. Chap. XIV. § 4: "That we have our notion of succession and duration from this original, viz., from reflection on the train of ideas which we find to appear one after another in our own minds, seems plain to me, in that we have no perception of duration, but by considering the train of ideas that take their turns in our understandings. When that succession of ideas ceases, our perception of duration ceases with it; which every one clearly experiments in himself, whilst he sleeps soundly, whether an hour or a day, a month or a year; of which duration of things, while he sleeps or thinks not, he has no perception at all, but it is quite lost to him; and the moment wherein he leaves off to think, till the moment he begins to think again, seems to him to have no distance. And so I doubt not it would be to a waking man, if it were possible for him to keep only one idea in his mind, without variation and the succession of others."

In this whole passage there is:

1st, A confusion of two very distinct ideas, duration and succession;

2d, An evident paralogism, for in it duration is explained by succession, which is explicable only by duration. In fact, where would the elements of succession succeed each other, unless in some duration? Where could there be succession, that is, distance between ideas, unless in the space of ideas and of minds, that is, in time ?

3d, Moreover, see to what results the theory of Locke conducts. If succession is no longer simply the measure of time, but time itself; if the succession of ideas is no longer simply the condition of the conception of time, but this conception itself, time is nothing else than what the succession of our ideas makes it. The succession of our ideas is more or less rapid; therefore time is more or less short, not in appearance, but in reality: in absolute sleep, in lethargy, all succession of ideas, all thought, ceases; therefore at that time we do not endure, and not only we do not endure, but nothing has endured, for not only our time, but time in itself is only the succession of our ideas. Ideas exist only under the eye of consciousness; now, there is no consciousness in lethargy, in sleep; consequently during sleep and lethargy there has been no time; the horologe has vainly moved on, the horologe has been wrong; and the sun, like the horologe, should have stopped. These are the very extravagant results, and yet the necessary results of the confusion of the idea of succession with that of time; and this confusion is itself necessary in the general system of Locke, which derives all our ideas from sensation and reflection. Sensation had given space, reflection gives time; but reflection, that is, consciousness with memory, attains only the succession of our ideas, of our voluntary acts, a finite and contingent succession, and not the necessary and unlimited time in which this succession is carried on: experience, whether external or internal, attains only the measure of time, not time itself. Now, Locke was forbidden every other source of knowledge than sensation and reflection; it was therefore necessary that he should make it explicable by the one or the other: he very clearly saw that it was not explicable by sensation; and it could not be by reflection except on the condition of being reduced to the measure of time, to succession. It is true that Locke thus destroyed time, but he saved his system:

it is at the same price that he will save it again in regard to the idea of the infinite.*

The character of time and space is, that they are unlimited and infinite. Without doubt the idea of the infinite is applied to something else than time and space; but since we hitherto have treated only of time and space, we will refer the idea of the infinite only to time and space, as Locke gives us the example.

Space and time are infinite; now the idea of the infinite may be detached from the ideas of time and space, and considered in itself, provided the subject from which it is borrowed be always kept in mind. The idea of the infinite incontestably exists in the human understanding, since there incontestably is in the understanding the idea of infinite time and space. The infinite is distinct from the finite, and consequently from the multiplication of the finite by itself, that is, from the indefinite. That which is not infinite, added as many times as you please to itself, will not become infinite. You no more draw the infinite from the finite, than you have been able to draw space from body, time from succession.

As to the origin of the idea of the infinite, recollect that if you had not had the idea of any body and any succession, you would neither have had the idea of time nor that of space, and that at the same time you cannot have the idea of body and succession, without having the idea of space and time. Body and succession are the finite, space and time are the infinite. Therefore, without the finite, there is for you no infinite; but, at the same time, as soon as you have the idea of the finite, you cannot avoid having the idea of the infinite. Recollect again the difference between the order of the acquisition of our ideas and their logical order. In the logical order, the finite supposes the infinite, as its necessary foundation; but, in the chronological order, it is the idea of the finite which is the necessary condition of the acquisition of the idea of the infinite.

---

* On the idea of the infinite, see First Series, Vol. 3, Lect. 1, p. 58, Lect. 3, p. 134; Vol. 4, Lect. 12, p. 64 and p. 74; Vol. 5, Lect. 6, p. 218, etc.

These facts are evident; but Locke has a system; this system consists in admitting no other origin of all our ideas than sensation and reflection. The idea of the finite, which is resolved into that of body and succession, easily comes from sensation or reflection; but the idea of the infinite, which is resolved neither into the idea of body nor into that of succession, since time and space are neither the one nor the other of these two things, can come neither from sensation nor reflection. The system of Locke, if the idea of the infinite subsist, will therefore be false; the idea of the infinite, therefore, must not subsist; and Locke shuns it and eludes it as much as he can. He begins by declaring that it is a very obscure idea, whilst that of the finite is very clear and comes easily into the mind (Book II. Chap. XVII. § 2). But obscure or not obscure, is it in the intelligence? That is the question, and obscure or not obscure, it is your duty as a philosopher, if it is real, to admit, whether you can elucidate it or not. And then, in regard to the obscurity, let us understand ourselves. The senses attain only body; consciousness or reflection attain only succession. The objects of the senses and the understanding are therefore body and succession, that is, the finite. Thus nothing is more clear for the senses and consciousness than the finite; whilst the infinite is and ought to be very obscure, for the very simple reason that the infinite is the object neither of the senses nor of consciousness, but of reason alone. If then it is with the senses or consciousness that you wish to attain the infinite, it is necessarily obscure and even inaccessible to you; if with the reason, nothing is clearer, so far that it is then the finite which becomes obscure to your eyes and escapes you. And behold how empiricism, which is exclusively grounded on internal or external experience, is quite naturally led to the denial of the infinite; whilst idealism, which is exclusively grounded on the reason, very easily forms a conception of the infinite, but finds great difficulty in admitting the finite, which is not its proper object.

After sporting a little with the idea of the infinite as obscure,

Locke objects that it is purely negative, that it has nothing in it positive. Book II. Chap. XVII. § 13: "We have no positive idea of infinity." § 16: "We have no positive idea of infinite duration." § 18: "We have no positive idea of infinite space." This is the source of the accusation so often repeated since against the conceptions of reason, that they are not positive. But, at first, observe that there is no more an idea of succession without the idea of time, than an idea of time without the previous idea of succession; and no more an idea of body without the idea of space, than an idea of space without the previous idea of body, that is, that there is no more an idea of the finite without the idea of the infinite, than there is an idea of the infinite without the previous idea of the finite, whence it follows that, in strictness, these ideas suppose each other, and, if any one wishes to say it, reciprocally limit each other; consequently, the idea of the infinite is no more the negative of that of the finite, than the idea of the finite is the negative of that of the infinite; they are negatives on the same ground, or they are both positive, for they are both simultaneous affirmations, and every affirmation contains a positive idea. Or do we understand by positive that which falls under experience, external or internal; and by negative that which does not fall under it? Then I agree that the idea of body, of succession, of the finite, falls alone under experience, under sensation, and consciousness, and that it alone is positive; and that the idea of time, of space, of the infinite, falls only under the reason, is purely negative. But it is necessary to maintain, according to this explanation, that all rational conceptions, and, for example, those of geometry and morals, are also purely negative, and have nothing positive. Or if we understand by positive every thing that is not abstract, every thing that is real, every thing that falls under the immediate and direct action of any of our faculties, it must be admitted that the idea of the infinite, of time and space, is as positive as that of the finite, of succession, and body, since it falls under the reason, a faculty quite as real and quite as positive as the senses and consciousness, although its proper objects are not objects of experience.*

Finally, being obliged to explain himself categorically, after many contradictions, for Locke often speaks here and elsewhere of the infinity of God (Book II. Chap. XVII. § 1), and even of the infinity of time and space (*ibid.*, § 4 and 5), he ends by resolving the infinite into number (*ibid.*, § 9): "*Number affords us the clearest idea of infinity.*—But of all other ideas, it is number, as I have said, which, I think, furnishes us with the clearest and most distinct idea of infinity we are capable of. For even in space and duration, when the mind pursues the idea of infinity, it there makes use of the ideas and repetitions of numbers, as of millions and millions of miles, or years, which are so many distinct ideas, kept best by number from running into a confused heap, wherein the mind loses itself." But what is number? it is, in the last analysis, such or such a number, for every number is a determinate number; it is, therefore, a finite number, whatever it may be, as high as you please. Number is the parent of succession, not of duration; number and succession measure time, but do not equal it and exhaust it. The reduction of the infinite to number is, therefore, the reduction of infinite time to its indefinite or finite measure, which is at bottom the same thing; as in regard to space, the reduction of space to body is the reduction of the infinite to the finite. Now, to reduce the infinite to the finite, is to destroy it; it is to destroy the belief of the human race, but, once more, it is to save the system of Locke. In fact, the infinite can enter the understanding neither by consciousness nor by the senses; but the finite enters the understanding marvellously well by these two doors; it alone enters the understanding: therefore there is nothing else either in the understanding or in nature; and the idea of the infinite is only a vague and obscure idea, entirely negative, which is re-

---

* On the infinite and the necessary as proper objects of reason, see 1st Series, Vol. 5, Lecture 6, p. 223.

solved, when reduced to its just value, into number and succession.

Let us examine the theory of personal identity* in the system of Locke, as we have examined that of infinity, of time, of space.

Is the idea of personal identity in the human understanding, or is it not? Each one of you can answer for himself: is there any one of you who doubts of his personal identity, who doubts that he is the same to-day that he was yesterday, and that he will be to-morrow? If no one doubts of his personal identity, it only remains to determine what is the origin of this idea.

I suppose that no one of you would know that he exists, unless he thought and were conscious of his thought. Seek whether, in the absence of all thought and consciousness, you could have any idea of your existence, and, consequently, of your existence as one and identical. On the contrary, can you have a consciousness of a single operation of your mind, without irresistibly believing, at the same instant, in your existence? No, in every act of consciousness there is the consciousness of some operation, of some phenomenon, thought, volition, sensation, and at the same time the conception of our existence; and when memory comes after consciousness, we conceive that the same being, the same *me*, which just before was the subject of the phenomenon of which I had a consciousness, exists still, and is the same that memory recalls to me. Thus consciousness and memory cannot be exercised without the reason suggesting to me the irresistible conviction of my personal existence, one and identical.

Now, if you again distinguish the two orders which I have several times designated to you, the logical order and the chronological order of knowledge, it is evident that, in the order of nature and reason, it is not consciousness and memory which are the foundation of personal identity, and that it is, on the contrary, personal identity, the continuous existence of the being, which is

---

* On personal identity, see 1st Series, Vol. 1, Lectures 19–22; Vol. 3, Lecture 1, p. 70, etc.; Vol. 4, Lecture 20, p. 368; and Lecture 21, p. 446.

the foundation of consciousness and memory. Take away being, and there are no more phenomena, and these phenomena come no longer to consciousness and memory; in the order of nature and reason, it is therefore consciousness and memory which presuppose personal identity: but it is not thus in the chronological order; and if in this order we cannot have the consciousness and the memory of any phenomenon without instantly having a rational conception of our identical existence, nevertheless it is necessary, in order that we may have this conception of our identity, that there should have been some act of consciousness and memory. Without doubt, the act of memory and consciousness is not consummated, unless we conceive our personal identity; but some act of memory and consciousness must have taken place, in order that the conception of our identity may take place in its turn. In this sense, I say that some operation, some acquisition of memory and consciousness, is the necessary chronological condition of the conception of our personal identity.

Analysis may raise, in regard to the phenomena of consciousness and memory, which suggest to us the idea of our personal identity, the same problem which it has already raised in regard to the phenomena of consciousness, which suggest to us the idea of time: it may seek what, among the numerous phenomena of which we have consciousness and memory, are those on occasion of which we acquire at first the conviction of our existence. At bottom, it is to seek what are the conditions of memory and consciousness. Now, as we have seen, the condition of memory is consciousness; and, as we have again seen, the condition of consciousness is attention, and the principle of attention is the will. It is, therefore, the will, attested by consciousness, which suggests to us the conviction of our existence, and it is the continuity of the will, attested by memory, which suggests the conviction of our personal identity. It is, again, to M. de Biran that I refer the honor and the responsibility of this theory.*

* Works of M. de Biran, Vol. i., Introduction of the Editor.

Let us look at the theory of Locke. Locke has very clearly seen (Book II. Chap. XXVII. § 9) that where there is no consciousness (and, as it has been very well remarked, Locke should have added memory to consciousness), where, I say, there is neither memory nor consciousness, there can be for us no idea of our personal identity, so that the sign, the character and measure of personality, is consciousness. I cannot render too much praise to this part of Locke's theory: it attains and puts into light the true sign, the true character, the true measure of personality; but the sign is one thing, and the thing signified another; the measure is one thing, and the thing measured another; the eminent and fundamental character of the *me* and personal identity is one thing, and this identity itself is another. Here, as in regard to the infinite, as in regard to time, as in regard to space, Locke has confounded the condition of an idea with this idea itself; he has confounded identity with consciousness and memory, which suggest the idea of it. Book II. Chap. XXVII. § 9: "Since consciousness always accompanies thinking, and it is that which makes every one to be what he calls self, and thereby distinguishes himself from all other thinking things; in this alone consists personal identity, *i. e.*, the sameness of a rational being: and as far as this consciousness can be extended backwards to any past action or thought, so far reaches the identity of that person; it is the same self now it was then; and it is the same self with this present one that now reflects on it, that that action was done." § 10: "Consciousness makes personal identity." § 16: "Consciousness makes the same person." § 17: "Self depends on consciousness." § 23: "Consciousness alone makes self." But, the confusion of consciousness and personal identity destroys personal identity, as the confusion of number and the infinite destroys the infinite, as the confusion of succession and time destroys time, as the confusion of body and space destroys space. In fact, if personal identity is altogether in consciousness, then when there is an enfeeblement, or loss of consciousness, there must be an enfeeblement or loss of personal identity; deep sleep, lethargy, which is a species of sleep, revery, intoxication, passion, which often destroy consciousness, and with it memory, must also destroy, not only the sentiment of existence, but existence itself. It is not necessary to follow all the consequences of this theory. It is evident that if memory and consciousness not only measure our existence, but constitute it, he who has forgotten that he has done a thing, really has not done it; he who has badly measured by memory, the time of his existence, has really had less existence. Then there is no more moral imputation, no more juridical action. A man no longer recollects to have done such or such a thing, therefore he cannot be tried for having done it, for he has ceased to be the same. The murderer can no longer bear the penalty of his crime, if, by a fortunate chance, he has lost the memory of it.

To sum up, there is no doubt that personality has for its distinguishing sign the will and the operations of which we have a consciousness and a memory, and that if we had neither consciousness nor memory of any operation and any voluntary act, we should never have the idea of our personal identity; but when this idea is introduced into the intelligence by consciousness and memory, it continues there independently of the memory of that which introduced it. There is no doubt that what declares and measures the personality and moral accountability of our acts, is the consciousness of the free will which produced them; but these acts once performed by us with consciousness and free-will, memory of them may fade or even entirely vanish, and the responsibility, as well as personality, may remain complete. It is not, therefore, consciousness and memory which constitute our personal identity. And not only consciousness and memory do not constitute personal identity, but personal identity is not even the object of consciousness and memory; none of us has a consciousness of his own nature, otherwise the depths of existence would be easy to sound, and the mysteries of the soul would be perfectly known; we should perceive the soul as an airy phenomenon of consciousness which we directly attain, a sensation, a volition, a thought. In point of fact it is not so, because personal existence, the being which we are, does not fall under the eyes of consciousness and memory; nothing falls under it but the operations by which this being manifests itself. These operations are the proper objects of consciousness and memory; personal identity is a conviction of reason. But all these distinctions could find no place in the theory of Locke. The pretension of this theory is to draw all ideas from sensation and reflection; not being able to make the idea of personal identity proceed from sensation, it is therefore necessary that this theory should make it come from reflection, that is, that it should make of this idea an object of memory and consciousness; that is, that it should destroy personal existence by confounding it with the phenomena which manifest it, and which would be impossible without it.

It only remains for us, in this lecture, to examine the theory of substance.* We are no more frightened by the idea of substance than by that of the infinite. The infinite is the character of time and space; so the idea and the name of substance, are the generalization of the fact of which I have just been treating. Consciousness attests to you, with memory, an operation, or several successive operations, and at the same time suggests to you a belief in your personal existence. Now, what is your personal existence, the being which you are and which reason reveals to you, relatively to the operations which consciousness and memory attest to you? The subject of these operations; and these operations are its characters, its signs, its attributes. These operations vary, and are renewed; they are accidents; on the contrary, your personal existence always subsists the same; you are to-day the same that you were yesterday and that you will be to-morrow, amidst the perpetual diversity of your acts. Personal identity is the unity of your being opposed to the plurality

* On the idea of substance, see the first Series, Vol. 1st, course of 1816; Vol. 2, Lectures 9 and 10, p. 19; Vol. 3, Lecture 3, p. 125; Vol. 4, Lecture 12, p. 56, Lecture 21, p. 433, Lecture 22, p. 448; Vol. 5, Lecture 6, pp. 156–72, etc.

of the acts of consciousness and memory; now being, one and identical, opposed to variable accidents, to transitory phenomena, is substance.

This, you see, is personal substance; it is the same in regard to exterior substance, which I still do not wish to call material substance. Touch gives you the idea of solid; sight and the other senses give you the idea of other qualities, primary or secondary. But what! is there nothing but these qualities? Whilst the senses give you solidity, color, figure, softness, hardness, etc., do you not believe that these qualities are not in the air, but that they are rather in something which really exists, which is solid, hard, soft, etc.? You would not have had the idea of this something, if the senses had not given you the idea of these qualities; but you cannot have the idea of these qualities without the idea of something existing; this is the universal belief, which the distinction between qualities and the subject of these qualities implies, the distinction between accidents and substance.

Attributes, accidents, phenomena, being, substance, subject, are the generalizations drawn from the source of the two incontestable facts of belief in my personal existence, and belief in the existence of the exterior world. Every thing that has been said of body and space, of succession and time, of the finite and the infinite, of consciousness and personal identity, all this should be said of attribute and subject, of qualities and substance, of phenomena and being. If we seek the origin of the idea of phenomena, of quality, of attribute, it is given us by the senses if the object of search be an attribute of external substance; by consciousness if the object of search be an attribute of the soul. As to substance, whether it be material or spiritual, it is given us neither by the senses nor by consciousness; it is a revelation of reason in the exercise of the senses and the consciousness, as space, time, the infinite, and personal identity, are revealed by reason in the exercise of sensibility, consciousness, and memory. Finally, as body, succession, the finite, variety, logically suppose space, time, the infinite and unity; so, in the order of reason and nature, it is evident that attribute and accident presuppose subject and substance. But it is not less evident that, in the order of the acquisition of our ideas, the idea of attribute and accident is the necessary condition in order to arrive at that of substance and subject, as in the same order the idea of body, of succession, of number, of variety, is the condition of the idea of space, of time, of the infinite and identity. This being settled, let us see what place the idea of substance occupies in the system of Locke.

"I confess," says he, Book I. Chap. IV. § 18, "there is another idea, which would be of general use for mankind to have, as it is of general talk, as if they had it; and that is the idea of substance, which we neither have, nor can have, by sensation or reflection." Locke, therefore, systematically denies the idea of substance. Doubtless many passages might be cited in which he implicitly admits it; but here he openly rejects it as "of little use in philosophy," Book II. Chap. XIII. § 19; there, as obscure, Book II. Chap. XXIII. § 4: "We have no clear idea of substance in general." But take away from substance this character of abstraction and generality, and restore it to its reality; substance is then *me*, is body. What! is substance of little use in philosophy, that is, does the belief in my personal identity, the belief in the exterior world, play an unimportant part in my understanding and in human life? Without doubt, to the eyes of the senses as well as to the eyes of consciousness, all substance is obscure; for no substance, material or spiritual, is the proper object of the senses and of consciousness; but, once more, it is not obscure to the eyes of reason, which has its proper objects, which it reveals to us with the same evidence that consciousness and the senses reveal their objects to us. Notwithstanding, Locke everywhere repels the idea of substance; and, when he officially explains himself in regard to it, he resolves it into a collection of simple ideas of sensation and reflection. Book II. Chap. XXIII. §§ 3, 4, 6: "We have no other idea of substances than what is framed by a collection of simple ideas." . . . "It is by such combinations of simple ideas, and nothing else, that we represent particular sorts of substances to ourselves. . . ." § 37: *Recapitulation.* "All our ideas of the several sorts of substances are nothing but collections of simple ideas, with a supposition of something to which they belong, and in which they subsist; though of this supposed something we have no clear distinct idea at all." And he declares that we know nothing of matter but the collection of its qualities, and nothing of mind but the collection of its operations. Nothing is more true than this in a certain respect. It is certain that we know nothing of mind but what its operations teach us in regard to it; that we know nothing of matter but what its qualities teach us in regard to it; as we have already granted that we know nothing of time except what succession teaches us in regard to it, of space except what body teaches us in regard to it, of the infinite except what the finite teaches us, of *me* except what consciousness teaches us. Body is the only measure of space, succession of time, the finite of the infinite, the operations of consciousness of our identity; so attributes and qualities are the only signs and the only measures of substances, whether material or spiritual. But because we know nothing of a thing except what another thing teaches us in regard to it, it does not follow that the former thing is the latter, and that substance is only the collection of its qualities, because it is by the collection alone of its qualities that substance is manifested. Hence a thousand extravagances and paralogisms which have everywhere been produced. It is evident that the collection into which substance is resolved is in every way impossible, without the supposition of substance. M. Royer-Collard* has perfectly shown the different phases of this impossibility. I will refer only to one. Among all the conditions under which a collection is possible, here is one which is incontestable: there must be some one, some mind, to make this collection. Numbers placed under each other do not make addition; arithmetic is not made entirely by itself, it sup-

* Works of Reid, Vol. iv., p. 305.

poses and demands an arithmetician. Now Locke, by denying substance, has destroyed the arithmetician necessary in order to make the addition; the human mind no longer exists, you are no longer a mind one and identical, capable of adding the different quantities of which a collection is composed, and there only remain quantities which must add themselves to each other, must themselves perceive the relations which bind them together. But pass over this difficulty, which, among several others, is a radical one; admit that the collection is possible without some one, some mind which makes it; suppose it made, made by itself alone, what will this collection be? All that a collection can be, an abstraction, a mere word. Behold, therefore, at what you definitely arrive; and, without speaking of God, who is nevertheless also a substance, the substance of substances and being of beings, behold, therefore, mind, behold matter reduced to mere words. Scholasticism had converted many collections into substances, many words into entities; by an exaggeration in a contrary sense, Locke converted substance into collection, and made words of things; and this, mark it well, necessarily and by the force of his system. Admitting only ideas explicable by sensation or reflection, and being able to explain the idea of substance by neither, it was necessary for him to deny it, to reduce it to qualities which are easily attained by sensation or reflection. Hence the systematic confusion of qualities and substance, of phenomena and being, that is, the destruction of being, and consequently of beings. Nothing, therefore, substantially exists, neither God nor the world, neither you nor I; all is resolved into phenomena, into abstractions, into words; and, strange enough, it is the very fear of abstraction and verbal entities, it is the badly understood taste for reality which precipitates Locke into an absolute nominalism, which is nothing else than an absolute nihilism.

LECTURE XIX.

ESSAY, SECOND BOOK. OF THE IDEA OF CAUSE.

Continuation of the examination of the Second Book of the *Essay on the Human Understanding.* Of the idea of cause.—Refutation of the theory which puts the origin of the idea of cause in the sensation.—Origin of the idea of cause in reflection, in the sentiment of the will.—Distinction between the idea of cause and the principle of causality. That the principle of causality is inexplicable by the sentiment of the will alone.—Of the true formation of the principle of causality.

Locke's first fault in regard to the ideas of space, of time, of the infinite, of personal identity, and of substance, is a fault of method. Instead of searching out and recognizing at first, by an impartial observation, the characters which these ideas actually have in the human understanding, he begins by the obscure and perilous question of the origin of these ideas. Then Locke resolves this question concerning the origin of the ideas of space, of time, of the infinite, of personal identity, and of substance, by his general system concerning the origin of ideas, which consists in admitting no idea which has not entered the human understanding either by reflection or by sensation. Now, the ideas of space, of time, of the infinite, of personal identity, and of substance, with the characters by which they are now incontestably marked, are inexplicable by sensation and reflection, and consequently incompatible with the system of Locke. To Locke, then, there remained but one resource, to wit, to mutilate these ideas with their characters, so as to reduce them to the dimensions of other ideas which enter in fact into the human understanding by reflection or sensation, for example the ideas of body, of succession, of number, that of the direct phenomena of consciousness and of memory, and that of the qualities of exterior objects and of our own qualities. But we think that we have shown that these last ideas, which are certainly the condition of the acquisition of the first, are not the first, that they are their chronological antecedent, but not the logical reason: that they precede them, but that they do not explain them. Thus facts disfigured and confounded, save the system of Locke; established and elucidated, they overturn it.

These observations are equally and particularly applicable to the theory of one of the most important ideas that are in the human understanding, the idea which plays the greatest part in human life and in the books of philosophers: I mean the idea of cause.* Locke would have acted wisely to have begun by recognizing it and describing it exactly, such as it now is and such as it is manifested by our actions and by our discourses. Far from this, he at first investigates the origin of the idea of cause, and refers it, without hesitation, to sensation. Observe the following passage from Locke:

Book II. Chap. XXVI. § 1.—*Of cause and effect. Whence their ideas got.*

"In the notice that our senses take of the constant vicissitude of things, we cannot but observe that several particulars, both qualities and substances, begin to exist; and that they receive this their existence from the due application and operation of some other being. From this observation we get our ideas of cause and effect. That which produces any simple or complex idea, we denote by the general name, cause; and that which is produced, effect. Thus finding that in that substance which we call wax, fluidity, which is a simple idea that was not in it before, is constantly produced by the application of a certain degree of heat; we call the simple idea of heat, in relation to fluidity in wax, the cause of it, and fluidity, the effect. So also, finding that the substance wood, which is a certain collection of simple ideas so called, by the application of fire is turned into another substance called ashes, that is, another complex idea, consisting

* On the idea of cause and the principle of causality, see 1st Series, Vol. 1st, course of 1817, programme, p. 216, Vol. 4, Lecture 22, p. 487, etc.

of a collection of simple ideas quite different from that complex idea which we call wood; we consider fire, in relation to ashes, as the cause, and ashes as effect."....§ 2: "Having thus, from what our senses are able to discover in the operations of bodies on one another, got the notion of cause and effect...."

This is positive; the idea of cause has its origin in sensation. It behooves us to examine this question. But since we wish to ascertain whether sensation gives us the idea of cause, our first care should be not to suppose what is a matter of question; we must divest sensation of every foreign element and interrogate it alone, in order to see what it can render in regard to the idea of cause.

I suppose myself reduced to sensation, and I take the example of Locke, that of a piece of wax, which melts, which enters into a fluid state by the contact of fire. What is there here for the senses? There are two phenomena, the wax and the fire, which are in contact with each other. The senses show me this; moreover, they show in the wax a modification which did not before exist in it. A moment since they showed me the wax in one condition, now they show it to me in another, and this other condition they show me even while showing me, or immediately after having shown me the presence of the other phenomena, to wit, the fire; that is, the senses show me the succession of one phenomenon to another phenomenon. Do the senses show me any thing more? I do not see, and Locke does not pretend, that they do; for according to him, the senses give us the idea of cause in the observation of the constant vicissitude of things. Now, the vicissitude of things is certainly the succession of phenomena to each other: let this succession often reappear, several times, constantly even, you will have a constant succession; but let this succession be so far constant as to be perpetual, or let it be limited to a very small number of cases, the greater or less number of cases have no influence over the nature of succession: succession is succession alone. Thus the constant vicissitude of things is, at bottom, reduced to their vicissitude, which is simply their succession. I grant, with Locke, that the senses give me this succession, and Locke does not pretend that they give any thing more. The only question then between us is to know whether the succession, rare or constant, of two phenomena, explains, exhausts the idea which we have of cause.

Because a phenomenon succeeds another and succeeds it constantly, is it the cause of that phenomenon? Is that all the idea that you form of cause? When you say, when you think that the fire is the cause of the fluid state of the wax, I ask you, whether you simply understand that the phenomenon of fluidity succeeds the phenomenon of the approach of the fire; I ask you whether you do not believe, whether the entire human race does not believe that there is in the fire a something, an unknown property, an explanation of which is not here required, to which you refer the production of the phenomenon of the fluidity of the wax. I ask you whether the conception of a phenomenon which appears after another phenomenon is not one thing, and whether the conception in a phenomenon of a certain property which produces the modification which the senses show us in the phenomenon which follows, is not another thing. I will make use of an example often employed, and which expresses perfectly the difference between the relation of succession and the relation of cause to effect. I will suppose that I now wish to hear a harmony, a succession of sounds, and that my desire is scarcely expressed when this succession of sounds is heard in a neighboring apartment and strikes my ear; there is evidently here nothing but a relation of succession. But suppose that I wish to produce sounds, and that I produce them myself: do I simply place between my volition and the sounds which are heard the relation of succession which I just now placed between my desire and the accidental sounds which were heard? Besides the relation of succession, do I not place between my will to produce sounds and the sounds heard, still another relation and a relation very different? Is it not evident that in the last case I believe that not only the first phenomenon, to wit, the will, precedes the second, to wit, the sounds, but moreover that the first phenomenon produces the second, that in short my will is the cause, and the sounds the effect? This is incontestable; it is incontestable that in certain cases we perceive between phenomena simply the relation of succession, and that in certain others we place between them the relation of cause and effect, and that these two relations are not identical with each other. The conviction of every person and the universal belief of the human race leave no doubt on this point. Our acts are not only phenomena which appear in the sequence of the operation of the will; they are judged by us and recognized by others as the direct effects of our will. Hence moral imputation, legal imputation, and three quarters of human life and conduct. If there is only a relation of succession between the act of the murderer and the death of the victim, there is an end of the universal belief and all civil life. Every civil action is founded on this hypothesis, universally admitted, that man is a cause; as the science of nature is founded on the hypothesis that exterior bodies are causes, that is, have properties that can produce and do produce effects. Thus, because the senses give the succession of phenomena, their vicissitude more or less constant, it does not follow that they explain this connection of phenomena with each other, much more intimate and profound, which is called the relation of cause and effect: they do not then explain the origin of the idea of cause. In regard to this I refer to Hume, who perfectly distinguished vicissitude, that is, succession from causation, and who clearly established that the latter cannot proceed from sensation.* This is already sufficient to ruin the theory of Locke on the origin of the idea of cause by sensation.

This is not all: not only is there in the human mind the idea of cause; not only do we believe ourselves to be the cause of our acts, and believe that certain bodies are the cause of the movements of certain others; but we judge in a general manner that

* Essay on the Human Understanding.

no phenomenon can begin to exist either in space or in time without having its cause. Here is something more than an idea, here a principle exists; and the principle is as incontestable as the idea. Imagine a movement, any change whatever: as soon as you conceive this change, this movement, you cannot avoid supposing that this change, that this movement, is made by virtue of some cause. It does not concern us to know what this cause is, what is its nature, how it has produced such a change: the only question is to know whether the human mind can conceive a change and a movement, without conceiving that it is produced by virtue of a cause. Hereon is founded the curiosity of man, who seeks the causes of all phenomena, and the legal action of society, which intervenes as soon as any phenomenon appears which interests it. An assassination, a murder, a theft, any phenomenon whatever which comes under the action of law, being given, an author is supposed, a thief, a murderer, an assassin, and investigation follows: these are all things which would not be done, if there were in the mind a veritable impossibility of not conceiving a cause where there is a phenomenon which begins to exist. Observe that I do not say that there is no effect without a cause; it is evident that this is a frivolous proposition, one term of which contains the other, and expresses the same idea in a different manner. The word effect being relative to the word cause, to say that effect supposes cause is to say no more than that effect is an effect. But we do not suppose an identical and frivolous proposition, when we affirm that every phenomenon which begins to exist has necessarily a cause. The two terms of this proposition do not reciprocally contain each other; the one is not the other, they are not identical, and nevertheless the mind places a necessary connection between them. This is what we call the principle of causality.

This principle is real, certain, incontestable. And what are its characters? First, it is universal. I ask if there is a savage, a child, an old man, a healthy man, a sick man, an idiot even, provided that he may not be completely an idiot, who, a phenomenon being given that begins to exist, does not immediately suppose a cause? Assuredly, if no phenomenon is given, if we have no idea of change, we do not suppose, we cannot suppose a cause; for, where no term is known, what relation can be seized? But it is a fact that in this instance, a single term being given, we suppose the other and their relation, and that universally; there is not a single case in which we do not judge thus. Moreover, not only do we judge thus in all cases, naturally and by the instinctive power of our understanding, but try to judge otherwise; try, a phenomenon being given to you, not to suppose a cause; you cannot do it: the principle is not only universal, it is necessary; whence I conclude that it cannot be derived from the senses. In fact, should it be granted that sensation may give the universal, it is evident that it cannot give the necessary; for the senses give what appears or even what is, such as it is or appears, such or such a phenomenon, with such or such an accidental character: but it is impossible that they should give what ought to be, the reason of a phenomenon, still less its necessary reason.

It is so true that it is not the senses and the exterior world that give us the principle of causality, that, without the intervention of this principle, the exterior world, from which Locke borrows it, would not exist for us. Suppose that a phenomenon may begin to appear in time or in space, without your necessarily seeking a cause; when the phenomenon of sensation appears under the eye of consciousness, not seeking a cause for this phenomenon, you would not seek any thing to which to refer it; you would stop at this phenomenon, that is, at a simple phenomenon of consciousness, that is again at a modification of yourself; you would not go out of yourself, you would not attain the exterior world. What is necessary in order that you may attain the exterior world and suspect its existence? It is necessary that, a sensation being given, you be compelled to ask yourself what is the cause of this new phenomenon, and that, in the double impossibility of referring this phenomenon to yourself, to the *me* that you are, and of not referring it to a cause, you be compelled to refer it to a cause other than yourself, to a foreign cause, to an exterior cause. The idea of an external cause of our sensations, such is the fundamental idea of a without, of exterior objects, of bodies, and of the world.* I do not say that the world, bodies, exterior objects, are only the cause of our sensations; but I say that at first they are given to us as causes of our sensations, on this condition and by this title; afterwards, or at the same time, if you please, we add to this property of objects still other properties; but it is upon this that all those which we may afterwards know are founded. Take away the principle of causality, sensation reveals to us only its relation to the *me* which proves it, without revealing to us that which produces it, the *not me*, external objects, the world. It is often said, and philosophers themselves, with all others, say that the senses discover to us the world. They are right, if they simply mean that without the senses, without some previous sensation, the principle of causality would lack the basis for attaining exterior causes, so that we should never conceive the world: but we should deceive ourselves entirely if we understood that it is the sense itself which, directly and by its own force, without the intervention of reason and of any foreign principle, makes us know the exterior world. To know in general, to know whatever it may be, is beyond the reach of the senses. It is reason, and reason alone, which knows, and knows the world; and it knows it at first only under a title of cause; it is at first for us only the cause of sensitive phenomena which we cannot relate to ourselves: and we should not seek this cause, and consequently we should not find it, if our reason were not provided with the principle of causality, if we could suppose that a phenomenon may begin to appear on the theatre of consciousness, of time or of space, without a cause. Therefore, the principle of causality, I do not fear to say it, is the father of the exterior world, and it is as far as possible from drawing it from the world and making it come from

* First Series, Vol. 1, Course of 1817, Lect. 11, p. 294, and Vol. 4, Lect. 21, p. 425.

sensation. When we speak of exterior objects and of the world without previously admitting the principle of causality, either we do not know what we say, or we are guilty of a paralogism.

The result of all this is that, if there is any question concerning the idea of cause, we cannot find it in the succession of exterior and sensible phenomena; that succession is the condition of the conception of cause, its chronological antecedent, not its principle and its logical reason; and that if the question is not only of the idea of cause, but of the principle of causality, the principle of causality escapes still more the attempt to explain it by succession and sensation. In the first case, that of the idea of cause, Locke confounds the antecedent of an idea with that idea; and in the second case, that of the principle of causality, he produces from the phenomena of the exterior world precisely that without which there would be for us no outward, no world; he supposes that which is yet a matter of question, he no longer confounds the antecedent with the consequent, but the consequent with the antecedent, the consequence with its principle; for the principle of causality is the necessary foundation of even the most trivial knowledge of the world, of the feeblest suspicion of its existence; and to explain the principle of causality by the spectacle of the world, which the principle of causality can alone discover to us, is, once more, to explain the principle by its consequence. Now, the idea of cause, and the principle of causality, are incontestable facts in the human understanding; therefore the system of Locke, which is condemned to obtain in their place only the idea of succession, of constant succession, does not account for facts and does not explain the human understanding.

But is there nothing more in Locke on the great question of cause? Does Locke never assign to the idea of cause any other origin than sensation? Do not expect from our philosopher this perfect consistency. I have already told you, I shall very often repeat it, nothing is so inconsistent as Locke; in his *Essay* contradictions exist not only from book to book, but in the same book from chapter to chapter, and almost from paragraph to paragraph. I have already read to you the positive passage from Book II. Chap. XXVI., in which Locke derives the idea of cause from sensation. Well, let us turn over a few pages, and we shall see him, forgetting both his assertion and the particular examples destined to justify it, conclude, to the great astonishment of the attentive reader, that the idea of cause comes no longer from sensation alone, but from sensation, or from reflection. *Ibid.*: "In which and all other cases, we may observe, that the notion of cause and effect has its rise from ideas, received by sensation *or* reflection; and that this relation, how comprehensible soever, terminates at last in them." This *or* is nothing less than a new theory: thus far Locke had not said a word concerning reflection; it is a manifest contradiction of the passage which I have cited to you. But is this contradiction thrown in here by chance, then abandoned and lost? Yes, in Chapter XXVI.: not in the entire work. Read another chapter of this same second book, Chapter XXI., on *power*. At bottom a chapter on power is a chapter on cause; for what is power, if not the power of producing something, that is, a cause?* To treat of power, then, is to treat of cause. Now, what is the origin of the idea of power, according to Locke, in the express chapter which he devotes to this investigation? As in Chapter XXVI., it is at the same time sensation and reflection.

Book II. Chap. XXI. *Of Power*, § 1. "*This idea how got.* The mind being every day informed, by the senses, of the alteration of those simple ideas it observes in things without, and taking notice how one comes to an end, and ceases to be, and another begins to exist which was not before: reflecting, also, on what passes within itself, and observing a constant change of its ideas, sometimes by the impression of outward objects on the senses, and sometimes by the determination of its own choice; and concluding from what it has so constantly observed to have been, that the like changes will for the future be made in the

* The famous Essay of Hume, on Cause, is entitled *Idea of Power.*

same things by like agents, and by the like ways; considers in one thing the possibility of having any of its simple ideas changed, and in another the possibility of making that change; and so comes by that idea which we call power."

Of these two origins, I have demonstrated that the first, sensation, is insufficient to explain the idea of cause, that is, of power. The second origin remains. But does this second origin precede, or does it follow the first? According to Locke, we derive the idea of cause both from sensation and from reflection; but from which do we draw it first? One of the eminent merits of Locke, as I have already designated to you, is that of having shown, in the question concerning time, that the first succession which reveals to us the idea of time, is not the succession of exterior events, but the succession of our thoughts. Here Locke equally says, that it is first from the interior and not from the exterior, in reflection, and not in sensation, that the idea of power is given to us. It is a manifest contradiction, I agree, with his official chapter on cause; but it is an honor to Locke to have seen and established, while contradicting himself, that it is in reflection, in the consciousness of our operations, that the first and most clear idea of cause is given to us. I wish to read this entire passage from Locke, because it shows a true talent for observation and a rare psychological sagacity.

Book II. Chap. XXI. § 4. "*The clearest idea of active power had from spirit.* We are abundantly furnished with the idea of passive power by almost all sorts of sensible things. In most of them we cannot avoid observing their sensible qualities, nay, their very substances, to be in a continual flux: and therefore with reason we look on them as liable still to the same change. Nor have we of active power (which is the more proper signification of the word power) fewer instances: since whatever change is observed, the mind must collect a power somewhere able to make that change, as well as a possibility in the thing itself to receive it. But yet, if we will consider it attentively, bodies, by our senses, do not afford us so clear and distinct an idea of active power as we have from reflection on the operations of our minds. For all power relating to action,—and there being but two sorts of action whereof we have any idea, viz., thinking and motion,—let us consider whence we have the clearest ideas of the powers which produce these actions. 1. Of thinking, body affords us no idea at all: it is only from reflection that we have that. 2. Neither have we from body any idea of the beginning of motion. A body at rest affords us no idea of any active power to move; and when it is set in motion itself, that motion is rather a passion than an action in it. For when the ball obeys the stroke of a billiard-stick, it is not any action of the ball, but bare passion: also, when by impulse it sets another ball in motion that lay in its way, it only communicates the motion it had received from another, and loses in itself so much as the other received: which gives us but a very obscure idea of an active power of moving in body, whilst we observe it only to transfer, but not produce, any motion. For it is but a very obscure idea of power, which reaches not the production of the action, but the continuation of the passion. For so is motion in a body impelled by another; the continuation of the alternation made in it from rest to motion being little more an action than the continuation of the alternation of its figure by the same blow, is an action. The idea of the beginning of motion we have only from reflection on what passes in ourselves, where we find by experience, that barely by willing it, barely by a thought of the mind, we can move the parts of our bodies which were before at rest. So that it seems to me, we have, from the observation of the operation of bodies by our senses, but a very imperfect, obscure idea of active power, since they afford us not any idea in themselves of the power to begin any action, either motion or thought."

Locke evidently feels that he has contradicted himself, and therefore adds: "But if from the impulse bodies are observed to make one upon another, any one thinks he has a clear idea of power, it serves as well to my purpose, sensation being one of those ways whereby the mind comes by its ideas: only I thought it worth while to consider here, by the way, whether the mind doth not receive its idea of active power clearer from reflection on its own operations than it doth from any external sensation."

Now, this power of action, of which reflection gives us the distinct idea, which sensation alone cannot furnish, what is it? This power is that of the will.

Book II. Chap. XXI. § 5: "This at least I think evident, that we find in ourselves a power to begin or forbear, continue or end several actions of our minds, and motions of our bodies, barely by a thought or preference of the mind ordering, or, as it were, commanding the doing or not doing such or such a particular action. This power which the mind has thus to order the consideration of any idea, or the forbearing to consider it—or to prefer the motion of any part of the body to its rest, and *vice versa*, in any particular instance—is that which we call the *will*. The actual exercise of that power, by directing any particular action, or its forbearance, is that which we call *volition*, or willing. The forbearance of that action, consequent to such order or command of the mind, is called *voluntary*. And whatsoever action is performed without such a thought of the mind, is called *involuntary*."

Behold, then, the will considered as a power of action, as a productive power, and consequently as a cause. This is the germ of the beautiful theory of M. de Biran on the origin of the idea of cause. According to M. de Biran,* as well as according to Locke, the idea of cause is not given to us in the observation of exterior phenomena, which, considered solely with the senses, do not manifest to us any causative power and appear simply successive: it is given from within in the reflection, in the consciousness of our operations and of the power which produces them, to wit, the will. I make an effort to move my arm, and I move it. When we analyze attentively this phenomenon of the effort which M. de Biran considers as the type of the phenomena of the will, we find therein: 1st, the consciousness of a voluntary act; 2d, the consciousness of a movement produced;

* Works of M. de Biran, *passim*.

3d, a relation of the movement to the voluntary act. And what is this relation? Evidently it is not a simple relation of succession. Repeat in yourselves the phenomenon of effort, and you will recognize that you all attribute, with a perfect conviction, the production of the movement of which you are conscious, to the anterior voluntary operation, of which you are also conscious. For you the will is not only a mere act without efficiency, it is a productive energy, it is a cause.

Moreover, this movement of which you are conscious, which you all refer as an effect to the anterior operation of the will as a producing operation, as a cause, I ask you, do you refer this movement to another will than your own? Do you consider this will, could you consider it, as the will of another, as the will of your neighbor, as the will of Alexander, or of Cæsar, or of some foreign or superior power? For you is it not your own? Do you not impute to yourself every voluntary act? In a word, is it not from the consciousness of will, in so far as your own, that you derive the idea of your personality, the idea of yourself? The peculiar merit of M. de Biran is in having established that the will is the constituent character of our personality. He went farther, too far perhaps. As Locke had confounded consciousness and memory with personality and the identity of the *me*, M. de Biran went so far as to confound the will with the personality itself; it is at least its eminent character; so that the idea of cause, which is given to us in the consciousness of the producing will, is for the same reason given to us in the consciousness of our personality, and that we are the first cause of which we have any knowledge.

In fine, this cause which we are, is implied in every fact of consciousness. The necessary condition of every phenomenon perceived by the consciousness, is, that attention be given to it. If we do not pay attention to it, the phenomenon may still exist; but the consciousness not applying itself to it, not taking cognizance of it, it is for us as if it did not exist. Attention is then the condition of every apperception of consciousness. Now, attention is the will; I have proved it more than once. Therefore the condition of every phenomenon of consciousness, and consequently of the first phenomenon as of all the others, is the will; and as the will is a causative power, it follows that in the first act of consciousness, and in order that this first act may take place, it is necessary that there be an apperception of our personal causality in our will; whence it follows again, that the idea of cause is the primary idea, that the apperception of the voluntary cause, which we are, is the primary apperception and the condition of all others.

Such is the theory to which M. de Biran* has elevated that of Locke. I adopt it; I believe that it gives a perfect account of the origin of the idea of cause; but it remains to know whether the idea of cause which proceeds from this origin, and from the sentiment of voluntary and personal activity, is sufficient to explain the idea that all men have of exterior causes, and to render an account of the principle of causality. For Locke, who treats of the idea of cause, and never of the principle of causality, the problem does not even exist. M. de Biran, who scarcely lays it down, resolves it too soon, and arrives immediately at a result, the only one which the theory of Locke and his own permit, but which a sound psychology, and a sound logic, cannot adopt.

According to M. de Biran, after having drawn the idea of cause from the sentiment of our voluntary and personal activity, from the phenomenon of the effort of which we are conscious, we transport this idea outwardly, we project it into the exterior world, by virtue of an operation which he, as well as M. Royer-Collard, has called a natural induction.† Let us understand this. If by that M. de Biran merely means, that before knowing exterior causes, whatever they may be, we first obtain the idea of cause from ourselves, I agree with him; but I deny that the knowledge

* See particularly in the Works of M. de Biran, Vol. i., the *Examination* of the Lectures of M. Laromiguière, Chap. VIII.

† *Ibid.*, article *Leibnitz*. See also Lectures of M. Royer-Collard, Works of Reid, Vols. iii. and iv.

which we have of external causes, and the idea which we form of these causes, are an importation, a projection, an induction of ours.* In fact, this induction could take place only on conditions which are in manifest contradiction with facts and reason. I here invoke all your attention.

According to Locke and M. de Biran, it is reflection, consciousness which gives us the idea of cause. But what idea of cause does it give us? Observe that it does not give us the idea of a general and abstract cause, but the idea of the *me* which wills, and which, willing, produces, and is thereby a cause. The idea of cause which consciousness gives us is, then, an idea, entirely particular, individual, determinate, since to us it is entirely personal. All that we know of cause by consciousness is concentrated in personality. It is this personality, and in this personality it is the will, the will alone, and nothing more, which is the power, which is the cause that consciousness gives us. This being settled, let us see what are the conditions of the induction of this cause. Induction is the supposition that, in certain circumstances, a certain phenomenon, a certain law, being given to us, under analogous circumstances, the same phenomenon, the same law, will take place. Induction supposes then, 1st, analogous cases; 2d, a phenomenon which must remain the same. Induction is the process of the mind which, having thus far perceived a phenomenon only in certain cases, transports this phenomenon, this phenomenon I say, and not another, into different cases, and different necessarily, since they are only analogous and similar, and since they cannot be absolutely identical. The peculiar character of induction is precisely in the contrast of the identity of the phenomenon, or of the law, and of the diversity of the circumstances from which it is first borrowed, and then transported. If, then, the knowledge of external causes is only an in-

* A sketch of this discussion will be found 1st Series, Vol. 2, Lectures 2–4, p. 58, etc., and a summary in the Introduction to the Works of M. de Biran, p. xxxv.

duction from our personal cause, it is strictly our cause, the voluntary and free cause which we are, that induction should transport into the exterior world; that is, that wherever any movement or change whatever shall begin to appear in time and in space, then we must suppose, what? a cause in general? No; for remember we have not yet the general idea of cause, we have simply the idea of our personal causality; we can suppose only that which we already have, otherwise it would no longer be the proper and legitimate process of induction; we must then suppose, not the general and abstract idea of cause, but the particular and determinate idea of the particular and determinate cause that we are; whence it follows that it is our causality which we must suppose wherever any phenomenon begins to appear: that is, that all causes which we can farther conceive, are and can be merely our own personality, the only cause of all the effects, accidents, or events which begin to appear. And observe that the belief in the world and in exterior causes is universal and necessary. All men have it, all men cannot avoid having it. If, then, induction explains all our conception of exterior causes, this induction must be universal and necessary; it must be a necessary and universal fact that we believe ourselves the cause of all the events, movements, and changes which happen and can happen.

Yes, strictly speaking, the induction, the transferring of our causality without ourselves, is nothing less than the substitution of our personal causality for all the causes of this world, the substitution of human liberty for destiny and nature. M. de Biran would have doubtless repelled this consequence as overstrained; but here is one which he almost accepted. If external causes are only an induction from our own, and if, nevertheless, we are unwilling to admit them to be identical with our own, they must, at least, be similar to our own, that is, endowed with consciousness, free, animated, living. In fact, without pretending that this is our whole conception of exterior causes, M. de Biran contends that such is the conception which we at first form of them. In proof of it, he says that children and savages, that is, infant peoples, conceive all external causes on the model of their own; that thus the child revolts against the stone that strikes him, as if it had had the intention of striking him, and that the savage personifies and deifies the causes of natural phenomena.

To this I reply: let us not forget that the belief in the world and in external causes is universal and necessary, and that the fact which explains it must itself be a universal and necessary fact: if, then, our belief in the world and in exterior causes resolves itself into the assimilation of these causes to our own, this assimilation must be a universal and necessary fact. Now here I look to psychology; I expect that it will prove that all intellectual and moral beings conceive external causes by reason of their own, as endowed with consciousness, and animated; I look to it to prove that this opinion of children and of savages is not only a frequent fact, but a universal fact, and that there is not a child, not a savage who does not thus begin. And when it shall have proved that this fact is universal, it must necessarily go still farther: it must necessarily prove that this fact is not only universal, but that it is necessary. But the character of a necessary fact is, that it must unavoidably exist; and the necessity of an idea, of a law, implies the domination of that idea, of that law, in the whole extent of its duration, and so long as the human mind subsists. Although I should grant that all children, and all infant peoples, begin by believing that external causes are animated, living, free, personal, it would not be enough to establish a necessary fact; it would be necessary that all men, without any distinction, should have this belief, as they believe every thing, without distinction, in the principle of causality. Far from this, we do not in the least admit such an opinion, and it is our honor not to admit it. That which would be a necessary truth, reproduced invariably from century to century, is simply, in our eyes, an extravagance which endured for a longer or shorter period, and which now has forever passed away. For the reason that induction has languished a single day, and for this reason alone, we must conclude that this induction is not a universal and necessary law of the human mind, and that it does not explain the universal and necessary belief in the existence of the world, and of external causes.

We all have the perfect conviction that this world exists, that there are external causes; and these causes we believe to be neither personal nor voluntary. This is the belief of the human race; it belongs to philosophy to explain it, without destroying it, without altering it. But if this belief is universal and necessary, the judgment which contains it, and which gives it, must have a principle which is itself universal and necessary; and this principle is none other than the principle of causality, the principle which logic and grammar now present under this form: every phenomenon, every movement which begins to appear has a cause. Suppress this principle and leave the simple consciousness of our personal causality, and we should never have the least idea of external causes and of the world. Let a phenomenon appear of which we are not the cause, take away the empire of the principle of causality, and no longer does any reason exist for demanding the cause of this phenomenon, we should not seek its cause; it would be for us without cause: for observe that, even for the induction of which we speak, even in order to fall into this absurdity of giving to sensation as its cause, either ourselves or something similar to ourselves, we must be under the necessity of assigning causes to every phenomenon, and in order to do it universally and necessarily, this necessity must be universal and necessary, that is, it must have the principle of causality. Thus, without the principle of causality, every phenomenon is for us as if it had no cause, and we cannot even attribute to it an extravagant cause. On the contrary, suppose the principle of causality, and as soon as a phenomenon of sensation begins to appear upon the theatre of consciousness, immediately the principle of causality marks it with the character that it cannot avoid having a cause. Now, as consciousness attests that this cause is not our own, and that, nevertheless, this phenomenon must have a cause, it follows that it has a cause, and a cause other than ourselves, which is neither personal nor voluntary, and which, nevertheless, is a cause, that is, a simple efficient cause. This is precisely the idea which all men form of external causes; they consider them as causes capable of producing the movements which they refer to them, but not as intentional and personal causes.* The universal and necessary principle of causality is the only principle that can give us such causes; it is, then, the veritable and legitimate process of the human mind in the acquisition of the idea of the world and of external causes.

After having demonstrated that our belief in exterior causes is not an induction from the consciousness of our personal cause, but a legitimate application of the principle of causality, it is necessary to show how we proceed from the consciousness of our particular personality to the conception of the general principle of causality.

I admit and I firmly believe that the consciousness of our own causality precedes all conception of the principle of causality, consequently all application of this principle, all knowledge of exterior causality; and behold, in my opinion, how in the depths of the intelligence the passage is made from the first fact, from the fact of consciousness to the ulterior fact of the conception of the principle. I wish to move my arm, and I move it. We have seen that this fact, being analyzed, contains three elements: 1st, Consciousness of a volition which is mine, which is personal; 2d, Movement produced; 3d, Finally, a relation of this movement to my will, which relation is, as we have seen, a relation of production, of causation; a relation which I no more question than the other two terms; a relation which is given me with these two terms, which is not given to me without the two terms, and without which the two terms are not given to me; so that the three terms are given to me in a single and even indivisible

---

* On the reality of causes, natural, efficient, and not voluntary, see in Vol. 4 of the 1st Series, pp. 542–564, the Examination of the Essay of Reid on the *Active power*.

fact, which is the consciousness of my personal causality. Now, what is the character of this fact? The character of this fact is that of being particular, individual, determinate, for the very simple reason that this fact is entirely personal. This productive will is my own, consequently it is a particular and determinate will; this movement which I produce is mine, consequently it is particular and determinate. And, again, the character of all that is particular is that of being susceptible of more or less. I myself, a voluntary cause, have at such a moment more or less energy, which gives to the movement produced by me more or less force. But does the most feeble movement belong to me less than the most energetic movement? Is there between the two terms, between the cause *me* and the effect movement, a less relation in one case than in the other? No, the two terms may vary and continually vary in intensity; the relation does not vary at all. Still farther: not only do the two terms vary, but they might be totally different; they might even not exist; they are merely accidental; but the relation between these two determinate, variable, contingent terms, is itself neither variable nor contingent; it is universal and necessary. At the same time that the consciousness seizes the two terms, the reason seizes their relation, and, by an immediate abstraction which has no need of relying on a number of similar facts, it disengages in a single fact the invariable and necessary element of its variable and contingent elements. Does it strive to put in question the truth of this relation; it cannot do it: intelligence in vain makes the attempt, it cannot be done. Whence it follows that this truth is a necessary and universal truth. Reason is then under the empire of this truth; it is impossible for it not to suppose a cause wherever the senses or the consciousness present any phenomenon whatever. This impossibility for the reason not to suppose a cause where the senses or the consciousness present any phenomenon whatever, is what is called the principle of causality, not in its actual logical formula, but in its internal, primitive energy. If it be asked how the universal and the necessary are in the relative and the contingent, and may be perceived in them, I reply that the reason also is in us with the will and the senses, and that it is, at the same time, developed with them.*

What I have just said of the principle of causality may be said of all the other principles. It is a fact which must not be forgotten, and which is much too often forgotten, that our judgments are at first particular and determinate judgments, and that it is under the form of a particular and determinate judgment, that all universal and necessary truths, all universal and necessary principles make their first appearance. Thus the senses attest to me the existence of a body, and at once I judge that this body is in space, not in general space, in mere space, but in a certain space; it is a certain body that the senses attest to me, and it is in a certain space that the reason places it. Then when we consider the relation which exists between this particular body and this particular space, we find that this relation is not itself particular, but that it is universal and necessary; and when we try to conceive a body without any space whatever, we cannot do it. It is the same in regard to time: when the consciousness or the senses give us a succession of events or of thoughts, we at once judge that this succession of events takes place in a determinate time. Every thing is determinate in time and succession, such as they are primitively given to us. The question is concerning such or such a succession, of an hour, of a day, or of a year, etc.; but that which is not determinate and particular, is the relation which we place between this succession and this time. We vary the two terms, we vary the succession and the time which embraces the succession, but the relation of succession to time does not vary. Thus it is again that the principle of substance is given to us. When a phenomenon occurs in my consciousness, this phenome-

* On this delicate point, the formation of our actual conception of the universal and necessary relation of cause and effect, and in general on the formation of the rational principles, see 1st Series, Vol. 1, Course of 1817, *programme*, pp. 216–218; and Vol. 2, Course of 1818, *programme*, p. 24, Lectures 2–4, pp. 47–58; and Lecture 11, p. 134.

non is a particular and determinate phenomenon, and not any phenomenon whatever; and then I judge that under this particular phenomenon, is a being which is its subject, not a general and abstract being, but real and determinate, *me*. All our primitive judgments are personal and determinate, and nevertheless in the depths of these personal and determinate judgments, are already relations, truths, principles which are not personal and determinate, although they determine and individualize themselves in the determination and in the individuality of their terms. Such is the first form of the truths of geometry and of arithmetic. Behold for example* two objects and two objects; here all is determinate; these quantities to be added are concrete and not discrete. You judge that these two objects and these two objects make four objects. Well, what is there in this? Once more, every thing is here contingent and variable, except the relation. You may vary the objects, put stones instead of these books, hats instead of these stones, and the relation does not vary. Still farther: why have you judged that these two determinate objects added to two other determinate objects make four determinate objects? Think of it; it is by virtue of this truth that two and two make four. Now, this truth of relation is entirely abstract and independent of the nature of the two terms, whatever they may be. It is then the abstract truth which makes us decide that two concrete objects and two concrete objects, different or similar, make four objects. The abstract is given to us in the concrete, the invariable and the necessary in the relative and the contingent, reason in the senses and the consciousness. It is the senses that attest to you the existence of concrete quantities and bodies; it is the consciousness that attests to you the presence of a succession of thoughts and that of all the phenomena under which is your personal identity. At the same time reason intervenes and decides that the relations of the quantities in question are abstract, universal, and necessary rela-

* See this same example, Vol. 1st of this same Series, Lecture 3.

tions; as the reason decides that the relation of body to space is a necessary relation; that the relation between succession and time is a necessary relation; that the relation between the phenomenal plurality which our thoughts form in the consciousness, and the identical and one being which is their subject is also a necessary relation. In the infancy of knowledge, the action of the senses and of the consciousness are mingled together with that of the reason. The senses and consciousness give external and internal phenomena, the variable, the contingent; reason discovers to us universal and necessary truths mingled with accidental and contingent truths which result from the apperception of internal or external phenomena; and these universal and necessary truths constitute universal and necessary principles. It is with the principle of causality as with other principles; the human mind would never conceive it in its universality and its necessity, if at first, a particular fact of causation were not given to us; and this primitive particular fact is that of our own personal causality manifested to the consciousness in effort or voluntary action. But this fact is not itself alone sufficient to explain the knowledge of external causes, because then external causes would necessarily be an induction from our own, that is, it would be necessary to resolve the belief of the human race, its universal and necessary belief, into an absurdity, and into a transitory absurdity, which experience contradicts, and which is now abandoned: this explanation is then inadmissible. It is necessary to conceive that in the contingent and determinate fact, I wish to move my arm and I move it, is a relation of the movement as effect to the will as cause, which relation, disengaged from its two terms, is seized by reason as a universal and necessary truth. Hence the principle of causality, by the aid of which we can reach external causes, because this principle surpasses the reach of our consciousness, and because with it we may judge universally and necessarily that every phenomenon, whatever it may be, has a cause. Thus armed, so to speak, let a new phenomenon present itself, and we refer it universally and necessarily to a cause; and this cause not being ourselves, according to the infallible testimony of our consciousness, we do not the less judge universally and necessarily that this cause exists; only we judge that it is other than ourselves, that it is foreign to us: here again is the idea of exteriority and the basis of our conviction of the existence of the exterior causes of the world; a universal and necessary conviction, because the principle of the judgment which gives it to us is itself universal and necessary.

Without doubt, at the same time that we conceive causes, exterior, foreign to us, other than ourselves, not intentional, not voluntary, causes such as the application of the general principle of causality can give us, the child, the savage, the human race in its infancy adds sometimes, very often even, to this idea of exteriority, of purely efficient cause, the idea of a will, of a personality similar to our own. But because this second fact sometimes accompanies the first, it does not follow that it must be confounded with it: in order to be attached to a universal and necessary fact, this new fact is not thereby necessary and universal, as I have demonstrated; it gives nothing but error and temporary superstitions, instead of the permanent and inviolable truth which the principle of causality engenders. But in short the fact is real, the errors which it produces are incontestable although local and temporary; it must then be explained; and the explanation is very simple. As the principle of causality, although universal and necessary, arises in us from the consciousness of our own causality, it preserves, in its first applications, the trace of its origin, and the belief in the exterior world is accompanied with some vague assimilation of exterior causes to our own. Add that here as in all things, it is truth which serves as a support to error; for the arbitrary and senseless personification of exterior causes presupposes their existence. Induction then misleads the principle of causation; but it does not constitute it.

It is thus that a sound psychology, determined never to abandon the natural conceptions of the human mind, ascends little by little to their veritable origin; while the systematic psychology of Locke, plunging into the question of the origin of our ideas and of our principles, before having determined with precision the characters by which they are actually marked, and admitting no other origin than sensation or reflection, believes that it can find the origin of the idea of cause in sensation; then forced to abandon this origin, it goes from sensation to reflection; but this origin which can give us the idea of voluntary personal cause, can give only this idea, and not the principle of causality, and consequently cannot explain the knowledge of purely efficient external causes. If then we wish to stop at this narrow origin, what must be done? With this universal and necessary result, that we conceive causes out of ourselves which are not ourselves, it is necessary to confound this other purely accidental fact, that we sometimes conceive these causes, as personal causes; so as to explain the knowledge of exterior causes by simple induction from our own causality, and the principle of causality by reflection, that is, by one of the two adopted origins of all knowledge. But again the conception of exterior causes, as personal and endowed with consciousness, is but an error of the infancy of human reason, and not a law of this reason: we cannot draw from it an explanation of the legitimate, universal, and necessary belief of the human race.

In closing, I must ask pardon for the length of this lecture; but I owed this discussion, though very imperfect, both to the importance of the subject and to the memory of the great metaphysician, who by his very sagacity and his profoundness was led astray by following Locke. Endowed with an admirable psychological acuteness, M. de Biran penetrated so far into the intimacy of the fact of consciousness which gives us the idea of cause, the idea of the voluntary and personal cause which we are, that he scarcely went out from this fact and from this idea, and neglected too much the principle of causality, confounding thus, like Locke, the antecedent of the principle with the principle itself; or when he tried to explain the principle of causality, explaining it by *a natural induction* which transports into the external world consciousness, the will, and all the peculiar attributes of its model, taking a particular, transient, and erroneous application of the principle of causality for this principle, in itself true, universal, and necessary; that is, confounding by a single error, no more the antecedent with the consequent, but the consequent with the antecedent. The theory of M. de Biran is the development of that of Locke; it reproduces it with more extent and profoundness, and exhausts at once its merits and its defects.

LECTURE XX.

ESSAY, SECOND BOOK. OF GOOD AND EVIL. THIRD BOOK. OF WORDS.

Continuation of the examination of the Second Book of the *Essay on the Human Understanding*. Of the idea of good and evil. Refutation.—Of the formation and mechanism of ideas in the understanding. Of simple and complex ideas.—Of the activity and passivity of the mind in the acquisition of ideas.—Of the most general characters of ideas.—Of the association of ideas.—Examination of the Third Book of the *Essay on the Human Understanding*, in regard to words.—Praise due to the author.—Examination of the following propositions: 1st, Do words take their first origin from other words which signify sensible ideas?—2d, Is the signification of words purely arbitrary?—3d, Are general ideas merely words? Of nominalism and realism.—4th, Are words the sole cause of error, and is all science only a well-constructed language? Conclusion of the examination of the Third Book.

It is* an incontestable fact that, when we have done right or wrong, when we have fulfilled the law of justice or have broken it, we judge that we merit a reward or a punishment; and it is also a fact that we really do receive reward or punishment, 1st, in the approval of conscience or in the bitterness of remorse; 2d, in the esteem or blame of our fellow-men, who, being also moral beings, judge as we do of good and evil, and punish us and reward us according to our acts, sometimes by the pain or the moral recompense of their blame or of their esteem, sometimes by the rewards or the physical pains which positive laws, the legitimate interpreters of natural law, hold ready for generous actions or for derelictions and crimes; 3d, finally, if we look beyond this world, if we conceive of God as we ought to conceive of him, not only as the author of the physical world, but as the

* On the idea of good and evil, of obligation, of merit and demerit, see 1st Series, *passim*, and particularly Vol. 2, Lecture 20.

father of the moral world, as the substance itself of good and of the moral law, we cannot help conceiving that God holds ready rewards or punishments for those who have fulfilled or broken the law. But suppose that there is neither good nor evil, neither justice nor injustice in itself; suppose that there is no law: there can then be neither merit nor demerit in having broken or fulfilled it; there is no place for punishment or reward; there is no place either for the pleasures of conscience or the pangs of remorse; there is no place either for the approbation or disapprobation of men, either for their esteem or their blame; there is no place either for the punishments or the rewards of society in this life, or in the life to come for the rewards and punishments of the supreme Legislator. The idea of reward and punishment rests, therefore, upon that of merit and demerit, which again rests upon that of a law. Now, what does Locke here do? he draws the idea of good and evil, the moral law and all the rules of our duties, from the fear and the hope of rewards and punishments, human or divine, that is,—to shun every other consideration, and to rest upon the solid ground of scientific method,—he founds the principle upon the consequence; he confounds, no longer as heretofore, the antecedent with the consequent, but the consequent with the antecedent. And whence comes this confusion? from that same source of confusion which we have so many times signalized, the premature search for causes before a sufficient study of effects, the search for the origin of the idea of good and evil, before having carefully stated the characters, and all the characters, of this idea. Permit me to dwell a moment on this important matter.

First, that there is in the human understanding, such as it now is, the idea of good, and the idea of evil, entirely distinct from each other, is what the most superficial observation, provided it be impartial, easily demonstrates. It is a fact, that in the presence of certain actions reason qualifies them as good or bad, as just or unjust, as honest or dishonest. And it is not only in some superior men that reason bears this judgment: there is not a man, ignorant or instructed, civilized or savage, provided he be a reasonable and moral being, who does not bear the same judgment. As the principle of causality errs and rectifies itself without ceasing to be, so the distinction between right and wrong may be incorrectly made, may vary in its objects, and be elucidated with time, without ceasing to be at bottom the same in all men; it is a universal conception of reason, and this is why all languages, those faithful images of thought, reproduce it. Not only is this distinction a universal conception, it is also a necessary conception. In vain the reason, after having conceived it, tries to deny it and put its verity in question, it cannot; we are not able at will to call the same action just or unjust; these two ideas resist every attempt to interchange them: they may change in regard to objects, never in regard to their nature. Furthermore: reason cannot conceive the distinction between good and evil, just and unjust, honest and dishonest, without conceiving at the same instant that the one ought to be done, and that the other ought not to be done: the conception of good and evil immediately gives that of duty and law, and as the one is universal and necessary, the other is equally so. Now, a law necessary for reason in respect to action is, for a reasonable but free agent, a simple obligation, not an absolute obligation. Duty obligates us without forcing us; if we can violate it, we cannot deny it; and even when the feebleness of liberty and the ascendency of passion, make the action, as it were, belie its law, the independent reason maintains the violated law as an inviolable law, and still imposes it with a supreme authority upon unfaithful action, as its imprescriptible rule. The sentiment of reason, and that of moral obligation which it reveals to us and imposes on us, is the moral consciousness properly so called.

Remark distinctly upon what obligation bears: it bears upon doing right; it bears only upon this point, but here it is absolute. It is, therefore, independent of every foreign consideration; it has nothing to do with the facilities or the perils which its fulfilment encounters, nothing to do with the consequences which it brings, with pleasure or pain, that is, with happiness and misery, that is, with any motive, whatever it may be, of utility; for pleasure and pain, happiness and misery, are only objects of sensibility; good and moral obligation are conceptions of reason; utility is only an accident which may or may not be; duty is a principle.

Now, is not good always useful to him who performs it, and to others? This is another question which does not pertain to reason, but to experience. Does experience always decide in the affirmative? Even should it, and were the useful always inseparable from the good, the good and the useful would not be less distinct in themselves, and it would not be on the ground of utility that virtue would be obligatory, and that it would obtain universal veneration and admiration. We admire it, therefore we do not take it solely as useful; for admiration is not the expression of interest.*

If the good were only the useful, the admiration which virtue excites would always be in the ratio of its utility: but this is not so. There are no virtues which, for utility, can be compared with certain natural phenomena which everywhere diffuse and sustain life. And who has ever felt for the sun, whose influence is so beneficent, the sentiment of admiration and respect with which the most sterile virtuous act inspires us? It is because the sun is simply useful; while the virtuous act, useful or not, is the fulfilment of a law, to which the agent, whom we qualify as virtuous, and whom we admire, is voluntarily conformed. We can profit by an action without admiring it, as we can admire it without profiting by it. The foundation of admiration is not, therefore, the utility which the admired object procures for others; it is still less the utility which the action procures for him who does it. Virtuous action would then be only a calculation of happiness; we might congratulate its author, but we should not be tempted to admire him. Humanity demands in its heroes

* On the moral phenomenon of admiration, see 1st Series, Vol. 2, Lecture 17, p. 214, etc.

some other merit than that of a sagacious merchant; and, far from the utility of the agent and his personal interest being the title and measure of admiration, it is a fact that, all other things being equal, the phenomenon of admiration decreases and increases just in proportion to the sacrifices which the virtuous action costs.* But do you wish a manifest proof that virtue does not rest upon the personal interest of him who practises it? take the example which I have already given,† that of an honest man whose virtue ruins him instead of being useful to him; and, in order to prevent all idea of calculation, suppose a man who gives his life for the truth, who dies upon the scaffold in the flower of his age, for the cause of justice. Here no future chance of happiness, at least in this world, therefore no calculation, no personal interest, is possible. This man, if virtue is only the useful, is a fool, and humanity which admires it, is in delirium. This delirium is nevertheless a fact, and an incontestable fact; it unanswerably demonstrates that, in the human understanding, such as it has pleased its Author to make it, the idea of good and evil, of vice and virtue, is one thing, and the idea of utility, of pleasure and pain, of happiness and misery, is another.

I have just shown you the essential and metaphysical difference between these ideas; it is now necessary to exhibit their relation. It is certain that the idea of virtue is distinct from that of happiness; but I ask whether, when you meet a virtuous man, a moral agent who, free to obey or not to obey a strict law, obeys it at the expense of his dearest affections; I ask whether this man, this moral agent, does not inspire you, independently of the admiration which is attached to the act, with a sentiment of benevolence which is attached to the person? Is it not true that you would be disposed, if happiness were in your hands, to bestow it upon this virtuous man? Is it not true that he would

* On sacrifice, as the foundation and measure of moral approbation, see 1st Series, Vol. 4, Lecture 15, p. 170, etc.

† Preceding Vol., Lecture 8, and 1st Series, Vol. 1, Course of 1817, Lecture 18, p. 313, and Vol. 2, Lecture 23, p. 355.

appear to you to merit happiness, and that in regard to him happiness would appear to you no longer as merely an arbitrary fact, but as a right? At the same time, when the culpable man finds himself in misery through the effect of his vices, do we not judge that he has deserved it? Do we not judge, in general, that it would be unjust for vice to be happy and virtue miserable? Such is evidently the opinion of all men; and this opinion is not only universal, it is a necessary conception. In vain reason tries to conceive of vice as worthy of happiness, it cannot succeed in it; it cannot succeed in denying an intimate harmony between happiness and virtue. And in this we are not beings of sensation who aspire after happiness, nor beings of sympathy who desire it for our fellow-men; we are rational and moral beings who judge thus for others, as well as for ourselves; and when facts do not accord with our judgments, it is not our judgments that we condemn, we maintain them before all the contrary facts. In a word, the idea of merit and demerit is for the reason inseparable from that of the moral law, fulfilled or violated.

Where virtue and vice have their recompense and punishment, there is order for us; whenever vice and virtue are without punishment and reward, or where they are equally treated, there for us is disorder. Rewards and punishments are diverse, according to cases which it is not necessary here to determine and classify with perfect precision. When vicious acts do not pass beyond the sphere of the person who commits them, we do not impose upon them any punishment but contempt: we punish them by opinion. When they pass beyond this sphere and attain that of others, then they fall under positive laws; hence penal laws. In all times, in all places, these two kinds of punishment, moral and material, have been inflicted upon vicious agents. Without any doubt, it is useful for society to inflict contempt upon him who violates the moral order; without any doubt, it is useful for society to effectively punish him who corrupts the foundations of social order; this consideration of utility is real, it is powerful; but I say that it is not the only one, that it is not the first, that it is only accessory, and that the principle of all penalty is the idea of the essential merit and demerit of actions, the general idea of order, which imperiously demands that the merit and demerit of acts, which is a law of reason and order, shall be realized in a society that pretends to be rational and well ordered. On this ground, and on this ground alone, of realizing this law of reason and order, the two powers of society, opinion and the State, appear to us faithful to their primary law. Then comes utility, the immediate utility of repressing evil, and the indirect utility of preventing it by example, that is, by fear. But this consideration of the utility of punishment, would not be sufficient for the foundation. Suppose, in fact, that there is in itself neither good nor evil, and consequently neither essential merit nor demerit: what right have you, I ask, to dishonor a man, to make him mount the scaffold, or to put him during his whole life in irons, solely for the benefit of others, when the action of this man is neither good nor bad, and merits in itself neither blame nor punishment? Suppose that it is not just in itself to blame this man and punish him, and there is an end made of the justice of infamy and glory, of the justice of every species of reward and punishment. I say farther: if penalty has no other foundation than utility, then there is made an end of its very utility; for, in order that a penalty may be useful, it is necessary, 1st, that he upon whom it is inflicted, provided he be endowed with the principle of merit and demerit, should regard himself as justly punished, and accept his punishment with a befitting disposition; 2d, that the spectators, equally endowed with the principle of merit and demerit, should find the criminal justly punished according to the extent of his criminality, should apply to themselves by anticipation the same justice, and should be kept in harmony with the general order by view of these legitimate forfeitures. Take away from punishment this foundation of justice, and you destroy its utility; you substitute indignation and abhorrence for a salutary lesson and for repentance both in the condemned and in the public; you put courage, sympathy, all that is noble and great in human nature, on the side of the victim; you rouse all energetic souls against society and its artificial laws. Thus even the utility of punishment rests upon its justice. The punishment is the sanction of the law, not its foundation. The idea of right and wrong is founded only upon itself and upon the reason which discovers it to us; it is the condition of the idea of merit and demerit, which is the condition of the idea of punishment and reward: this is therefore, to the two first, especially to the idea of good and evil, in the relation of the consequence to the principle.*

This relation, which contains all moral order, inviolably subsists, even when we pass from the sphere of this life and from human society to that of religion and of the world where God reigns alone, where destiny gives place to the pure action of Providence, where fact and right are one and the same thing. The idea of merit and demerit, transported in some sort beyond this world, is the true reason of the idea of the punishments and the rewards of another life. It is not in the caprice of a being superior to us in power that resides the legitimacy of future punishments and rewards. Take away the justice of God; his power, absolute as it is, does not sufficiently authorize punishments and rewards. Take away his justice: what remains? an order, and not a law; and, instead of the sublime realization of the idea of merit and demerit, religion is no longer any thing but the menace of a tyrannical force against a feeble being, condemned to the part of patient and victim.† In heaven, as upon earth, and in heaven much more than upon earth, the sanction of law is not its foundation; punishment and reward are derived from good and evil, but good and evil are not constituted by punishment and reward.

Let us apply to all this the distinctions which we have previously established. We have distinguished the logical order of

* First Series, *passim*, particularly Vol. 2, part 3, Lecture 17, p. 218; Lecture 21 and 22, p. 341; see also the *Translation of Plato*, Vol. 3, argument of the *Gorgias*.

† First Series, Vol. 1, p. 333; Vol. 2, Lecture 19, p. 278–284.

ideas from the order of their acquisition. In the first order, one idea is the logical condition of another idea when it explains it; in the second order, one idea is the chronological condition of another idea when it is produced in the human mind before it. Now, in regard to the question which occupies us, the idea of justice, the idea of moral law, violated or fulfilled, is: 1st, the logical condition of the idea of merit or of demerit, which without it is incomprehensible and inadmissible; 2d, the antecedent, the chronological condition of the acquisition of the idea of merit or of demerit, which certainly never would have been produced in the mind, if the idea of justice and injustice had not been previously given it. Locke, after having often confounded, as we have seen, the logical condition of an idea with its chronological condition, here confounds at once the logical and chronological condition of an idea with this idea itself, and even with a consequence of this idea; for the idea of punishment and reward is only a consequence of the idea of merit and demerit, which, in its turn, is only a consequence of the idea of good and evil, of just and unjust, which is the supreme principle beyond which it is impossible to ascend. Locke reverses this order: instead of first laying down the idea of good and evil, then that of merit and demerit, then that of punishment and reward, it is the reward or the punishment, that is, the pleasure or the pain that results from it, which, according to Locke, is the foundation of good and evil, and of the moral rectitude of actions.

Book II. Chap. XXVIII. § 5. "*Moral good and evil.*—Good and evil, as hath been shown, Book II. Chap. XX. § 2, and Chap. XXI. § 42, are nothing but pleasure or pain, or that which occasions or procures pleasure or pain to us. Moral good and evil, then, is only the conformity or disagreement of our voluntary actions to some law, whereby good or evil is drawn on us by the will and power of the law-maker; which good and evil, pleasure or pain, attending our observance or breach of the law, by the decree of the law-maker, is what we call reward and punishment."

Hence, Locke distinguishes three laws or rules, to wit: the divine law, the civil law, the law of opinion or reputation.

Ibid. § 7. "By the relation they bear to the first of these, men judge whether their actions are sins or duties; by the second, whether they be criminal or innocent; and by the third, whether they be virtues or vices."

Ibid. § 8. "*Divine law, the measure of sin and duty.*—First, The divine law, whereby I mean that law which God has set to the actions of men, whether promulgated to them by the light of nature, or the voice of revelation. That God has given a rule whereby men should govern themselves, I think there is nobody so brutish as to deny. He has a right to do it; we are his creatures: he has goodness and wisdom to direct our actions to that which is best; and he has power to enforce it by rewards and punishments, of infinite weight and duration, in another life; for nobody can take us out of his hands. This is the only true touchstone of moral rectitude, and by comparing them to this law it is that men judge of the most considerable moral good or evil of their actions; that is, whether as duties or sins, they are like to procure them happiness or misery from the hand of the Almighty."

You see then that the punishments and rewards of another life are declared the sole touchstone, the sole measure of the rectitude of our actions. But suppose that the law which God has given us were not just in itself, independently of the punishments and rewards which are attached to it, the act which obeys it or breaks it would be neither good nor bad in itself; and then the divine will would have in vain attached to this law, indifferent in itself, both in regard to its fulfilment and its violation, punishments the most dreadful and rewards most alluring, these promises and these threats, addressed only to the sensibility and not to the reason, would excite in us fear or hope, not respect and the sentiment of duty. And we must not say, like Locke, that God has the right to do it, that is, to establish this law, indifferent in itself, since we are his creatures; for this means nothing, unless that he is the strongest and that we are weakest: it is simply invoking the right of might. In general, the tendency of this theory is to make of God an arbitrary* king, to substitute in God will and power for reason and wisdom. It is a theodicea of the senses, not of the reason, made for slaves and brutes, not for intelligent and free beings.

§ 9. "*Civil law, the measure of crimes and innocence.*—Secondly, the civil law, the rule set by the commonwealth to the actions of those who belong to it, is another rule, to which men refer their actions to judge whether they be criminal or no. This law nobody overlooks; the rewards and punishments that enforce it being ready at hand, and suitable to the power that makes it; which is the force of the commonwealth, engaged to protect the lives, liberties, and possessions of those who live according to its laws, and has power to take away life, liberty, or goods, from him who disobeys: which is the punishment of offences committed against this law."

Society assuredly has this right; this right is even a duty for it; but upon the condition that the laws which it shall enact be just: for suppose the law which society establishes to be unjust, the violation of this law ceases to be unjust, and then the punishment of an act not unjust which has transgressed an unjust law is itself an injustice. Take away, I repeat, the legitimacy and the justice of the law, and you destroy the justice and the legitimacy of the punishment. Punishment loses all character of morality and only keeps that of purely physical force, which could not be, as Hobbes† clearly saw, too great, too absolute, since it subsists only through the fear which it inspires.

§ 10. "*Philosophical law, the measure of virtue and vice.*—Thirdly, the law of opinion or reputation. Virtue and vice are names pretended and supposed everywhere to stand for actions in their own nature right and wrong; and as far as they really

---

* *Translation of Plato*, Vol. 1, argument of the *Euthyphrôn*.

† First Series, Vol. 3, Lect. 9, etc.

are so applied, they so far are coincident with the divine law above mentioned. But yet, whatever is pretended, this is visible, that these names, virtue and vice, in the particular instances of their application, through the several nations and societies of men in the world, are constantly attributed only to such actions as in each country and society are in reputation or discredit. Nor is it to be thought strange, that men everywhere should give the name of virtue to those actions which among them are judged praiseworthy, and call that vice which they account blamable; since otherwise they would condemn themselves if they should think any thing right to which they allowed not commendation, any thing wrong which they let pass without blame. Thus the measure of what is everywhere called and esteemed virtue and vice, is the approbation or dislike, praise or blame, which by a secret and tacit consent establishes itself in the several societies, tribes, and clubs of men in the world; whereby several actions come to find credit or disgrace among them according to the judgment, maxims, or fashion of that place. For though men, uniting into politic societies, have resigned up to the public the disposing of all their force, so that they cannot employ it against any fellow-citizens any farther than the law of the country directs; yet they retain still the power of thinking well or ill, approving or disapproving of the actions of those whom they live among and converse with; and by this approbation and dislike, they establish among themselves what they will call virtue and vice."

§ 11. "That this is the common measure of virtue and vice, will appear to any one who considers that though that passes for vice in one country which is counted a virtue, or at least not vice in another, yet, everywhere, virtue and praise, vice and blame, go together."

Upon this point Locke cites all pagan antiquity, which excited to virtue by appeal to glory. He even cites a passage of St. Paul, which he forces and turns aside from its natural sense in order to arrive at the conclusion that there is no other measure of virtue than good or bad renown. Read also § 12: *The "enforcements" of this law are "condemnation and discredit."*

But you perceive that it is the same with opinion, the pretended philosophic law, as it is with public chastisements or the civil law, as it is with the chastisements of another life or the divine law. Suppose that virtue is not virtue in itself, and that it is praise and approbation which constitute it, then it is clear that there is no longer any morality; there is no longer any law; there is no longer any thing but arbitrary customs, local and changing; there is no longer any thing but fashion and opinion. Now, opinion is nothing but a lying noise, or it is the echo of the public conscience, and in this case it is an effect and not a cause; its legitimacy and its force lie in the energy of the sentiment of good and evil. But to elevate the effect to the rank of the cause, to establish good and evil upon opinion alone,* is to destroy good and evil, is to pervert and corrupt virtue by giving fear as its only source; it is to make courtiers, not virtuous men. Popularity is one of the sweetest things in the world, but only when it is the echo of our own conscience and not the price of complaisance; when it is acquired by a course of truly virtuous actions, by constancy to character, fidelity to principles and to friends, in the common service of country. Glory is the crown, not the foundation of virtue. Duty is not measured by reward. Without doubt it is easier to perform it upon a public theatre, with the applauses of the crowd; but it does not decrease in obscurity, it does not perish in ignominy: there, as elsewhere, it remains the same, inviolable and obligatory.

The conclusion, to which I continually recur, is, that here Locke evidently takes the consequence for the principle, the effect for the cause. And remark that this confusion is a necessity of the system of Locke. This system admits no idea which does not come from reflection or from sensation. Reflection not

---

* This is the fundamental error of Smith's *Theory of the Moral Sentiments*, First Series, Vol. 4, Lect. 16, p. 234–240, etc.

being here admissible, Locke addresses himself to sensation; and sensation not being able to explain the idea which men have of good and evil, the question is to find an idea more or less resembling it, which can enter into the human understanding by sensation, and take the place of the former. This idea is that of punishment and reward, which is resolved into that of fear and hope, of pleasure and pain, of happiness and misery, and in general of utility. Once more, this confusion was necessary to the system of Locke, and it saves his system; but, this confusion being dispelled and the facts being re-established in their real value and true order, there is an end to the system of Locke.

Let us therefore see where we are in regard to this system. Locke has tried his system upon a certain number of particular ideas, the idea of space, the idea of the infinite, the idea of time, the idea of personal identity, the idea of substance, the idea of cause, the idea of good and evil, undertaking to explain all these ideas by sensation and by reflection. We have followed Locke upon all those points which he has himself chosen; and, upon all these points, an attentive examination has demonstrated to us that we can explain none of these ideas by sensation or reflection, except on the condition of entirely misconceiving the real characters with which these ideas are now marked in the understanding of all men, and of confounding, by the aid of this alteration, these ideas with other ideas which are more or less intimately connected with them but which are not the same, with ideas which precede them but do not constitute them, or which follow them and do not any the more constitute them, such as the ideas of body, of succession, of number, of the phenomena of consciousness and memory, of collection and totality, of reward and punishment, of pain and pleasure. Without doubt, sensation and reflection explain these last ideas; but these ideas are not those which he undertook to explain, and the system of Locke is thereby convicted of not being able to account for all the ideas which are in the human understanding.

The theories which we have exhibited and discussed fill three-fourths of the second book of the *Essay on the Human Understanding*. Locke has then only to deduce generalizations; he has nothing more to do but to see how, the ideas which we have examined, and all ideas analogous to them, being furnished by sensation and reflection, upon these bases the whole edifice of the human understanding can be erected. On our side, the most important part of our task is accomplished. It was necessary to accompany the exposition of the principles of the system of Locke with a thorough discussion. Now that these principles are overturned, we can proceed more speedily; it will be sufficient to run rapidly over the last part of the second book, tracing the principal propositions, elucidating them with some reflections.

Locke calls all those ideas which are immediately derived from sensation and reflection, simple ideas. Simple ideas are the elements with which we form all other ideas. Locke calls those ideas which we subsequently form from the combination of simple and primitive ideas, compound ideas, complex ideas; so that the whole development and play of the human understanding is reduced to acquiring immediately, by the senses or reflection, a certain number of simple ideas which Locke believes he has determined; then to forming from these materials, by way of composition and association, complex ideas; then to forming again, from these complex ideas, ideas more complex than the first, and so on, until all the ideas which are in the human understanding are exhausted (Book II. Chap. II. and Chap. XII.)

I must here expose an error, of idea or of word, just as you please.

It is not true that we commence by simple ideas, and then proceed to complex ideas: on the contrary, we commence by complex ideas, then from complex ideas proceed to simple ideas; and the process of the human mind in the acquisition of ideas, is precisely the inverse of that which Locke assigns. All our primary ideas are complex ideas, for the evident reason that all our faculties, or at least a great number of our faculties, enter at once into exercise; their simultaneous action gives us, at the same time, a certain number of ideas connected with each other, and which form a whole. For example, the idea of the exterior world, which is given us so quickly, is a very complex idea, which contains a multitude of ideas. There is the idea of the secondary qualities of exterior objects; there is the idea of their primary qualities; there is the idea of the permanent reality of something to which you refer those qualities, to wit, bodies, matter; there is the idea of space which contains bodies; there is the idea of time in which their movements are accomplished, etc. And do you believe that you have at first by itself the idea of primary qualities and secondary qualities, then the idea of the subject of these qualities, then the idea of time, then the idea of space? Not at all; it is simultaneously, or nearly simultaneously, that you acquire all these ideas. Moreover, you do not have them without knowing that you have them. Now, consciousness implies a certain degree of attention, that is, of will; it implies, also, the belief in your own existence, in the real and substantial *me* which you are. In a word, you have a multitude of ideas which are given in each other, and all your primitive ideas are complex ideas. They are complex for still another reason, because they are particular and concrete, as I have shown in the last lecture. Abstraction then comes, which, applying itself to these primitive, complex, concrete, and particular data, separates what nature had given you united and simultaneous, and considers by itself each of the parts of the whole. This part isolated from the whole to which it belongs, this idea detached from the total picture of the primitive ideas, becomes an abstract and simple idea, until a more sagacious abstraction decomposes this pretended simple idea, and makes several other ideas spring from it, which it considers still abstractedly from each other; until finally, from decomposition to decomposition, abstraction and analysis arrive at ideas so simple that they are, or appear to be, indecomposable. The more simple an idea is, the more general it is; the more abstract an idea is, the more extensive it is. We start with the concrete, and proceed to the abstract; we start with the determined and the particular, to proceed to the simple and the general. The course of the understanding is, therefore, as I have said to you, entirely the inverse of that which Locke imputes to it. I must render this justice to the school of Locke, that it has not suffered an error so grave to remain in the analysis of the understanding, and that the true process of the human mind was restored by Condillac.

It has not been thus in regard to another opinion of Locke mingled with the former, that the mind is passive in the acquisition of simple ideas, and active in the acquisition of complex ideas (Book II. Chap. I. § 25; Chap. XII. § 2). Without doubt the mind is more active, and its activity is more easily seized in abstraction and the formation of general ideas (this is what must be understood by the complex ideas of Locke); but it is also active in the acquisition of particular ideas (simple ideas of Locke), for in that there is still consciousness, and consciousness supposes attention, activity. The mind is active whenever it thinks, it cannot always think, as Locke has clearly seen (Book II. Chap. I. § 18, 19); but whenever it does think, and it assuredly thinks in the acquisition of particular ideas, it is active. Locke had too much diminished the intervention of the activity of the mind; we shall see that the school of Locke, far from extending it, have diminished it still more.

All ideas are obtained, or supposed to be obtained: their mechanism has been described; it only remains to search out their most general characters. Locke divides them into clear and distinct ideas, and into obscure and confused ideas (Book II. Chap. XXIX.), into real and chimerical ideas (Book II. Chap. XX.), into complete and incomplete ideas (Book II. Chap. XXXI.), into true and false ideas (Book II. Chap. XXXII.). In this last chapter is found the remark, so often repeated since, that, strictly, all our ideas are true, and that error does not fall upon the idea considered in itself: for, even when you have the idea of a thing that does not exist, the idea of a centaur, of a chimera, it is certain that you have the idea which you have; only this idea that you really have has no object really existing in nature; but the idea in itself is not less true. The error pertains then, not to the idea, but to the affirmation that is sometimes joined to it, that this idea has an object really existing in nature. You are not in error because you have the idea of a centaur, but you are in error when to this idea of the centaur you join the affirmation, that the object of such an idea exists. It is not the idea taken in itself, it is the judgment that is joined to it, which contains the error. The school of Locke has developed and elucidated this judicious observation.

The second book terminates with an excellent chapter on the association of ideas (Book II. Chap. XXXIII.). Not only are ideas clear or obscure, distinct or confused, real or chimerical, complete or incomplete, true or false; they have also the incontestable property, that by occasion of one we conceive the other, that they are recalled and suggested by each other. There are natural, necessary, and rational associations of ideas; and there are false, arbitrary, and vicious associations of ideas. Locke clearly saw and forcibly designated the danger of the last; he has shown by a multitude of examples how frequently, simply because we have seen two things by chance united, this purely accidental association remains in the imagination and subjugates the understanding. Hence, the source of a crowd of errors, and not only of false ideas, but of false sentiments, of arbitrary antipathies or sympathies, of aberrations which often degenerate into folly. We find here in Locke the wisest counsels for the education of the soul and of the mind, on the art of breaking up in good time the false connections of ideas, and of establishing in their place rational connections, which spring from the nature itself of ideas and from the nature of the human mind. I regret only one thing: it is, that Locke has not pushed this analysis far enough, and that he has still left so much vagueness and indecision on this important subject. It should not have been enough for him to establish that there are true, natural, and rational connections, and false, accidental, and irrational connections; it was necessary to show in what true connections consist; it was necessary to determine what are the most important, the most usual of these legitimate connections, and to endeavor to ascend to the laws which govern them. A precise theory of these laws would have been an immense service rendered to philosophy, for the laws of the associations of ideas rest upon the laws of the understanding itself. Finally, when Locke passed to vicious associations, he should have shown what is the root of these associations, and what is the relation between false and true connections. We see only the extravagant side of the human understanding, until we ascend to the source, to the reason of extravagance. Thus Locke continually recommends, and very justly, to break up in the mind of children the habitual connection of phantoms with darkness. A wiser analysis would have sought upon what rests this association of ideas between mysterious beings and night, darkness, obscurity. The idea of phantoms or of spectres has never been united in the mind or in the imagination with the idea of the sun and a clear light. There is certainly in this association an extravagance, but an extravagance which has its reason, which it would have been curious and useful to search out; there is in it a vicious connection which analysis can completely explain only by referring it to another connection of ideas, natural and legitimate, perverted in this particular case. Otherwise, I repeat, this whole chapter is that of an ingenious observer, a true philosopher; and we shall see hereafter that the association of ideas has become in the hands of the school of Locke, a rich subject of experiment and wise results, a fruitful theme which this school has particularly loved and studied, and upon which it has rendered incontestable service to the human reason.

Such is the exact and faithful analysis of the second book. Locke has made all our ideas spring from sensation or from reflection, has exhibited the different general characters under which they may be classified, and their most remarkable, most useful, or most dangerous property: ideology, psychology, at least that of Locke, is achieved. It remains to pass to the applications of ideology, to the knowledge of objects and beings by the aid of ideas: such will be the subject of the fourth book. But Locke, having clearly seen what is the relation of words to ideas, and how fruitful a cause of error to the human understanding words are, devotes an entire book to the examination of the great question of signs and language.

You know that this too is one of the favorite subjects of the school of Locke; and I freely acknowledge that this is the question, with that of the association of ideas, upon which it has merited most of philosophy. I am thankful for a multitude of sound, ingenious, even original ideas, which are scattered through this third book. Locke has seen with wonderful clearness what is the necessary intervention of signs, of words, in the formation of abstract and general ideas; what is the influence of signs and words in definitions, and consequently in a considerable part of logic: he has seen and signalized the advantages of a good system of signs, the utility of a well-formed language, the disputes of words to which a defective language too often reduces philosophy, and on all these points he has opened the route upon which his school have entered. If he has not been far, yet he it is who has opened the way; if he has let many profound observations escape him which have been the conquest of his successors, he has in return shunned many systematic errors into which they have fallen. Faithful to his method of seeking much more the origin of things than their actual characters, Locke has not been wanting in seeking, although very briefly, what is the origin of words, of signs, of language. He has recognized that the materials of language pre-exist in nature, in sounds, in that of our organs which is fitted for their formation; but he has perfectly comprehended that, if there were nothing else than sounds, even articulate sounds, there would be the materials of signs, yet there would be no signs. The understanding must attach a sense, some meaning to a sound, in order that this sound may become a sign, a sign of the internal conception of the understanding. "Parrots and several other birds," says Locke (Book III. Chap. I. § 1 and 2), "will be taught to make articulate sounds distinct enough; which yet by no means are capable of language. Besides articulate sounds, therefore, it was farther necessary that man should be able *to use these sounds as signs of internal conceptions,* and to make them stand as marks for the ideas within his own mind." Whence it follows: 1st, that the intelligence is not the product of languages, but that on the contrary languages are the products of intelligence; 2d, that, most words having, as Locke has very well remarked, an arbitrary signification, not only are languages products of intelligence, but that they are in great part even products of the will; whilst, in the school of Locke and in a school quite opposite, intelligence has been made to come from language, and language from sensation and sound, without doubting that there is an abyss between sound as sound and sound as a sign, and that what makes it a sign is the power of comprehending it, that is, the mind, the intelligence. Sounds, and the organs which perceive them and produce them, are the conditions of language; its principle is intelligence. Here, at least, I congratulate Locke for not having confounded the condition of a principle with the principle itself: we shall see that his successors have not been as wise.*

I will now draw from this third book as a whole, and from the theories which it contains, a certain number of important points which appear to me suspicious, doubtful, or false: in regard to which you shall judge.

I. Locke affirms (Book III. Chap. I. § 5) that "words ultimately derive their origin from such as signify sensible things;" that is, that in the last analysis all words have for their roots elementary words, which are signs of sensible ideas.

At first, we may deny the absolute truth of this proposition. I

---

* First Series, Vol. 3, Lecture 2, on Condillac, p. 94, etc., and Lecture 3, p. 140. See also Vol. 1, p. 365.

will give you two words, and I will ask you to reduce them to primitive words which express sensible ideas. Take the word *I* or *me*. This word, at least in all the languages that are known to me, is irreducible, indecomposable, primitive; it expresses no sensible idea, it represents nothing but the sense which the intelligence attaches to it; it is a pure sign, with no relation to any sensible idea. The word *being* is in exactly the same case; it is primitive and entirely intellectual. I know no language in which the word *being* is expressed by a corresponding word which represents a sensible idea; therefore it is not true that all the roots of language are, in the last analysis, signs of sensible ideas. Moreover, were it true, even absolutely true, which is not the fact, behold the only conclusion which could be drawn from it. Man is at first led by the action of all his faculties out of himself and towards the exterior world; the phenomena of the exterior world first strike him; these phenomena therefore receive the first names; these names are naturally borrowed from their objects; they are, as it were, tinged with their colors. Then when man, falling back upon himself, distinctly perceives the intellectual phenomena of which he had at first only confused glimpses, and when he wishes to express these new phenomena of the soul and of thought, analogy leads him to attach the signs for which he is seeking to the signs which he already possesses, for analogy is the law of all language, nascent or developed: hence the metaphors into which analysis resolves the greater part of the most abstract moral ideas. But it does not at all follow that man has thereby wished to mark the generation of his ideas; and because the signs of certain ideas are analogous to the signs of certain other ideas, it is necessary to conclude that the former were formed after the latter and upon the latter, and not that the ideas of all these signs are in themselves identical or analogous. It is, however, on account of these analogies, purely verbal, and which, I repeat, do not account for all the phenomena of language, that the school of Locke, availing itself of the relations of words to each other and of the sensible character of the greater part of their roots, has pretended that, all the signs being derived in the last analysis from sensible signs, all ideas are equally derived from sensible ideas. This is the foundation of the great work of Horne Tooke,* who, with respect to grammar, has developed with a hardy fidelity the system already clearly indicated in the *Essay on the Human Understanding* (Book III. Chap. I. § 5), a system more or less in accordance with the necessary intervention of intelligence in the formation of language which Locke had himself signalized, and with the power of reflection distinct from sensation in the acquisition of our knowledge. "It may also lead us a little towards the original of all our notions and knowledge," says Locke, "if we remark how great a dependence our words have on common sensible ideas; and how those, which are made use of to stand for actions and notions quite removed from sense, have their rise from thence, and from obvious sensible ideas are transferred to more abstruse significations, and made to stand for ideas that come not under the cognizance of our senses; v. g., *to imagine, apprehend, comprehend, adhere, conceive, instil, disgust, disturbance, tranquillity*, &c., are all words taken from the operations of sensible things, and applied to certain modes of thinking. *Spirit*, in its primary signification, is *breath*; *angel*, a *messenger*; and I doubt not, but if we could trace them to their sources, we should find, in all languages, the names, which stand for things that fall not under our senses, to have had their first rise from sensible ideas. By which we may give some kind of guess, what kind of notions they were, and whence derived, which filled their minds, who were the first beginners of languages; and how nature, even in the naming of things, unawares suggested to men the originals and principles of all their knowledge. . . . . . "

II. Another proposition of Locke: "The signification of words is perfectly arbitrary" (Book III. Chap. II. § 8). I have just acknowledged that the greater part of words are arbitrary, and

---

* See Lecture 14 in this Vol.

come not only from the intelligence, but from the will. I firmly believe that the greater part of words are conventional; but the question is to know whether all words are conventional; the point to determine is whether there is absolutely not a single root in language which carries its signification with itself, which has its natural meaning, which is the foundation of subsequent convention, instead of coming from this convention. It is a great question which Locke has cut off with a single word, and which his whole school has regarded as definitively resolved; it has not even agitated it. In all cases, even when I should grant (which I cannot grant in an absolute manner) that all words are arbitrary, I should except the laws of the relation of words to each other. A language is not a simple collection of words; it is the system of the various relations of words to each other. These relations so variable may be reduced to invariable relations, which constitute the foundation of each language, its grammar, the common and identical part of all languages, that is, general grammar, which has its laws, its necessary laws, which are derived from the nature itself of the human mind. Now, it is remarkable that, in the book on words, Locke treats continually of words, never of their relations, never of syntax, never of the true foundation of languages; there is a multitude of particular reflections which are ingenious; but no theory, no real grammar. The school of Locke has converted the isolated remarks of the master into a grammatical system, true or false, which we shall encounter hereafter.

III. But here is a proposition of Locke which is quite as important. Locke declares that what is called general and universal is a work of the understanding, and that real essence is nothing else than nominal essence. Book III. Chap. III. § 2: "General and universal belong not to the real existence of things; but are the inventions and creatures of the understanding, made by it for its own use, and concern only signs, whether words or ideas." You see it is the very foundation of nominalism. It is important to examine, although succinctly, this proposition, which has become in the school of Locke an unquestioned principle, a prejudice placed above discussion.

I perceive a book, then another book, then another book still; I neglect by abstraction their differences of position, of size, of form, of color; I attend to their relations of resemblance which it is useless to enumerate, and I arrive by known processes to the general idea of book; and this general idea is expressed for me by the word book. What is then beneath this word? Neither more nor less than this: 1st, the supposition that among the different books placed under my eyes there is, besides the differences which separate them, resemblances, common qualities, without which any generalization would be impossible; 2d, the supposition that there is found a mind capable of understanding these common qualities; 3d, finally, the supposition that there are objects really existing, real books, subjects of these common qualities. The word book represents all this: different books existing in nature, common qualities among these different books, and a mind capable of conceiving these common qualities, and of elevating them to their general idea. But independently of these different and real books, of their common qualities, and of the mind which conceives them, does the word book express something existing which is neither such nor such a book, but book in itself? No, certainly. Therefore the word book is merely a word, a pure word, which has no special type, no real object existing in nature: it is therefore certain that the general essence of book is confounded with its nominal essence, that the existence of book is only a word; and here I entirely agree with Locke and nominalism.

But are there not other general ideas? Let us examine: I perceive a body, and at the same instant my mind cannot but suppose that it is in a certain particular space, which is the place of this particular body. I perceive another body, and my mind cannot help believing that this other particular body is also in a particular space; and thus I arrive, and I arrive very soon, as you have seen, without the necessity of passing through a long course of experiments, at the general idea of space. It remains to know whether this general idea of space is exactly the same as the general idea of book, and whether the word space signifies nothing more than the word book. Let us consult the human mind, and the truth of interior facts. It is an incontestable fact that, when you speak of book in general, you do not add to the idea of book that of real existence. On the contrary, I ask whether, when you speak of space in general, you add or do not add to this idea belief in the reality of space? I ask whether it is the same with space as with book; whether you believe, for example, that there is out of you only particular spaces, that there is not a universal space capable of embracing all possible bodies, a space one and continuous, of which different particular spaces are only arbitrary portions and measures? It is certain that when you speak of space, you have the conviction that there is something beyond you which is space, as, when you speak of time, you have the conviction that there is something out of you which is time, even when you know neither the nature of time, nor that of space. Different times, different spaces, are not the constituent elements of time and space; time and space are for you not merely the collection of those different times and those different spaces; but you believe that space and time exist by themselves, and that it is not two or three spaces, two or three centuries which constitute space and time; for every thing that is borrowed from experience, whether in regard to space, or in regard to time, is finite, and the character of space and time is for you that of being infinite, of being without commencement and without end: time is resolved into eternity, as space is resolved into immensity. In a word, an invincible belief of the reality of time and space is attached for you to the general idea of time and space. This is what the human mind believes; this is what is attested by consciousness. Here the phenomenon is precisely the inverse of that which I just before designated to you; and whilst the general idea of book does not suppose in the human mind a conviction of the existence of any thing which is book, here, on the contrary, to the general idea of time and space is attached the invincible conviction of the reality of something which is space and time. Without doubt, the word space is a pure word like that of book; but this word bears with it the supposition of a thing, of something real in itself: herein is the root and reason of realism.

Nominalism thinks that general ideas are only words; realism thinks that general ideas suppose something real: on both sides there is equal truth, equal error. Yes, without doubt, there is a large number of general ideas which are purely collective, and which express nothing else than the common qualities of objects, without implying any existence; and in this sense nominalism is right. But it is also certain that there are general ideas which imply the supposition of the real existence of their object: realism rests upon this basis, which is incontestable. Now behold the error of nominalism and realism! The force of realism resides in general ideas which invincibly imply the exterior existence of their objects; they are, you know, general, universal, necessary ideas; it starts thence; but in the circle of these superior ideas it attracts and envelops ideas which are purely collective and relative, born of abstraction and language. That which it had a right to affirm of the former, it affirms of the latter. It was right upon one point; it claims an absolute right: therein it is wrong. On its side, nominalism, because it evidently demonstrates that there are many general ideas which are only collective, relative ideas, and pure words, hence concludes that all general ideas are nothing but general, collective, and relative ideas, pure signs. The one converts things into words, the other converts words into things. Both are right in the starting point; both err in the conclusion by their excessive and absolute pretensions. In general, the sensualistic school is nominalistic, and the idealistic is realistic. Once more, on both sides, as it always is with the incomplete and the exclusive, there is a mixture of truth and error.*

* On the difference of genera' collective ideas, and general necessary ideas, see First Series, Vol. 2, Lectures 2–4, p. 55; and on realism, nominalism,

IV. I conclude by designating to you another proposition, or rather another pretension of Locke, which it is important to confine within just limits. Everywhere Locke attributes to words (Book III. Chap. II. § 4; Book IV. *passim*) the greatest part of our errors; and if you expound the master by the pupils, you will find in all the writers of the school of Locke that all disputes are disputes of words; that science is nothing but a language, and consequently that a well-constructed science is a well-constructed language. I declare my opposition to the exaggerations of these assertions.* No doubt words have a great influence; no doubt they have much to do with our errors, and we should strive to make the best language possible. Who questions it? But the question is to know whether every error is derived from language, and whether science is merely a well-constructed language. No; the causes of our errors are very different; they are both more extended and more profound. Levity, presumption, indolence, precipitation, pride, a multitude of moral causes influence our judgments. The vices of language may be added to natural causes and aggravate them, but they do not constitute them. If you look more closely, you will see that the greater part of disputes, which seem at first disputes of words, are at bottom disputes of things. Humanity is too serious to become excited and often shed its best blood, for the sake of words. Wars do not turn upon verbal disputes: I say as much of other quarrels, of theological quarrels, and of scientific quarrels, the profundity and importance of which are misconceived when they are resolved into pure logomachies. Assuredly every science

---

and conceptualism, First Series, Vol. 4, Lecture 21, p. 457–463, and the *Introduction to the unpublished Works* of Abelard.

* First Series, Vol. 3, Lecture 1, p. 63. "In order that this should be true, it would be necessary that our thought might take place without the aid of language, which is not the case. I will give but one example among a thousand. Is it by the aid of the word *me* or of the word *existence* that I feel that I exist? Have I here been from the word to the thing? The very supposition is absurd. Consciousness directly perceives its phenomena by the virtue which is in it, and not by that of words; words powerfully aid it, they do not constitute it."

should seek a well-constructed language; but to suppose that there are well-constructed sciences because there are well-constructed languages, is to take the effect for the cause. The contrary is true: sciences have well-constructed languages when they are themselves well constructed. The mathematics have a well-constructed language. Why? Because in mathematics the ideas are perfectly determined; the simplicity, the rigor, and the precision of ideas have produced rigor, precision, and simplicity of signs. Precise ideas cannot be expressed in confused language; and if in the infancy of a language it were so for a while, soon the precision, the rigor, and the fixedness of the ideas would dissipate the vagueness and the obscurity of the language. The excellence of physical and chemical sciences evidently comes from well-made experiments. Facts having been observed and described with fidelity, reason has been able to apply itself to these facts with certainty, and to deduce from them legitimate consequences and applications. Hence has sprung, and should have sprung, a good system of signs. Make the contrary supposition; suppose badly made experiments: the more strict the reasoning, founded upon these false data, shall be, the more errors will it draw from them, the greater reach and extent will it communicate to the errors. Suppose that the theories which result from these imperfect and vicious experiments were represented by the most simple, the most analogous, the best determined signs; of what importance will the goodness of the signs be, if that which is concealed under this excellent language is a chimera or an error? Take medicine. The complaint is made that this science has advanced so little. What do you think must be done to bring it up from the regions of hypothesis, and to elevate it to the rank of a science? Do you think that at first you could, by a well-constructed language, reform physiology and medicine? Or do you not think that the true method is experiment, and with experiment the severe employment of reasoning? A good system of signs would of itself follow; it would not come before, or it would uselessly come. It is the same in philosophy. It has been unceasingly repeated that the structure of the human mind is entire in that of language, and that philosophy would be finished the day in which a philosophical language should be achieved; and starting thence an endeavor has been made to arrange a certain philosophical language more or less clear, easy, elegant, and it has been believed that philosophy was achieved. It was not; it was far from being achieved. This prejudice has even retarded it, by separating experiment from it. Philosophical science, like every science of observation and reasoning, lives by well-made observation and strict reasonings. There, and not elsewhere, is the whole future of philos-

LECTURE XXI.

ESSAY, FOURTH BOOK. THEORY OF REPRESENTATIVE IDEAS.*

Examination of the Fourth Book of the *Essay*, in regard to knowledge. That knowledge, according to Locke, depends, 1st, on ideas; 2d, on ideas conformed to their object.—That the conformity or nonconformity of ideas with their objects, as the foundation of the true or of the false in knowledge, is not a simple metaphor in Locke, but a veritable theory.—Examination of the theory of representative ideas, 1st, in relation to the exterior world, to secondary qualities, to primary qualities, to the *substratum* of these qualities, to space, to time, etc.; 2d, in relation to the spiritual world.—Appeal to revelation. Paralogism of Locke.

Being in possession of all the ideas which are in the human understanding, their origin, their generation, their mechanism, and their characters; being in possession of the signs by which they are expressed, manifested, and developed, it concerns us to see what man does with these ideas, what knowledge he derives from them, what is the extent of this knowledge, and what are its limits. Such is the subject of the fourth book of the *Essay on the Human Understanding:* it treats of knowledge, that is, not simply of ideas taken in themselves, but in relation to their objects, in relation to other beings; for knowledge goes thus far; it attains to God, to bodies, and to ourselves. Now here, at the outset, is presented a prejudicial question. Knowledge reaches as far as beings, the fact is incontestable; but how does this fact take place? Having set out from ideas which are in it, how does the understanding attain to beings which are without it? What bridge is there between the faculty of knowing which is within us, and the objects of knowledge which are without us? When we shall have arrived on the other shore, we shall see what

* On the theory of representative ideas, see 1st Series, Vol. 1, Lecture 8, pp. 36–42; Lecture 10, p. 71, etc.; Vol. 3, Lecture 1, p. 63; especially Vol. 4, Lecture 20, pp. 356–370; Lecture 21, pp. 417–431.

route we should pursue, and how far we can go; but in the first place it is necessary to know how to make the passage. Before entering upon ontology, it is necessary to know how to pass from psychology to ontology, what is the foundation, and legitimate foundation, of knowledge. It is this preliminary question which we shall at first address to Locke.

The fourth book of the *Essay on the Human Understanding* begins by asserting that all knowledge depends on ideas.

Book IV. *Of knowledge.* Chap. I. *Of knowledge in general.* § 1: "Since the mind in all its thoughts and reasonings, hath no other immediate object but its own ideas, which it alone does or can contemplate, it is evident that our knowledge is only conversant about them."

But, as you have seen, Locke recognizes, and with reason, that ideas in themselves are always true. It is always true that we have the idea which we have, which is actually under the eye of consciousness: let this idea be a chimera, a centaur, still we have it, and, under this relation, the idea cannot be false, it cannot but be true, or rather, strictly speaking, it is neither false nor true. Where can error then begin, and wherein does truth reside? Both evidently reside and can reside only in this supposition of the mind, that this idea is related or is not related to an object, to such or such an object really existing in nature. It is in this relation that truth or error lies for the human mind. If this relation may be seized, human knowledge is possible; if this relation cannot be seized, human knowledge is impossible. Now, in supposing that this relation is possible, what is it, and in what does it consist? It behooves us on this point to interrogate Locke with precision and severity, for here must be the foundation of the theory of the true and the false in human knowledge, that is, the foundation of the fourth book which we have to examine.

Throughout the whole of this fourth book, as at the close of the second, Locke declares expressly that the true or the false in ideas, on which all knowledge turns, consists in the supposition of a relation between these ideas and their object; and still, everywhere he declares expressly that this relation is, and can be, only a relation of conformity or nonconformity. The idea, on which falls, properly speaking, neither error nor truth, is conformed to its object, or is not conformed to it; if it is conformed to it, not only knowledge is possible, but it is true, for it rests upon a true idea, upon an idea conformed to its object; or the idea is not conformed to its object, and the idea is false, and the knowledge which is derived from it is equally so. This is what we find from one end of the fourth book of the *Essay* on knowledge to the other; it is what we find at each step in the last six chapters of the second book, where Locke treats of true and false ideas.

Book II. Chap. XXXII. § 4: "Whenever the mind refers any of its ideas to any thing extraneous to them, they are then capable to be called true or false. Because the mind in such a reference makes a tacit supposition of their conformity to that thing."

Book IV. Chap. IV. § 3: "It is evident, the mind knows not things immediately, but only by the intervention of the ideas it has of them. Our knowledge, therefore, is real, only so far as there is a conformity between our ideas and the reality of things."

These two passages are positive; they clearly reduce the question of the true and the false in knowledge to the question of conformity or nonconformity of ideas with their objects.

But is this necessity of the conformity of an idea with its object in order to be true, in Locke, a veritable philosophical theory, or is it only a simple manner of speaking, a metaphor more or less happy? If it is a metaphor, I ask what is the theory concealed under this metaphor, and where in Locke's work may this theory be found a single time expressed? I find throughout it nothing but the metaphor itself. If, in the complete absence of every other theory, the two passages which I have just cited, were insufficient to establish that the necessity of the conformity of the idea to its object, in order to constitute truth, is not a metaphor, but a serious theory, I could bring here a multitude of other passages which would not leave any doubt in this respect. Thus, when at the close of the second book Locke treats of ideas as real or chimerical, as complete or incomplete, he rests upon his theory of conformity or nonconformity of ideas with their objects.

Book II. Chap. XXX. § 1: "*Real ideas are conformable to their archetypes.* First, by real ideas I mean such as have a foundation in nature; such as have a conformity with the real being and existence of things, or with their archetypes. Fantastical or chimerical I call such as have no foundation in nature, nor have any conformity to that reality of being to which they are tacitly referred as to their archetypes."

And what is a complete or incomplete idea? A complete idea will be completely conformed to its archetype; an incomplete idea, that which will be conformed only in part.

Book II. Chap. XXXI. § 1: "Those I call adequate which perfectly represent those archetypes, which the mind supposes them taken from."

The theory of complete or incomplete ideas rests on the theory of real and chimerical ideas, which rests on the theory of true or false ideas, which is wholly in the theory of the conformity of the idea to the object. This point is of so much importance, that to take away all uncertainty, I wish once more to quote a passage in which Locke lays down the problem itself; and the manner in which he lays it down excludes all ambiguity in the solution which he gives of it.

Book IV. Chap. IV. § 3: "But what shall be here the criterion? How shall the mind, when it perceives nothing but its own ideas, know that they agree with things themselves? This, though it seems not to want difficulty, yet, I think, there be two sorts of ideas that, we may be assured, agree with things . . . ." § 4: "Simple ideas carry with them all the conformity which is intended, or which our state requires; for they represent to us things, under those appearances, which they are fitted to produce in us;" and farther on: "This conformity between our simple ideas, and the existence of things, is sufficient for real knowledge."

It is impossible to express one's self more categorically. It is not then a mere manner of speaking, a metaphor thrown off in passing; it is wholly a theory, wholly a system: let us examine it seriously.

Behold truth and error, reality and chimera resolved into the representation or non-representation of the object by the idea, into the conformity or nonconformity of the idea to the object. There is knowledge on this condition and on this condition alone, that the idea represents its object, is conformed to it. But on what condition does an idea represent its object and is conformed to it? On this condition, that this idea resembles it, that this idea is with its object in the relation of a copy to the original. Estimate the value of the words: the conformity of an idea to its object cannot signify any thing else, except the resemblance of this idea taken as a copy, with the object taken as an original. This is certainly what Locke expresses by the word archetypes, which he uses to designate the objects of ideas. Now, if the conformity of the idea to the object is only the resemblance of the copy with the original, with its archetype, I say that in this case the idea is taken only as an image. The idea must evidently be an image, in order to resemble something, in order to represent something. Behold, then, the representative idea reduced to an image. But observe it closely, and you will see that every image implies something material. Can we conceive an image of any thing that is immaterial? Every image is necessarily sensible and material, or it is merely a metaphor, a supposition which we have abandoned. Thus, in the last analysis, to say that there is knowledge if the idea is conformed to its object, and that no knowledge is possible except on this condition, is to pretend that there is no knowledge except on the condition that a thing be the image of this thing, that is, its material image. All knowledge is, then, involved in the following question: Have we, concerning beings, ideas which represent them to us, which resemble them, which are their images, which are their material images? or, have we not such images? If we have, knowledge is possible; if we have not, it is impossible. But, in fact, human knowledge embraces the exterior world, the soul, and God. If, then, the knowledge of these objects is possible and real, it is so only on the aforesaid condition, to wit, that concerning these beings we have ideas which are conformed to them, ideas which represent them, which resemble them, which are images of them, and, once more, material images. Have we or have we not idea-images, material images of God, of the soul, of the exterior world? Such is the question. Let us apply it at first to the external world; it is there especially that the theory of Locke appears admissible; let us see what is its solidity, its value even upon this ground.

The idea of the exterior world is the idea of bodies. Bodies are known only by their qualities. These qualities are primary or secondary. We understand, as you know, by the secondary qualities of bodies, those which might not exist notwithstanding the existence of the body; for example, the qualities of which we acquire an idea by the sense of smell, by the sense of hearing, by the sense of taste, by all the senses, except that of touch, and perhaps also that of sight. The primary qualities of bodies are those which are given to us as the fundamental attributes of bodies, without which bodies would not exist for us. The primary quality, *par excellence,* is solidity, which implies more or less extension, which directly implies form. We have the conviction that every body is solid, extended, that it has form. We are convinced, again, that bodies have the property of causing in us those particular modifications which we call taste, sound, odor, perhaps even that modification which we call color. Locke grants all this, and it is he who has greatly contributed to spread the distinction between the primary qualities and the secondary qualities of bodies, upon which it is not our business here to enlarge. See how he accounts for the acquisition of ideas of the primary qualities and of the secondary qualities.

Book II. Chap. VIII. § 11. "*How primary qualities produce*

their ideas.—The next thing to be considered is, how bodies produce ideas in us; and that is manifestly by impulse, the only way which we can conceive bodies to operate in."

§ 12. "If then external objects be not united to our minds, when they produce ideas therein, and yet we perceive these original qualities in such of them as singly fall under our senses, it is evident that some motion must be thence continued by our nerves or animal spirits, by some parts of our bodies, to the brain, or the seat of sensation, there to produce in our minds the particular ideas we have of them. And since the extension, figure, number, and motion of bodies, of an observable bigness, may be perceived at a distance by the sight, it is evident some singly imperceptible bodies must come from them to the eyes, and thereby convey to the brain some motion, which produces these ideas which we have of them in us."

§ 13. "*How secondary.*—After the same manner that the ideas of these original qualities are produced in us, we may conceive that the ideas of secondary qualities are also produced, viz., by the operations of insensible particles on our senses. For it being manifest that there are bodies, each whereof are so small that we cannot, by any of our senses, discover either their bulk, figure, or motion, as is evident in the particles of the air and water, and others extremely smaller than those, perhaps as much smaller than the particles of air and water as the particles of air and water are smaller than peas or hailstones; let us suppose at present that the different motions and figures, bulk and number of such particles, affecting the several organs of our senses, produce in us those different sensations which we have from the colors and smells of bodies; *v. g.*, that a violet, by the impulse of such insensible particles of matter of peculiar figures and bulks, and in different degrees and modifications of their motions, causes the ideas of the blue color and sweet scent of that flower to be produced in our minds, it being no more impossible to conceive that God should annex such ideas to such motions, with which they have no similitude, than that he should annex the idea of pain to the motion of a piece of steel dividing our flesh, with which that idea hath no resemblance."

§ 14. "What I have said concerning colors and smells may be understood also of tastes and sounds, and other the like sensible qualities; which, whatever reality we by mistake attribute to them, are in truth nothing in the objects themselves, but powers to produce various sensations in us, and depend on those primary qualities, viz., bulk, figure, texture, and motion of parts, as I have said."

If you go back to the principle of all this theory, badly discussed and badly exposed in Locke, you will find that it is founded in the last analysis on this supposition, that, as bodies act upon each other only by contact, and consequently by impulsion, so the mind can be in relation with corporeal things only on this condition, that there be contact between mind and body, and consequently only by so much as there shall be impulsion of the one upon the other. Now, in sensible ideas which are involuntary, and in which, according to Locke, the mind is passive, the impulse must come from bodies upon the mind, and not from the mind upon bodies, and the contact cannot take place directly, but indirectly, by means of particles. Thus the necessity of contact involves that of particles, which, emitted by bodies, are introduced by organs into the brain, and thence introduce into the soul what are called sensible ideas. The whole theory sets out with the necessity of a contact, and terminates in intermediate particles and their action. These particles are in other terms the sensible species of the peripatetic scholasticism, to which modern physics have done justice. There is at present no question concerning sonorous, visible, tangible species; nor can there be any question concerning their emission, nor consequently concerning the principle which had engendered them, to wit, the necessity of contact and of impulsion, as the condition of the acquisition of sensible ideas. All this is at present an abandoned hypothesis upon which it would be superfluous to stop. Sensible ideas thus formed, once obtained on this condition, which is a chimera, behold in what these ideas differ from each other.

According to Locke the ideas which we have of the primary qualities of matter, have this peculiarity, that they resemble their object; while the ideas which we have of the secondary qualities of matter have this peculiarity, that they do not resemble their objects.

Book II. Chap. VIII. § 15. "The ideas of primary qualities of bodies are resemblances of them, and their patterns do really exist in the bodies themselves; but the ideas produced in us by these secondary qualities, have no resemblance of them at all."

The ideas of secondary qualities do not resemble these qualities; very well: I immediately conclude, that, according to the theory of Locke, the ideas of secondary qualities are mere chimeras, and that we have no knowledge of these qualities. Remember that all knowledge, according to Locke, rests upon ideas, and that knowledge depends upon the resemblance of the idea to its object; now, by the confession itself of Locke, the ideas of secondary qualities do not resemble these qualities; these ideas, then, do not contain any knowledge. Let it not be said that we have only an incomplete knowledge of the secondary qualities of bodies. If Locke had simply intended to say this, he should have said, according to his theory, that the ideas of secondary qualities represent but incompletely their objects; but he says that they do not represent them in any manner. Therefore they do not contain even the most imperfect knowledge, they do not contain any knowledge; they are mere chimeras, as the idea of the centaur, etc. The consequence is necessary in the theory of Locke. But does this consequence accord with the facts which it is our business to explain and not to destroy? Is it, in fact, true that we have any knowledge of the secondary qualities of bodies? Far from this, the secondary qualities of bodies, odor, sound, savor, and color, are for us real properties in bodies, to which we attribute the power of exciting in us certain modifications or sensations. We not only have the consciousness of these sensations, but we believe that they have causes, and that these causes are in bodies. As we might conceive bodies independently of these causes or powers, or properties or qualities, we call these qualities secondary qualities; we know them, I confess, only in so far as causes of our sensations: but in short we know them by this title, and this is a real knowledge incontestably found in all men. But, according to Locke, knowledge is always on this condition, that the idea upon which knowledge turns shall represent its object. You have certainly the idea of the secondary qualities of bodies in so far as causes of several of your sensations. Well, this idea which you all have, and upon which is founded almost all your conduct and human life entire, is true, constitutes a legitimate knowledge, only on condition that it shall be conformed to its object, to the causes of your sensations, to the secondary qualities of bodies. And when I say that it shall be conformed to them, think that the condition of the conformity is nothing less than that of resemblance, that the condition of the resemblance is nothing less than the condition of being an image, and that the condition of every image is nothing less than the condition of being a sensible and material image: for there is no immaterial image. The question, then, is, whether you have or have not the material image of the secondary qualities of bodies, that is, of those properties of bodies which cause in you the sensations of color, of sound, of savor, and of odor. Let us see what the material image of a cause can be. A cause, in so far as cause (and the properties or secondary qualities of bodies are nothing else), has no form, no color; consequently, what material image can be made of it? A cause, whatever it may be, whether you place it in the soul or in what is called matter, is always a cause, is never any thing but a cause; and in so far as cause, it falls neither under the hand nor under the eye, it falls under none of the senses: it is therefore something of which you cannot have, strictly, a sensible idea, an image-idea, a material image. Therefore since you have not, and cannot have the image of a cause, and since the secondary qualities of bodies are given to you only as causes, it follows that you should not have any legitimate knowledge of the secondary qualities of bodies; it follows even, strictly speaking, that you cannot have any legitimate or illegitimate knowledge of them, and that these qualities must be for you as if they were not, since you have been able to reach them only by the more or less faithful images which you make of them, images which are here absolutely wanting to you. The denial of the secondary qualities of bodies is then the inevitable result of the theory that every idea must represent its object in order to be true. This result is inevitable; nevertheless experience contradicts it, and in contradicting it, refutes the principle. The ideas of secondary qualities do not in any manner resemble their objects, and nevertheless they contain a certain knowledge: therefore it is not true that all knowledge supposes the resemblance of the idea to its object.

The theory of Locke is destroyed upon the secondary qualities of bodies, let us see if it will be more happy in regard to the primary qualities.

Solidity is the primary quality of bodies *par excellence.* Solidity with its degrees and its shades, hardness or softness, impenetrability or penetrability, envelops extension, which contains dimension and form: these are almost all the primary qualities of bodies. Locke affirms that the ideas of the primary qualities resemble these qualities. It is, in his eyes, their title of legitimacy. This theory seems true on one point, in that which regards form. In fact, the form of objects, which appertains to extension, which appertains to solidity, is painted upon the retina. Experience testifies to it, and the conformity of these images to their objects seems certainly the foundation of the truth of the ideas which we have of the form of objects; but this is only a false semblance.

If the resemblance of the image upon the retina to the form of the exterior object is the foundation of the knowledge of the form of this object, it follows that this knowledge could never have been acquired except on the following conditions:

1st, That we should know that some image is upon the retina.

2d, That by some process, comparing the image upon the retina with the exterior object, we should find in fact the image which is on the retina similar to the object in respect to form.

These two conditions are necessary; but are they, in reality, fulfilled, in the fact of the knowledge of the forms of exterior objects? Not at all. First, the knowledge of the image upon the retina is a tardy acquisition of experience and of physiology. The first men who believed that they had before them figured bodies, did not in the least know that there were images upon the retina. They were still farther from calling into question the resemblance between these images, which they knew not, and the forms of the bodies which they knew; and, consequently, the condition which is imposed upon the human mind of knowing the image upon the retina and verifying the conformity of this image with its object, is not the process which abandoned to itself, and without any system, it naturally employs to know the forms of bodies. Afterwards, observe that if the faithful picture of the object on the retina explains the secret of the perception of this form, it is necessary that this image should go from the retina to the optic nerve, from the optic nerve to the brain, which, as Locke says, is the audience-chamber of the soul, and that from this audience-chamber it should be introduced into the soul itself: but it may be stopped at each step. From the retina the image must be transmitted by the optic nerve. Now, who does not know that the optic nerve is in a dark region, impenetrable to light? The optic nerve is dark; no image can then be painted upon it: and the image thus abandons us. Besides, the brain, this audience-chamber, is also in a dark region; the soul, which, according to the theory of Locke, must look upon the retina in order to encounter an image of the form of the body, and which must see this image, and see it conformed to its original, can make this observation neither upon the optic nerve, nor upon the brain.

We have, thus to speak, closed all the avenues of the soul to the hypothesis of the idea-image; in the perception of the form of objects, we do not find the three things—figured objects—a soul capable of perceiving the figures of these objects—an intermediate image between the real form of objects and the soul; figured objects alone exist, and a soul endowed with the faculty of perceiving them with their forms. The existence of the image of the figure of objects upon the retina is a real fact, which is, doubtless, the previous condition of the perception of visible appearances, but not the foundation of this perception, which precedes it, but does not constitute it nor in any wise explain it. The existence of the image of the figure of objects upon the retina, a simple condition and an exterior condition of the phenomenon of vision, transformed into a complete explanation of this phenomenon, is the source of the hypothesis of the idea-image, as to the perception of the forms of objects. It has still another. Not only is the soul endowed with the faculty of perceiving the forms of present objects, certain organic conditions being fulfilled; but again, when these objects are absent, it is endowed with the faculty of recalling them, not only of knowing that they were, but of representing them such as they were, and with the forms which we had perceived in them when they were present. The memory has really this imaginative power; we imagine objects precisely as we perceive them; this is incontestable. But in the imagination of the forms of absent objects, as in the perception of the forms of present objects, there are but two terms, the absent objects, and the soul which can represent them when absent; or rather, in this case, there is really nothing but the soul, which, in the absence of the objects, recalls them with their forms, as if they were before it. Now, in the soul which represents past objects, poetry may very well detach the representation itself from the objects and consider it apart, as a proper element and subsisting by itself: it is the right of poetry, but not that of philosophical analysis, which cannot legitimately convert abstractions into realities. Abstraction realized, the participle or adjective converted into a substantive, is the second source of the hypothesis of the idea-image, not to call to mind vicious conditions of the communication between bodies imposed upon the intelligence.

As yet we have only discussed the phenomenon of vision, of the form of external objects: what would it then be, if we discussed other primary qualities of bodies, for example, the primary quality *par excellence,* solidity? Would you dare to revive the scholastic hypothesis of the tangible species, in order to make a match for the visual image upon the retina? Would you place this tangible species upon the mysterious avenues of the nerves and of the brain, which the image of the form was unable to traverse? Be it so: let us suppose that this tangible species, this idea-image of solidity, has arrived as far as the soul, and let us see if it satisfies the fundamental condition of the theory of Locke, if it is conformed or not conformed to its model, to solidity itself. What is solidity? Solidity, as we have seen, is resistance. Where there is no resistance, there is for us nothing but ourselves. When resistance begins, then, for us, begins something besides ourselves: the outward, the exterior, nature, the world. If solidity is something that resists, it is a resisting cause; and again, for the primary qualities of bodies as well as for their secondary qualities, we are brought back to the idea of cause; here again it is necessary, in order that we may have the legitimate knowledge of the resisting cause, of solidity, it is necessary, I say, that we should have an idea which is conformed to it, which is similar to it, which is the image of the resisting cause, and which is its material image. Such is the systematic condition of the knowledge of the primary quality of bodies. But I have shown that there cannot be a material image of any cause; there cannot then be one of a resisting cause, of solid, that is, of the fundamental quality of bodies.

Thus we have not a more legitimate idea of the primary qualities of bodies, than of their secondary qualities, if we have this legitimate idea on condition that this idea shall be a material image of its object. But we have not yet finished; as yet we are only at the entrance of the exterior world. Not only has body secondary qualities and primary qualities, which I have just enumerated, and which I have just demonstrated as incompatible with the theory of Locke; but again, we believe that, under these secondary and primary qualities, there is something that is the subject of all these qualities, something which really exists in a permanent manner, whilst the qualities are in a movement and in a perpetual alteration; we all believe in the existence of a subject, of a substance of these qualities. Now, according to the theory, the idea of this substance is legitimate only on condition that it is conformed to its object, to wit, the substance of the body; and the idea, in order to be conformed to its object, in order to resemble it, must be its image, and every image must be material. But I ask you, if it is possible to have a material image of substance? it is evidently impossible; then you have no idea of substance and of the reality of bodies.

Not only do you believe in the real and substantial existence of bodies, but you believe that these bodies, whose fundamental attribute is solidity, resistance, are somewhere, in a place, in space. You all have the idea of space. But you can have it only on condition that the idea which you have of it represents it, is its material image; and as we have seen, one of the characters of space is, that it cannot be confounded with the bodies which fill it and measure it, but which do not constitute it. Then it is impossible *à fortiori*, that you can have a material image of that which does not materially exist, when you cannot have such an image of bodies and of their fundamental attributes or accessories.

It is the same in regard to time. You believe that the movements of bodies and the succession of their movements are accomplished in time, and you do not confound the succession of the movements of bodies with the time which it measures, and which it no more constitutes than the collection of bodies constitutes space. You have the idea of time distinct from all succession: if you have it, it is again, by the theory of Locke, on the condition that you have an idea which is conformed to it, an idea-image. But you cannot have an idea-image of time, since time is distinct from the movements of bodies, and does not fall under any sense; then you cannot have a legitimate idea of it.

I could pursue this discussion much farther; but I think that I have carried it far enough to demonstrate that if, relatively to the exterior world, our ideas are true only on condition that they are representative ideas, ideas conformed to their objects, images and material images of their objects, we should have no legitimate idea of the exterior world, nor of secondary qualities, nor of primary qualities, nor of their subject, nor of space, nor of time. Therefore the theory of the material image concludes by destroying the legitimate knowledge of matter and of the exterior world.

The objections which I have just presented to you are so natural and so simple, that Locke could not even lay down the problem as he has laid it down without suspecting them in part; and they presented themselves to him with sufficient strength to shake his conviction of the existence of the exterior world. He does not call this existence in question, but he confesses that on the sole foundation of the representative idea, the knowledge of bodies has not a perfect certainty; he thinks, at the same time, that it goes beyond simple probability. "But yet, if after all," says Locke, "any one will question the existence of all things, or our knowledge of any thing, I must desire him to consider that we have such an assurance of the existence of things without us, as is sufficient to direct us in the attaining the good, and avoiding the evil, which is caused by them; which is the important concernment we have of being made acquainted with them." This is almost the language of skepticism.

Nevertheless, Locke is not skeptical in regard to the existence of bodies; notwithstanding his theory of ideas, he is clearly idealistic. He is attached to the great peripatetic and sensualistic family, in which the theory of species, and sensible species, had the authority of a dogma, and the duty of giving and explaining the exterior world. Of sensible species, the seventeenth century in general, and Locke in particular, have made sensible ideas, provided with all the qualities of species, representatives of their objects and emanating from them. There is, then, no idealistic design in Locke's theory of ideas. On the contrary, Locke is convinced that these ideas, in so far as representatives, are the only solid foundation which can be given for the knowledge of exterior objects; only he acknowledges, partly against his will, the peripatetic hypothesis of species, transformed into the modern theory of sensible ideas, turns against his aim, and that, although this hypothesis has an evidently materialistic character, since in it ideas are necessarily images and material images, it has not the power to give matter legitimately. Judge what it must be in regard to the spiritual world, the soul, and God: I shall be brief.

Remember the general principle of Locke. We have no legitimate knowledge whatever, except on condition that the ideas which we have of it be conformed to their object. Now, every one believes in the existence of his soul, that is, in the existence of something in us, which feels, which wills, which thinks. Those even who do not believe in the spiritual existence of this subject, have never doubted the existence of its faculties, the existence of the sensibility, for example, that of the will, that of the thought. Well, think of it: you have no legitimate knowledge of thought, of will, of sensibility, except on condition that the ideas which you have of them represent them; and these ideas must be images, and consequently material images. See into what an abyss of absurdities we have fallen. In order to know thought and will, which are immaterial, we must necessarily have a material image which resembles them. But what is a material image of thought and of will? The same absurdity exists in regard to the sensibility. The absurdity is greater, if possible, in regard to the substance of these faculties, in regard to the soul, and then in regard to the unity and identity of this soul, and then in regard to the time in which the operations of the faculties of this soul are fulfilled, sensations, volitions, thoughts.

Behold, then, the spiritual world crumbling like the material world. Simply because we have no legitimate ideas of our faculties and of their subject, except on the condition of these ideas being material images, it is evident that we have no legitimate knowledge of our soul, of its faculties, and of our whole interior being, intellectual and moral. The difficulty here even seems greater than in regard to the material world, or at least it shakes still more the successor of Bacon and of Hobbes. As to the material world, he had acknowledged that many objections existed against his theory of ideas, but these objections did not seem insurmountable, and he believed that they still left us a certain knowledge of the material world, sufficient for our wants; by this he pretended to open the door only to a semi-skepticism. It was doubtless a weakness; for the idea of Locke, a material image, in nowise representing bodies, either complete or incomplete, no idea of bodies should have been admitted; he should have gone on to absolute skepticism. Locke is arrested by good sense and by the evidence which, in his school, surrounds the objects of sense and the physical world. But when he arrives at the spiritual world, to which the sensualistic school adheres less closely, the arguments which naturally arise from his own theory, strike him more forcibly, and see what he declares, Book IV. Chap. XI. § 12: "We can no more know that there are finite spirits really existing, by the idea we have of such beings in our minds, than by the ideas any one has of fairies, or centaurs, he can come to know that things answering those ideas do really exist." This seems to me to be absolute skepticism; and you, perhaps, think that the last conclusion of Locke will be that there is no knowledge of finite spirits, consequently none of our soul, consequently again, none of any of the faculties of our soul; for the objection is as valid against the phenomena of the soul as against its substance. It is here he should have terminated; but he did not dare to do it, because there is no philosopher at the same time more wise and more inconsistent than Locke. What does he then do?

In the danger in which his philosophy throws him, he abandons his philosophy, and all philosophy, and he appeals to Christianity, to revelation, to faith; and by faith and revelation, he does not understand a faith, a natural revelation; he understands faith and revelation in the peculiar theological sense, and he concludes thus: "Therefore concerning the existence of finite spirits, as well as several other things, we must content ourselves with the evidence of faith." Thus, Locke himself anticipates the inevitable consequences to which I wished to lead him. Speaking as a philosopher and not as a theologian, I said that if we have no other reason for believing in the existence of spirit than the hypothesis of the representative idea, we have no good reason for believing in it. Locke grants it, proclaims it himself, and throws himself into the arms of faith. I shall not leave him there. The world of faith is interdicted to him as well as the world of spirit and that of matter; he could penetrate it only by the grossest paralogism. Locke has no more right, he has still less right to believe in faith, in revelation, in Christianity, than to believe in the finite spirits which we are and in the matter which is before us.

Revelation supposes two things: 1st, doctrines emanating from God; 2d, a book in which these doctrines are deposited and preserved. This book, although its contents are divine and sacred, is itself material; it is a body, and I here refer Locke to the objections which I have made against the legitimate knowledge of bodies, if we have no other foundation for believing in them than the idea-image which represents them to us. Thus we can have no legitimate knowledge of the book in which the sacred doctrines, revealed by God, are contained. If it is thus in regard to the book, what become of the doctrines which it contains? Besides, these doctrines come from God.

And what is God? a spirit, and, apparently, an infinite spirit. Now, we have just seen that Locke was unable, according to his theory, to admit the legitimate existence of finite spirits; and, incredible as it may seem, in order to make me admit the existence of finite spirits, he proposes to have me begin by admitting the existence of an infinite spirit! But is not this explaining *obscurum per obscurius?* A while since the human mind was condemned to have no knowledge of finite spirits, because it could have no ideas conformed to them, and now, for greater facility, it must have an idea of the infinite spirit, which perfectly represents it! But if it cannot represent a finite it will be still less able to represent an infinite spirit; evidently it cannot do it on the condition of Locke, that is, on the condition of forming an image of it, and moreover a material image; therefore there is no infinite spirit, no God; therefore no possible revelation. Everywhere at each step, in the theory of Locke, we have an abyss of paralogism.

If it is true that we have no legitimate knowledge, no true idea except on the condition that this idea represents its object, that it be conformed to an image, and a material image of this object, which I have shown to be the rigorous condition of the hypothesis of ideas, it follows that we have no legitimate idea of the exterior world, of the world of spirits, of souls, of ourselves, and still less of God, to whom Locke appeals. Consequently it follows in the last analysis that we have no true idea of beings, and that we have no other legitimate knowledge than that of our ideas, still less their object, whatever it may be, beginning by our own personal being itself. Such a consequence overwhelms the theory of ideas, and this consequence proceeds invincibly from this theory.

LECTURE XXII.

ESSAY, FOURTH BOOK. REPRESENTATIVE IDEAS CONTINUED.

Summary and continuation of the preceding lecture.—Of the idea, no longer in relation to the object which it should represent, but in relation to the mind which perceives it and in which it is found.—The idea-image, taken materially, implies a material subject; whence materialism.—Taken spiritually, it can give neither bodies nor spirit.—That the representative idea laid down as the only primitive datum of spirit in the search after reality, condemns to a paralogism, it being impossible that any representative idea can be judged to represent well or ill, except by comparing it with its original, with reality itself, to which, in the hypothesis of the representative idea, we can arrive only by the idea.—That knowledge is direct and without intermediation.—Of judgments, of propositions, of ideas.—Return to the question of innate ideas.

I AM now about to resume and complete the last lecture. According to Locke, knowledge is entirely in the relation of the idea to its object; and this knowledge is true or false according as the relation of the idea to the object is a relation of conformity or of nonconformity: the idea in order to be true, in order to be the foundation of legitimate knowledge, must be similar to its object, must represent it, and be its image. Now, what is the condition of an idea-image? There is no image without figure, without something extended, without something sensible and material. The idea-image implies then something material; and if the truth of knowledge is resolved into the conformity of the idea to its object, it is resolved into the conformity of an image, taken materially, to its object, whatever it may be.

Remark that the theory of the representative idea, as the basis of consciousness, is in Locke a universal theory, without limit, without exception: it must therefore account for all knowledge; it must go as far as human knowledge can go; it embraces God, spirits, bodies; for all this falls more or less under knowledge. If then we can know nothing, neither God, nor spirits, nor bodies, except by the ideas which represent them, and which represent them on condition of being material images of them, the question is to know whether we have of these objects, of these beings, ideas, faithful images, taken materially.

The problem, thus reduced to its most simple expression, has been easily resolved. I think that it has been clearly demonstrated that the exterior world itself, which the idea-image seems able most easily to give us, entirely escapes us if it can come only by the idea-image; for there is no sensible idea which may be an image of the world, of exterior objects, of bodies.

We have first considered in regard to bodies the qualities called secondary qualities, which are, you know, properties beyond our grasp in their nature, and appreciable solely by their effects, that is, pure causes, the causes of our sensations. Now it is evident that there is not, that there cannot be an image, a material image of a cause. As to the primary qualities of bodies, there is among them one, figure, which seems proper to be represented by the idea-image; and in fact, it is certain that the visible appearance, the figure of exterior bodies placed before us, before the organ of vision, is painted upon the retina. But, 1st, the first one who knew the visible figure of a body was perfectly ignorant that this visible figure was painted upon the retina: it was not then to the knowledge of this picture upon the retina, and to the knowledge of the conformity of this picture to its object, that he owed the knowledge of the reality of the external figure; 2d, then this picture is confined to the retina; in order to go to the brain, which is the audience-chamber of the soul, as Locke says, it would be necessary that it should traverse the optic nerve, which is in an obscure region; and were the optic nerve in a luminous region, the image, after having traversed the optic nerve, would arrive at the brain, which is itself incontestably obscure, and there the idea-image would perish, before arriving at the soul. Thus it is a condition of the phenomena of vision that there should be on the retina an image of the object;

but it is only the exterior condition, unknown to the soul itself; it is neither the direct foundation nor the explanation. Besides, if the idea-image plays a certain part in the phenomena of vision, it is not at all applied to other phenomena, to those of touch, for example, by which we derive the knowledge of the primary quality of bodies, to wit, solidity, resistance. We have demonstrated that there can be no idea-image of resistance, of solidity; for the idea of solidity and resistance is resolved into the idea of a cause, of a resisting cause, and it has been demonstrated that there can be no idea-image of cause.

So much for the primary as well as secondary qualities of bodies. If the idea-image represents no quality of bodies, still less does it represent the subject of these qualities, that *substratum* which escapes the reach of the senses, and consequently does not fall under an image borrowed from the senses. Also space, which must not be confounded with the bodies which it contains, cannot be given by the idea-image. It is the same with time; it is the same with all cognitions which are attached to the general knowledge of the exterior world. Therefore, as the idea-image can represent only forms, and as it plays a part only in the circle of the phenomena of vision, and as even there it is only the condition of these phenomena, it follows that if the exterior world has no other way of arriving at the intelligence than that of the representative idea, it does not and cannot arrive there.

The difficulties of the hypothesis of the representative idea are redoubled when the spiritual world is considered. Locke recognizes them; he admits that, since in fact the idea-image cannot represent the qualities of spirits, inasmuch as there is no image of that which has no figure, either the knowledge of spirit must be renounced, or, to obtain it, we must have recourse to faith, to revelation. But revelation is for us a book which contains doctrines revealed by God. There are here, therefore, two things, a book and God. As to the book, we refer it to the exterior world: no representative idea being able to give certain knowledge of a sensible object, can consequently give that of a book; the book, sacred or not, cannot be certainly known and be the certain foundation of the existence of spirit. God remains; but to have recourse to God in order to justify the knowledge of spirit, is to have recourse to spirit in order to justify the knowledge of spirit, and to take for granted what is in question. The sole difference between the spirit of God and our spirit, is that the spirit of God is infinite, whilst ours is finite, which, far from diminishing the difficulty, increases it. Thus the representative idea, examined in every way, can give no real knowledge, neither that of body, nor that of spirits, and still less the knowledge of the infinite spirit to which Locke gratuitously appeals.

Absolute skepticism is therefore the inevitable consequence of the theory of the representative idea; and absolute skepticism is here nothing less than absolute nihilism. In fact, you legitimately have in this theory neither secondary qualities, nor primary qualities of bodies, nor the subject of these qualities, nor space in which bodies are placed, nor time in which their motions are accomplished and their duration lapses. Still less have you legitimately the qualities of your spirit; the spirit itself, the spirit of your fellow-beings, the finite spirit; much less God, the infinite spirit: you have then nothing, absolutely nothing, except the idea itself, that idea which should represent every thing and which represents nothing, and lets no real knowledge come to you. Behold where we now are, and the difficulties are far from being exhausted. We have thus far considered the idea, the idea-image, in its relation with its object which it ought to represent, to wit, bodies, our spirits, and God; let us now consider it on another side, in its relation with mind, which should perceive it and in which it should be found.

The idea represents neither body, nor spirit, nor God; it can give no object, as we have demonstrated: but is necessarily in a subject. How is it there? What is the relation of the idea, not with its object, but with its subject?

Recollect to what condition we have condemned the representative idea. If it represents, it must have in itself some figure, something material: it is, therefore, something material. Behold then the representative idea, which is something material in the subject where it is found. But it is clear that the subject of the idea, the subject which perceives, contains, and possesses the idea, can be of no other nature than the idea itself. The representative idea is something with figure, like the shadows which are painted in a magic lantern; it can, therefore, exist only in something analogous, in a subject of the same nature, figured like the idea, having parts, like it, extended and material. Hence the destruction of the simplicity and the spirituality of the subject of the idea, that is, of the soul, or, in a single word, materialism, is the necessary consequence of the theory of the representative idea in relation to its subject.

The result was already in the principle, and this consequence only brings to view the vice of the origin of the representative idea. In fact, the origin of this theory, you know, is in the hypothesis that the mind knows bodies, communicates with bodies, only in the same manner that bodies communicate with each other. Now bodies communicate with each other either by immediate impulsion upon each other, or indirectly by the intermediation of one or several bodies, which, receiving an impulse from the preceding, communicate it to that which follows; so that it is always impulsion, whether immediate or mediate, that makes the communication of bodies. If, therefore, the mind knows bodies, it can know them only in the manner in which bodies communicate with each other, by impulsion. But we do not see that there is immediate and direct impulsion of bodies upon the mind, nor of mind upon bodies; the communication, the impulsion must be made at a distance, that is, through an intermediate. This intermediate is the idea. The idea emanates from bodies, such is its first character; its second character is, that it represents them, and it will easily represent bodies, since it comes from them. The representation is founded upon emission. But the emission, which is the first root of the representative idea, condemns it to be material. This is already a strong inclination to materialism; see now what renders this inclination much stronger. Not only the mind knows not bodies except as bodies communicate with each other, but the mind knows minds only as it knows bodies; and as it knows bodies only through the intermediate of the representative idea, it knows minds only through the same intermediate. A theory, materialistic in its origin, is applied at first to the knowledge of bodies, then is transferred to the knowledge of spirit; it was then quite natural that its last expression should be materialism. And I do not impose upon this theory consequences logically necessary, but which it has not borne; in fact, the school of Locke grounds in part upon the theory of the representative idea, its denial of the soul's spirituality. According to his school, several ideas in the soul, taken materially, suppose something extended in the soul; and even a single idea, being an image, is already something figured which supposes an analogous subject. The common expression: Objects make an impression upon the mind, is not a metaphor for this school, it is reality itself. I refer you to Hartley, to Darwin, to Priestley, and to their English or other successors. We shall meet with them again at the proper time and place.

Does any one wish to save the spirituality of the soul, and, at the same time, the theory of the representative idea? He has, on the one side, material ideas, material images; on the other, a simple soul, and, consequently, an abyss between the modification and its subject. How is this abyss to be bridged over? what relation is there between the material image and the subject of this image, if we wish to maintain that this subject is simple, extended, spiritual? Intermediates must then be found between the idea-images and their subject, the soul. Images were already the intermediates between body and soul; now there must be intermediates between these first intermediates, or idea-images, and the soul; there must be new intermediates, that is, new ideas. But these new ideas, in order to serve as intermediates between the first idea and the soul, should represent these ideas;

in order to represent images they should be images themselves; and if they are images, they are material. The difficulty then continually returns: either the idea-images do not enter into the soul, or they stamp it with materiality. It is in vain to subtilize these ideas, it is vain to refine the intermediate; either, notwithstanding all these refinements, it is left material, and the material image stamps its subject with materiality; or, rather, it is necessary absolutely to renounce the idea-image, the material idea, and, while preserving the theory of the representative idea, to make the idea spiritual.

This has been done, the material idea-image has been abandoned for the spiritual idea. But what is the result of this modification of the theory which we are examining? I admit that, if the idea is spiritual, it permits a spiritual subject, and there is place for the simplicity and the immateriality of the soul; but then the hypothesis of emission is evidently destroyed, and with it the hypothesis of representation. In fact, I pray you, what is a spiritual idea as an image of a material object? Spirit is that which admits none of the properties which constitute what is called matter; it is, therefore, that which admits neither solidity, nor extent, nor figure. But how could that which is neither solid, nor extended, nor figured, represent what is extended, solid, figured? What can be the spiritual idea of solid? What can be the spiritual idea of extension, of form? It is evident that the spiritual idea cannot represent body. Does it represent spirit any more? No better; for, once more, there is no representation where there is no resemblance, and there is resemblance only between figures. That which is figured can represent that which is figured; but where there is no figure, there is no possible matter for resemblance, consequently, none for representation. Spirit cannot represent spirit. A spiritual idea, therefore, can in no manner represent any spiritual quality or any spiritual subject; and the spiritual idea which destroys the possible knowledge of body destroys not less, destroys even more the possible knowledge of spirit, of finite spirits such as we are, and of the infinite spirit, God. Hence, even from the bosom of sensualism, there springs a kind of idealism which, together with matter, would dispense with spirit and God himself. Do not believe, I pray you, that it is only reasoning which imposes these new consequences on the theory of ideas. As Hartley and Priestley prove that I have not gratuitously borrowed materialism from the theory of ideas, taken as material images, so the history of another branch of the school of Locke demonstrates that it is not I who condemn the theory of the spiritual idea to destroy both body and spirit. It destroys body, as Berkeley* testifies, who is armed with this theory in order to deny all material existence. It destroys spirit, testifies Hume†, who, taking from the hands of Berkeley the arms which had served to destroy the material world, and turning them against the spiritual, has destroyed with them both the finite spirit which we are, and the infinite spirit: the human soul and God.

It is necessary to go to the extent of these principles: the representative idea, considered relatively to its subject and as its material image, leads to materialism; and, taken spiritually, it leads to the destruction of both body and spirit, to absolute skepticism and to absolute nihilism. Now, it is an incontestable fact that we have the knowledge of bodies, that we have the knowledge of our spirit. We have this double knowledge, and yet we could not have obtained it by the theory of the representative idea; therefore, this theory does not reproduce the true process of the human mind. According to Locke, the representative idea is the only way of legitimate knowledge; therefore, this way being wanting to us, we are in the absolute impossibility of ever arriving at knowledge: we do arrive at it, however; consequently, we arrive at it by some other way than that of the representative idea, and consequently, again, the theory of the representative idea is a chimera.

---

* First Series, Vol. 1, Lecture 8, p. 43, etc., and Vol. 4, Lecture 20, p. 359.
† First Series, Vol. 1, Lecture 10, and Vol. 4, Lecture 20, pp. 360–369, etc.

I go farther; I change ground altogether; I admit that the idea has a representative virtue, I admit the reality of the representation; I will indeed believe, with Locke and all his partisans, that we know only by representative ideas, and that, in fact, ideas have the marvellous property of representing their objects. Let it be so: but upon what condition do ideas represent things? You know, on the condition of being conformed to them. I suppose that if we knew not that the idea is conformed to its object, we should not know what it represents; we should have no real knowledge of this object. And yet upon what condition can we know that an idea is conformed to its object, that it is a faithful copy of the original which it represents? Nothing is more simple: upon this condition, that we should know the original. We must have under our eyes the original and the copy, in order to be able to relate the copy to the original, and to pronounce that the copy is, in fact, a faithful copy of the original. But suppose we have not the original, what can we say of the copy? Can you say, in the absence of the original, that the copy, which alone is under your eyes, is a faithful copy of the original, which you do not possess, which you have never seen? No, certainly; you cannot be sure that the copy is a faithful copy, nor that it is an unfaithful copy; you cannot even affirm that it is a copy. If we know things only by ideas, and if we know them only on condition that ideas faithfully represent them, we can know that the ideas faithfully represent them only on condition that, on the one hand, we see the things, and, on the other, the ideas; it is then, and only then, that we can decide that the ideas are conformed to the things. Thus, in order to know whether you have a true idea of God, of the soul, of bodies, you must have, on the one hand, God, bodies, and the soul, and, on the other, the idea of God, the idea of the soul, the idea of body, to the end that, comparing the idea with its object, you may decide whether it is or is not conformed to its object. Let us choose an example.

I wish to know whether the idea which I have of body is true.

I must have both the idea which I form of body and the body itself, and then I must compare them and judge.

I take, therefore, from the hands of Locke, the idea of body such as Locke himself has furnished it to me. In order to know whether it is true, I must compare it with body itself. This supposes that I know body; for if I do not know it, with what can I compare the idea of body in order to know whether it is true or false. It is necessary to suppose that I know body. But how have I been able to know it? In the theory of Locke, you are aware, you can know only the ideas which represent things to you. Now, I know this body; therefore, in the theory of Locke, I know it only by the ideas which represent it to me; therefore I know not this body itself, this body which it would be necessary for me to know in order to compare it with the idea which I have of it; I only know its idea, that is, I could compare an idea with an idea, a copy with a copy. Here is still no original: therefore the comparison, the verification, is impossible. In order that the verification might conduct me to a result, it is necessary that this second idea, which I have of body, in the knowledge which I suppose I have of body, should be a true idea, an idea conformed to its object; but I am able to know whether this second idea is true only on the condition that I compare it; and with what? with the body, with the original; therefore it is necessary that I should in some other way have cognizance of the body, in order to know whether this second is conformed to it. Let us see then. I know the body; but how do I know it? In the theory of Locke, I always know it only by the idea which I can have of it; there is still only an idea here with which I must compare the second idea which I have of body; I cannot pass beyond the idea: continue thus as long as you please, you will go round in an impassable circle of ideas which will never let you arrive at a real object, and will never lay the foundation of a comparison, since a legitimate comparison would suppose that you have, on the one hand, the copy, and on the other hand, the original, and since you would never have any thing but an idea, then another idea, and so on; therefore you could never compare any thing but ideas, but copies. And still in order to say that there are copies, it would be necessary that you should have the original itself, which escapes you, and will forever escape you, in every theory of knowledge which condemns the mind to know only by the intermediate of representative ideas.

Thus, in the last analysis, the object, the original, continually escaping the immediate grasp of the human mind, can never be brought under the eyes of the human mind, nor consequently authorize a comparison with the copy, with the idea. You will therefore never know whether the idea that you have of body is conformed or non-conformed, faithful or unfaithful, true or false. You will have this idea without knowing even whether it has an object or not.

We cannot remain thus, and, in order to assist Locke, I will make a supposition. I will suppose that, in fact, we have under our eyes, not only the idea of the original, but the original itself. I will suppose that we directly know the original; then the comparison is possible: let us proceed to make it. But I remark, beforehand, that the supposition which I make, that of an original directly known, which supposition is the necessary basis of every comparison, which comparison is the necessary basis of even Locke's theory, I remark, I say, that this supposition exactly destroys this theory. In fact, if we suppose we have an original directly known, we suppose that we can know otherwise than by representative ideas.

But I proceed, and ask whether this original which we know directly, otherwise than by representative ideas, is a chimera? No. If it were a chimera, to compare the idea with a chimerical object would lead you to nothing. You therefore suppose that it is indeed the original, the true original, the object itself, the body; and you suppose that the knowledge which you have of it is a certain knowledge, a knowledge which leaves nothing to be desired. Then see what is your position. You have on the one hand the certain knowledge of body, and, on the other hand, you have of this body an idea in regard to which you wish to know whether it is faithful or not. On such terms the comparison is very easy; it is made of itself; having the copy and the original, you can easily say whether one represents the other. But this comparison, necessary in the theory, and now possible and easy, is also perfectly useless. What was the end of this comparison? it was to obtain a certain knowledge of body; for that is what you are seeking. In order to arrive at it, you have put the original in presence of the copy. But if you suppose that you have the original, that is, a certain knowledge of body, all is finished, there is nothing more to do; leave there your comparison, your verification; do not trouble yourself to seek whether the idea is conformed or not to this original: you possess it, which is sufficient; you possess the very knowledge which you wish to acquire. Thus, without the certain knowledge of the original, you could never know whether the idea which you have is faithful or not, and all comparison is impossible; and as soon as you have the original, without doubt it is then easy to compare the idea with the reality: but since you have this reality, it is entirely useless for you to compare the idea with it; you have what you are searching for; and the very condition of the theory and the comparison which it requires, is precisely the supposition of the knowledge which you are seeking from this theory, that is, a paralogism.

Such is the examination, somewhat subtile, but exact, which, following in all its windings the theory of the representative idea, confounds it on all sides. Either the representative idea does not represent and cannot represent, and in this case, if we have no other means of knowing things, we are condemned to not know them; we are condemned to skepticism more or less extensive, according as we are more or less consistent, and, if we wish to be perfectly consistent, to absolute skepticism in respect to body and in respect to mind, that is, to absolute nihilism. Or rather do we wish that the idea should represent its object? In this case, we can know that it faithfully represents it only so far as we have the original, only so far as we know by other means body, mind, things themselves; and then the intervention of the representative idea is possible, but it is useless. Its truth, the conformity of the idea to its object, can be demonstrated only by a supposition which overthrows the very theory which it is designed to sustain.*

---

* We believe the following, from Sir Wm. Hamilton (Edinburgh Review, Oct. 1830, p. 182), is the only true history of the word idea. We regard Sir Wm. Hamilton as the profoundest analyst who has appeared since Aristotle, and his erudition, both in its extent and in its exactness, is perfectly provoking. A collection of his philosophic papers would be useful in several ways.—*Tr.*

"The history of the word *idea* seems completely unknown. Previous to the age of Descartes, as a philosophical term, it was employed exclusively by the Platonists, at least exclusively in a Platonic meaning; and this meaning was *precisely the reverse* of that attributed to the word by Dr. Brown; the idea *was not an object of perception*—the idea *was not derived from without.* In the schools, so far from being a current *psychological* expression, as he imagines, it had no other application than a *theological.* Neither, after the revival of letters, was the term extended by the Aristotelians even to the objects of *intellect.* Melancthon indeed (who was a kind of semi-Platonist), uses it on *one* occasion as a synonym for notion, or intelligible species (*De Anima*, p. 187, ed. 1555); but it was even to this solitary instance, we presume, that Julius Scalliger alludes (*De Subtilitate*, vi. 4) when he castigates such an application of the word as neoteric and abusive ('*Melanch.*' is on the margin). We should have distinctly said that, previous to its employment *by Descartes himself*, the expression had never been used as a comprehensive term for the immediate objects of thought, had we not in remembrance the *Historia Animæ Humanæ* of our countryman, David Buchanan. This work, originally written in French, had for some years been privately circulated previous to its publication at Paris in 1636. Here we find the word *idea* familiarly employed, in its most extensive signification, to express the objects, not only of intellect proper, but of memory, imagination, sense; and this is the *earliest* example of such an employment. For the *Discourse on method*, in which the term is usurped by Descartes in an equal latitude, was at least a year later in its publication—viz., in June, 1637. Adopted soon after also by Gassendi, the word under such imposing patronage gradually won its way into general use. In England, however, Locke may be said to have been the first who naturalized the term in its Cartesian universality. Hobbes employs it, and that historically, only once or twice; Henry More and Cudworth are very chary of it, even when treating of the Cartesian philosophy; Willis rarely uses it; while Lord Herbert, Reynolds, and the English philosophers in general, between Descartes and Locke, do not apply it psycho-

Let us deduce the consequences of this discussion.

First consequence: we know matter and spirit, the world, the soul, and God, otherwise than by representative ideas. Second and more general consequence: in order to know beings, we have no need of an intermediate; we know things directly, without the intermediation of ideas, and without any other intermediation; the mind in its exercise is subjected to certain conditions, but these conditions, once fulfilled, it enters into exercise and knows, for the sole reason that it is endowed with the virtue of knowing.

The true history of the understanding confirms this important result, and succeeds in putting the theory of ideas in its full light.

Primitively nothing is abstract, nothing is general; every thing is particular, every thing is concrete. The understanding, as I have demonstrated, does not start with these formulas, that there is no modification without subject, that there is no body without space, etc.; but a modification being given it, it conceives a particular subject of this modification; a body being given, it conceives that this body is in a space; a particular succession being given, it conceives that this succession is in a determinate time, etc. It

logically at all. When in common language employed by Milton and Dryden, *after* Descartes as *before* him, by Sidney, Spenser, Shakspeare, Hooker, etc., the meaning is Platonic. Our lexicographers are ignorant of the difference.

"The fortune of this word is curious. Employed by Plato to express the real forms of the intelligible world, in lofty contrast to the unreal images of the sensible, it was lowered only when Descartes extended it to the objects of our consciousness in general. When, after Gassendi, the school of Condillac had analyzed our highest faculties into our lowest, the *idea* was still farther degraded from its high original. Like a fallen angel, it was relegated from the sphere of divine intelligence to the atmosphere of human sense; till at last by a double blunder in philosophy and Greek, IDEOLOGIE (for IDEALOGIE), a word which could only *properly* suggest an *a priori* scheme, deducing our knowledge from the intellect, has in France become the name peculiarly distinctive of that philosophy of mind which exclusively derives our knowledge from sensation. Word and thing, *idea*, has been the *crux philosophorum*, since Aristotle cursed it to the present day:—τὰς δὲ ἰδέας χαιρέτω· τερετίσματα γάρ ἐισι."

is so with all our primitive conceptions; they are all particular, determinate, concrete. Moreover, and I have demonstrated this too, they are mingled with each other, all our faculties entering into exercise simultaneously, or nearly simultaneously. There is no consciousness of the smallest sensation without an act of attention, that is, without some unfolding of the will; there is no volition without the sentiment of an interior causative force; there is no sensation perceived without reference to an external cause and the world, which we at that moment conceive as in a space and in a time, etc. Finally, our primitive conceptions present still two distinct characters; on the one hand they are contingent, on the other they are necessary. Under the very eye of consciousness is a sensation of pain or pleasure, which I perceive as really existing; but this variable sensation changes, disappears, and hence very soon arises the conviction that this sensible phenomenon which I perceive is real no doubt, but which might or might not exist, and which, being able to exist or not to exist, I might or might not perceive: it is this character which, subsequently, philosophy will designate under the name of contingence. But when I conceive that a body is in space, if I attempt to conceive the contrary, to conceive that a body can exist without space, I do not succeed; and this conception of space is what philosophy will subsequently designate under the name of necessary conception. But whence come all our necessary or contingent conceptions? From the faculty of conceiving which is in us, whatever name you apply to this faculty of which we have a consciousness,—mind, reason, thought, understanding, intelligence. The acts of this faculty, our conceptions, are essentially affirmative, if not orally, at least mentally. To deny even, is to affirm; for it is to affirm the opposite of that which has been affirmed. To doubt, is also to affirm; it is to affirm uncertainty. Moreover, we evidently begin neither by doubt nor negation, but by affirmation. Now, to affirm in any manner, is to judge. If, therefore, every intellectual operation is resolved into the operation of judgment, all our conceptions, either contingent or necessary, are resolved into judgments, either contingent or necessary; and all our primitive operations, being concrete and synthetical, it follows that all the primitive judgments which these operations suppose, are also exercised under this form.

Such is the primitive scene of intelligence. Little by little intelligence is developed. In this development supervenes language which reflects the understanding, and puts it, thus to speak, out of itself. If you open grammars, you will see that they all commence with elements, to go thence to propositions; that is, they commence with analysis to end with synthesis. But, in reality, it is not so. When the mind translates itself by the use of language, the first expressions of its judgments are, like the judgments themselves, concrete and synthetical. It does not at first produce words, but phrases, propositions, and very complex propositions. A primitive proposition is a whole which corresponds to the natural synthesis by which the mind begins. These primitive propositions are in nowise abstract propositions, such as the following: There is no quality without a subject, no body without a space which contains it, and other similar ones; but they are all particular, like these: I exist, this body exists, such a body is in this space, God exists, etc.; these are propositions which refer to a particular, determinate object, which is either *me*, or body, or God. But after having expressed by concrete and synthetic propositions, its primitive, concrete, and synthetic judgments, the mind operates upon its judgments by abstraction; it neglects the concrete in them to consider only their form; for example, this character of necessity with which several are invested, and which, disengaged and developed, gives, instead of those concrete propositions: I exist, those bodies are in such a space, etc.; the abstract propositions: There can be no body without space, there can be no modification without subject, there can be no succession without time, etc. The general was at first enveloped in the particular; then, you disengage the general from the particular, and you express it alone. But I have elsewhere sufficiently explained the formation of general propositions.*

Language is the sign of the mind, of its operations, and of their development. It expresses primitive, concrete, and synthetic judgments, by propositions themselves primitive, concrete, and synthetic. The judgments are gradually generalized by abstraction, and in their turn propositions become general and abstract. In these abstractions, abstraction operates upon new abstractions. Abstract propositions, signs of abstract judgments, are themselves composed of several elements. We abstract these elements in order to consider them separately; these elements are what we call ideas. It is a great error to suppose that we have at first these elements without having the whole of which they form a part. We do not begin even by propositions, but by judgments: judgments do not come from propositions, propositions come from judgments, which themselves come from the faculty of judging, which rests upon the original virtue of the mind; for a still stronger reason, we do not begin by ideas; for ideas are given to us in these propositions. Take, for example, the idea of space. It is not given to us as a solitary idea, but in the complete proposition: There is no body without space, and this proposition is only the form of a judgment. Take away the propositions, which would not exist without the judgments, and you will have no ideas; but as soon as language has enabled you to translate your judgments into propositions, then you can consider separately the different elements of these propositions, that is, the ideas separate from each other. Strictly speaking, there are no propositions in nature, neither concrete propositions, nor abstract propositions, neither particular propositions, nor general propositions; for a still stronger reason, there are no ideas in nature. If by ideas is meant something real, which exists independently of language, which is an intermediate between beings and the mind, I say that there are absolutely no ideas. There is nothing real but

---

* Lecture 19 of this volume.

things, and the mind with its operations, to wit, its judgments. Then come languages, which create in some sort a new world, at once material and spiritual, those symbolic beings which are called signs, by the aid of which they give a sort of exterior and independent existence to the results of the operations of the mind. Thus, in expressing judgments or propositions, they have the appearance of making these propositions : it is the same with ideas. Ideas are not more real than propositions, and they are just as real ; they have all the reality which propositions have, the reality of abstractions to which language gives a nominal and conventional existence. Every language is at once an analyst and a poet ; it makes abstractions, and gives to them reality. This is the condition of language : we must be resigned to it, and speak by figures, provided we know what we are doing. Thus everybody speaks of having an idea of such a thing, of having a clear or obscure idea of it ; and by this no one means to say that he knows things only by means of intermediates, called ideas ; it is only meant to mark by this the action of the mind in regard to such a thing, the action by which the mind knows this thing, knows it more or less, etc. We also say that a thing is represented, and often a thing which does not fall under the senses, in order to say that we know it, that we comprehend it, by using a metaphor borrowed from the phenomena of the senses, from the sense whose use is the most frequent, that of sight. The taste is usually the sole judge of the employment of these figures. We can and often do go very far in this metaphorical style, without obscurity and without error. I absolve then the ordinary language of the greater part of men, and I believe that we may also absolve that of the most part of philosophers, who often speak like the people, without being more absurd than the people. It is impossible, in fact, to interdict the philosopher all metaphor ; the only law which it is necessary to impose on him is that he shall not stop at metaphors, and convert them into theories. Perhaps the Scotch school, which revived in the eighteenth century the ancient controversy against the representative idea, in the name of the common sense of the human race, was not always sufficiently mindful that philosophers are a part of mankind; perhaps it imputed too much to the schools, and was too willing to see everywhere the theory which it had undertaken to combat;* but it is certain that it rendered an eminent service to philosophy, by demonstrating that the idea-image is at bottom only a metaphor, and by doing justice to this metaphor, when any representative virtue is seriously attributed to it. This is the vice into which Locke has incontestably fallen, and which I have considered it necessary to designate to you as one of the most perilous rocks of the sensualistic school.

From the point at which we have arrived we can easily appreciate the doctrine of innate ideas, the refutation of which fills the entire first book of the *Essay on the Understanding*.† The moment has come to explain ourselves in regard to this doctrine, and in regard to the refutation which Locke has given of it. Locke divides the general doctrine of innate ideas into two points, general propositions or maxims, and ideas. And we also reject innate propositions and ideas, and for the very simple reason that there are in nature neither ideas nor propositions. What is there in nature? Besides bodies nothing but minds, among others that which we are, which directly conceives and knows things, minds, and bodies. And in the order of mind what is there innate? Nothing but mind itself, the understanding, the faculty of knowing. The understanding, as Leibnitz has profoundly said, is innate to itself; the development of the understanding is equally innate to it, in the sense that it cannot but be developed, the understanding once being given with the virtue which is its own; and, as you have seen, the development of the understanding is the judgments which it passes at the outset, and the knowledge implied in these judgments. Without doubt these judgments have conditions which belong to the domain of experience. Take

* See the development and confirmation of this doubt, First Series, Vol. 4, *Scotch School*, Lecture 22, p. 508 and p. 518, etc.

† Lecture 17 of this volume.

away experience, and there is nothing in the senses, nothing in consciousness, consequently nothing in the understanding. Is this the absolute law of the understanding? Could it not still judge and develop itself without the aid of experience, without an organic impression, without a sensation? I neither affirm it nor deny it: *Hypotheses non fingo*, as Newton said, "I am not making hypotheses;" I am stating what is, without seeking what might be. I say that, in the limits of the present state, it is an undeniable fact that so long as certain experimental conditions are not fulfilled, the mind does not enter into exercise, does not judge; but I say at the same time that as soon as these conditions are fulfilled, the mind, by its own virtue, develops itself, judges, thinks, conceives, and knows a multitude of things which fall neither under the consciousness nor under the senses, as time, space, exterior causes, existences, and its own existence. There are no more innate ideas than innate propositions; but there is an innate virtue of the understanding, that is produced in primitive judgments, which, when languages come, are expressed in propositions, which propositions being decomposed engender under the hand of abstraction and analysis distinct ideas. As the mind is equal to itself in all men, the primitive judgments which it passes are the same in all men; and consequently the propositions in which language expresses these judgments, and the fundamental ideas of which these propositions are composed, are at once and universally admitted. A condition however is necessary: they must be comprehended. When Locke pretended that these propositions: Whatever is, is, and it is impossible for the same thing to be and not to be, are neither universally nor primitively admitted, he was both right and wrong. Assuredly the first comer, the peasant, to whom you should say: Whatever is, is, it is impossible for the same thing to be and not to be, would not admit these propositions, for he would not comprehend them, because you would speak to him in a language not his own, that of abstraction and analysis. But that which the peasant does not admit and does not comprehend in its abstract form, he at once and necessarily admits under the concrete and synthetic form. Ask this man who does not comprehend your metaphysical language, ask him whether, under the diverse actions or sensations which consciousness attests to him, there is not something real and substantial which is himself; whether he is not the same to-day as he was yesterday. In a word, instead of abstract formulas, put to him particular, determinate, concrete questions, and then human nature will respond to you, because human nature and the human understanding are in the peasant just as well as in Leibnitz. What I have just said of abstract and general propositions, I say of the simple ideas which analysis draws from these propositions. For example, ask a savage whether he has the idea of God; you put him a question to which he cannot respond, for he does not understand it. But if you know how to interrogate this poor savage, you will see spring from his intelligence a synthetic and confused judgment which, if you know how to read it, already contains every thing that the most refined analysis will ever give you; you will see that under the confusion of their natural judgments, which they know neither how to separate nor to express, the savage, the infant, the idiot even, if he is not entirely an idiot, primitively and universally admit all the ideas which analysis subsequently develops without producing, or of which it produces only the scientific form.

There are no innate ideas, there are no innate propositions, because there are neither ideas nor propositions really existing; and again, there are no ideas and general propositions, universally and primitively admitted under the form of general ideas and propositions, but it is certain that the understanding of all men is, as it were, pregnant with natural judgments, which may be called innate* in the sense that they are the primitive, universal, and necessary development of the human understanding, which, once more, is innate to itself and equal to itself in all men.

---

* This is the recognized and at present incontestable sense of the Cartesian theory of innate ideas.

LECTURE XXIII.

ESSAY, THEORY OF JUDGMENT.*

Examination of the Fourth Book of the *Essay on the Human Understanding* continued.—Of knowledge. Its different modes. Omission of inductive knowledge.—Its degrees. False distinction of Locke between knowing and judging.—That Locke's theory of knowledge and of judgment is resolved into that of the perception of a relation of agreement or of disagreement between ideas. Detailed examination of this theory.—That it is applied to abstract judgments and in nowise to primitive judgments, which imply existence.—Analysis of this judgment: I exist. Three objections to the theory of Locke: 1st, impossibility of arriving at real existence, by the abstraction of existence; 2d, that to begin by abstraction is contrary to the true process of the human mind; 3d, that the theory of Locke contains a paralogism.—Analysis of the judgments: I think, This body exists, This body is colored, God exists, &c.—Analysis of the judgments upon which arithmetic and geometry rest.

We have stopped some time at the beginning of the fourth book of the *Essay on the Human Understanding:* we will now enter farther into it.

The fourth book of the *Essay on the Human Understanding* treats of knowledge in general, of its different modes, of its different degrees, of its extent, and of its limits, with some applications: this is, properly speaking, logic with a little ontology. The principle of this logic rests on the theory which we have examined, that of the representative idea. We have seen that the condition of all legitimate knowledge, for Locke, is the conformity of the idea to the object; and we have in every way shown this conformity to be a mere chimera. We have then overturned in advance the general theory of knowledge; but we have overturned it in its principle only. It is in some sort a

* On the true theory of judgment, see 1st Series, Vol. 4, Lecture 20, p. 370–376, Lecture 21, p. 414, and Lecture 22, p. 464–477.

prejudicial question, an exception which we have raised against this theory; it is necessary now to examine it in itself, independently of the principle of the representative idea, to follow it in the development which is proper to it, and in the consequences which belong to it.

Whether the idea represents or does not represent, in the system of Locke, we always find that the understanding begins with things only by ideas; that ideas are the only objects of the understanding, and consequently the only foundations of knowledge. Now, if all knowledge necessarily rests upon ideas, where there is no idea there can be no knowledge, and wherever there is knowledge, there has necessarily been an idea. But the reciprocal is not true; and wherever there is an idea, it does not follow that there is knowledge. For example, in order that you should have a profound knowledge of God, it is first necessary that you should have some idea of God; but because you have some idea of him, it does not follow that you have a true or sufficient knowledge of him. Thus knowledge is limited by ideas, but it does not go as far as ideas go.

Book IV. Chap. III. § 1. "*We can have knowledge no farther than we have ideas.*" *Ibid.*, § 6. "*Our knowledge is narrower than our ideas.*"

If knowledge never surpasses the ideas, and sometimes fails of coming up to them, and if all knowledge turns only on ideas, it is clear that knowledge cannot be any thing more than the relation of one idea with another idea, and that the process of the human mind in knowledge is simply the perception of some relation between ideas.

Book IV. Chap. I. § 1. "Since the mind, in all its thoughts and reasonings, hath no other immediate object but its own ideas, which it alone does, or can contemplate, it is evident, that our knowledge is only conversant about them."

§ 2. "Knowledge then seems to me to be nothing but the perception of the connection or agreement, or disagreement and repugnancy of any of our ideas. In this alone it consists.

Where this perception is, there is knowledge: and where it is not, there, though we may fancy, guess, or believe, yet we always come short of knowledge."

Thence follow different modes and different degrees of knowledge in the system of Locke. We simply know whether we perceive a relation of agreement or disagreement between two ideas. Now we can perceive this relation in two ways: either we perceive it immediately, and then knowledge is intuitive, or we do not perceive it immediately, and it is necessary that we should have recourse to another idea or to several other ideas, which we place between the two ideas whose relation cannot be perceived, so that by means of this new idea or of these new ideas we may seize the relation which escapes us. Knowledge in this case is called demonstrative knowledge. Book IV. Chap. II. § 1. Ibid., § 2.

Here Locke makes an excellent remark, which I ought not to omit, and of which it is just to give him the honor. Doubtless we are often compelled to recur to demonstration, to the intermediation of one idea or of several other ideas, in order to perceive the hidden relation of two ideas; but this new idea which we, in some way, interpose between the two others, it is necessary that we should see its relation with both. Now if the perception of this relation between this idea and the two others was not intuitive, if it were not demonstrative, it would be necessary to have recourse to the intermediation of a new idea. But if between this idea and the anterior ideas the perception of relation were not intuitive, but demonstrative, it would still be necessary to have recourse to a new idea, and so on without end. The perception of the relation between the middle idea and the extreme terms must then be intuitive, and thus it must be in all the degrees of deduction, so that demonstrative evidence is founded on intuitive evidence and constantly supposes it. Book IV. Chap. II. § 7: "*Each step must have intuitive evidence.*—Now in every step reason makes in demonstrative knowledge, there is an intuitive knowledge of that agreement or disagreement it seeks with the next intermediate idea, which it uses as a proof: for if it were not so, that yet would need a proof; since without the perception of such agreement or disagreement, there is no knowledge produced. If it be perceived by itself, it is intuitive knowledge: if it cannot be perceived by itself, there is need of some intervening idea, as a common measure to show their agreement or disagreement. By which it is plain, that every step in reasoning that produces knowledge has intuitive certainty; which when the mind perceives, there is no more required, but to remember it, to make the agreement or disagreement of the ideas, concerning which we inquire, visible and certain. So that to make any thing a demonstration, it is necessary to perceive the immediate agreement of the intervening ideas, whereby the agreement or disagreement of the two ideas under examination (whereof the one is always the first, and the other the last in the account) is found. This intuitive perception of the agreement or disagreement of the intermediate ideas, in each step and progression of the demonstration, must also be carried exactly in the mind, and a man must be sure that no part is left out."

This intuition and demonstration are the different modes of knowledge according to Locke. But are there no others? Is there no knowledge which we acquire except by intuition or by demonstration? How do we acquire knowledge of the laws of exterior nature? Take what you please, gravitation, for example. Certainly here is not simple intuition and immediate evidence; for experiments multiplied and combined are necessary for the least law, and still, alone, they would not be sufficient, the least law surpassing the number, whatever it may be, of particular experiments drawn from it. There must then be an intervention of some other operation of the mind besides intuition. Is it demonstration? This is impossible. What in fact is demonstration? It is the perception of a relation between two ideas by means of a third, but on the condition that the third be more general than the other two, in order to embrace them and bind them. To demonstrate is in the last analysis to draw the particular from the general. But what physical law is more general than that of gravitation, and from what is it deduced? The knowledge of gravitation is not deduced from any other knowledge anterior to it and which contains it. How then have we obtained this knowledge which we certainly have, and how in general have we obtained the knowledge of physical laws? A phenomenon having been presented to us with such a character, in such circumstances we have judged that if this phenomenon should present itself anew in analogous circumstances, it would have the same character; that is, we have at first generalized the particular character of this phenomenon: instead of descending from the general to the particular, we have risen from the particular to the general. This general character is what is called law; we have not deduced this law from a more general law or character; we have drawn it from particular experiments, in order to transfer it beyond; there is here neither simple intuition nor demonstration; it is what is called induction.* It is to induction that we owe all our conquests over nature, all our discoveries of the laws of the world. Natural philosophers, for a long time, contented themselves either with immediate observations, which resulted in nothing of importance, or with reasonings which simply gave hypotheses. For a long time induction was merely a natural process of the human mind, of which all men made use in order to acquire the knowledge of which they had need relatively to the exterior world, without accounting for it or without its passing from practice into science. It is especially to Bacon that we owe, not the discovery, but the exposition and greatest use of this process. It is strange that Locke, the compatriot of Bacon, and who belongs to his school, should, in his classification of the modes of knowledge, have suffered to escape the very one which Bacon has rendered most celebrated and placed in the clearest light. It is strange that the whole sensual-

---

* On induction, see Lecture 13 of this Series, and 1st Series, Vol. 4, Lectures 20 and 22.

istic school, which pretends to be the legitimate offspring of Bacon, should, after the example of Locke, have almost forgotten the evidence of induction, among the different species of evidence, and that, contrary to what an experimental school should have done, it should have neglected induction to plunge into demonstration. Such is the reason of this singular but incontestable phenomenon, that in the eighteenth century the logic of the sensualistic school was little else than a reflection of the peripatetic scholasticism of the middle age, of that scholasticism which admitted no other processes in knowledge than intuition and demonstration.

Let us now see what, according to Locke, are the different degrees of knowledge.

We know sometimes in so positive a manner that no doubt whatever is mingled with our knowledge. Often instead of a positive knowledge, we have simply a probable knowledge. Probability itself has many degrees, and it has particular foundations. Locke treats fully of this subject. I entreat you to read with care the chapters not very profound, but sufficiently exact, in which he treats of the different degrees of knowledge. I cannot enter into all these details, and content myself with pointing out to you chapters XIV. XV. and XVI. of the fourth book. I shall dwell on but one distinction to which Locke attaches the greatest importance, and which, in my opinion, has no foundation.

We either know in a certain and absolute manner, or we know only in a more or less probable manner. Locke wishes that the expression knowledge should be exclusively applied to knowledge absolute, placed above all probability, and he uses the term judgment for knowledge which is wanting in certainty, simple conjecture, presumption more or less probable. Book IV. Chap. XIV. § 4: "The mind has two faculties conversant about truth and falsehood. First *knowledge*, whereby it certainly perceives and is undoubtedly satisfied of the agreement and disagreement of any ideas. Secondly *judgment*, which is the putting ideas together, or separating them from one another in the mind, when their certain agreement or disagreement is not perceived, but presumed to be so; which is as the word imports, taken to be so, before it certainly appears."

But the general usage of all languages is contrary to so limited an employment of the word *to know*. A certain knowledge, or a probable, or even a conjectural knowledge, is always knowledge in different degrees. It is the same with judgment. As languages have not confined the term knowledge to absolute knowledge, so they have not confined the term judgment to knowledge simply probable. In certain cases we pass certain judgments; in other cases we pass judgments which are only probable, or merely conjectural. In a word, judgments are either infallible, or doubtful, to such or such a degree: but doubtful or infallible, they are still judgments; and this distinction between knowledge as being exclusively infallible, and judgment as being exclusively probable, doubtful, or conjectural, is a verbal distinction entirely arbitrary and sterile. Time has done justice to it; but it seems to have respected the theory which is at the basis of this distinction, a theory which makes knowledge and judgment consist in the perception of a relation of agreement between these two ideas. All verbal distinction aside, to judge or to know, to know or to judge, is for Locke simply to perceive, whether intuitively or demonstratively, a relation of agreement or of disagreement, certain or probable, between two ideas: such is Locke's theory of knowledge and of judgment reduced to its most simple expression; it is from Locke that it passed into the sensualistic school, where it still enjoys undisputed authority and forms the settled theory of judgment: it therefore claims and merits a scrupulous examination.

Let us at first ascertain the extent of this theory: it not only pretends that there are judgments which are nothing else than perceptions of the relation of agreement or disagreement between two ideas; it pretends that every judgment is subject to this condition: this is what it concerns us to verify.

Let us take any knowledge whatever, any judgment whatever. I propose the following judgment: two and three make five;

this is not a chimera; it is clearly a knowledge, it is clearly a judgment and a certain judgment. How do we acquire this knowledge, what are the conditions of this judgment?

The theory of Locke supposes three: 1st, that there are here two ideas before the understanding, known anterior to the perception of the relation; 2d, that there is a comparison between these two ideas; 3d, that succeeding this comparison there is a perception of some relation between these two ideas. Two ideas, a comparison between them, a perception of relation derived from this comparison: such are the conditions of the theory of Locke.

Let us resume: two and three make five. Where are the two ideas? two and three, and five. Suppose that I had not these two ideas, these two terms, on the one hand two and three, and on the other five: could I never perceive that there is between them a relation of equality or of inequality, of identity or of diversity? no. And if, having these two terms, I did not compare them, would I never perceive their relation? not at all. And if comparing them, notwithstanding all my efforts, their relation escaped my understanding, would I never arrive at this result, that two and three make five? in nowise. On the contrary, these three conditions being fulfilled, is not this result infallibly obtained? Without doubt, and I do not see that any thing is wanting. Thus, to this point the theory of Locke seems very good. Shall I take another arithmetical example? but arithmetical examples have this peculiarity, that they all seem alike. What, in fact, are arithmetical truths except the relations of numbers? Arithmetical truths are nothing else; therefore arithmetical truths enter into Locke's general theory of knowledge; and arithmetical judgment, if we may so express it, is nothing else than a perception of the relation of numbers: thus far, again, the theory of Locke is perfectly justified.

Shall we take geometry? But if geometrical truths are only relations of magnitude, it is clear that no geometrical truth can be obtained except on condition of previously having two ideas of magnitude, then of comparing them, then of drawing from them a relation of agreement or of disagreement. And as all mathematics are, according to Newton, only a universal arithmetic, it must be granted that the mathematical judgment is only a perception of relations.

Let us take still other examples a little at random. I wish to know whether Alexander was a truly great man: it is a question frequently agitated. It is evident that if, on one hand, I had no idea of Alexander, and if, on the other, I formed no idea of a truly great man, if I did not compare these two ideas, if I did not perceive between them any relation of agreement or of disagreement, I could not decide that Alexander was a great man, or that he was not. Here again, we have, and must necessarily have, two ideas, the one particular, that of Alexander, the other general, that of the great man, and we compare these two ideas, in order to know whether they agree or disagree with each other, whether the predicate can be affirmed of the subject, whether the subject comes within the predicate, etc.

I wish to know whether God is good. At first, I must have the idea of the existence of God, the idea of God in so far as existing; then I must have the idea of goodness, a more or less extended, more or less complete idea of goodness, so as to be able to affirm, after comparison of the one idea with the other, that these two ideas have a relation of agreement between them.

These are clearly the conditions of knowledge, the conditions of judgment in these different cases. But let us account for the nature of these different cases. Let us examine the mathematical truths which so easily lend themselves to the theory of Locke. Do arithmetical truths, for example, exist in nature? no. And why do they not exist in nature? because these relations, which are called arithmetical truths, have for terms not concrete quantities, that is, real, but discrete quantities, that is, abstract. One, two, three, four, five, all this does not exist in nature; consequently the relations between these abstract and not real quantities have no more existence than their terms: arithmetical truths are mere abstractions. And then, the human mind operates at first on concrete quantities, and it is only at a later period that it ascends from the concrete to the conception of these general relations, which are arithmetical truths properly so called. They have two characters: 1st, they are abstract; 2d, they are not primitive; they suppose anterior concrete judgments, in the midst of which they rest, until abstraction draws them therefrom, and elevates them to the height of universal truths. I may say as much of the truths of geometry. The magnitudes with which geometry is occupied are not concrete magnitudes, they are abstract magnitudes, which do not exist in nature; for imperfect figures alone exist in nature, and the condition of geometry is to operate upon perfect figures, on the perfect triangle, the perfect circle, etc., that is, on figures which have no real existence, and which are pure conceptions of the mind. The relations of abstractions can therefore be nothing more than abstractions. Besides, the human mind did no more begin by conceiving perfect figures, than it began by conceiving the abstract relations of numbers; it first conceived the concrete, the imperfect triangle, the imperfect circle, from which it afterwards drew, by an abstraction, rapid, it is true, the triangle and the perfect circle of geometry: the truths of geometry are not, therefore, primitive truths in the human understanding. The other examples which we have taken, to wit, that Alexander is a great man, that God is good, are characterized by being problems instituted by a tardy reflection and a learned curiosity. In a word, we have thus far only verified the theory of Locke as regards abstract judgments and judgments which are not primitive: let us take judgments marked by other characters.

Behold another knowledge, another judgment which I propose for your examination: I exist. You no more doubt the certainty of this knowledge, than you do that of the first knowledge which I cited to you. Two and three make five: you would even sooner doubt the first than the second. Well, let us submit this certain knowledge, this certain judgment, I exist,* to the conditions of Locke's general theory of knowledge and of judgment.

I will remind you of the conditions of this theory: 1st, two ideas; 2d, comparison between these two ideas; 3d, perception of some relation of agreement or disagreement.

What are the two ideas which should be the two terms of this relation and the bases of the comparison? It is the idea of I or *me,* and the idea of existence, between which it concerns us to find a relation of agreement or disagreement.

Let us be careful as to what we are about doing. It is not the idea of our existence which will be one of the ideas upon which the comparison will be made; for what are we seeking? our existence. If we have it we should not seek it: we must not take for granted that which is a matter of question, our own existence; therefore the idea of existence which must here be one of the two terms of the comparison, is the idea of existence in general, and not the particular idea of our own existence: this is the rigorous condition of the problem. And what is the other idea, the second term of the comparison? the idea of the *me.* But what are we seeking? the existing *me.* Let us not therefore suppose it, for we should take for granted that which is in question. It is not therefore the existing *me* which will be the second term of the comparison, but a *me* which must be necessarily conceived as distinct from the idea with which it concerns us to compare it, to wit, the idea of existence, a *me* which must consequently be conceived as not possessing existence, that is, an abstract *me,* a general *me.*

The idea of an abstract *me,* and the idea of abstract existence, are then the two ideas upon which we must make the comparison from which the judgment is to proceed. Think of it, I pray you. What are you seeking? your personal existence. Do not suppose it, since you are seeking it; do not place it in either of the

* We have several times taken this example against the theory of representative ideas, and that of comparative judgment, 1st Series, Vol. 1, Lecture 8, p. 37, and Vol. 4, Lecture 20, p. 371, and Lecture 22, p. 474.

two terms from the comparison of which you demand it. Since it must only be the fruit of the relation of these two terms, it should not be supposed in either of them, for the comparison would be useless, and the truth would then be anterior to the perception of their relation; it would not be the result of it. Such, then, are the imperious conditions of the theory of Locke: two abstract ideas, the abstract idea of the *me* and the abstract idea of existence. It concerns us now to compare these two ideas, to know whether they agree or disagree with each other, to perceive the relation of agreement or disagreement which separates them or unites them. I might at first cavil in regard to this expression of agreement or disagreement, and show how it is wanting in precision and clearness: I shall not do it. I take the words as Locke gives them to me; I leave his theory to unfold itself freely, I do not arrest it; I merely wish to know where it will arrive. It sets out from two abstract terms, it compares them, and seeks a relation of agreement or disagreement between them, between the idea of existence and the idea of the *me*. It compares them then, so be it; and in what does it terminate? in a relation, a relation of agreement. So be it again; I would here remark but one thing; it is that this relation, whatever it may be, must necessarily be of the same nature as that of the two terms upon which it is founded. The two terms are abstract: the relation will, therefore, necessarily be abstract. What will then result from the perception of the relation, which I am willing to suppose, of agreement, between the general and abstract idea of existence and the general and abstract idea of the *me?* A truth of relation of the same nature as the two terms upon which it is founded, an abstract knowledge, a logical knowledge of the non-contradiction which is found between the idea of existence and the idea of the *me*, that is, the knowledge of the mere possibility of the existence of a *me*. But when you believe that you exist, I ask whether you simply pass this judgment that there is no contradiction between the general idea of the *me* and that of existence? Not at all. There is no question concerning a possible *you* or a possible *me*, but of a real *me*, of that very determinate *me* which no one confounds with a logical abstraction; there is no question concerning existence in general, but of your own, of your entirely personal and individual existence. On the contrary, the result of the judgment which is derived from the perception of a relation of agreement between the general and abstract idea of existence, and the general and abstract idea of the *me*, does not imply real existence; it gives, if you please, a possible existence, but it does not give and cannot give any thing more.

Such is the first vice of the theory of Locke. We proceed to show another.

The judgment, I exist, is a primitive judgment *par excellence;* it is the starting point of knowledge; you, evidently, can know nothing anterior to yourself. But in the theory of Locke, the two ideas upon which judgment depends, and between which it must perceive the relation of agreement, are necessarily two abstract ideas. Therefore the radical supposition of the theory of Locke is, that the human mind sets out by abstraction in knowledge, a supposition gratuitous and disproved by facts. In fact, we begin by the concrete and not by the abstract; and, although it were possible, which I deny, and which I have demonstrated to be impossible, to draw reality from abstraction, it would not be less true that the process which Locke imputes to the human mind, were it legitimate, would not be that which the human mind employs.

The theory of Locke can give only an abstract judgment, and not a judgment which reaches to real existence; it is not the true process of the human understanding, since the process of which it makes use is entirely abstract and nowise primitive; besides, this theory contains a paralogism.

In fact, Locke proposes to arrive at the knowledge of real and personal existence by comparison of the idea of existence and the idea of the *me*, in bringing them together in order to perceive their relation. But, in general, and to finish the question at a single stroke, the abstract being given to us only in the concrete, to draw the concrete from the abstract, is to take as a principle what could have been obtained only as a consequence, it is to demand what is sought from the very thing which could have been known only by means of what is sought. And in this particular case, on what condition have you obtained the general and abstract idea of existence, and the general and abstract idea of the *me*, which you compare in order to deduce from it the knowledge of your own existence? On the condition that you have had the idea of your own existence. It is impossible that you should have ascended to the generalization of existence, except through knowledge of some particular existence; and neither the knowledge of the existence of God, nor that of the existence of the external world preceding or being able to precede your own, it follows that the knowledge of your own existence cannot have been one of the bases of the abstract and general idea of existence: consequently, to attempt to draw the knowledge of your own existence from the general idea of existence, is to fall into an evident paralogism. If Locke had not known that he existed, if he had not already acquired the knowledge of his real and existent *me*, he never would have had either the general and abstract idea of a *me*, nor the general and abstract idea of existence, those same ideas from which he demands the knowledge of the *me* and of personal existence.

We thus have three radical objections against the theory of Locke:

1st, It sets out from abstractions; consequently it gives only an abstract result, and not that which you are seeking;

2d, It sets out from abstractions, and consequently it does not set out from the true starting point, the human intelligence;

3d, It sets out from abstractions which it could have obtained only by aid of this same concrete knowledge which it pretends to draw from abstractions which suppose it; consequently it takes for granted what is in question.

The theory of Locke falls under these three objections, and the judgment, I exist, escapes in every way from the theory of Locke.

This judgment has two characters:

1st, It is not abstract: it implies existence;

2d, It is a primitive judgment: all others suppose it, and it supposes none.

We have before seen that it was on abstract judgments, and on judgments slowly formed in the human mind, that the theory of Locke was verified. Here judgment implies existence, and it is primitive; the theory is no longer verified. It is, therefore, necessary to choose between the theory and the certitude of personal existence.

So much for personal existence. It is the same with all modes of this existence, with our faculties, with our operations, whether sensation, will, or thought.

Take whatever phenomenon you please: I feel, I will, I think. Take, for example, I think. This is said to be a fact of consciousness; but consciousness is still to know (*conscire sibi*), it is to know since it is to know one's self; it is to believe, it is to affirm, it is to judge. When you say, I think, it is a judgment which you pass and express; and when you have a consciousness of thinking without saying it, it is still a judgment which you pass without expressing it. Now this judgment, expressed or not, implies existence; it implies that you, a real being, actually accomplish the real operation of thought. Still more, it is a primitive judgment, at least contemporaneous with the judgment that you exist.

Upon this judgment then let us verify the theory of Locke, as we have verified it on this other primitive and concrete judgment: I exist.

Three conditions are necessary in the theory of Locke in order to explain and justify this judgment, I think: two ideas, their comparison, a perception of relation between them. What are here the two ideas? Evidently the idea of the thought on the one hand, and on the other the idea of the *I* or *me*. But if it is the idea of thinking distinct from the *me*, if it is a thought considered aside from the subject *me*, of this subject *me*, which is, do not forget, the first basis of every idea of existence, it is thought abstracted from existence, that is, abstract thought, that is, the simple power of thinking and nothing else. On the other hand, the *me*, which is the other necessary term of the comparison, cannot be a *me* which thinks, for you have just now separated it from thought; it is, therefore, a *me* which you must consider as abstracted from thought. In fact, if you suppose it thinking, you would have what you are seeking, and it would be needless for you to enter upon a laborious comparison; you could stop at one of the terms which would give you the other, the *me* as thinking, or I think: but in order to avoid the paralogism, it is necessary to suppose it as not thinking, and as your first legitimate term is thought separated from the *me*, your second legitimate term must also be a *me* separated from thought, a *me* not thinking. And you wish to know whether this *me* taken independently of the thought, and this thought taken independently of the *me*, have between them a relation of agreement or of disagreement. It is, then, two abstractions which you are going to compare; but, once more, two abstract terms can produce only an abstract relation, and an abstract relation can produce only an abstract judgment, the abstract judgment, that the thought and the *me* are two ideas which do not imply contradiction; so that the result of the theory of Locke, applied to the judgment, I think, as well as to the other judgment, I exist, is still merely an abstract result, an abstract verity, which in nowise represents what is passing in your mind when you judge that you think, and when you say: I think.

Besides, the theory makes the human mind begin by abstraction; and it is not thus that it begins.

Finally it begins by abstraction, and seeks therefrom to draw the concrete, whilst you would never have had the abstract if you had not previously had the concrete. You first passed, naturally, this determinate, concrete, synthetic judgment, I think; and then as you have the faculty of abstraction, you made a division in the primitive synthesis; you considered separately, first the thought, that is, the thought without the subject, without *me*, that is, the possible thought, and secondly, *you, I*, without the real attribute of thought, without thought, that is, the simple possibility of existence; and now you are pleased to unite artifically and too late, by a pretended relation of agreement, two terms which, primitively, had not been given to you separated and disjoined, but united and confounded in the synthesis of reality and of life.

Thus the three preceding objections return here with the same force, and the theory of Locke cannot legitimately give you either the knowledge of your own existence, or even the knowledge of any of your faculties, of any of your operations; for what I have said of *I think* I could equally say of *I will*, of *I feel*, and I could say the same of all the attributes and of all the modes of personal existence.

The theory of Locke cannot, moreover, give external existence. Take the judgment: this body exists. The theory demands that you should have this knowledge only on condition of having perceived it in a relation of agreement between two ideas compared together. What are these two ideas? Assuredly it is not the idea of a body really existing, for you would have what you seek; neither is it the idea of real existence: it is then the idea of a possible body and the idea of a possible existence, or two abstractions. From them you can only draw this other abstraction: There is no logical incompatibility between the idea of existence and the idea of body. Then you begin by abstraction, contrary to the natural order. Finally, you begin by an abstraction which you would never have had, if you had not previously obtained the concrete knowledge, that precisely which you wish to draw from the comparison of your abstractions.

What I say of the existence of bodies, I say of the attributes by which body is known to us; I say the same of solid, of form, of color, etc. Take for example the knowledge of color, a quality which is reckoned among the secondary qualities, and which is perhaps more inherent in figure than is believed. Whatever it may be, whether color be a simple secondary quality or a primary quality of bodies, as well as figure, let us see on what condition in the theory of Locke we acquire the knowledge of it. In order to pass the judgment: This body is colored, white or black, etc., is it true that we must have had two ideas, must have compared them and perceived their relation? The two ideas should be that of body and that of color. But the idea of body cannot here be the idea of a colored body; for this single term would imply the other, would render the comparison superfluous, and would suppose what is in question: it must then be the idea of a body not colored. Nor can the idea of color be the idea of a color really existing; for a color is real, exists, only in a body, and the condition itself of the operation which we wish to make is the separation of the color from the body: the question here is not then of a real color having such or such a determinate shade, but of color, abstracted from all that determines it and realizes it; the question is simply concerning the abstract and general idea of color. Whence it results that the two ideas which you have are two general and abstract ideas; and abstractions can only give abstractions. And again you begin by abstractions: you go therefore contrary to the ways of nature. Finally, and this is the most overwhelming objection, it is evident that you have obtained the general idea of color only from the idea of such or such a particular and positive color, and that you have obtained this only with the idea of a figured and colored body. It is not by aid of the general idea of color, and of the general idea of body, that you have learned that bodies are colored; but it is, on the contrary, because you know previously, that such a body was colored, that, separating afterwards what was united in the previous synthesis, you were able to consider, on the one hand, the idea of body, and on the other the idea of color, abstractly one from the other; and it was then alone that you were able to institute a comparison, in order to account for what you already knew.

In general, judgments are of two sorts: either they are judgments in which we acquire that of which we were before ignorant, or they are reflex judgments, in which we account for what we already knew. The theory of Locke can explain the second up to a certain point; but the first escape him entirely.

For example, if we now wish to render an account to ourselves of the existence of God, which we already know, we take, or we may take, on the one hand, the idea of God, and on the other the idea of existence, and ascertain whether these two ideas agree or disagree. But it is one thing to give an account of a knowledge already acquired, and it is another thing to acquire that knowledge; now, certainly we did not first acquire the knowledge of the existence of God by placing on one hand the idea of God, and on the other the idea of existence, and by seeking their relation; for, in order not to weary you with superfluous repetitions, in order not to go over again the circle of the three ordinary objections, and to lay hold upon the third, this would be to suppose what is a matter of question. It is very evident that when we consider on one hand the idea of God, and on the other the idea of existence, and when we are seeking the knowledge of the existence of God in the comparison of these two ideas, we simply labor to obtain what we already have, and what we never should have if we were reduced to the theory of Locke. It is clearly understood that it is with the attributes of God as with his existence: everywhere and always we meet the same objections, everywhere and always the same paralogism.

The theory of Locke, then, cannot give God, or body, or the *me*, or their attributes: at this price, I grant, if you please, that it may give every thing else.

It gives mathematics, you will say. Yes, I have said so myself, and I repeat it; it gives mathematics, geometry and arithmetic, in so far as sciences of the relations of magnitudes and of numbers; it gives them, but on one condition, it is that you consider these numbers and these magnitudes as abstract magnitudes and numbers, not implying existence. Now, it is very true that geometrical science is an abstract science; but it has its bases in concrete ideas and real existences. One of these ideas is that of space, which, you know,* is given to us in the judgment: Every body is in space; this is the proposition, this is the judgment which gives space, a judgment accompanied by the perfect certainty of the reality of its object. We have but a single idea as a starting point, the idea of body; then the mind, by its power, as soon as the idea of body is given to it, conceives the idea of space, and its necessary connection with body. A body being known, we cannot avoid judging that it is in a space which contains it. From this judgment abstract the idea of space, and you have the abstract idea of space. But this idea was not anterior to the conception of the necessary relation of space to body, any more than the relation was anterior to it; neither is it posterior to the relation, nor is the relation posterior to it; they mutually imply each other, and are given to us in the same judgment as soon as body is known. It is overturning the order of the development of mind, to lay down first the idea of space, and the idea of body, and then to seek from their comparison the relation which binds them; for the idea alone of space supposes already this judgment, that every body is necessarily in space. The judgment cannot then come from the idea, it is the idea on the contrary which comes from the judgment. It is not difficult to draw the judgment from the idea which supposes it; but it remains to explain whence the idea comes, anterior to the judgment. It is not difficult to find a relation between body and space when we know body and space; but we must ask Locke how he has obtained this idea of space, as just now we asked him how he had obtained the idea of body, the idea of God, the idea of color, the idea of existence, etc. To suppose that the necessary idea of space is given to us by the comparison of two ideas, of which one is already the idea of space, is a vicious circle and a ridiculous paralogism. It is the rock upon which the theory of Locke perpetually strikes.

---

* See Lecture 17.

The other idea upon which geometry rests, is the idea of magnitude, which involves the idea of point, the idea of line, etc Magnitude, point, line, are abstract conceptions which presuppose the idea of some real body, of a solid existing in nature. Now, the idea of solid is given to us in a judgment like every idea; and we must have judged that such a body exists, in order to conceive apart the idea of solid. How then do we judge that such a solid exists? According to the theory of Locke, two ideas would be necessary, a comparison between these two ideas, and a perception of agreement between these two ideas. And what could be the two ideas which would serve as terms to this judgment: This solid exists? I confess that I do not clearly see. Compelled, for the sake of the hypothesis, to find them, I can think of no others than the idea of solid and that of existence, which we should compare, in order to know whether they agree or disagree. The theory demands all this scaffolding. But is there any need of destroying it piece by piece, in order to overthrow it? Is it not sufficient to remember that the solid in question being deprived of existence, since it is separated from the idea of existence, is simply the abstraction of the solid, and that this abstraction could have never existed without the anterior conception of a solid really existing? The abstraction, line, point, etc., presupposes such or such a real solid, a primitive and concrete knowledge, which cannot be obtained from ulterior abstractions without falling into a vicious circle, and without taking away from all geometrical conceptions their natural basis.

We then see that the two fundamental ideas of geometry, the idea of space and the idea of solid, escape Locke's theory of knowledge and of judgment.

So it is with the fundamental idea of arithmetic. This idea is evidently that of unity, and it is not a collective unity, for example, 4 representing 2 and 2, 5 representing 2 and 3, it is a unity which is found in all collective unities, measures them, and values them. Arithmetic conceives this unity in an abstract manner; but abstraction not being the point of departure for the human mind, the abstract unity must have been first given in some concrete unity really existing. What then is this concrete unity, really existing, the source of the abstract idea of unity? It is not body; this is divisible, ad infinitum: it is the *me,* the *me* identical, and consequently one, under the variety of its acts, of its thoughts, of its sensations. And how, in the theory of Locke, can the knowledge of the unity of the *me* be acquired? It would be necessary for us to have, on one hand, the idea of the *me* as not being one, that is, without reality, the identity and unity of the *me* being implied from the first act of memory, and on the other hand the idea of a unity distinct from the *me,* without subject, and consequently without reality; and it would be necessary that, bringing these two ideas together, we should perceive their relation of agreement. Now, here all my objections return; and, in closing, I ask your permission to recapitulate them.

1st, It is an abstract unity and an abstract *me* from which you set out; but the abstract unity and the abstract *me,* brought together and compared, will only give you an abstract relation and not a real relation, an abstract unity and not a real unity of the *me;* you will not therefore have that concrete idea of unity, the necessary basis of the abstract idea of unity, which is the basis of arithmetic, the general measure of all numbers;

2d, You start from abstraction without having passed through the concrete, and this is contrary to the natural order of the understanding;

3d, You make a paralogism, since you wish to obtain the real unity of the *me,* by the comparison of two abstractions which suppose precisely what you are seeking, to wit, the real unity of the *me.*

The theory of Locke cannot, therefore, furnish the basis of arithmetic and of geometry, that is, of the two most abstract sciences. It has its place in the field of arithmetic and of geometry in so far as abstract sciences; but these abstract sciences and all mathematics rest in the last analysis on primitive cognitions, which imply existence; and these primitive cognitions, which imply existence, escape on all sides the theory of Locke. Now, we have seen that the knowledge of personal existence, that of bodies, and that of God equally escape it, and for the same reason. It follows that in the last result the theory of Locke is worth nothing except in mere abstraction, and that it dissolves as soon as it is confronted with any reality to be known, whatever that reality may be. Therefore this general and unlimited pretension of Locke, that every cognition, every judgment, is only the perception of a relation of agreement or of disagreement between two ideas, this pretension is convicted in every way of error and even of absurdity.

I fear very much lest this discussion of the theory of Locke in regard to judgment and knowledge may have appeared to you somewhat subtile; but when we wish to follow error in all its windings, and untie methodically by analysis and dialectics the knot of sophistical theories, instead of at once cutting it by simple good sense, we are condemned to engage in apparent subtilties, according to the example of those whom we wish to combat; it is at this price alone that we can reach them and confound them. I fear also lest this discussion may have appeared to you very long, and still it is not finished, for it has not yet penetrated to the real root of Locke's theory. In fact, this theory, that every judgment, every knowledge is only the perception of a relation between two ideas supposes and contains another theory, which is the principle of the first. The examination of the one is indispensable in order to complete that of the other, and to determine the definitive judgment which we ought to pass upon it.

LECTURE XXIV.

ESSAY, FOURTH BOOK. CONTINUATION OF THE THEORY OF JUDGMENT.

Continuation of the last lecture. That the theory of judgment as the perception of a relation of agreement or disagreement between ideas supposes that every judgment is founded upon a comparison. Refutation of the theory of comparative judgment.—Of axioms.—Of identical propositions.—Of reason and faith.—Of the syllogism.—Of enthusiasm.—Of the causes of error.—Division of sciences. End of the examination of the Fourth Book of the *Essay on the Human Understanding.*

I BELIEVE I have sufficiently refuted, by its results, the theory of Locke which makes knowledge and judgment consist in a perception of the relation of agreement or disagreement of ideas; I believe I have demonstrated that this theory cannot give reality, existences; that it is condemned to start from abstraction and to result in abstraction. I now come to examine this theory under another aspect, no longer in its results, but in its principles, in its essential principle, in its very condition.

It is evident that the judgment can be the perception of a relation of agreement or disagreement between ideas only on condition that there may have been a comparison between these ideas: every judgment of relation is necessarily comparative. This is, if we pay attention to it, the first and the last principle of the theory of Locke; a principle which the infallible analysis of time has successively disengaged and put at the head of the sensualistic logic; it is at least in germ in the fourth book of the *Essay on the Human Understanding.* It is this which we must take up and examine.

Once more, the theory of comparative judgment,* as that of

* On the theory of comparative judgment, see 1st Series, Vol. 4, Lecture 20, p. 370, etc.

which it is the foundation, is an unlimited, absolute theory whose pretension is to account for all our knowledge, for all our judgments; so that if the theory is exact, that is, if it is complete, there should not be a single judgment which is not a comparative judgment. Thus I might, I should even, in this lecture as in the preceding, go from judgments to judgments, asking whether in fact they are or are not the fruit of comparison. But this superfluity of method would carry me too far, and the long space which remains to run over admonishes me to hasten. I will therefore say all at once, that if there are many judgments which are incontestably comparative judgments, there are also many which are not, and that here again every judgment which implies reality and existence excludes all comparison.

Let us begin by clearly recognizing the conditions of a comparative judgment, then let us verify these conditions in regard to judgments which imply existence. We shall without doubt return somewhat to our former reasonings; but it is necessary in order to pursue and force in its last hold the theory of Locke.

In order that there may be a comparison, there must be two terms to compare. Whether these terms are abstractions or realities, is a point which it is no longer necessary to examine; there always must be two terms, or the comparison is impossible. These two terms must be known and present to the mind before the mind can compare and judge them. This is very simple: well! this is sufficient to overturn the theory of comparative judgment, in regard to reality and existence. Here, in fact, I maintain that the judgment does not and cannot depend upon two terms.

Let us again take, for example, personal existence, and let us see what are the two terms which it is necessary to compare in order to draw from them this judgment: I exist. Let us, for this time, pass over the abstraction of *me* and the abstraction of existence, which, we have seen, can give only an abstract judgment; let us take a more favorable hypothesis; let us approach reality. It is indubitable that if we never thought, if we never acted, if we never felt, we never should know that we exist. Sensation, action, thought, some phenomenon must appear upon the theatre of consciousness, in order that the understanding may relate this phenomenon to the subject that experiences it, to that subject which we are. If then knowledge is here the fruit of a comparative judgment, the two terms should be, on the one side, action, sensation, thought, and in general every phenomenon of consciousness; on the other side, the subject *me:* I see no other possible terms of comparison.

But what is the nature of these two terms? and at first what is that of the phenomenon of consciousness? The phenomenon of consciousness is given by an immediate apperception which attains it and directly knows it. Behold already a knowledge; I say a knowledge, for, either we are disputing about words, or an apperception of consciousness pertains to knowledge, or it is nothing. But if there is knowledge there has been judgment, for apparently there has been a belief that there has been knowledge, there has been affirmation of the truth of this knowledge; and, whether this affirmation may have been tacit or express, whether it may have taken place solely in the depths of intelligence or may have been pronounced from the lips and expressed in words, it has in fine taken place; and to affirm is to judge. There has then been judgment. Now, there is here only a single term, sensation, action, or thought, in a word, a phenomenon of consciousness. Therefore there can have been no comparison; therefore again, according to Locke, there can have been no judgment, if every judgment is comparative. All our cognitions are resolved, in the last analysis, into affirmations of truth or falsehood, into judgments; and it is a contradiction to suppose that the judgment which gives the first knowledge, the knowledge of consciousness, is a comparative judgment, because this knowledge has only a single term, and two terms are necessary for a comparison; and yet this single term is a knowledge, and consequently it supposes a judgment, but a judgment which escapes the conditions that the theory of Locke imposes on every judgment.

Thus, the two necessary terms of the comparison from which should result the judgment: I exist, the first by itself alone already comprehends a knowledge, a judgment which is not and cannot be comparative: it is the same with the second term as with the first. If every phenomenon of consciousness, so far as known, already implies a judgment, it is evident that the *me* which should also be known in order to be the second term of the comparison, for the very reason that it is known implies also a judgment, and a judgment that cannot have been comparative. In fact, if it is the relation between a sensation, a volition, a thought, and the *me* which constitutes the judgment: I exist, it follows that neither the phenomenon of consciousness, nor the being *me*, which are the two terms of this comparison, neither ought nor can, either of them, cause the comparison that has not yet taken place: nevertheless both of these terms constitute cognitions; the second especially is an important and fundamental cognition which evidently implies a judgment. The theory of comparative judgment is therefore destroyed in regard to the second term as well as in regard to the first; and the two terms,—necessary, according to Locke, in order that a judgment may take place,—contain each a judgment, and a judgment without comparison.

But there is a second difficulty, much more important than the first. The special character of every cognition of consciousness is that of being an immediate and direct cognition. There is immediate and direct apperception of a sensation, of a volition, of a thought, and behold the reason why you can observe them and describe them in all their modes, in all their shades, in all their relative or particular, fugitive or permanent characters. Here the judgment has no other principle than the faculty itself of judging, and the consciousness itself. There is no general or particular principle upon which consciousness must rest in order to perceive its own objects. Without doubt any phenomenon whatever takes place in vain; without an act of attention we do not perceive it; an act of attention is the condition of every cognition of consciousness; but, this condition being given, the phenomenon is directly perceived and known. But it is not with being as with phenomenon; it is not with the *me* as with sensation, volition, or thought. Any phenomenon having been directly perceived, suppose that the understanding be not pervaded with the principle that every phenomenon implies being, that every quality implies a subject, and the understanding would never judge that, under sensation, volition, or thought, there is being, the subject *me*. And observe that I do not mean to say that the understanding should know this principle under its general and abstract form, I have elsewhere shown that such was not the primitive form of principles;* I only say that the understanding should be directed, consciously or unconsciously, by this principle, in order to judge, in order to suppose even,—which is still to judge,—that there is any being under the phenomenon which consciousness perceives. This principle is, properly speaking, the principle of being; it is that which reveals the *me:* I say reveals, for the *me* does not fall under the immediate apperception of consciousness; the understanding conceives it and believes it, although the consciousness does not attain it and see it. Sensation, volition, thought, are believed because they are seen, as it were, in the internal intuition of consciousness: the subject of sensation, of volition, of thought, is believed without being seen either by the external senses, or by consciousness itself; it is believed because it is conceived. Phenomenon alone is visible to the consciousness, being is invisible; but the one is the sign of the other, and the visible phenomenon reveals the invisible being, on the faith of the principle in question, without which the understanding would never come from consciousness, from the visible, from phenomenon, and would never attain the invisible, substance, the *me*. There is still this eminent difference between the character of the

---

* See Lecture 19 of this volume.

knowledge of the *me*, and that of the knowledge of the phenomena of consciousness: the one is a judgment of fact which gives a truth, but a contingent truth, the truth that there is, at such or such a moment, under the eye of consciousness, such or such a phenomenon; whilst the other is a judgment which is necessary, its condition once being supplied; for as soon as a perception of consciousness is given, we cannot help judging that the *me* exists. Thus, in regard to the second term, the subject *me*, there is not only knowledge, and consequently judgment, as in regard to the first term, but there is knowledge and judgment marked with characters quite peculiar. It is, therefore, absurd to draw the judgment of personal existence from the comparison of two terms, the second of which, in order to be known, supposes a judgment of so remarkable a character. It is very evident that this judgment is not a comparative judgment; for from what comparison could the *me* proceed? Invisible, it cannot be brought under the eye of consciousness with the visible phenomenon, in order that they may be compared together. No more is it from a comparison of two terms that is drawn the certainty of the existence of the second; for this second term is given us all at once with a certainty which neither increases nor decreases, and which has no degrees. The knowledge of the *me* and personal existence is so far from coming from a comparison between a phenomenon and the *me* taken as correlative terms, that it is sufficient to have a single term, a phenomenon of consciousness, in order that at the instant, and without the second term *me* being already known, the understanding, by its innate virtue and that of the principle which directs it in this circumstance, conceives, and as it were divines, but infallibly divines, this second term, so far as it is the necessary subject of the first. It is after thus having known the second term that the understanding can, if it pleases, place it by the side of the first, and compare the subject *me* with the phenomena of sensation, volition, thought; but this comparison teaches it only what it already knows, and it can do it only because it already has two terms, which contain all the knowledge which is sought in their comparison, and have been acquired previously to all comparison by two different terms, the only resemblance of which is that they are not comparative.

The judgment of personal existence, therefore, does not rest upon the comparison of two terms, but upon a single term, the phenomenon of consciousness: the latter is immediately given, and with it the understanding conceives the former, that is, the *me* and personal existence itself—thus far unknown, and, consequently, incapable of serving as the second term of a comparison. Now, what is true of personal existence is true of all other existences, and of the judgments which reveal them to us: primitively, these judgments rest only upon a single datum.

How do we know the exterior world, bodies, and their qualities, according to the theory of Locke? To begin with the qualities of bodies, if we know them, we must know them only by a judgment founded upon a comparison, that is, upon two terms previously known. Such is the theory; but it is falsified by facts.

I experience a sensation, painful or agreeable, which is perceived by consciousness: this is all that is directly given me, and nothing more; for the thing in question, qualities of bodies, must not be taken for granted; the question is to arrive at a knowledge of them, it must not be supposed that they are already known. And you know how we arrive at a knowledge of them, how we pass from sensation, from the apperception of a phenomenon of consciousness, to the knowledge of the qualities of exterior objects. It is by virtue of the principle of causality,* which, as soon as any phenomenon begins to appear, irresistibly leads us to search out the cause of it; in our inability to refer to ourselves the cause of an involuntary phenomenon of sensation which is actually under the eye of consciousness, we refer it to a cause other than ourselves, foreign to us, that is, exterior; we make as many causes as there are distinct classes of sensations, and these different causes are the powers, properties, qualities of

* See Lecture 19 of this volume, and 1st Series, Vol. 4, Lecture 21, p. 425.

bodies. It is not then a comparison which causes us to arrive at the knowledge of the qualities of bodies, for, at first, involuntary sensation is alone given us, and it is after this sensation that the mind passes the judgment that it is impossible that sensation should be sufficient for itself, that it is, therefore, referred to a cause, to an exterior cause, which is such or such a quality of bodies.

The theory of comparison cannot give the qualities of bodies; still less does it give the *substratum*, the subject of these qualities. You do not believe that there is before you merely extension, resistance, solidity, hardness, softness, savor, color, etc.; you believe that there is something which is colored, extended, resisting, solid, hard, soft, etc. Now we must not commence by supposing this something at the same time with its qualities, so as to have these two terms, solidity, resistance, hardness, etc.; and something really solid, resisting, hard, etc.; two terms which you might compare, in order to decide whether they agree or disagree. No, such is not the case: at first you have only the qualities which are given you by the application of the principle of causality to your sensations; then, upon this single datum, you judge that these qualities cannot but be referred to a subject of the same nature, and this subject is body. Therefore it is not to the comparison of two terms, one of which, the subject of sensible qualities, was at first profoundly unknown to you, that you owe the knowledge of body.

It is the same with space. Here, again, you have only a single term, a single datum, to wit, bodies; and, without having another term, upon this alone you judge and cannot but judge that bodies are in space: the knowledge of space is the fruit of this judgment, which has nothing to do with any comparison; for you knew not space previous to your judgment; but a body being given you, you judge that space exists, and it is then only that comes the idea of space, that is, the second term.*

* Lecture 17.

The same thing is true in regard to time. In order to judge that the succession of events is in time, you have not, on one hand, the idea of succession, on the other, the idea of time; you have only a single term, the succession of events, whether external or internal events, of our sensations, our thoughts, or our acts; and this single term being given, without comparing it with time which is still profoundly unknown to you, you judge that the succession of events is necessarily in time: hence the idea, the knowledge of time. Thus this knowledge, far from being the fruit of a comparison, becomes the possible basis of an ulterior comparison only on condition that it shall at first have been given you in a judgment, which does not depend upon two terms, but upon one, upon the succession of events.*

This is still more evident in regard to the infinite. If we know the infinite, we must know it, according to the theory of Locke, by a judgment, and by a comparative judgment; now, the two terms of this judgment cannot be two finite terms, which could never give the infinite; it must be the finite and the infinite, between which the understanding discovers a relation of agreement or disagreement. But I think I have demonstrated, and I here only need to refer to it, that it is sufficient that the idea of the finite be given us, in order that at the instant† we may judge that the infinite exists, or, not to pass beyond the limits of the subject we are discussing, the infinite is a character of time and of space, which we necessarily conceive, on occasion of the contingent and finite character of bodies and of all succession of events. The understanding is so constituted, that on occasion of the finite it cannot but conceive the infinite. The finite is previously known; but it is known entirely alone: the finite is known directly by the senses or the consciousness; the infinite is invisible, and beyond the grasp; it is only conceivable and comprehensible; it escapes the senses and consciousness, and falls only under the understanding; it is neither one of two terms, nor the fruit of a comparison;

---

* Lecture 18.

† Lecture 18.

it is given us in a judgment which rests upon a single term, the idea of the finite. So much for the judgments which pertain to existence in general.

There are many other judgments which, without being related to existence, present the same character. I will limit myself to citing the judgment of good and evil, of the beautiful and the ugly. In either case, the judgment rests upon a single datum, upon a single term; and it is the judgment itself which attains and reveals the other term, instead of resulting from the comparison of the two.

According to the theory of Locke, in order to judge whether an action is just or unjust, good or bad, it would be necessary first to have the idea of this action, then the idea of the just and the unjust, and to compare the one with the other. But in order to compare an action with the idea of the just and the unjust, it is necessary to have this idea, this knowledge, and this knowledge supposes a judgment; the question is to know whence this judgment comes and how it is formed. Now we have seen* that in presence of such or such an act, destitute of any moral character to the eyes of the senses, the understanding takes the lead, and qualifies this act, indifferent for the sensibility, as just or unjust, as good or bad. It is from this primitive judgment, which doubtless has its law, that subsequently analysis draws the idea of the just and the unjust, which then serves as a rule for our ulterior judgments.

The forms of objects are, for the sense, whether external or internal, neither beautiful nor ugly. Take away intelligence, and there is no longer any beauty for us in exterior forms and in things. What, in fact, do the senses teach you in regard to form? Nothing, except that they are round or square, colored, etc. What does consciousness teach you concerning them? Nothing, except that they give you agreeable or disagreeable sensations; but between the agreeable or the disagreeable, the

* Lecture 20.

square and the round, the green or the yellow color, etc., and the beautiful or the ugly, there is an immense abyss. Whilst the senses and the consciousness perceive such or such a form, such or such a sensation more or less agreeable, the understanding conceives the beautiful, as well as the good and true, by a primitive and spontaneous judgment, the whole force of which resides in that of the understanding and its laws, and of which the only datum is an exterior perception.*

I believe, then, that I have demonstrated, and too much at length, perhaps, that the theory of Locke, which makes knowledge depend upon comparison, that is, upon two terms previously known, does not render an account of the true process of the understanding in the acquisition of a multitude of cognitions; and, in general, I here reproduce the criticism which I have many times made upon Locke, that he always confounds either the antecedents of a knowledge with this knowledge itself, as when he confounds body with space, succession with time, the finite with the infinite, effect with cause, qualities and their collection with substance; or, what is not less important, the consequences of a knowledge with this knowledge itself. Here, foi example, the comparative judgments which pertain to existence, and even in other cases, demand two terms, which suppose a previous judgment founded upon a single term, and consequently not comparative. Comparative judgments suppose judgments not comparative. Comparative judgments are abstract, and suppose real judgments; they teach us scarcely any thing but what the first have already taught us; they explicitly mark what the others teach implicitly, but decisively; they are arbitrary, at least in form: the others are universal and necessary; they need the aid of language; the others, strictly speaking, pass beyond language, beyond signs, and suppose only the understanding and its laws; these pertain to reflection and artificial logic; those constitute the natural and spontaneous logic of the human race; to

* First Series, Vol. 2, Lecture 11 and Lecture 12; Vol. 4, Lecture 13 and Lecture 23.

confound these two classes of judgments, is to vitiate at once the whole of psychology and the whole of logic. Nevertheless, such a confusion fills a great part of the fourth book of the *Essay on the Human Understanding.*

I will rapidly run over the fundamental points of which this fourth book is composed, and you will see that in regard to the most part we shall always find the same error, the results of judgments confounded with the judgments themselves: this criticism particularly applies to Chapter VII., on *axioms.*

If I made myself understood in my last lecture, it must be evident to you that axioms, principles, general truths, are the remains of primitive judgments. There are no axioms in the first development of the understanding; there is an understanding which, certain exterior or interior conditions being fulfilled, and by the aid of its own laws, passes certain judgments, sometimes contingent and local, sometimes universal and necessary: these last judgments, when we operate upon them by analysis and language, are resolved, like the others, into propositions; these universal and necessary propositions, like the judgments which they express, are what we call axioms. But it is clear that the form of primitive judgments is one thing, and that the form of these same judgments reduced to propositions and axioms is another thing. At first concrete, particular, and determined, at the same time that they are universal and necessary, language and analysis elevate them to that abstract form which is the actual form of axioms. Thus, primitively, such a phenomenon being under the eye of your consciousness, you instinctively refer it to a subject which is yourself; on the contrary, at present, instead of abandoning your thought to its laws, you recall them to it, you submit it to the axiom. Every phenomenon supposes a subject to which it is referred; and to these every succession supposes time, every body supposes space, every effect supposes a cause, every finite supposes the infinite, etc. Observe that these axioms have no force except what they borrow from the primitive judgments whence they are drawn. Primitive judgments give us all our real and fundamental knowledge, the knowledge of ourselves, of the world, of time, of space, and even (I have demonstrated it in the last lecture) the knowledge of magnitude and that of unity. But in regard to axioms, it is not so; you acquire no real knowledge by the application of the axiom: every effect supposes a cause. It is the philosopher, and not the man, that uses this axiom. The savage, the peasant, the common man, do not understand it; but all, as well as the philosopher, are provided with an understanding which causes them to pass certain judgments, concrete, positive and determinate, as well as necessary, the result of which is the knowledge of such or such a cause. I repeat, judgments and their laws produce all knowledge; axioms are only the analytical expressions of these judgments and these laws, whose last elements they express under the most abstract form. Locke, instead of stopping at these limits, pretends that axioms are of no use (*ibid.*, § 11), and that they are not principles of science; he rather contemptuously asks that a science shall be shown him founded on axioms: "It has been my ill luck," says he, "never to meet with any such science; much less any one built upon these two maxims, *what is, is;* and, *it is impossible for the same thing to be, and not to be.* And I would be glad to be shown where any such science, erected upon these or any other general axioms, is to be found; I should be obliged to any one who would lay before me the frame and system of any science so built on these or any such like maxims, that could not be shown to stand as firm without any consideration of them." Yes, without doubt axioms, under their actual form of axioms, have engendered no science; but it is not less true that, in their source and under their primitive form, that is, in the laws of the natural judgments whence they are drawn, they have served as the basis for all the sciences. Besides, if in their actual form they have produced and could produce no science, and if they give no particular truth, it must be recognized that with them no science, either general or particular, subsists. Try to deny axioms; suppose, for example, that there may be a quality without a subject, a body without space, a succession without time, an effect without cause, etc.; attempt to make abstractions of the axioms with which Locke prefers to amuse himself, to wit, what is, is; it is impossible for the same thing to be, and not to be; that is, make an abstraction of the idea of being and of identity, and there is made an end of all sciences, they can neither advance nor be sustained.

Locke also pretends (*ibid.*, § 9) that axioms are not the truths which we first know. Yes, without doubt, once more, under their actual form, axioms are not primitive knowledge; but, under their real form, as laws attached to the exercise of the understanding and implied in our judgments, they are so truly primitive that without them no knowledge could be acquired. They are not primitive in the sense that they are the first truths which we know, but in the sense that without them we could know nothing. Here again recurs the perpetual confusion of the historical order and the logical order of human knowledge. In the chronological order, we do not commence by knowing axioms, the laws of our understanding; but, logically, without axioms, all truth is impossible; without the action, unperceived, but real, of the laws of thought, no thought, no judgment, is either legitimate or possible.

Finally, Locke combats axioms by a celebrated argument, very often renewed since, to wit, that axioms are only frivolous propositions, because they are identical propositions (*ibid.*, § 11). It is Locke, I believe, who introduced, or at least gave currency to the expression, identical proposition, in philosophic language. It signifies a judgment, a proposition, in which an idea is affirmed by itself, or in which we affirm of a thing what we already know of it. Elsewhere (Chap. VIII., *of trifling propositions;* § 3, *of identical propositions*), Locke shows that identical propositions are only propositions purely verbal. "Let any one repeat as often as he pleases, that the will is the will . . . a law is a law . . . obligation is obligation . . . right is right . . . wrong is wrong . . ., what is this more than trifling with words?" "It is," says he, but like a monkey shifting his oyster from one hand to the other; and had he but words, might, no doubt, have said, Oyster in right hand is subject, and oyster in left hand is predicate: and so might have made a self-evident proposition of oyster, *i. e.*, oyster is oyster." Hence the condemnation of the axiom: What is, is, etc. But it is not exact, it is not equitable to concentrate all axioms, all principles, all primitive and necessary truth into the axiom: What is, is; it is impossible for the same thing to be, and not to be; and to the vain and ridiculous examples of Locke, I oppose as examples, the following axioms, which you already know: Quality supposes a subject, succession supposes time, body supposes space, the finite supposes the infinite, variety supposes unity, phenomenon supposes substance and being; in a word, all the necessary truths which so many lectures must have fixed in your minds. The question is to know whether these are identical axioms. Locke therefore maintains that time is reducible to succession, or succession to time; space to body, or body to space; the infinite to the finite, or the finite to the infinite; cause to effect, or effect to cause; plurality to unity, or unity to plurality; phenomenon to being, or being to phenomenon, etc.; and according to his system, Locke ought to have maintained this; but it must now be evident enough to you that this pretension, and the system upon which it is founded, do not bear the scrutiny of reason.

This proscription of axioms as identical, Locke extends to other propositions which are not axioms; in general, he perceives many more identical propositions than there are. For example, gold is heavy, gold is fusible, are for Locke (*ibid.*, §§ 5 and 13) identical propositions; however, nothing is less true: we do not in these propositions affirm the same of the same. A proposition is called identical whenever the attribute is contained in the subject, so that the subject cannot be conceived as not containing the attribute. Thus, when you say body is solid, I say that you make an identical proposition, because it is impossible to have the idea of body without that of solid. The idea of body is perhaps more extended than that of solid, but it is primarily and essentially the same. The idea of solid being then for you the essential quality of body, to say that body is solid, is to say nothing else than that body is body. But when you say that gold is fusible, you affirm of gold a quality which may be contained in it, and which may not be contained in it. It implies a contradiction to assert that body is not solid; but it does not imply a contradiction to assert that gold is not fusible. Gold may have been a long time known solely as solid, as hard, as yellow, etc.; and if such or such an experiment had not been made, if it had not been put in the fire, it would not be known as fusible. When therefore you affirm of gold that it is fusible, you recognize a quality of it which you may not have previously known in regard to it; you do not then affirm the same of the same, at least the first time that you express this proposition. Without doubt, at the present time, in the laboratory of modern chemistry, when the fusibility of gold is a quality perfectly and universally known, to say that gold is fusible, is to repeat what is already known, is to affirm of the word gold what is already comprehended in its received signification; but the first one who said that gold is fusible, far from making a tautology, expressed, on the contrary, the result of a discovery, and a discovery not without difficulty and importance. I ask whether, in his times, Locke would have made merry with this proposition: Air has weight, as an identical and frivolous proposition? No, certainly; and why? Because at that time weight was a quality of air which had scarcely been demonstrated by the experiments of Toricelli and Pascal. Those which have proved the fusibility of gold are older by some thousands of years; but if: Air has weight, is not an identical proposition, on the same ground as: Gold is fusible, it is not an identical proposition, since the first who announced it did not affirm in the second term what he had already affirmed in the first.

Moreover, wonder at the destiny of identical truths: Locke sees many more than there are, and ridicules them; the school of

Locke sees many more still, but far from accusing identity, it applauds it, and goes so far as to say that every proposition is true only on condition of being identical. Thus, by a strange progress, what Locke had branded with ridicule, as a sign of frivolity, became in the hands of his successors a title of legitimacy and truth. The identity which Locke ridiculed was only an illusory identity, and behold now this pretended identity, so much mocked at, and indeed very wrongly, since it was not real, behold it celebrated and vaunted, with less reason still, as the triumph of truth and the last conquest of science and analysis. Now, if all true propositions are identical, since every identical proposition, frivolous or not, as we follow Locke or his disciples, is, according to both, only a verbal proposition, it follows that the knowledge of all possible truths is only a verbal knowledge; and thus, when we think we are learning sciences or systems of truth, we are only translating one word into another, we are only learning words, we are only learning language: hence the famous principle that all sciences are only languages, dictionaries well or badly made, and hence the reduction of the human mind to grammar.*

I pass to other theories which remain to be examined in the fourth book of the *Essay on the Human Understanding.*

Chap. XVII. "*Of Reason.*"—I have scarcely any thing but eulogy to bestow upon this chapter. Locke in it shows that the syllogism is not the only nor the principal instrument of reason (§ 4). The evidence of demonstration is not the only evidence; there is also the intuitive evidence upon which Locke himself has founded the evidence of demonstration, and a third sort of evidence which Locke has misconceived, the evidence of induction. Now, the syllogism is of no service to the evidence of induction,

---

* See on the pretended identity of certain propositions, First Series, Vol. 1, Course of 1817, Lecture 8, p. 269–274; Lecture 9, p. 277–284; Vol. 3, Lecture 8, p. 186; Vol. 5, Lecture 3, p. 57, etc.; and on the famous principle that all science is only a well-made language, see especially First Series, Vol. 3, Lecture 3, p. 140; see also in this Vol. the close of Lecture 20, on Words.

for it goes from the general to the particular, whilst induction goes from the particular to the general. The syllogism is of no more use to intuition, which is direct knowledge, without any intermediation. It is therefore only useful for the evidence of demonstration. But Locke does not stop there; he goes so far as to pretend that the syllogism adds nothing to our knowledge, that it is only a means of disputing (§ 6). Here I recognize the language of a man belonging to the close of the seventeenth century, still engaged in the movement of the reaction against scholasticism. Scholasticism had admitted, like Locke, intuitive evidence and demonstrative evidence: like Locke also it had forgotten the evidence of induction; besides, condemned not to choose for itself and not to examine its principles, it had scarcely employed any thing else than demonstration, and consequently it had made the syllogism its favorite weapon. A reaction against scholasticism was therefore necessary and legitimate: but every reaction goes too far; hence, the proscription of the syllogism, a blind and unjust proscription; for deductive knowledge is real knowledge. There are two things in the syllogism, the form and the foundation. The foundation is the special process by which the human mind goes from the general to the particular; and this is certainly a process of which particular account must be taken in a faithful and complete description of the human mind. It is not the work of the schools, it is common to the ignorant and the learned, and it is an original and fecund principle of knowledge and truth, since it is that which gives all consequences. As to the form so well described and so well developed by Aristotle, it can without doubt be abused; but it has a very useful employment. In general, all reasoning which cannot be put under this form is vague reasoning, which must be guarded against; whilst every true demomstration naturally lends itself to this form. The syllogistic form, it is true, is often only a counterproof by which we account for a deduction already obtained, but it is a valuable counterproof, a sort of guarantee of rigor and exactness of which it would not be wise to deprive ourselves. It is not true to say that the syllogism lends itself to the demonstration of the false as well as the true ; for let one take in the order of deduction any error, and I defy him to put it into a regular syllogism. The only remark which holds good is, that the human mind is not altogether in the syllogism, neither in the process which constitutes it, nor in the form which expresses it, because the reason is not entire in reasoning, and because all evidence is not reducible to the evidence of demonstration. On the contrary, as Locke has very well seen, the evidence of demonstration would not exist, if the evidence of intuition were not previously given : within these limits must be confined the criticism of Locke on the syllogism.

This same Chap. XVII. contains several passages, § 7th and the following, upon the necessity of other aid than that of the syllogism for making discoveries. Unfortunately, these passages promise more than they fulfil, and furnish no precise indication. To find this new aid, Locke had only to open the *Novum Organum*, wherein he would have found perfectly described, both sensible intuition and rational intuition, and especially induction. We are compelled to suspect that he had very little acquaintance with Bacon, when we see him, without being able to find it, groping after the new route opened more than half a century before, and already made so luminous by his illustrious countryman.

One of the best chapters of Locke is the XVIII., on *Faith and Reason*. Locke assigns in it the exact part to each ; he indicates their relative office and their distinct limits. He had already said, at the end of Chap. XVII. § 24, that faith in general is so little contrary to reason, that it is the assent of reason to itself. "I think it may not be amiss to take notice, that however faith be opposed to reason, faith is nothing but a firm assent of the mind ; which if it be regulated, as is our duty, cannot be offered to any thing but upon good reason, and so cannot be opposite to it."

And when he comes to positive faith, that is, to revelation, in spite of his respect, or rather by reason of his profound respect for Christianity, and even while admitting the celebrated distinction between things according to reason, contrary to reason, and above reason (Chap. XVIII. § 7), he declares that no revelation, whether immediate or traditional, can be admitted contrary to reason. These are the words of Locke:

Ibid., § 5. "No proposition can be received for divine revelation, or obtain the assent due to all such, if it be contradictory to our clear intuitive knowledge. Because this would be to subvert the principles and foundations of all knowledge, evidence, and assent whatsoever; and there would be left no difference between truth and falsehood, no measures of credible and incredible in the world, if doubtful propositions shall take place before self-evident, and what we certainly know give way to what we may possibly be mistaken in. In propositions, therefore, contrary to the clear perception of the agreement or disagreement of any of our ideas, it will be in vain to urge them as matters of faith. They cannot move our assent under that or any other title whatsoever. For faith can never convince us of any thing that contradicts our knowledge. Because though faith be founded on the testimony of God (who cannot lie) revealing any proposition to us; yet we cannot have an assurance of the truth of its being a divine revelation greater than our own knowledge; since the whole strength of the certainty depends upon our own knowledge that God revealed it; which, in this case, where the proposition supposed revealed contradicts our knowledge or reason, will always have this objection hanging to it, viz., that we cannot tell how to conceive that to come from God, the bountiful Author of our being, which, if received for true, must overturn all the principles and foundations of knowledge he has given us; render all our faculties useless; wholly destroy the most excellent part of his workmanship, our understandings."*

* I cannot refrain from giving, upon this important subject, the passage of the *Nouveaux Essais*, corresponding to that of Locke, a passage which entirely accords with the opinion which we have elsewhere more than once expressed. Leibnitz had even begun to question the celebrated distinction,

I could wish to be equally satisfied with Chapter XIX., *On Enthusiasm*. But it seems to me that Locke has not sufficiently

---

according to reason and above reason: "I find something to remark on your definition of that which is above reason, at least if you refer it to the received usage of this phrase; for it seems to me that, from the manner in which this definition is worded, it is much too one-sided. . . . I applaud you much when you wish to found faith upon reason; without this, why should we prefer the Bible to the Alcoran, or to the ancient books of the Brahmins? Thus our theologians and other learned men have recognized it, and it is this which has caused us to have such fine works on the truth of the Christian religion, and so many fine proofs which have been advanced against pagans and other infidels, ancient and modern. Thus learned persons have always regarded as suspicious those who have pretended that it is not necessary to trouble one's self about reasons and proofs, when believing is a subject of discussion; a thing impossible, in fact, unless to believe signifies to recite or repeat, and to let pass, without troubling ourselves, as many persons do, and as it is even the character of some nations more than others. This is why some Aristotelian philosophers of the fifteenth and sixteenth centuries, whose remains have since subsisted . . ., having wished to sustain two opposite truths, the one philosophical, the other theological, the last Council of Lateran, under Leo X., rightly opposed them. And a similar dispute formerly arose at Helmstadt between Hoffman, the theologian, and Martin, the philosopher; but with this difference, that the philosopher would reconcile philosophy with revelation, whilst the theologian would reject the use of it. But Duke Julius, the founder of the university, decided for the philosopher. It is true that in our times a person of highest eminence has declared that, in regard to articles of faith, it is necessary to shut the eyes in order to see clearly; and Tertullian somewhere says: This is true, for it is impossible; it is to be believed, for it is an absurdity. But if the intention of those who explain themselves in this way is good, the expressions are always extravagant, and may do harm. Faith is founded on motives of belief, and on the internal grace which immediately determines the mind. [This theological distinction of Leibnitz is, at bottom, our philosophical distinction between spontaneous reason and reflective reason.] It must be granted that there are many judgments more evident than those which depend upon these motives: some are more advanced in them than others, and there are even many persons who have never known, still less have weighed them, and who, consequently, have not even what might be called a motive of belief. But the internal grace of the Holy Spirit immediately supplies it . . . . It is true that God never gives it except when that which he causes to be believed is founded upon reason, otherwise he would destroy the means of knowing the truth; but it is not necessary that all those who have this divine faith should know those reasons, and still less that they should always have them before their eyes; otherwise simple people and idiots would never have true faith, and the most enlightened would not have it when they might have most need of it, for they cannot at all times recollect the reasons of belief. The question of the use of

fathomed his subject, and that he rather made a satire than a philosophic description.

What, in fact, is enthusiasm, according to Locke? It is: 1st, the pretension of attributing to a privileged and personal revelation, to a divine illumination made in our favor, sentiments which are peculiar to ourselves, and which are often nothing but extravagances; 2d, the still more absurd pretension of imposing upon others these imaginations as superior orders invested with divine authority, §§ 5 and 6. These are, it is true, the follies of enthusiasm; but is enthusiasm nothing but this?

Locke has elsewhere clearly seen that the evidence of demonstration is founded upon that of intuition. He has even said that in regard to these two kinds of evidence, the evidence of intuition is not only anterior to the other, but that it is superior to it, that it

---

reason in theology has been greatly agitated, as much between the Socinians and those called Catholics in a more general sense, as between the Reformers and the Evangelicals. . . . We may say, in general terms, that the Socinians go too far in rejecting every thing that is not conformed to the order of nature, even whilst they might not prove its impossibility; but their adversaries also sometimes go too far, and push mystery as far as to the borders of contradiction, by which they do harm to the truth which they undertake to defend. . . . How can faith establish any thing that overturns a principle without which all belief, affirmation, or denial would be vain? . . . . But it seems to me that there remains a question which the authors of whom I have just spoken have not sufficiently examined, which is this: Suppose that, on one hand, the literal sense of a text of Holy Scripture is found, and that, on the other, is found a great appearance of logical impossibility, or at least a recognized physical impossibility, is it more reasonable to rely upon the literal sense or the philosophical principle? It is certain that there are passages in which we find no difficulty in departing from the letter, as when . . . Here come in the rules of interpretation . . . The two authors that I have just named (Videlius and Musæus) dispute still in regard to the undertaking of Kekerman, who wished to demonstrate the Trinity by reason, as Raymond Lully also had attempted before. But Musæus acknowledged with sufficient fairness that if the demonstration of the reformed author had been good and sound, he should have had nothing to say, and that he would have been right in maintaining that the light of the Holy Spirit could be illuminated by philosophy." Leibnitz speaks with force in regard to the employment of reason in theological questions, such as the salvation of pagans, and that of infants dying without baptism, and he concludes thus: "Good proves to us God is more philanthropic than men."

is the highest degree of knowledge. Chap. XVII. § 14. "Intuitive knowledge is certain, beyond all doubt, and needs no probation, nor can have any; this being the highest of all human certainty. In this consists the evidence of all those maxims, which nobody has any doubt about, but every man (does not, as is said, only assent to, but) knows to be true as soon as ever they are proposed to his understanding. In the discovery of, and assent to these truths, there is no use of the discursive faculty, no need of reasoning, but they are known by a superior and higher degree of evidence. And such, if I may guess at things unknown, I am apt to think that angels have now, and the spirits of just men made perfect shall have, in a future state, of thousands of things, which now either wholly escape our apprehensions, or which, our short-sighted reason having got some faint glimpse of, we in the dark grope after." I accept this proposition, whether it accords or not, as the case may be, with the general system of Locke. I add that intuitive knowledge, in many cases, for example, in regard to time, space, personal identity, the infinite, all substantial existences, as also the good and the beautiful, has, you know, this peculiarity, that it is founded neither upon the senses nor upon the consciousness, but upon the reason, which, without the intermediation of reasoning, attains its objects and conceives them with certainty. Now, it is an attribute inherent in the reason to believe in itself, and from this is derived faith. If, then, intuitive reason is above induction and demonstrative reason, the faith of reason in itself in intuition is purer, more elevated than the faith of reason in itself in induction and in demonstration. Recollect, also, that the truths which reason intuitively discovers are not arbitrary, but necessary; that they are not relative, but absolute: the authority of reason is therefore absolute, and it is a character of faith, attached to reason, to be absolute like reason. These are the admirable characters of reason, and of the faith of reason in itself.

This is not all: when we demand of the reason the source of this absolute authority which distinguishes it, we are forced to recognize that this reason is not ours, nor, consequently, is the authority which belongs to it ours. It is not in our power to make the reason give us such or such a truth, or not to give them to us. Independently of our will, reason intervenes, and certain conditions being fulfilled, suggests to us, I was going to say imposes upon us, those truths. Reason makes its appearance in us, though it is not ourselves, and can in no way be confounded with our personality.* Whence then comes this wonderful guest within us, and what is the principle of this reason which enlightens us without belonging to us? This principle is God,† the first and the last principle of every thing. When the reason knows that it comes from God, the faith which it had in itself increases, not in degree, but in nature, as much as, thus to speak, as the eternal substance is superior to finite substance. Then there is a redoubling of faith in the truths which the supreme reason reveals to us in the midst of the shadows of time and in the limits of our feebleness.

Behold, then, reason become to its own eyes divine in its principle. This state of reason which listens to itself and takes itself as the echo of God upon the earth, with the particular and extraordinary characters which are attached to it, is what we call enthusiasm. The word sufficiently explains the thing: enthusiasm, as the breath of God within us,‡ is immediate intuition opposed to induction and demonstration, is primitive spontaneity opposed to the tardy development of reflection, is the apperception of the highest truths by reason in the greatest independence both of the senses and of our personality. Enthusiasm in its highest degree, and, thus to speak, in its crisis, belongs only to certain in-

---

* See first volume of this Series, *Introduction to the History of Philosophy*, Lectures 5 and 6, and 1st Series, *passim*.

† First volume of this Series, Lectures 5 and 6, and 1st Series, Vol. 2, Lectures 7 and 8, *God, the principle of necessary truths;* Lecture 13, *God, the principle of the beautiful;* Lecture 23, *God, the principle of the idea of the good:* Vol. 3, *Opening discourse*, p. 31.

‡ On enthusiasm, 1st Series, Vol. 2, Lecture 12, p. 138; 2d Series, **Vol. 1,** Lecture 6, etc.

dividuals, and to them only in certain circumstances; but in its most feeble degree, enthusiasm does not belong to such or such an individual, to such or such an epoch, but to human nature, in all men, in all conditions, and almost at every hour. It is enthusiasm which makes spontaneous convictions and revolutions, in small as well as great, in heroes and in the feeblest woman. Enthusiasm is the poetic spirit in all things; and the poetic spirit, thanks to God, does not belong exclusively to poets; it has been given to all men in some degree, more or less pure, more or less elevated; it appears especially in certain men, and in certain moments of the life of these men, who are the poets *par excellence.* Enthusiasm also makes religions; for every religion supposes two things: that the truths it proclaims are absolute truths, and that it proclaims them in the name of God himself, who reveals them to it.

Thus far all is well; we are still within the bounds of reason, for it is reason which is the foundation of faith and enthusiasm, of heroism, of poetry and religion; and when the poet and the priest repudiate reason in the name of faith and enthusiasm, they do nothing else, whether they know it or are ignorant of it,—and it is the affair neither of poets nor priests to render an account of what they do,—they do, I say, nothing else than put one mode of reason above the other modes of this same reason; for if immediate intuition is above reasoning, it none the less belongs to reason: we in vain try to repudiate reason, we always use it. Enthusiasm is a rational fact which has its place in the order of natural facts and in the history of the human mind; only this fact is extremely delicate, and enthusiasm may easily turn it into folly. We are here upon the doubtful border between reason and extravagance. This is the legitimate, universal, and necessary principle of religions, a principle which must not be confounded with the aberrations which may corrupt it. Thus disengaged and elucidated by analysis, philosophy ought to recognize it, if it wishes to recognize all the essential facts, all the elements of reason and humanity.

Behold now where error commences. Enthusiasm is, I repeat, this spontaneous intuition of truth by reason, as independent as possible of personality and the senses. But it often happens that the senses and personality are introduced into inspiration itself, and with it mingle details which are material, arbitrary, false, and ridiculous. It also happens that those who participate, in a superior degree, in this revelation of God, made to all men by reason and by truth, imagine that it belongs to themselves, that it has been refused to others, not only in this same degree, but totally and absolutely; they institute in their minds, to their advantage, a sort of privilege of inspiration; and as in inspiration we feel the duty of submitting ourselves to the truths which it reveals to us, and the sacred mission of proclaiming them and of spreading them, we often go so far as to suppose that it is also a duty for us, while submitting ourselves to its truths, to subject others to them, to impose on them these truths, not in virtue of our power and of our personal illumination, but in virtue of the superior power from which emanates all inspiration: on our knees before the principle of our enthusiasm and our faith, we also wish to make others bow to the same principle, and to make them adore and serve it for the same reason that we adore and serve it ourselves.* Hence religious authority; hence also tyranny. We begin by believing in special revelations made in our favor, and end by regarding ourselves as delegates of God and providence, charged not only to enlighten and save docile souls, to enlighten and save, whether they are willing or not, those who would resist the truth and God.

But the folly and the tyranny, which are often derived, I grant, from the principle of inspiration, because we are feeble, and consequently exclusive, and therefore intolerant, are essentially distinct from this principle. We may and should honor this principle, and at the same time condemn its aberrations. Instead of this, Locke confounds the abuse of the principle, the

---

* See especially, 1st Series, Vol. 2, Lecture 10, *Of mysticism*, etc.

extravagant enthusiasm, peculiar to some men, with the principle itself, true enthusiasm, which has been given in some degree to all men. In all enthusiasm he sees only a disordered movement of imagination, and everywhere applies himself to erecting barriers to passing beyond the circle of authentic and legitimately interpreted passages of holy books. I approve of this prudence, admit it at all times, and prize it much more still when I think of the extravagances of puritan enthusiasm, the spectacle of which Locke had under his eyes; but prudence should not degenerate into injustice. What would the sensualistic school say if, by prudence also, idealism should wish to suppress the senses on account of the excesses to which they might lead and often do lead, or reasoning, on account of the sophisms which it engenders? It is necessary to be wise with measure, *sobrie sapere;* it is necessary to be wise within the limits of humanity and nature; and Locke was wrong in considering enthusiasm much less in itself than in its consequences, and in its foolish and mournful consequences.

There follows Chap. XX., *On the Causes of Error.* Nearly all those which Locke signalized had been already recognized before him; they are: 1st, want of proofs; 2d, want of ability to use them; 3d, want of will to use them; 4th, many measures of probability, which Locke reduces to the four following: 1st, propositions that are not in themselves certain and evident, but doubtful and false, taken up for principles; 2d, received hypotheses; 3d, predominant passions or inclinations; 4th, authority. This chapter of Locke may be read with profit; I wish to dwell only upon the last paragraph, thus entitled: § 18: "Men not in so many errors as is imagined." I confess that the title of this chapter singularly pleased me, on account of the optimism which you know I cherish. I hoped to find in the good and wise Locke these two propositions which are so dear to me: first, that men do not believe in error so much as in truth, and that there is no error in which there is not some truth. Far from this, I perceived that Locke made an apology for humanity, in respect to error, very unfavorable to it. According to Locke, if men are not so foolish as they appear to be, it is because they put very little faith in the foolish opinions with which they seem to be penetrated, which they follow only from habit, excitement, or interest. "They are resolved to stick to a party that education or interest has engaged them in; and these, like the common soldiers of an army, show their courage and warmth as their leaders direct, without ever so much as examining or knowing the cause they contend for. . . . . . It is enough for a man to obey his leaders, to have his hand and his tongue ready for the support of the common cause, and thereby approve himself to those who can give him credit, preferment, or protection in that society." Here, again, Locke suffered himself to be troubled by the spectacle of his times, when, in the midst of so many follies, there might have been some dissemblers; but all were not and could not be so. I grant that, in revolutionary times, ambition often takes the standard of extravagances in which it cannot believe, in order to lead the crowd; but ambition must not be calumniated. All is in all in humanity, and one can be at the same time both very ambitious and very sincere. Cromwell, for example, was, in my opinion,* a Puritan sincere even to fanaticism, and greedy of domination even to hypocrisy; and yet the hypocrisy is in him more doubtful and obscure than fanaticism. Probably it only led him to exaggerate the opinions which were in his heart, and to arouse the passions which he shared himself. His tyranny is not a proof of the imposture of his republican ardor. There are times when the most popular cause has need of a master, and when the good sense which recognizes the necessity, and the genius which feels its own force, easily impel an ardent soul to arbitrary power, without indicating an excess of selfishness. Pericles, Cæsar, Cromwell, and others still, might have very sincerely loved equality in the midst of a dictatorship.

* This opinion concerning the sincerity of the fanaticism of Cromwell, which caused astonishment in 1829, is now demonstrated by the publication of his letters, by Carlyle.

There is, perhaps, now in the world a man whose ambition is the last hope of the country which he has twice saved,* and which alone he can save again by applying a firm hand. But let us leave great men, who, in expiation of their superiority and their glory, are condemned not to be comprehended; let us leave the chiefs, let us come to the multitude: there, the explanation of Locke falls of itself. In fact, we can explain, up to a certain point, the foolish opinions of some men by the interest which they have in simulating those of the masses upon whom they wish to support themselves; but the masses cannot receive false opinions by imposture, for apparently they do not wish to deceive themselves. No, it is not thus that error and humanity can be justified. Their true apology is that which I have so many times given, and which I will not cease to repeat, that there is no complete error in an intelligent and rational being. Men, individuals and nations, men of genius and ordinary men, yield to many errors without doubt, and attach themselves to them, but not on account of that which makes them errors, but on account of the part of truth which is in them. Examine at bottom all celebrated errors, political, religious, philosophical; there is not one which has not a considerable portion of truth in it, and it is by this truth that it has been able to find credence in the minds of great men who have introduced it upon the stage of the world, and in the minds of the multitude who have followed these great men. It is the truth joined to the error which gives the force of error, which produces it, sustains it, spreads it, explains it, and excuses it; and errors succeed each other in the world only by carrying with them, and offering, as it were, for their ransom, so many truths which, piercing through the clouds which envelop them, enlighten and guide the human race. Thus I entirely approve the title of the paragraph of Locke, but I reject its development.†

* Allusion to Bolivar.

† I am again happy to confirm an opinion which is so dear to me, by the great authority of Leibnitz. Here is his reply to Locke: "This justice

The XXI. and last chapter contains a division of sciences into physics, practics, and logic or grammar. Locke here understands by physics, the nature of things, not only the nature of bodies, but of minds, God and the soul; it is the ancient physics and the modern ontology. I have nothing to say of this division, except that it is very old, evidently arbitrary and superficial, and much inferior to the celebrated division of Bacon, reproduced by d'Alembert. I have difficulty in persuading myself that the author of this paragraph could have known the division of Bacon. I rather see in this, as in the third book on signs and words, a recollection of the reading of Hobbes.

We have now arrived at the end of this long analysis of the fourth book of the *Essay on the Human Understanding*. I have followed, step by step, chapter by chapter, all the important propositions contained in this fourth book, as I have done in regard to the third, in regard to the second, and in regard to the first. Nevertheless, I should not give you a complete view of the *Essay on the Human Understanding*, if I did not exhibit to you some theories which are scattered throughout the work of Locke, but have an intimate relation to the general spirit of his system, and have acquired in the sensualistic school an immense authority. It has therefore appeared to me proper to reserve these diverse theories for a particular examination: I propose to make them known to you and to discuss them in the next lecture, which will be the last of this year, and will contain my definite judgment in regard to the philosophy of Locke.

---

which you render to the human race does not turn to its credit, and men would be much more excusable in sincerely following their opinions than in counterfeiting them by considerations of interest. Perhaps, however, there is more sincerity in fact than you seem willing to understand; for, without any knowledge of the cause, they may come to exercise implicit faith by submitting themselves generally and blindly, but often in good faith, to the judgments of others, whose authority they have once recognized. It is true that the interest they find in it often contributes to this submission; but this does not hinder opinion being formed."

LECTURE XXV.

ESSAY, LIBERTY. SOUL. GOD. CONCLUSION.

Examination of three important theories which are found in the *Essay on the Human Understanding;* 1st, Theory of Liberty: that it inclines to fatalism. 2d, Theory of the nature of the Soul: that it inclines to materialism. 3d, Theory of the existence of God: that it relies almost exclusively on proofs borrowed from the sensible world. Recapitulation of all the lectures on the *Essay on the Human Understanding;* Of the merits and defects which have been pointed out.—Of the spirit which has guided this examination of Locke.—Conclusion.

THE theories which I must to-day present to you are those of liberty, of the soul, and of God. I will unfold to you these three theories in the same order in which they are found in the *Essay on the Human Understanding.*

In order that you may clearly understand the true character of Locke's theory of Liberty, some preliminary explanations are indispensable.*

All the facts which can fall under the consciousness of man and under the reflection of the philosopher, are resolved into three fundamental facts which contain all the others, three facts which without doubt in reality, are never solitary, but which are not the less distinct, and which a scrupulous analysis must discern, without dividing them, in the complex phenomenon of intellectual life. These three facts are: *to feel, to think, to act.*

* On the true notion of liberty, see 1st Series, Vol. 1, Course of 1816, Lectures 23 and 24, p. 189, and Course of 1817, Lecture 23; Vol. 2, 3d Part, Lecture 18 and Lecture 20; Vol. 3, Lecture 1, *Locke*, p. 71, Lecture 3, *Condillac*, p. 149, etc.; Vol. 4, Lecture 23, *Morals of Reid*, p. 541–574. This last passage contains, with the other, sufficiently developed, all our doctrine on human liberty.

I open a book and I read; let us decompose this fact, and in it we shall find three elements.*

Suppose that I do not see the letters of which each page is composed, the shape and the order of these letters; it is very evident that I will not comprehend the sense which usage has attached to these letters, and that thus I shall not read. To see, then, is here the condition of reading. On the other hand, to see is not still to read; for the letters being seen, nothing would be done if the intelligence were not added to the sense of sight in order to comprehend the signification of the letters placed before my eyes.

Behold then two facts which the most superficial analysis immediately discerns in reading: let us investigate the characters of these two facts.

Am I the cause of vision, and in general of sensation? Have I the consciousness of being the cause of this phenomenon, of beginning it, of continuing it, of interrupting it, of augmenting it, of diminishing it, of maintaining it, and of abolishing it as I please? I will take other examples more striking. Suppose I press upon a sharp instrument; a painful sensation follows. I approach a rose; an agreeable sensation succeeds. Is it I who produce these two phenomena? can I make them cease? do the suffering and enjoyment come and go at my bidding? No; I am subject to the pleasure as well as to the pain; both come, subsist, disappear, without the concurrence of my will; finally, sensation is a phenomenon marked in the eyes of my consciousness, with the incontestable character of necessity.

Let us examine the character of the other fact which sensation precedes and does not constitute. When the sensation is accomplished, the intelligence applies itself to this sensation, and first it pronounces that this sensation has a cause, the sharp instrument, the rose, and to return to our example, the letters placed

* We have already chosen this example in the *Examination of the Lectures of M. Laromiguière*, *Philosophical Fragments*, in order to authorize the distinction here established.

before my eyes: this is the first judgment which the intelligence passes. Besides, as soon as the sensation has been referred by the intelligence to an external cause, to wit, the letters and the words which they form, this same intelligence conceives the sense of these letters and of these words, and judges that the propositions which these words form are true or false. The intelligence, therefore, judges that the sensation has a cause; but, I ask you, could it judge the contrary? No, the intelligence can no more judge that this sensation has not a cause, than it was possible for the sensation to exist or not to exist when the sharp instrument was in the wound, or the rose under the nose, or the book before my eyes. And not only does the intelligence necessarily judge that the sensation is related to a cause, but it judges quite as necessarily that the propositions, contained in the lines perceived by the eye, are true or false: for example, that two and two make four, and not five, etc. I ask again whether it is in the power of the intelligence to judge at will that such an action of which the book speaks is good or bad, that such a form which it describes is beautiful or ugly? In nowise. Doubtless different intelligences, or the same intelligence at different moments of its exercise, will often pass very different judgments in regard to the same thing; often it will be deceived; it will judge that which is true to be false; that which is good to be bad, that which is beautiful to be ugly, and the reciprocal: but at the moment when it judges that a proposition is true or false, that an act is good or bad, that a form is beautiful or ugly, at that moment it is not in the power of the intelligence to pass another judgment than that which it passes; it obeys laws which it has not made; it yields to motives which determine it without any concurrence of the will. In a word, the phenomenon of intelligence, to comprehend, to judge, to know, to think, whatever name may be given to it, is marked by the same character of necessity as the phenomenon of sensibility. If then the sensibility and the intelligence are under the empire of necessity, it is not in them, assuredly, that we must seek for liberty.

Where shall we seek it? We must find it in the third fact mingled with the other two, which we have not yet analyzed, or we shall find it nowhere, and liberty is only a chimera.

To see and feel, to judge and comprehend, do not exhaust the complex fact submitted to our analysis. If I did not look at the letters of this book, should I see them, or at least should I see them distinctly? If, seeing these letters, I paid no attention to them, would I comprehend them? No, certainly. Now, what is it to pay attention, to consider any thing? It is neither to feel nor to comprehend; for to look is not to perceive, if the organ of vision is wanting or is unfaithful; to give attention is not to comprehend; it is certainly an indispensable condition, but not always a sufficient reason; it is not sufficient to be attentive to the exposition of a problem in order to resolve it: and attention no more contains the understanding* than it is contained in the sensibility. To be attentive is a new phenomenon which it is impossible to confound with the first two, although it is continually mingled with them, and with them completes the total fact of which we wish to render an account to ourselves.

Let us examine the character of this third fact, the phenomenon of activity. Let us first distinguish different sorts of actions. There are actions which man does not relate to himself, although he may be the theatre of them. Others may tell us that we perform these actions; we, ourselves, know nothing of them; they are performed in us; we do not perform them. In lethargy, in real or artificial sleep, in delirium, we execute a multitude of movements which resemble actions, which are actions even, if you please, but actions which present the following characters:

We have no consciousness of them even at the moment when we appear to be performing them;

We have no remembrance of having performed them;

Consequently, we do not refer them to ourselves, neither while we are performing them, nor after having performed them;

---

* See the *Philosophical Fragments, Examination of the Lectures M. Laromiguière.*

Consequently, again, they do not belong to us, and we no more impute them to ourselves than to our neighbor or to an inhabitant of another world.

But are there no other actions than these? I open this book, I look at the letters, I give my attention to them; these are certainly actions also: do they resemble the preceding?

I open this book: am I conscious of doing it? yes.

This action being done, have I a remembrance of it? yes.

Do I refer this action to myself as having done it? yes.

Am I convinced that it belongs to me? Could I impute it to such or such another person as well as to myself, or am I not alone and exclusively responsible in my own eyes? Here I again answer to myself, yes.

Finally, at the moment in which I perform this action, have I not, with the consciousness of performing it, the consciousness of being able not to perform it? When I open this book, have I not the consciousness of opening it, and the consciousness of being able not to open it? When I look, do I not know at the same time that I am looking, and that I am able not to look? When I give my attention, do I not know that I am giving it, and that I am able not to give it? Is not this a fact which each of us can repeat as many times as he pleases and on a thousand occasions? And is not this a universal belief of the human race? Let us generalize and say that there are movements and actions which we do with the double consciousness of doing and of being able not to do them.

An action which is done with the consciousness of being able not to do it, is what men have called a free action; for there is no longer in it the character of necessity. In the phenomenon of sensation I could not avoid enjoying when joy fell under my consciousness; I could not avoid suffering when it was pain; I had the consciousness of feeling with the consciousness of inability not to feel. In the phenomenon of intelligence, I could not avoid judging that two and two make four: I had the consciousness of thinking this and that, with the consciousness of being unable not to think it. In certain movements, again, I had so little consciousness of being able not to perform them, that I had not even the consciousness of performing them at the moment when I performed them. But in a very great number of cases, I do certain acts with the consciousness of doing them and of being able not to do them, of being able to suspend them or to continue them, to finish them or to abolish them. This is a class of very real acts; they are very numerous: but although there should be but one of them, this one would be sufficient to attest in man a special power, liberty. Liberty belongs neither to the sensibility nor to the intelligence; it belongs to the activity, and only to acts which we perform with the consciousness of performing them and of being able not to perform them.

After having stated the free act, it is necessary to analyze it more attentively.

The free act is a phenomenon which contains many different elements mingled together. To act freely is to perform an action with the consciousness of being able not to perform it: now, to perform an action with the consciousness of being able not to perform it, supposes a choice of doing it or of not doing it; to commence an action, being able at the same time not to commence it, is choosing to commence it; to continue it, being able to suspend it, is choosing to continue it; to carry it on to the end, being able to abandon it, is choosing to accomplish it. But to choose supposes motives for choice, motives for doing this action, and motives for not doing it, that these different motives are known, and that these are preferred to those. Whether these motives are passions or ideas, errors or truths, this or that, is of little consequence; what is important, is to know what is here the faculty in play, that is, what knows these motives, what prefers the one to the other; what judges that one is preferable to the other; for this is to prefer. And what knows, what judges, if it is not the intelligence? The intelligence is then the faculty that prefers. But in order to prefer some motives to others, to judge that some are preferable to others, it is not necessary merely to know these different motives, it is necessary to compare them and weigh them; it is necessary to deliberate and conclude. And what is deliberating? It is nothing else than examining with doubt, appreciating the relative goodness of different motives, without perceiving it by that evidence which decides the judgment, the conviction, the preference. But what is it that examines, what is it that doubts, what is it that concludes? Evidently the intelligence, that same intelligence which, subsequently, after having passed several provisional judgments, will abrogate all these judgments, will judge that they are less true, less reasonable than such another, and will pass this last judgment, that is, will conclude, that is, again, will prefer after having deliberated. It is from the intelligence that the phenomenon of preference and the other phenomena which suppose it spring. Thus far we are still in the sphere of intelligence, and not in that of action. Assuredly intelligence has its conditions; no one examines who does not wish to examine, and the will intervenes in deliberation; but it is the simple condition, it is not the basis of the phenomenon; for, if it is true that, without the faculty of willing, every examination and every deliberation is impossible, it is also true that the faculty itself which examines and which deliberates, and which passes a judgment, suspensive or decisive, is the intelligence. Deliberation, conclusion, or preference, are then purely intellectual facts. Let us pursue our analysis.

We have conceived different motives for doing or not doing an action. We have deliberated upon these motives, and we have preferred some of them to others; we have concluded to do it rather than not to do it; but to conclude to do it and to do it are not the same thing. When the intelligence has judged it necessary to do this or that, from such or such motives, it remains to pass on to action, at first to resolve, to say to itself, not I ought to do, but I will to do. But the faculty which says I ought to do, is not and cannot be the faculty which says I will to do, I take the resolution to do. Here the part of the intelligence ceases. I ought to do is a judgment; I will to do is not a judgment. Behold then a new element, which must not be confounded with the preceding; this element is the will. Just now we were at the point of judging and of knowing; now we are at the point of willing. I say willing, and not doing; for, as judging that it is necessary to do any thing is not willing to do it, so to will to do any thing is not doing it. To will to do is an act, not a judgment, but an act entirely internal. It is evident that this act is not an action properly so called; in order to arrive at action, it is necessary to pass from the sphere of the will to that of the external world, in which the action is definitively accomplished which at first you conceived, deliberated upon, and preferred, which afterwards you willed, and which must be executed. If there were no exterior world, there would be no terminated action; and not only is it necessary that there should be an exterior world, but it is necessary that the power of willing, which we recognized after the power of comprehending and of judging, should be connected with another power, with a physical power which may serve it in reaching the external world. Suppose that the will is not connected with the organization, there is no longer any bridge between the will and the external world; there is no external action possible. The physical power necessary to action, is the organization; and in this organization it is recognized that the muscular system is the special instrument of the will. Take away the muscular system, there is no more effort possible, consequently there is no locomotion, no movement possible, and if there is no movement possible, there is no exterior action possible. Thus, in order to resume, the total action which we were to analyze is resolved into three perfectly distinct elements: 1st, the intellectual element, which is composed of the knowledge of motives for or against, of deliberation, of preference, of choice; 2d, the voluntary element, which consists neither more nor less in the resolution to do; 3d, the physical element, or external action.

The question now is, to which of these three elements does liberty precisely belong, that is, the power of doing with the consciousness of being able not to do. Does this power of doing, with the consciousness of being able not to do, belong to the first element, the intellectual element of free action? No, for we are not masters of our preference; we prefer such a motive to such another, the *for* or the *against*, according to our intellectual nature, which has its necessary laws, without having the consciousness of being able to prefer or to judge otherwise, and even with the consciousness of not being able to prefer and to judge otherwise than we do. It is not then in this element that we must seek liberty. Neither is it in the third element, in the physical action; for this element supposes the external world, an organization which corresponds with it, and in this organization a muscular system, healthy and suitable, without which the physical action is impossible. When we accomplish it, we have the consciousness of acting, but under the condition of a theatre of which we have not the disposal, and under the condition of instruments of which we can but poorly dispose, which we cannot recover if they escape us, and which may escape us at every moment, nor repair if they become deranged and betray us, and which betray us very often, and obey their own laws, over which we have no power, and which even we scarcely know; whence it follows that we do not act here with the consciousness of being able to do the contrary of that which we do. It is then no more to the third than to the first element that liberty belongs; it can then be only in the second, and it is there, in fact, that we encounter it.

Neglect the first and the third element, the judgment and the physical action, attach yourself to the second element, to the will: analysis discovers in this single element two terms still, a special act of willing, and the power of willing to which we refer it. This act is an effect by a relation to the power of willing, which is its cause; and this cause, in order to produce its effect, has no need of another theatre, of another instrument than itself.* It produces it directly, without intermediation and without condition,

* On this essential point, see 1st Series, Vol. 4, Lecture 13, p. 545, etc.

continues it and consummates it, or suspends it and modifies it, creates it entirely or destroys it entirely; and at the moment even when it exercises itself by such a special act, we have the consciousness that it could exercise itself by a special act entirely contrary, without being thereby exhausted; so that after having changed its acts ten times, a hundred times, the faculty would remain integrally the same, inexhaustible and identical with itself, in the perpetual variety of its applications, being always able to do what it does not do, and not to do what it does. Here in all its plenitude is the character of liberty.

Should the entire world be wanting to the will, if the organization and muscular system remained, the will would still be able to produce muscular effort, and consequently a sensible fact, although this fact would not pass beyond the limits of the organization; this was perfectly established by M. de Biran,* who placed the type of causality, of the will and of liberty, in the phenomenon of muscular effort. But whilst with him I cheerfully grant that in muscular effort, in the consciousness of this effort and of the sensation which accompanies it, we find the most eminent and the most easily appreciable type of our causative power, voluntary and free, I say that this is but an exterior and derivative type, and not the primitive and essential type; or M. de Biran ought to have carried his theory so far as to say, that where there is absence or paralysis of muscles, there can never be causation, volition, active and free phenomenon. Now, I maintain the contrary; I maintain that if the exterior world be taken away, and the muscular and locomotive system also, and if there remained to man, with a purely nervous organization, an intelligence capable of conceiving motives, of deliberating, of preferring, and of choosing, there would remain to him the power of willing, which would still be exercised in special acts, in volitions, in which would be visible the proper causality and freedom of the will, although these effects, these free volitions would not pass beyond the in-

* See Lecture 19; and Works of M. de Biran, *passim*.

ternal world of the will, although they would have no counter-stroke in the organization through the muscular system, and would not produce the phenomenon of effort, an internal phenomenon without doubt in relation to the interior world, but itself external in relation to the will. Thus, suppose I will to move my arm without being able for want of muscles, there will still be in this: 1st, the act of willing to move my arm, a special volition; 2d, the general power of willing, which is the direct cause of this volition; there will then be the cause and the effect; there will be consciousness of this effect and of this cause, of an action caused and of an internal causative force, sovereign in its own world, in the world of will, though it might be absolutely unable to pass to external action, because the muscular and locomotive system were wanting to it.

The theory of M. de Biran considers the free act only in its external manifestation, in a remarkable fact without doubt, but which itself supposes the fact quite as profound and intimate, the fact of willing with its immediate and proper effect. Here, in my opinion, is the primitive type of liberty, and this is the entire conclusion of this analysis too long for its place, and too brief in itself in order not to be still very large.* When we seek freedom in an act, we may be deceived in two ways:

* *Fragments Philosophiques*, preface of the first edition. It is a fact, that in the midst of the movements which exterior agents determine in us, in spite of us, we have the power of taking the first step of a different movement, first of conceiving it, then of deliberating whether we will execute it, finally that of resolving and passing to the execution of it, of commencing this execution, of continuing or suspending it, of accomplishing or arresting it, and always of being master of it. The fact is certain, and what is not less certain is, that the movement executed on these conditions takes in our eyes a new character; we impute it to ourselves, we refer it as an effect to ourselves, considering ourselves then as the cause of it. This is for us the origin of the notion of cause, not of an abstract cause, but of a personal cause, of ourselves. The proper character of the *me* is causality or will, since we refer to ourselves, and impute only to ourselves, that which we cause, and that we cause only what we will . . . We must not confound the will or the internal causality which produces at first effects, that are internal as well as their cause, with the external instruments of this causality, which, as instruments, appear

Either we seek it in the intellectual element of the act, the consciousness of the motives, the deliberation, the preference, the choice, and then we cannot find it; for it is evident that the different motives for or against command the intelligence, which is not free to judge this or that, to prefer this to that; we do not find liberty in the intellectual part of the action, and we therefore say that there is no liberty, and doubtless it is not there, but it may be elsewhere.

Or we seek liberty in the physical element of the act, and we do not find it there, at least constantly, and we are tempted to conclude that liberty is but an accident, which sometimes takes place, and which, three-fourths of the time, does not take place, depending on physical conditions external or internal; we herein see no sign of the proper and fundamental power of human nature.

---

also to produce effects, but without being the true cause of them. When I strike one ball against another, it is not the ball which really causes the movement which it impresses, for this movement has been impressed upon it by the muscles, which, in our organization, are at the service of the will. Properly speaking, these actions are only effects joined to each other, alternately seeming to be causes without actually being so, and all being referable as effects, more or less remote, to the will as first cause. Do we search for the primitive notion of cause in the action of the ball upon the ball, as was done before Hume, or of the hand upon the ball, or of the first muscles upon their extremities, or even in the action of the will upon the muscles, as M. de Biran did? We do not find it in any of these cases, not even in the last; for it is possible that there might be a paralysis of the muscles, which would deprive the will of its power over them, which would render it unproductive, incapable of being a cause, and, consequently, of suggesting the notion of it. But that which paralysis cannot destroy, is the action of the will upon itself, the production of a resolution, that is, a causation wholly spiritual, a primitive type of the causality of which all the exterior actions, commencing with muscular effort, and ending with the movement of the ball against the ball, are only the more or less imperfect symbols. The first cause for us, then, is the will, whose first effect is a volition. This is the source, at once the highest and the purest, of the notion of cause, which is there confounded with that of personality. . . The phenomenon of will presents the following momenta: 1st, to predetermine an act to be done; 2d, to deliberate; 3d, to form a resolution. If we take notice of the operation, we shall find that it is the reason which constitutes the first entire, and even the second; for it is the reason which deliberates; but it is not the reason which resolves and determines."

If we wish to refer these two sorts of errors to their most general causes, that is, to consider them in regard to method, we may say that they consist, the first, in seeking the phenomenon of liberty in the antecedent of this phenomenon, to wit, the intellectual fact which always precedes the free will, but which does not engender it and does not contain it as the cause engenders and contains the effect; and the second, in seeking the phenomenon of liberty, not in the antecedent, but in the consequent, thus to speak, of this phenomenon, in the sensible fact which sometimes follows and sometimes does not follow the will, but which is not directly derived from it and contains it only as borrowed. This brings us back to the general source of all the errors of Locke, the confusion of an idea with that which precedes it or with that which follows it. You have seen it in regard to space, to time, to the infinite, to substance, to cause, to good and evil; you will see it here in the theory of liberty.

Locke begins, Book II. Chap. XXI., *Of Power*, § 5, by dividing all the phenomena of consciousness, not into three classes, but into two, the understanding and the will. Then follows the classification of actions.

"All the actions that we have any idea of, reduce themselves to two: namely, thinking and motion." *Ibid.* § 8.

Sometimes, in Locke, the will includes the thought and the movement; sometimes it is applied only to movement.

"This power which the mind has to order the consideration of any idea, or the forbearing to consider it, or to prefer the motion of any part of the body to its rest, and *vice versa,* in any particular instance, is that which we call the will. The actual exercise of that power, by directing any particular action, or its forbearance, is that which we call volition or willing." *Ibid.* § 5.

Here we have the will applied to the acts of the understanding as to the movements of the body. In the following, on the contrary, it is applied only to the latter:

"Volition, it is plain, is an act of the mind knowingly exerting that dominion it takes itself to have over any part of the man, by employing it in, or withholding it from, any particular action." *Ibid.* § 15.

It may be seen that the theory of the will in Locke is quite as uncertain as the other theories which I have exhibited to you. Besides, there is equal error on both sides. Does Locke refer the will to the understanding? it is clear that he will not there find liberty, for the intelligence is not free, and we do not think as we please. Locke is then deceived by confounding a phenomenon with that which precedes and does not include it. Does Locke wish to understand by the will, only the faculty of moving one's body? it is clear, again, that it is not in this faculty that he will find liberty; for, as you know, our physical power is a power limited on all sides, and of which we cannot always dispose with the consciousness of being able to do the contrary of what we do; and in this case Locke is deceived in confounding the internal phenomenon of the will with the external phenomenon of movement which often follows the will, but which is not the will itself. This is, however, in the midst of many inconsistencies, the ruling theory of Locke, a theory which, like that of M. de Biran, but with less profoundness, puts the will into one of its applications, concentrates it into exterior action. Now, if the will is only the power of motion, it is certain that the will is not always and essentially free. So Locke arrives at this conclusion.

Ibid. § 14. "*Liberty belongs not to the will.* If this be so (as I imagine it is), I leave it to be considered whether it may not help to put an end to that long agitated, and I think unreasonable, because unintelligible question, viz., whether man's will be free or no. . . . . The question itself is altogether improper; and it is as insignificant to ask whether man's will be free, as to ask whether his sleep be swift or his virtue square. . . . ."

§ 10. "Our idea of liberty reaches as far as that power, and no farther. For wherever restraint comes to check that power, or compulsion takes away that indifferency of ability on either side to act, or to forbear acting, there liberty, and our notion of it, presently ceases."

Now, as it is unquestionable that a thousand obstacles oppose or may continually oppose our power of acting, evidently here physical, it follows that liberty sometimes exists, and sometimes does not; and when it does exist, it would exist or not exist, according to such or such exterior circumstances. To explain liberty thus, is to destroy it. Liberty is not and cannot be either in the power of thinking or in that of acting, which have their necessary laws, but in the pure power of willing, which alone is always accompanied by the consciousness of power, I do not say to think, I do not say to do, but to will the contrary of what it wills. Locke has then suppressed liberty, by refusing it to the will, and by seeking it either in the thought or in the motive power; he destroys it, and he believes that he has destroyed the question itself of liberty. But the belief of the human race protests against the destruction of liberty, and the whole history of philosophy protests against the destruction of the question.

I now pass to another point, to the celebrated theory of Locke in regard to the nature of the soul.*

It is impossible, as you have seen,† to know any phenomenon of consciousness, the phenomena of sensation or of volition, or of intelligence, without instantly referring them to a subject one and identical, which is the *me*; so we cannot know the external phenomena of resistance, of solidity, of impenetrability, of figure, of color, of smell, of taste, etc., without judging that these are not phenomena in appearance, but phenomena which belong to something real, which is solid, impenetrable, figured, colored, odorous, savory, etc. On the other hand, if you did not know any of the phenomena of consciousness, you would never have the least idea of the subject of these phenomena; if you did not know any of the external phenomena of resistance, of solidity, of

* On the spirituality of the soul, 1st Series, Vol. 1st, Lecture 10, p. 74; Lectures 19–22, p. 85; Vol. 2, Lecture 23, p. 357; Vol. 3, 1st Lecture, p. 71; Lecture 3, p. 143, etc.; Vol. 4, Lecture 12, pp. 55–60; Lecture 21, pp. 448–454; Vol. 5, pp. 155–172, etc.

† See Lecture 18.

impenetrability, of figure, of color, etc., you would not have any idea of the subject of these phenomena: therefore the characters, whether of the phenomena of consciousness, or of exterior phenomena, are for you the only signs of the nature of the subjects of these phenomena. In examining the phenomena which fall under the senses, we find between them grave differences upon which it is useless here to insist, and which establish the distinction of primary qualities and of secondary qualities. In the first rank among the primary qualities is solidity, which is given to you in the sensation of resistance, and inevitably accompanied by form, etc. On the contrary, when you examine the phenomena of consciousness, you do not therein find this character of resistance, of solidity, of form, etc.; you do not find that the phenomena of your consciousness have a figure, solidity, impenetrability, resistance; without speaking of secondary qualities which are equally foreign to them, color, savor, sound, smell, etc. Now, as the subject is for us only the collection of the phenomena which reveal it to us, together with its own existence in so far as the subject of the inherence of these phenomena, it follows that, under phenomena marked with dissimilar characters and entirely foreign to each other, the human mind conceives dissimilar and foreign subjects. Thus as solidity and figure have nothing in common with sensation, will, and thought, as every solid is extended for us, and as we place it necessarily in space, while our thoughts, our volitions, our sensations, are for us unextended, and while we cannot conceive them and place them in space, but only in time, the human mind concludes with perfect strictness that the subject of the exterior phenomena has the character of the latter, and that the subject of the phenomena of consciousness has the character of the former; that the one is solid and extended, and that the other is neither solid nor extended. Finally, as that which is solid and extended is divisible, and as that which is neither solid nor extended is indivisible, hence divisibility is attributed to the solid and extended subject, and indivisibility attributed to the subject which is neither extended nor solid. Who of us, in fact, does not believe himself an indivisible being, one and identical, the same yesterday, to-day, and to-morrow? Well, the word body, the word matter, signifies nothing else than the subject of external phenomena, the most eminent of which are form, impenetrability, solidity, extension, divisibility. The word mind, the word soul, signifies nothing else than the subject of the phenomena of consciousness, thought, will, sensation, phenomena simple, unextended, not solid, etc. Behold the whole idea of spirit, and the whole idea of matter! See, therefore, all that must be done in order to bring back matter to spirit and spirit to matter: it is necessary to pretend that sensation, volition, thought, are reducible in the last analysis to solidity, extension, figure, divisibility, etc., or that solidity, extension, figure, etc., are reducible to thought, volition, sensation. For spiritualism there will be but a single substance, spirit, because there will be but one general phenomenon, consciousness. For materialism there will be but a single substance, which is matter, because there is but a single fundamental phenomenon, which is solidity or extension. These are the two great systems; they both have their portion of truth and of error, which it is not my object to determine now. I simply wish to state this fact, that Locke is more inclined to the one than to the other, and that he is almost tempted to draw thought from extension, and consequently to make of mind a modification of matter. Locke is, doubtless, far from explaining himself clearly in this respect; but he says that it would not be impossible that matter, besides the phenomenon of extension, by a certain disposition and arrangement of the parts, might also produce the phenomenon of thought. He does not say that the soul is material, but he says that such might be the case.

See this important passage, Book IV. Chap. III. § 6: "We have the ideas of matter and of thinking, but possibly shall never be able to know whether any mere material being thinks, or no; it being impossible for us, by the contemplation of our own ideas without relation, to discover, whether omnipotency has not given to some systems of matter, fitly disposed, a power to perceive and think, or else joined and fitted to matter so disposed, a thinking immaterial. . . . . What certainty of knowledge can any one have that some perceptions, such as pleasure and pain, should not be in some bodies themselves after a certain manner modified, as well as that they should be in an immaterial substance, upon the motion of the parts of the body? . . . ."

Locke declares, then, that without revelation and within the limits of the reason alone, it is not certain that the soul is not material. Now, you conceive that if the soul is not immaterial, it runs great risk of not being immortal; for if the phenomenon of thought and of consciousness is only the result of the combination of material, extended and divisible parts, the dissolution of these parts may very well involve that of thought and of the soul. But Locke replies that this consequence is not to be feared; for, material or not, revelation declares to us that the soul is immortal. "And therefore," says he (*ibid.*), "it is not of such mighty necessity to determine one way or the other, as some over-zealous for or against the immateriality of the soul have been forward to make the world believe." And when his adversaries insist, when Dr. Stillingfleet objects that it is greatly diminishing the evidence of immortality to make it depend entirely upon what God gives, and of which it is not capable in its own nature, Locke is ready to charge him with blasphemy; "that is to say," replies he, "it is not as credible upon divine revelation, that a material substance should be immortal, as an immaterial; or which is all one, God is not equally to be believed when he declared it, because the immortality of a material substance cannot be demonstrated from natural reason. . . . ." Again he says, "Any one's not being able to demonstrate the soul to be immortal, takes not off from the evidence of its immortality, if God has revealed it; because the veracity of God is a demonstration of the truth of what he has revealed, and the want of another demonstration of a proposition, that is demonstratively true, takes not off from the evidence of it." And he goes so far as to say that this system is the only Christian system. I certainly believe nothing of this sort; but without descending upon this ground, which is not ours, see the consequences which follow such a system. If the immateriality of the soul is very doubtful and indifferent, and if the immortality of the soul, as doubtful in itself as its immateriality, has for its only foundation the promise of God, whose word must be believed, it follows that whoever should not have, like Locke, the happiness to be illumined by the lights of Christian revelation, and whoever should have no other resource than that of his reason, could legitimately believe neither in the immateriality nor in the immortality of the soul, which, previous to Christianity, condemns the entire human race to materialism, and subsequent to Christianity, at least the half of humanity. But facts repel this sad consequence; facts attest that this reason so impotent, according to Locke, is sufficient to establish, and sufficient too to maintain in humanity the double conviction of the immateriality and of the immortality of the soul. The universal and perpetual revelation of reason (*illuminat omnem hominem venientem in hunc mundum*), more or less vivid, more or less pure, has everywhere preceded, prepared, or supplied that which, in the designs of Providence and the progress of humanity, has come to confirm, extend, complete the first. Finally, I pray you to observe that it is the father of the sensualistic school of the eighteenth century, who here pronounces against reason, and substitutes theology for philosophy, and with perfect loyalty, too, for he firmly believes in revelation and in Christianity. We shall see, hereafter, what will become of the immateriality and of the immortality of our being in the hands of the successors of Locke, who, according to his example, will declare the reason impotent and incompetent on these two points, and will appeal, like him, to faith, to revelation, to theology, save believing or not believing in the authority which they invoke.*

* See Lecture 13, Priestley and Bonnet, who were sincerely religious and materialistic; and 1st Series, Vol. 3, Lectures 4 and 5, *Helvetius*, p. 168; Lecture 6, *Saint-Lambert*, p. 225.

I believe that I have proved that Locke, seeking liberty where it cannot be, in the power of motion, could not find it, and that thus, through many contradictions, he has put philosophy on the road to fatalism. I have proved again that, without affirming the soul to be material and perishable, he has at least said that revelation alone can give us the certainty of it, and that he has put philosophy on the road to materialism. Now, I am happy to declare that Locke has not, the least in the world, put philosophy on the road to atheism. Locke, not only as a Christian, but as a philosopher, admits and proclaims the existence of God, and he gives excellent natural proofs of it; but it is important to lay before you the particular character of these proofs, which belong also to the general spirit of the system of Locke.

There are different proofs of the existence of God.* The consoling result of my studies is, that these different proofs are more or less strict in their forms, but that they all have a depth of truth, which must be only disengaged and put in clear light, in order to give them an incontestable authority. Every thing leads us to God; there is no bad mode of arriving at him; but we go to him by different ways. In general, all the proofs of the existence of God have been arranged into two great classes, the proofs *a posteriori* and the proofs *a priori*. Either I devote myself, by the aid of my senses and of my consciousness, to the spectacle and to the study of the world and of my own existence, and this is simply by a more or less profound knowledge of nature and of myself, after sufficient observations, and by inductions founded on these observations, I arrive at the knowledge of God who made man and nature, and this is what is called demonstration *a posteriori* of the existence of God; or I neglect the exterior world and fall back upon myself, into the interior world of consciousness; and there, without engaging in the study of its numerous phenomena, I borrow at first from reason an idea, a sin-

---

* See the principal traits of the present discussion, 1st Series, Vol. 3, Lect. 1, *Locke*, p. 65, etc.

gle idea, which without the aid of experience, in the hands of this same reason, becomes the basis of a demonstration of the existence of God: it is this demonstration which is called *a priori*.

Behold, for example, the most celebrated proof *a priori* of the existence of God, and which contains almost all the others of the same kind.* When we fall back upon ourselves, the first look which we cast upon the phenomena of consciousness discovers to us this striking character, that they begin and that they are arrested, are renewed, and languish, that they have their suspensions, their abatements, their different degrees of energy, in a word they attest in us something imperfect, limited, finite. Now, this character of finite cannot be given to us, as we have seen,† without the reason instantly entering into exercise, and passing this judgment, that there is something infinite, if there is something finite. Although you should be unacquainted with the external world, consciousness would suffice to give you the idea of the finite, and consequently reason would have a sufficient base to suggest to you the idea of the infinite. The idea of the infinite opposed to the idea of the finite is nothing less than the idea of perfection opposed to the idea of imperfection. What, in fact, is consciousness for us except the sentiment of our imperfection and of our weakness? I do not control my sensations; they go and come at their pleasure; they appear and disappear, without, often, any power on my part to retain them or to avoid them. Nor do I control my judgments, which follow their own laws, which I have not made. I control my will, it is true, but often it terminates only in volitions, without being able to arrive at visible and external acts; and sleep and lethargy and delirium suspend it. On all sides, the finite and imperfection appear in me. But I cannot have the idea of the finite and of imperfection without

* We have very often exhibited the proof *a priori* of the existence of God, called the Cartesian proof from the name of its author, or rather from its most illustrious interpreter. See especially in this 2d Series, Vol. 2, Lect. 11, and 1st Series, Vol. 4, Lect. 12, p. 63–68, and Vol. 5, Lect. 6, p. 205–224.

† See Lect. 18.

having that of perfection and of the infinite. These two ideas are logically correlative ; and in the order of their acquisition, that of the finite and imperfect precedes the other, but scarcely precedes it. It is not in the power of reason, as soon as the consciousness furnishes it with the idea of the finite and imperfect not to conceive the idea of the infinite and the perfect. Now, the infinite and the perfect is God himself. Then it is sufficient for you to have the idea of the imperfect and the finite in order to have the idea of the infinite and the perfect, that is, of God, though you may or may not thus name him, though you may be able to express in words the spontaneous convictions of your intelligence, or for want of language and analysis, they may remain obscure and indistinct in the depths of your soul. Once more, do not consult savages, children, idiots, in order to know whether they have the idea of God; ask them, or rather, without asking them, see whether they have the idea of the imperfect and the finite; and if they have (and they cannot but have it if they have the least apperception), you may be sure that they have the obscure and confused idea of something infinite and perfect; you may be sure that what they see of themselves and of the world does not suffice them, and that they are humbled and exalted in the intimate faith in the existence of something infinite, perfect, that is, of God. The word may be wanting to them, because the idea is not yet clear and distinct; but it none the less exists under the veils of nascent intelligence, and there the philosophical observer easily discovers it.

The infinite and the perfect are given to you with the imperfect and the finite, and the finite and the imperfect are given to you immediately by your consciousness as soon as there are any phenomena under the eyes of your consciousness. Therefore the idea of the finite and imperfect being primitive, the correlative idea of the infinite and perfect, and consequently of God, is primitive also.

The idea of God is a primitive idea ; but whence does this idea come to you ? Is it a creation of your imagination, an illusion, a chimera? You can imagine a gorgon, a centaur, to exist, and you can imagine them not to exist; but is it in your power, the finite and the imperfect being given, to conceive or not to conceive the infinite and the perfect? No: the one being given, the other is necessarily so. It is not then a chimera; it is a necessary product of your reason: therefore it is a legitimate product. Either deny your reason, and then never more speak of reason, of truth, of consciousness, of philosophy, or accept the authority of your reason, and accept it here as elsewhere.

You are a finite being, and you have the necessary idea of an infinite being. But how could a finite and imperfect being have the idea of an infinite and perfect being, and have it necessarily, if this being did not exist? Take away God, the infinite, the perfect, leave only man, the finite and the imperfect, and I shall never draw from the finite the idea of the infinite, from the imperfect the idea of the perfect, from humanity the idea of God; but if the perfect, if the infinite, if God exists, then my reason will be able to conceive them. Finally, you see at what I wish to arrive: the single fact of the conception of God by reason, the idea alone of God implies the certainty and the necessity of the existence of God.

Such nearly is the celebrated demonstration of the existence of God *a priori*, that is, independently of all experience; behold now the proof *a posteriori*; a few words will suffice to make you comprehend it; it explains itself.

This proof consists in arriving at God only by an induction founded on an observation more or less extended. Instead of closing your senses and opening only your consciousness, you open your senses and close more or less your consciousness, in order to consider especially nature and this vast world which surrounds you; and by a contemplation more or less profound and studies more or less learned, you are penetrated with the beauty, order, intelligence, wisdom, and perfection spread throughout the universe; and as in the cause there must be at least what is in the effect, you reason from nature to its author, and from the existence and perfection of the one you conclude the existence and perfection of the other.

These two proofs are excellent, I repeat; and instead of choosing between them, it is necessary, like the human mind, to accept and employ them both. In fact, they so little exclude each other, that each of them contains somewhat of the other. The argument *a priori*, for example, supposes an element *a posteriori*, a datum of observation and experience; for if the idea of the infinite and of the perfect leads directly to God, and if this idea is given by reason and not by experience, it is not given to us independently of all experience, since reason would never give it to us without the simultaneous or anterior idea of the finite and of the imperfect, which is derived from experience; only here the experimental datum is borrowed from consciousness and not from the senses: and again we may say that every phenomenon of consciousness supposes a sensitive phenomenon, simultaneous or anterior. An element *a posteriori* intervenes, then, as a condition of the demonstration *a priori*. So if we reflect upon it, the proof by experience or *a posteriori* implies an element purely rational, or *a priori*. In fact, on what condition do you conclude from nature to God? On the condition that you admit or that at least you employ the principle of causality; for if you are deprived of this principle, you will contemplate, you will forever study the world, you will forever adore the order and the wisdom which reign in it, without ever elevating yourself to the supposition that all this is but an effect, that all this must have a cause. Take away the principle of causality, and there are no more causes for us, there is no longer either need or possibility of seeking or of finding any, and induction no longer goes from the world to God. Now, the principle of causality has clearly an experimental condition; but it is not itself borrowed from experience; it supposes it and is applied to it, but it governs and judges it; it belongs properly to the reason.* Behold then, in its turn, an element *a pri-*

---

* See Lecture 19.

ori in the proof *a posteriori*. Moreover, this world is full of harmony; I believe it; and the more we look at it, especially in placing ourselves at a certain point of view which the observation may confirm but which it does not give, the more we are struck with the order of the world; but we may also, in consulting only our senses, find appearances of disorder; we cannot comprehend the reason of volcanoes which devour flourishing cities, of earthquakes, tempests, etc.; in a word, observation, when employed alone and not directed by a superior principle, may well find evil in this world. If to this deceitful experience you add the principle, that all that is true of effect is true of cause, it will be necessary to admit in cause that which exists in effect, that is, not only intelligence, wisdom, and power, but degrading imperfections, as has been done by more than one distinguished mind, under the exclusive dominion of experience, and by more than one people in the infancy of humanity. Finally, so many different effects, of which experience does not always show the connection, might well conduct not to a single cause and to God, but to different causes and to a plurality of gods; and history justifies this belief. You then clearly see that the proof *a posteriori*, which at first needs the principle of causality, needs other principles still which direct the application of causality to experience, principles which, in order to govern experience, should not come from it, and should come from reason. The argument *a posteriori* therefore supposes more than one element *a priori*. Thus completed, it has its use and its excellence like the argument *a priori*, when well regulated and recalled to its true principles.

These two arguments do not exclude each other; but one or the other is more or less striking, according to the turn of mind and moral and religious disposition of nations and individuals. The Christian religion, which rests on the mind and not on the senses, chiefly employs proofs *a priori*. Neglecting nature, or looking at it under an idealistic point of view, it is from the depths of the soul, through reason and the Word, that it elevates itself to God. The proof *a priori* is the Christian proof *par excellence;* it belongs particularly to the reign of Christianity, to the middle age, and to the philosophy which represents it, scholasticism; it is thence that it has passed into the great modern spiritualistic school, that of Descartes,* where it was brilliantly developed during a half century by Malebranche, Fenelon, Bossuet, Leibnitz. On the contrary, the simple religions of the first age of humanity, which are not still religions in spirit and in truth, and which are almost only founded on the senses and appearance, make use of the proof *a posteriori;* so while the religions of the mind tend a little too much to separate God from nature, because the proof upon which they rest separates too much the reason and the consciousness from the senses and from experience, on their side the religions of nature make God in the image of nature, and reflect all the imperfections of the proof *a posteriori;* they are tempted to put in the cause all that is in the effect; and nature presenting very different phenomena, the harmony of which is often hardly visible, the religions of nature are polytheistic, physical, astronomical, anthropomorphic. As the Christian religion especially produces an idealistic philosophy, so the philosophy which springs from the religions of nature is a sensualistic philosophy, the theodicea of which delights in the proofs *a posteriori;* and one of two things then happens, either the sensualistic theodicea accepts the rational principle *a priori* of causality, contrary to the spirit of the school to which it belongs, and then it arrives at God through an inconsistency; or it rejects the principle of causality, and then it does not and cannot arrive at God: and as sensualism confounds the substance with the collection of qualities,† it recognizes no other God than the aggregate of the phenomena of nature, and the assemblage of the things of the world. Hence pantheism, the natural theodicea of paganism

---

* Descartes thought that he had created it, but he owed it, unconsciously, to his first studies, to scholastic tradition, and to Saint Anselm. See Vol. 2 of this 2d Series, Lectures 9 and 11.

† See Lecture 18.

and of the sensualistic philosophy.* Let us apply all this to Locke.

Locke believes in the existence of God, and he has demonstrated it well; but he springs from a sensualistic school; he therefore repels the arguments *a priori*, and hardly admits the arguments *a posteriori*. He is unwilling to employ the argument of Descartes, who proves the existence of God by the idea of him, by the idea of the infinite and of perfection. Book IV. Chap. X. § 7: "But yet, I think, this I may say, that it is an ill way of establishing this truth, and silencing atheists, to lay the whole stress of so important a point as this upon that sole foundation; and take some men's having that idea of God in their minds (for it is evident some men have none, and some worse than none, and the most very different) for the only proof of a Deity: and out of an over-fondness of that darling invention cashier, or at least endeavor to invalidate all other arguments, and forbid us to hearken to those proofs, as being weak or fallacious, which our own existence and the sensible parts of the universe offer so clearly and so cogently to our thoughts, that I deem it impossible for a considering man to withstand them. For I judge it as certain and clear a truth, as can anywhere be delivered, that the invisible things of God are clearly seen from the creation of the world, being understood by the things that are made, even his eternal power and Godhead. . . . ."

He sets out from this to develop particularly this kind of proof. If Locke had simply wished to establish that the argument *a priori* is not the only valid argument, and that the proof *a posteriori* must not be disdained, I would very willingly join with him; but he goes farther, and wanders into assertions which I cannot repel with too much vigor. I deny that there are people who have no idea of God; and here the Cartesian philosophy and all

* On Pantheism, see Vol. 1 of this Series, Lecture 5, with the Appendix, and in the Philosophical Fragments, Vol. 2, ANCIENT PHILOSOPHY, article Xenophanes.

idealistic philosophy which proves that the idea of God being at bottom that of the infinite, of perfection, of unity, and of absolute existence, cannot but be found in every man whose reason is ever so little developed. I deny also the sentiment which Locke has unfortunately but very naturally lent to Bayle, that is, sensualism to skepticism, to wit, that some men have such an idea of God that it would be better that they had none at all. I deny that it would be better to have no idea of God than to have an imperfect idea of him, as if we were not imperfect beings condemned to mingle the false with the true! If we would only have truths without mixture, very few beliefs would be left to humanity, and very few theories to science. That man must be a stranger to the history of philosophy who could desire to reject truth because it is mingled with a few errors, or even with many errors. Finally, I remark that, in developing his preference for the proof *a posteriori*, Locke often employs, and unconsciously, arguments *a priori*, idealistic, and even somewhat scholastic. § 8 : "Something must be from eternity." Although he chiefly seeks God in the external world, like Descartes he goes from man to God, §§ 2 and 3. Nowhere does he accept and disengage, but everywhere he employs the principle of causality, without which he could not take a single step beyond nature and man. Besides, the only consequence which I wish to draw from these observations is, that the theodicea of Locke, in repelling the argument *a priori*, and in employing through choice the argument *a posteriori*, retains still and develops the fundamental character of the philosophy of Locke, which rests particularly, and often even exclusively, on experience, and on sensible and exterior experience.

Here closes the long analysis which I was to present you of the *Essay on the Human Understanding;* it only remains to me to recapitulate and generalize the partial results which we have obtained.

1st, Considered under the most important point of view, that of method, the *Essay on the Human Understanding* has this excellence, that psychology is given in it as the basis of all sound philosophy. Locke begins by the study of man, of his faculties, and of the observable phenomena of consciousness; and thereby he attaches himself to the great Cartesian movement and to the genius of modern philosophy: this is the good side of the method of Locke. The bad side is, that, instead of observing man, his faculties, and the phenomena which result from the development of these faculties, in the condition and with the characters which these phenomena now present, he plunges at first into the obscure and perilous question of the primitive state of these phenomena, the first developments of our faculties, the origin of our ideas.

2d, The question of the origin of our ideas, which should come after that of their actual characters, being prematurely taken up without sufficient knowledge of the facts to be explained, casts Locke into a system which admits no other origin of all our knowledge and of all our ideas than sensation and reflection.

3d, And again, you must recollect that Locke does not hold the balance equal between these two origins, and that he lets it incline in favor of sensation.

4th, The resolution being taken to derive all ideas from sensation and reflection, and particularly from sensation, it imposes upon Locke the necessity of confounding certain ideas with certain others; for there are ideas (for example, the seven following: the idea of space, the idea of time, the idea of the infinite, the idea of personal identity, the idea of substance, the idea of cause, the idea of good and of evil) which, as we have demonstrated, cannot enter into the human understanding through sensation, or even through reflection. Locke is, therefore, compelled to confound them with the ideas of body, of succession, of the finite or of number, of consciousness, of the collection of qualities, of the succession of phenomena, of rewards and punishments, of pleasure and pain, which are, in fact, explicable by sensation or reflection; that is, he is forced to confound either the antecedents or the consequents of the idea of space, of time, of the infinite, of substance, of cause, of good and evil with these ideas themselves.

5th, This is the most general vice which governs the philosophy of Locke; it is fully discovered in the theory of knowledge and judgment. Locke founds knowledge and judgment on the perception of a relation between two ideas, that is, on comparison; while in many cases the relations, and the ideas of relation, far from being the foundation of our judgments and our knowledge, are, on the contrary, fragments of knowledge and of primitive judgments due to the natural power of the understanding, which judges and knows by its own power, resting often upon a single term, and consequently without comparing two in order to deduce ideas of relation.

6th, It is the same with the theory of language. Locke correctly attributes a great deal to language; but it must not be believed that every dispute is a dispute concerning words; every error a verbal error, every general idea the sole work of language, and that a science is only a well-made language, because, in fact, words play a great part in our disputes and our errors, because there are no general ideas without language, and because a well-made language is the condition or rather the consequence of a true science.

7th, Finally, in the great theories, by which all philosophies, in their last result, are judged, to wit, the theories of God, of the soul, and of liberty, you see Locke confounding the will with the faculty of moving, as he expresses it, with the power of acting, of doing such or such an exterior action, seeking liberty in the will thus understood, that is, where it is not; you see him yielding to the prejudices of empiricism, expressing a doubt whether thought is any thing else than a mode of matter, just like extension; you see him, finally, in theodicea always faithful to the spirit of his system, resting on the senses more than on the consciousness, interrogating nature rather than reason in regard to the existence of God, repelling the proof *a priori* of Descartes, and admitting only the proof *a posteriori*.

Such is my definitive judgment in regard to the work of Locke. If I have devoted the greatest part of the lectures of this summer to the examination of this single work, you will approve of what I have done, in consideration of its importance, of all that it embodies, and of all that it prepares. The *Essay on the Human Understanding* comprehends almost all the sensualistic tradition which concerns the eighteenth century. In general, modern philosophy (and I do not mean to except any school) is careless of the past, to say no more; it thinks only of the future, and knows only its most immediate history.* As the spiritualistic school of the eighteenth century does not ascend beyond Descartes, so the sensualistic school scarcely ascends beyond Locke; it has boasted much of Bacon, but its official starting-point is Locke; it is Locke and Locke continually that it cites, that it imitates, that it develops. In fact, now that you thoroughly know the *Essay on the Human Understanding* in its whole and in its details, you must see that it really contains the most marked traits of all the great sensualistic theories, whether of modern philosophy, of Greece, or of the East.

The essential character of sensualism is, as we have seen, the negation of all the great truths which escape the senses, and which the reason alone discovers, the negation of time and of infinite space, of good and evil, of human liberty, of the immateriality of the soul and of Divine Providence; according to the times and the greater or less degree of energy of its partisans, it openly proclaims these results, or it veils them by the distinction often sincere, often fictitious, of philosophy and of theology. It is the only difference which, in the seventeenth century, separates Gassendi, the Catholic priest, from Hobbes, the enemy of the Church. At bottom, their philosophical system is the same; they give an almost exclusive part to sensation in the consciousness; they almost maintain that all being is material (*substantia nobis datur sub ratione materiæ*); in spiritual beliefs, they see metaphors alone, and, after the senses, they attribute every thing

* I have shown it, in regard to Reid, 1st Series, Vol. 4, Lecture 22, p. 505, and in regard to Kant, Vol. 5, *passim*.

to signs and to language; but, beyond all this, Gassendi invokes revelation, and Hobbes does not invoke it.* In the sixteenth century the appeal to revelation was indispensable; it characterizes and it scarcely saves the sensualistic peripateticism of Pomponatius and of his school.† Before this, under the absolute reign of Christianity, this precaution was still more necessary; it ill protects the nascent sensualism and the avowed nominalism of Occam,‡ the negation of all absolute truth in itself, that of good and of evil, of the beautiful and of the ugly, of the true and of the false, in so far as founded on the nature of things, and their explanation by the sole will and arbitrary power of God. All these traits of the sensualism, manifest or hidden, of the middle age, of the sixteenth and seventeenth centuries, are reproduced in Locke. Who cannot see, too, in the bosom of paganism, the precursors of Gassendi and of Hobbes, and consequently of Locke, in Epicurus,§ and in Democritus, and in the school of Ionia?‖ Finally, in certain Oriental systems, and particularly in the Sankhya of Kapila,¶ in the midst of inconsistencies, apparent or real, and of a mysticism true or false, similar, perhaps, to the modern invocation of revelation, who cannot recognize the first lineaments of this theory, which, growing from epoch to epoch, and participating in all the progress of humanity, arrived, at the commencement of the eighteenth century, at its expression, uncertain still, but already elevated and truly scientific, in the *Essay on the Human Understanding?*

And not only did the *Essay on the Human Understanding* then recapitulate the past, but it contained the future. All these theories upon which I have so long dwelt, and which have often wearied you by their equivocal character, are going, in less than half a century, to become in the hardy hands of the successors of Locke, firm and precise theories, which, in more than

---

* On Hobbes and Gassendi, see the preceding volume, Lecture 11, and on Hobbes in particular, see 1st Series, Vol. 3, Lectures 7–10.

† Vol. 2, Lecture 10.

‡ *Ibid.*, Lecture 9.

§ *Ibid.*, Lecture 8.

‖ *Ibid.*, Lecture 7.

¶ *Ibid.*, Lecture 5.

one country of Europe, will obtain an authority almost absolute, and will seem to be the last word of the human thought. Thus Locke's theory concerning freedom tended to fatalism; this theory developed will arrive at it. Locke did not seem to fear materialism; his pupils will accept it and will proclaim it. Soon the principle of causality being no longer simply neglected, but repelled and destroyed, the proof *a posteriori* of the existence of God will lack a basis, and the sincere theism of the undecisive sensualism of Locke will terminate in an avowed pantheism, that is, in atheism. The two sources of human knowledge, sensation and reflection, will be resolved into a single one; reflection will be destroyed in sensation; nothing but sensation will remain to explain the entire human mind. Signs, the influence of which Locke had already exaggerated, will become, after sensation, the source itself of all ideas. In a word, you shall, on a future occasion,* see of what importance it was to throw, at first, an abundant and strong light on questions and theories which, rising little by little, must become the battle-field of all our ulterior discussions. It was necessary to become acquainted with it in advance, and to familiarize you with the ground upon which we must so often combat.

Permit me, in closing, to remind you of the engagements which I made at the beginning of this course both with you and with myself; I shall not cease to keep them constantly before my eyes.

I then divided all the schools of the eighteenth century into four fundamental schools, which appeared to me to embrace all the others. I was pleased to say to you:† Each of these schools has existed, therefore it had some reason for existing. If these schools had been entirely absurd and extravagant, they

---

* In default of the lectures here promised we may consult those of Vol. 3 of the 1st Series, where the school of sensation is presented under all its great metaphysical, moral, and political aspects in the person of Locke, of Condillac, of Helvetius, of Saint-Lambert, and of Hobbes.

† See the preceding volume, Lectures 4 and 13.

could not have existed: for absurdity alone could not have found either place or credit in the human mind, could not have procured so much lustre, could not have obtained so much authority in any century, still less in a century so enlightened as the eighteenth. Thus because the sensualistic school has existed, it has had reason for existing, and it possesses some element of truth. But there are four schools, and not simply one. Now, absolute truth is one; if one of these four schools contained the absolute truth, there would be one school alone, and not four. They exist; therefore they have reason for existing, and they contain some truth; and at the same time there are four; therefore neither the one nor the other contains the entire truth, and each of them with the element of truth which has made it exist, contains some element of error which reduces it to be, after all, only a particular school; and, bear in mind, error, in the hands of systematic genius, easily becomes extravagance. I should, therefore, as I had promised, have at once absolved and combated all the schools, and consequently that great school which is called the school of sensation, from the title itself of the only principle upon which it rests. I should have absolved the school of sensation as having had its share of truth; and I should have combated it as having mingled with the share of truth which recommends it many errors and extravagances. And by what means was I to combat the school of sensation? I had promised you to combat the errors of one school by means of the truth found in the opposing school; it was therefore my duty to combat the exaggerations of sensualism with whatever is sound and reasonable in idealism. This is what I have done. Perhaps there is a little of my own, if I may be permitted to say it, in the development of the arguments which I have opposed to the *Essay on the Human Understanding,* and in the management of the discussion, in some sort, especially in its general and moral character; but the arguments in themselves belong for the most part to the spiritualistic school in its most reasonable, that is, in its negative part, which is always the best part of every school. Hereafter I shall again seek out the spiritualistic school;* I shall examine it in itself, and I shall turn against it, against its sublime errors and its mystical tendencies, the solid arms which the good sense of empiricism and of skepticism shall furnish me. Meanwhile, it is with spiritualistic dialectics that I have combated the extravagances of the empiric school in its first representative in the eighteenth century. And it is not ancient idealism that I have invoked against modern empiricism, for the one does not answer to the other; ancient philosophy and modern philosophy only serve and only illumine each other on the heights of science and for a small number of elect thinkers: it is modern spiritualism which has served me against modern sensualism. I have opposed to Locke the great men who have followed him, and who were to combat him in order to surpass him, and put science on an onward march. It is not even from Leibnitz, already too far from us, it is from Reid and from Kant,† that I have borrowed arguments; but I have been, almost continually, obliged to change their form, for this form savors somewhat of the country and language of these two great men. Both express themselves as people do at Glasgow and at Kœnigsburg, which is not the manner of expression in France. I have therefore neglected the phraseology of Reid, and especially that of Kant, but I have preserved the basis of their arguments. You are not acquainted with Kant. At a future day I will try to make you acquainted with this mind so firm and so elevated, the Descartes of our age.‡ But you can read in the translation of one of the best pupils of the Normal School, now my colleague in this Faculty, the judicious Reid, with the truly superior commentary of M.

---

* The revolution of 1830 prevented this project. What I should have done in regard to transcendental idealism may be seen by what I did in 1820 in regard to apparent or real idealism, but certainly much tempered by the philosophy of Kœnigsburg.

† See 1st Series, Vols. 4 and 5.

‡ The 1st Series of my courses was not yet published.

Royer-Collard.* The Scotch philosophy will prepare you for the German philosophy. It is to Reid and to Kant that I refer in great part the polemics which I have instituted against empiricism in the person of Locke.

It was my duty also to be just towards the empiric school, while combating it; it was my duty to exhibit its share of good as well as evil, for both must equally exist in it. And I ask you whether I have not also done this? Have I not recognized and pointed out all the good that exists in the different parts of the *Essay on the Human Understanding?* Have I not carefully produced the happy commencements of the method and theories of Locke, before attacking the errors into which the spirit of system has thrown him? Finally, have I not rendered a proper tribute to his character and to his virtues? I have done it, and with all my heart; and on this point I am sure of being exempt from reproach both towards Locke and towards myself, and towards philosophy. In fact, philosophy is not such or such a school, but the common basis, and, thus to speak, the soul of all schools. It is distinct from all systems, but it is mingled with each of them, for it is manifested, it is developed, it is advanced only by them; its unity is their variety, so discordant in appearance, in reality so harmonious; its progress and its glory is their reciprocal perfectionment by their pacific struggles. When we attack without reserve a considerable system, we proscribe, unintentionally, some real element of the human mind, we wound philosophy itself in some of its parts; when we outrage an illustrious philosopher, to whatever school he may belong, we outrage philosophy, the human mind, in one of its choicest representatives. I hope that nothing like this will ever proceed from these lectures; for, what I profess before all else, what I teach,

* I have continually cited the translation of M. Jouffroy and the admirable lectures of M. Royer-Collard in Vol. 4 of the 1st Series; and I am happy to render homage to him who was and will always be for me a revered master, and to him whom I may now call the first of the independent pupils who have gone forth from my auditory.

is not such or such a philosophy, but philosophy itself; it is not attachment to such or such a system, however great it may be, admiration for such or such a man, whatever may have been his genius, but the philosophical spirit, superior to all systems and to all philosophers, that is, boundless love of truth, knowledge of all systems which pretend to possess it entire and which at least possess something of it, and respect for all men who have sought it and who are seeking it still with talent and loyalty. The true muse of history is not Hatred, it is Love; the mission of true criticism is not only to point out the too real and too numerous extravagances of philosophical systems, but to pick out and disengage from the midst of these errors the truths which may and must be mingled with them, and thereby raise the human reason in its own eyes, absolve philosophy in the past, embolden it, and illumine it in the future.

I cannot part with you, gentlemen, without thanking you for the remarkable zeal, honorable to yourselves and encouraging to me, which you have exhibited during the course of these lectures. Engaged in discussions, the length and dryness of which could have been spared you only at the expense of scientific rigor, your attention and kindness have never for a moment been wanting. I beseech you to preserve them both for me: I shall have need of them next year in the exposition and profound discussion of the consequences of the philosophy of Locke, that is, of all the systems which have been produced by this rich and fruitful sensualistic school in the eighteenth century, the father and first monument of which you now understand.

Other portions of Cousin's works are ready for the press, the publication of which will depend upon the success of these volumes.—[Tr.

THE END.

INDEX OF PROPER NAMES,

AND OF SUBJECTS NOT ALREADY SUFFICIENTLY INDICATED BY THE GENERAL HEADINGS OF THE LECTURES.

It may be well enough to remark here that this work of M. Cousin's is, in the original, divided into three volumes—which will explain the reference in the notes.

MISCELLANEOUS.

Hugh A. Garland.

LIFE OF JOHN RANDOLPH,

Of Roanoke. Including Letters, Speeches, Anecdotes, Personal Reminiscences, and Times. 2 vols. 12mo. Portraits. $2 50.

"The name of John Randolph, from his eccentricities of character, his patriotism, his independence, his keen sarcasm, his elegant and accomplished scholarship, and from his being contemporary with some of the most distinguished men of our annals, has become familiar to every American citizen. No biography has been published in this country that equals these remarkable volumes in interest and attraction."—*Hunt's Merchants' Mag.*

George Gilfillan.

THE BARDS OF THE BIBLE.

12*mo. Cloth,* 50 *cents.*

"This is truly one of the choicest and most acceptable books of the season. The views which it presents are original and striking, and yet at once commend themselves to the reader's approval and admiration. The Author has indulged freely in literary criticism, and in historical explanation, but his great aim has been to give artistic effect to his work—to make a real prose poem in honor of the poetry and poets of the Bible. Mr. Gilfillan has executed his task in a most masterly manner. No one can close this work without a better appreciation and a profounder reverence of the Book of Books. It will add greatly to Mr. Gilfillan's already widely extended fame."—*Courier & Enquirer.*

John Anthon.

THE LAW STUDENT;

Or, Guides to the Study of the Law in its Principles. Octavo. $3

"This book, which is put forth under the modest title of a text-book for students, is from the pen of one of our most eminent lawyers. Mr. ANTHON has brought to his task the store of legal knowledge and elegant learning, which is the accumulation of many years, united with the wisdom acquired by a long practice in the application of the principles which he has attempted to unfold. Hence, whether we regard this volume as an exposition of the elementary principles of the law, or as a guide to the better knowledge of those principles, it is worthy to rank among the best books that can be put into the hands of young students."—*Tribune.*

LETTERS FROM THREE CONTINENTS.

By the Arkansas Correspondent of the Louisville Journal. 12*mo. Cloth.*

"The Author writes with an off-hand freshness of manner entirely different from the hack neyed tourist."—*Picayune.*

"The impression left on laying down the volume is, that the traveller is a man of talent and cultivation, with an active mind and keen powers of observation and description, which have made a very entertaining book."—*Delta.*

William W. Lord.

CHRIST IN HADES: A POEM.

12*mo.* *Boards,* 75 *cents.*

"We are happy to say the work displays much powerful conception, true poetical genius, and taste; and affords many beautiful descriptions. The appearance of Christ in Paradise is finely imagined and grandly exhibited, so is the overthrow of Satan in the last book; and many other passages might be instanced."—*Churchman.*

Goethe.

IPHIGENIA IN TAURUS.

A Drama in Five Acts. Translated from the German, by G. J. Adler, A. M. 12*mo.* 75 *cents.*

H. R. Agnel.

THE BOOK OF CHESS;

Containing the Rudiments of the same, and Elementary Analysis of the most Popular Openings, exemplified in Games actually played by the great Masters; including Staunton's Analyses of the Kings and Queens, Gammits, Numerous Positions, and Problems on Diagrams, both Original and Selected: also, a Series of Chess Tales. With Illustrations, engraved from Original Designs by Robert W. Weir. *A New Edition.* 12*mo.* $1 25.

James Wynne, M. D.

LIVES OF EMINENT LITERARY AND SCIENTIFIC MEN OF AMERICA.

12*mo.* *Cloth*, $1.

"A good book, well chosen, and particularly adapted to the present time. We are happy to announce to our readers a volume of so much interest and utility, containing as it does, the brief but well-written biographies of Franklin, Rev. Jonathan Edwards, Fulton, Chief Justice Marshall, Dr. Rittenhouse, and Eli Whitney, either of which is a model in itself, and *all* together a combination of the great, good, and brilliant talents and virtues that adorn the human character, and ennoble the heart. This work will be perused with pleasure and profit, and we trust this is but the beginning of a series of volumes of the same class, for which we have so abundant material, and which cannot fail to be exceedingly interesting and eminently useful."—*Farmer and Mechanic.*

Jean Paul.

LIFE OF JEAN PAUL FREDERIC RICHTER.

Compiled from various Sources. Together with his Autobiography. Translated by Eliza Buckminster Lee, *Translator of "Walt and Valt."* 12*mo.* $1 25.

"The admirers of Jean Paul—and that is but another phrase for the literary world—will be gladdened to learn that an authentic life of the great German poet has made its appearance from the American press. The book before us is not merely a translation; and the accomplished author has a right to claim a higher title for her work. She has not only given us a translation of Richter's *own* biography, but has compiled and woven together, from *Spazier*, the Author's correspondence, and other sources, a work in which her taste and judgment in selection are only equalled by the patient industry and artistic skill with which she has arranged, blended, and elaborated the material at her command."—*Savannah Star.*

George Gilfillan.

MODERN LITERATURE AND LITERARY MEN.

Being a Second Gallery of Literary Portraits. Reprinted entire from the London Edition. 12*mo.* $1.

"He wields a powerful pen, and his style has a sway and a swing which are always exciting and often magnificent. The reader is caught up with an intense enthusiasm and hurried along in spite of himself, till the Author pleases to let him down. There is a rugged strength of manner, a bold beauty of imagery, and honest fearlessness of opinion, which mark the Author a man of genius, and leave a decided impression of some sort. In the main, we approve his criticisms: he comes nearer to a just award than usual. Especially of the poets, there is a keen and subtle appreciation. He generally strikes a key note with which all sober readers will harmonize, though it differs often widely from the popular opinion. He dares, too, to say what he thinks, and deals out some home truths well worth the study of thinking men."—*Home Journal.*